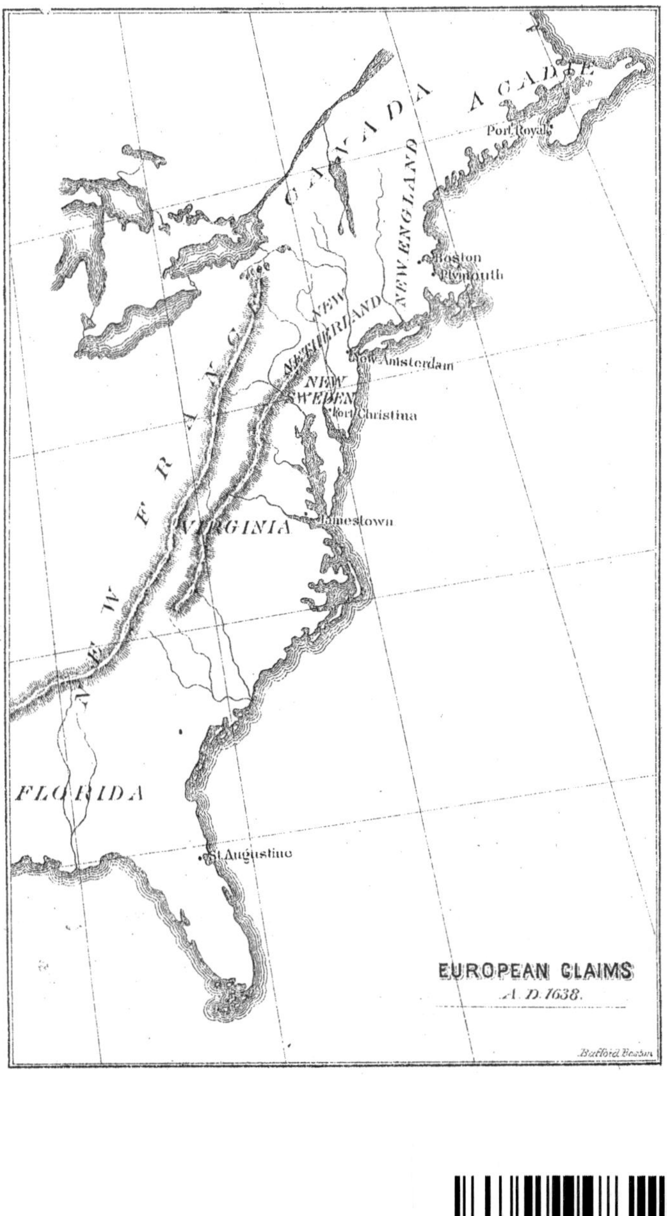

CANADA
ACADIE
Port Royal
NEW ENGLAND
Boston
Plymouth
NEW NETHERLAND
New Amsterdam
NEW SWEDEN
Fort Christina
NEW FRANCE
VIRGINIA
Jamestown
FLORIDA
St. Augustine

EUROPEAN CLAIMS

A. D. 1638.

Bufford, Boston.

HISTORY

OF THE

UNITED STATES.

FROM 1492 TO 1872.

BY

SAMUEL ELIOT.

BOSTON:
BREWER AND TILESTON.
FRANKLIN STREET.
1876.

Electrotyped at the Boston Stereotype Foundry,
19 Spring Lane.

PREFACE.

As I remarked in the preface to the original edition of this book, I have endeavored to observe the proper proportions. The same space is not given to every period or to every transaction. On the contrary, events are narrated at greater or less length, according to their importance — a few days occupying as many pages in some parts of the volume as a long series of years in others. By thus making inferior matters subordinate, I trust that I have done more justice than might be anticipated, from the appearance of the book, to the great passages in our history. It is nowhere, however, a book of details. I have confined myself intentionally to outlines — endeavoring to sketch these in such a way as to suggest comprehensive conceptions of the whole, rather than complete views of any single part.

In bringing down the history to the present time, I have made a few corrections and omissions in Parts I., II., and III., and almost wholly re-written Part IV.

CONTENTS.

PART I.

OCCUPATION.

1492—1638.

CHAPTER I.

DISCOVERY.

CHAPTER II.

SPANISH SETTLEMENTS.

CHAPTER III.

FRENCH SETTLEMENTS.

CHAPTER IV.

ENGLISH SETTLEMENTS.

PART II.

ENGLISH DOMINION.

1638—1763.

CHAPTER I.

THE THIRTEEN COLONIES.

CHAPTER II.

COLONIAL RELATIONS.

CHAPTER III.

INDIAN WARS.

CHAPTER IV.

DUTCH WARS.

CHAPTER V.

SPANISH WARS.

CHAPTER VI.

FRENCH POSSESSIONS.

CHAPTER VII.

FRENCH WARS.

CHAPTER VIII.

COLONIAL DEVELOPMENT.

CHAPTER IX.

THE MOTHER COUNTRY.

PART III.

INDEPENDENCE.

1763 – 1797.

CHAPTER I.

PROVOCATIONS.

CHAPTER II.

WAR.

CHAPTER III.

DECLARATION OF INDEPENDENCE.

CHAPTER IV.

WAR, CONTINUED. SECOND PERIOD.

CHAPTER V.

WAR, CONTINUED. THIRD PERIOD.

CHAPTER VI.

THE CONSTITUTION.

CHAPTER VII.

WASHINGTON'S ADMINISTRATION.

PART IV.

UNION.

1797–1872.

CHAPTER I.

PARTY ADMINISTRATIONS.

CHAPTER II.

WAR WITH GREAT BRITAIN.

CHAPTER III.

MISSOURI COMPROMISE.

CHAPTER IV.

THE MONROE DOCTRINE.

CHAPTER V.

TARIFF COMPROMISE.

2

CHAPTER VI.

ANTI-SLAVERY.

CHAPTER VII.

ANNEXATION OF TEXAS.

CHAPTER VIII.

WAR WITH MEXICO.

CHAPTER IX.

COMPROMISE OF 1850.

CHAPTER X.

KANSAS.

CHAPTER XI.

SECESSION.

CHAPTER XII.

CIVIL WAR.

CHAPTER XIII.

CIVIL WAR, CONTINUED.

CHAPTER XIV.

REUNION.

CHAPTER XV.

NATIONAL DEVELOPMENT.

PART I.

OCCUPATION.

1492–1638.

CHAPTER I.

Discovery.

Tradi-tional. The first man to discover the shores of the United States, according to Icelandic writings, was the Icelander Leif. A countryman of his, sailing from Greenland, had reached Newfoundland or Labrador, and Leif sailed in search of the same land, a few years afterwards. He is described as having found more than he sought, by keeping on to the southward and westward, until he arrived at a point which he called Vinland, from the wild grapes growing there, and which has been supposed to be our own Rhode Island. This was in the year 1000, and from that time, for upwards of three hundred years, voyages to these coasts continued to be made at intervals by Icelanders or Northmen. Other traditions bring over Madoc and his Welshmen in the twelfth century, and the Venetian brothers Zeni at the close of the fourteenth; but when they came, and if they came at all, cannot now be told.

Histori-cal. Whatever may be thought of these traditional discoveries, this much, at least, is historical about them: that they quickened the discoveries of a later period. The idea that land could be gained by sailing westward over the Atlantic was a very old one, but it needed to be revived. At last it triumphed, and Christopher Columbus, a Genoese in the Spanish service, discovered Guanahani, or San Salvador, one of the Bahama Islands, at dawn on

Friday, October 12, 1492. He thought he had succeeded in finding a western route to the Indies, and therefore called his discovery the West Indies. On his third voyage westward, in 1498, he reached the American continent off the Island of Trinidad; but if he knew it to be a continent, he supposed it to be Asiatic, and so he continued to suppose it till his death in 1506. The next year a German geographer, drawing from the descriptions given by Amerigo Vespucci, a Florentine who had crossed the ocean under the Spanish and Portuguese flags, coined the name of America. Several years still elapsed before Columbus was known to have discovered a New World.

Fulness of the time.

No event in history appears to have been more happily timed. The middle ages were closing, the modern were opening; the great nations of Europe were putting forth their energies, material and immaterial, when the discovery of America came just in season to help and be helped by the movements of these stirring years. Had it taken place before, or long before, it would have suffered from the want of those who could turn it to account; had it been delayed, or long delayed, generations would have languished without the golden opportunities which it gave them. The old world needed the new; the new needed the old.

CHAPTER II.

SPANISH SETTLEMENTS.

Spanish adventures. FROM almost every point first gained in America, as well as from the shores of Spain, adventures, some great, some small, some national, some individual, were urged by the Spaniards in all directions. The West Indies, at first the whole, soon became the mere centre of the Spanish possessions.

Ponce de Leon in Florida. The first to reach the territory of the present United States was Ponce de Leon, a companion of Columbus. Long visited by dreams of riches, and latterly, in his advancing age, excited by rumors of a fountain in which youth might be renewed, Ponce set sail from Porto Rico in search of the treasures in the north. On Easter Sunday, — in the Spanish calendar *Pascua Florida*, — he descried a land to which, in his mingled visions of resurrection and of abundance, he gave the name of *Florida* or Flower-land, (1512.) Nine years later, with a commission from the Spanish crown, as governor of Florida, Ponce returned to conquer and to colonize his discovery. But driven off by the natives of the coast, the old adventurer left Florida to return no more, (1521.)

Various expeditions. A series of expeditions had already begun to scour the Atlantic coast. The Portuguese Cortereal had led the way, twenty years before, in a cruise towards the north, (1501.) A line of Spanish adventurers, intent upon treasure and conquest, succeeded.

Vasquez de Ayllon twice made descents upon Chicora, the later Carolina, (1520–24.) Gomez sailed farther to the north in quest of a western passage to richer lands, (1525.) Pamphilo de Narvaez tried his fortune in Florida, (1528,) whither also De Soto directed his greater expedition, and pursued his wanderings northward and westward (1539–43) with no greater reward than the discovery of the Mississippi, (1541.) At the same time, Vasquez Coronado was penetrating from Mexico high up into the interior, (1540–42,) while De Cabrillo (1542) was coasting the Pacific shore, and, though dying on the voyage, leaving his pilot, Ferrelo, to ascend as far as Oregon, (1543.) Of these western explorations there were few if any results to satisfy the explorers. Nor were the adventurers in the east better contented; the only ones to gain any thing being those who laded their ships with slaves. The natives had been pressed into bondage almost from the moment when they were first seen in the West Indies.

Luis de Cancello. A figure of more Christian aspect appears in Luis de Cancello, a Dominican friar. Obtaining an order from Spain that all the slaves from the northern shore of the Gulf of Mexico should be returned, he set sail with such as he could collect. Instead of proposing to conquer the natives, he went with the hope of converting them to a religion of peace. But in his first interview with them on the coast, he and two priests accompanying him were slain, (1549.)

Menendez. Nearly twenty years elapsed, and our soil was still unoccupied by the Spaniards. At length a veteran commander, Menendez de Aviles, engaged to complete the conquest and to commence the colonization of Florida, with a train of soldiers, priests, and negro slaves. He was of a stern temper, without a vision of romance or a touch of sensibility to turn him from the severe enterprise which he had assumed. He began with the foundation of St. Augustine, (September 8, 1565,) the oldest town in the United States. Then he routed and slew some French settlers who had lately encamped upon the ground claimed by Spain, and whose destruction had been one of the great incentives to his expedition. Where they fell most thickly, the conqueror marked out the site of a Christian church. The colony thus resolutely founded brought none of the rich returns that had been looked for; but it was not abandoned.

De Espejio and Vizcaino.

Fifteen years afterwards, the expeditions from Mexico were renewed by Ruiz (1580) and De Espejio, (1581,) the latter of whom, followed by soldiers and Indians, marched northward, until he named the country New Mexico, and founded the settlement of Santa Fe, the second town of the United States in point of age. Twenty years later, (1602,) a squadron under Sebastiano Vizcaino explored the Californian shore, bestowing upon its headlands and its bays many of the names which they still bear. It was Vizcaino's hope to colonize the coast, but he died in the midst of his schemes, (1608.)

Motives.

The motives of the Spanish settler, as we perceive, were partly of a high and partly of a low nature. Devoted to great aims and to generous deeds, he encountered, as Luis de Cancello did in Florida, the perils of an unknown shore, in order to impart to others the faith in which he lived and for which he was willing to die. But in another aspect the Spanish character grows dark and threatening. Men, like the greater part of those who have been mentioned, sought our land for gold or for dominion; sometimes, indeed, with a national object, but more generally for merely selfish ends. Motives of this sort led to scenes of cruelty and of carnage, on which it is, fortunately, unnecessary to dwell.

Institutions. The institutions of Spain were those of an absolute monarchy. They lent but little aid to the development of the better elements in the national character. Indeed, they rather encouraged the opposite elements, both before and after the colonies of the nation were founded. A military rule was the only political institution of Florida. It was in the hands of a few officials, whose authority was kept up at the sacrifice of the general progress of the settlements. A rigid system of trade, upholding a monopoly in favor of the government, or of the capitalists dependent on the government at home, increased the obstacles with which the colony had to contend.

Circumstances Coming with these motives and under these institutions, the Spaniards found themselves in circumstances of similar tendency. Choosing the south for their first, and, as it proved, their only settlements, from its promising the richest harvest, they met the influences springing from the air above them and from the earth beneath them. The habits of indulgence and of repose which ensued were any thing but favorable to character or to prosperity.

Extent of Spanish claims. Few and far between were the Spanish settlements. But the Spanish claims were universal. In the first place, there was a papal bull of 1493, conveying a right to all America. In the next place, there were the successive discoverers from Ponce de Leon to Vizcaino, whose labors had won the continent anew. The name of Florida was stretched from the Gulf of Mexico to the Gulf of St. Lawrence; that of New Mexico was made equally extensive in the interior and on the west. Could names, and deeds, and papal bulls have sufficed to support the Spanish claim, it would have prevailed throughout the United States.

CHAPTER III.

French Settlements.

New France. The approaches of France to our country were made, first by fishermen, (1504,) and then by navigators. A Florentine, Verrazzano, in the French service, sailing along the coast from Florida to Newfoundland, was not deterred by any previous discoveries from giving to the continent the name of *New France*, (1524.) Ten years after, the Frenchman Cartier renewed the name in voyages in and about the Gulf of St. Lawrence, (1534–42.)

Carolina. Fate of its Huguenots. Nothing, however, was done in a persevering way to fix the name upon the territory, until Admiral De Coligny conceived the idea of a colony to which his brother Protestants, the Huguenots, might repair for refuge against persecution in France. After failing to make a settlement in South America, De Coligny despatched a party to the northern coast, where a fort, named Charlesfort in honor of the French king, was erected near Port Royal in the present South Carolina, (1562.) This settlement likewise falling through, another was made upon the St. John's in Florida, where a fort called Caroline was reared, (1564.) The mutinous dispositions of the colonists and their Indian wars had much reduced the settlement, when it was annihilated by the Spanish force under Menendez de Aviles, (1565.) Such of the French as did not escape or fall in battle were put to death by the Spaniard and the Catholic, "not as Frenchmen," he is said to have declared, "but as Lutherans." Such was the unhappy fate of the first fugitives from the old world to the new. Objects at once of religious and of national animosity, they were pursued by enemies enlisted against them as on a crusade. The passions of Europe obtained fresh space in America; the feeble fell, the strong triumphed as they had done in older lands.

Expedition to avenge them.

But there was something inspiring, after all, in the associations of the western shore. If the fugitives thither were murdered by their foes, they were not forgotten by their friends. Three years after their victory, the Spaniards were surprised on the same ground by a French expedition under De Gourgues, a soldier of Gascony, who had sold his estate in order to avenge his fallen countrymen. He took the Spanish forts, and hung his prisoners, with the inscription above them, "Not as Spaniards or Moriscoes, but as Traitors, Robbers, and Assassins." Thus was our soil a second time darkened with the slaughter of strangers. Without waiting an attack from the Spaniards at St. Augustine, De Gourgues sailed home, the last of the French to attempt the possession of Florida or of Carolina, (1568.)

Acadie and Maine. De Monts and De Saussaye.

A long period elapsed before the French reappeared, except as fishermen or as traders, in any part of America. At length, a grant of all the territory from Pennsylvania to New Brunswick, under the name of Acadie, was made by Henry IV. of France to the Sieur de Monts, (1603,) and he, after a hard winter, made the first permanent settlement of Frenchmen in America at Port Royal, (1604,) since Annapolis. A later attempt to make a settlement upon Cape Cod met with immediate failure on account of the hostility of the natives, (1606.) Some years afterwards, one or two Jesuit missionaries crossed over from that part of Acadie which was occupied, to a part as yet unoccupied, within the limits of the present Maine, (1612.) They were followed the next year, by De Saussaye, the agent of Madame de Guercheville to whom the earlier grant to De Monts was now reconveyed; the limits being extended so far as to reach from Florida to the St. Lawrence. De Saussaye, accompanied by a few Jesuits, began the colony of St. Sauveur upon Mount Desert Island, off the coast of Maine, (1613.) It was hardly begun, however, before it was broken up by an attack from an English armed vessel belonging to the then rising colony of Virginia.

Canada. Champlain. Meantime the banners of France had been carried up the St. Lawrence. Champlain, the greatest leader whom the French had as yet followed to the west, laid the foundations of Quebec in the heart of the province of Canada, (1608.) The next year, forming an alliance with the Algonquins, then at war with the Iroquois or Five Nations of New York, he marched southward to the lake which bears his name, (1609.) Six years later, he took the lead in another foray which penetrated the forests on the southern shore of Lake Ontario, (1615.) A new way appeared to be open to French settlements in the United States.

Collisions with the English. But nothing followed. The English arms, after an interval of several years, were carried against the northern settlements of the French. Acadie, already made the subject of an English grant, and Canada were conquered, but restored, (1628–32.) Then the French came down in their turn, and drove the English from the trading posts established by the Plymouth colony on the Maine coast, (1631–35.) The attempts to repel them were in vain; on the contrary, they forbade the English to pass Pemaquid, a point midway between the Kennebec and the Penobscot. The interior was at the same time in the occupation of the French priests, if of any Europeans.

Priests and missionaries. The priests and the missionaries of France were the most prominent amongst her settlers. They came full of adventure as of faith, hesitating at no danger, shrinking from no sacrifice. That there should be some less worthy amongst the number was a matter of course. It was equally natural that, among the most worthy, there should be many to magnify their work, to count their converts too freely, and to oppose their antagonists too fiercely. But taken all in all, the French missionaries have a higher place than most early comers deserve in our history. What they were and what they did will appear more clearly at a later period.

Other settlers. With the priest came the soldier, the explorer, and the trader, all animated by the love of enterprise, to say nothing of its rewards in fame or in riches. They form a less sinister group than the Spanish settlers, more supple, more gay, though by no means more gallant or more adventurous.

Institutions. Much of the difference may be ascribed to the influence of the French institutions. These, at the time in question, were the institutions of a comparatively limited monarchy. If there were arbitrary influences in the government, sufficient, as we shall hereafter observe, to oppress its subjects and its colonies, there was also something of a more generous nature, by which the devotedness of the missionary, the bravery of the soldier, and the zeal of the adventurer were sustained.

Circumstances. The circumstances in which the French settlers were placed tended to confirm all their enterprise and all their fortitude. Abandoning the southern Carolina and drawing in the limits of Acadie on the south, they were for a long time concentrated upon northern shores and in northern valleys. In these lands, adventure was not to be pursued, nor was sustenance to be obtained, without energy and hardihood.

Extent of French claims.

In following the French into Acadie and Canada, we have gone far beyond the limits of the United States. But their Acadie embraced our Maine, or a large portion of it; their Canada comprehended our Vermont and our New York, or large portions of them; not to speak of the western regions afterwards included in the same province. We shall return to the French at the epoch of their later acquisitions. For the present, we leave the name of New France, bestowed by Verrazzano and Cartier in their voyages, and adopted by De Monts, Champlain, and De Saussaye, in their settlements, extending in immense proportions along the seaboard and in the interior. It was a title to be set against the Florida and the New Mexico of Spain.

CHAPTER IV.

ENGLISH SETTLEMENTS.

SECTION I. — *Early Movements.* 1492 *to* 1606.

England and Columbus. THE English were first connected with America through Columbus. When his plans of discovery were declined by the Portuguese court, he sent his brother Bartholomew to make the same offers to the king of England, (1484.) Bartholomew, long upon his way and upon his return, was bringing back some favorable proposals from Henry VII., just as Christopher was returning from his first voyage, (1493.) It was too late for England to obtain the services of Columbus.

Voyages of the Cabots. But it was just in time for England to profit by his discoveries. Both the king and his subjects, at least those of his subjects who were interested in navigation, seem to have caught the impulse naturally springing from such an enterprise as had been achieved. Within three years from the first return of Columbus, Henry authorized a Venetian then belonging to Bristol, John Cabot, with his three sons, to start an expedition at their own expense, in order to do whatever they could for themselves, and at the same time to set up the banners of the English monarch, as his vassals and deputies, upon the lands supposed to exist northward of those discovered by Columbus, (1496.) The Cabots, setting sail in the following year, (1497,) reached a shore called by them *Prima*

Vista, the First View, since known by the name of Labrador. It was more than a year before the continent was gained by Columbus. Another voyage, made a year later (1498) by Sebastian Cabot, the second son of John, and a native of England, was directed along the coast of the new continent from the latitude of Labrador to that of the Chesapeake.

Interval. Gilbert and Drake.

So successful a beginning augured great ends. But there ensued a long interval, in which none but isolated and remote adventures towards the west were undertaken in England. The fisheries of the north were for many years the only objects of attraction in the direction of America. Then the opening of hostilities, at first rather of a private or piratical than of a national character, against Spain,* drew the English towards the southern regions. But the central territories, those of the present United States, were long unvisited except for some passing purpose. More than three quarters of a century had elapsed since the coasting voyage of Sebastian Cabot, and both the Spaniards and the French had several times seized upon the shores discovered by the English navigators, when a new permission to possess and settle the western lands was given by Queen Elizabeth to one of her noblest subjects, Sir Humphrey Gilbert, (1578.) At the same period, while Sir Francis Drake, the half hero, half freebooter of the English navy, was on his voyage of adventure and plunder round the world, he gave the name of New Albion to the coasts of California and Oregon. Thus gaining a foothold on the western as well as on the eastern side of the continent, England was recalled, at a moment of general activity throughout the nation, to her interests in America.

* Beginning about 1570, though there was no formal war until 1585.

Raleigh.

Sir Humphrey Gilbert perished in the course of a second attempt to reach his American possessions, (1583.) But his claims were immediately transferred to his half brother, Walter Raleigh, the courtier and the cavalier of the age in England, (1584.) A voyage of exploration was immediately made under his directions to the coast of our North Carolina, of which so flattering an account was returned to him and to his sovereign, that the name of Virginia, from the virgin Queen Elizabeth, was not thought too great for the new land.

Failures of his colonies.

In the following year, (1585,) Sir Richard Grenville, one of the chief commanders of the time, left a colony of one hundred and eighty persons at Roanoke Island; but such were the hardships which they encountered, that they were only too well satisfied to be taken home by Sir Francis Drake a year afterwards. They had scarcely gone when Grenville returned with supplies for them, and he, unwilling to have the colony abandoned, left fifteen of his mariners to keep possession until they could be reënforced, (1586.) The little band was gone, murdered, it was believed, by the natives, when, in the next year, (1587,) a fresh party of one hundred and seventeen arrived. Soon after they came, the first English child to see the light in America was born. She was the daughter of Ananias Dare, and the granddaughter of John White, the leader of the expedition, who gave her the name of Virginia. But the presence of the infant brought no better fate to the colony than had befallen its predecessors. The one hundred and eighteen disappeared, and though sought for at various times, were never heard of more. Raleigh lost heart as well as means. He made over his patent to a number of persons, (1589,) who, with less enterprise than he, met with still less success. North

Carolina was but a waste as far as English settlements were concerned, and Virginia but a name.

Gosnold and others. Many years passed before any further attempts were made to occupy the American coast. The cessation of hostilities with Spain * at length reopened the way to commercial and colonial enterprise. Bartholomew Gosnold, after landing on Cape Cod, sailed thence to Buzzard's Bay, where, on Elizabeth's Island, named after his queen, he commenced, but soon abandoned, a settlement, (1602.) The adjoining coasts were revisited the next year (1603) by Martin Pring, and again, the next year but one, (1605,) by George Weymouth, both, like Gosnold, commanders of distinction. The preparation for settlements was decidedly resumed.

Ill success of the English. It was high time. The Spaniards had their St. Augustine and their Santa Fe, the French their Port Royal, though this was beyond the limits of our United States. But the English, the first to discover the coast, were still without a single foothold upon it. Wherever they had gained one, it had slipped from beneath them.

Section II. — *Companies.* 1606 *to* 1635.

Organized efforts. Hitherto the efforts of the English in exploring and in settling the American shore had been those of individuals. No one, indeed, unless it were those who went on voyages for fishery or for trade, attempted his enterprise without the formal countenance of the sovereign. But there had been no organized efforts such as were now prepared.

* 1604. But it was some time since the war had been generally carried on.

Patent of Virginia.

A year or two after James I. succeeded to the English throne, he issued the patent of Virginia. This was a twofold grant of the American territory from what is now North Carolina to what is now Maine. Of this vast tract, the southerly half* was appropriated to the First Colony, and the northerly † to the Second Colony, each colony to be founded and governed by a separate council, to which the grant was made. The council or company, as it is generally styled, of the First Colony went by the name of London, from the residence of its prominent members. For a similar reason, the name of Plymouth was given to the council or company of the Second Colony. The great point, however, is this, that the parties to the patent were not colonists, but capitalists, not adventurers, but speculators, who, in their respective corporations in England, not in America, were declared possessors of the best portion of the American territory. At the same time, the companies were invested with ample powers to settle "colonists and servants," to impose duties, and to coin money. Their obligations, in return, were to pay over to the crown a share of their profits,‡ and to support the laws and the church of England. To exercise some sort of supervision over so great corporations as these, a council for Virginia was instituted by the king, who, to complete his work, put forth a code of laws and regulations for the direction of the various bodies which he had created.

* From lat. 34° to lat. 38°, with a right, if first in the field, to make settlements as far north as 41°.

† From lat. 41° to lat. 45°, with a right, if first in the field, to make settlements as far south as 38°.

‡ One fifth of the gold and silver, and one fifteenth of the copper, that might be found.

THE LONDON COMPANY.

Members and colonists. The moving spirit of the London Company appears to have been Richard Hakluyt, prebendary of Bristol, afterwards of Westminster, who had been interested in American colonization from the time of Raleigh's expeditions. Around him were gathered many eminent and energetic men, among them Sir George Calvert, the future founder of Maryland, but none of greater promise, in relation to the work before them, than Bartholomew Gosnold, the settler of Elizabeth's Island, and John Smith, a hero in the east long before he turned his face westward. Gosnold and Smith were both amongst the first colonists.

Jamestown. It was in midwinter, (December 19, 1606,) that an expedition, one hundred strong, set out from England. A feeble band as regarded their individual resources, they were strong in the company by which they were sent to stranger shores. The voyage was long, by the common route of the West Indies, but Virginia was reached at last. The spring (May 13, 1607) saw the beginning of the first English town in America. Its royal name of Jamestown is now a name alone.

New charters. The company had hardly begun its work when it sought new powers. Three years after the patent, a second charter was framed, giving additional authority to the English company, and extending the American limits to the latitude of Philadelphia, (1609.) Three years later, (1612,) a third charter vested the powers of the company in a General Court of the members, and added the Bermuda Islands to their domains. If charters were all that the company needed in order to flourish, it bade fair to be great and enduring.

The fortunes of the colony were less promising. Some-

Fortunes of the colony. times at peace, sometimes at war* with the natives, sometimes contented, sometimes despairing amongst themselves, the colonists went through great vicissitudes. One cause of feebleness is plain enough; it is the entire dependence of the colony upon the company and the company's representatives. Another cause of equal moment was the variety of rank and of character in the colony. The gentleman and the felon, the ardent seeker after adventure and the patient toiler for subsistence, the freeman, the apprentice, and the slave,† made up a community too mixed to possess any steadiness of growth. The three first years, (1607–9,) the colonists hung upon John Smith, who had become their president in the year following the settlement of Jamestown. It is curious to see how he led, rebuked, supported them; he, as the strong man, guiding them, as feeble children. One year, (1610,) the colony is all but abandoned; another, (1613,) it is strong enough to make the attack already mentioned upon the French settlements in the north. But the tendency to increase, though interrupted, continues, and not without support from the company in England.

Institutions. The first step to raise the colonists from a state of mere vassalage was the grant of an estate to each settler, (1615.) The progress from the landholder to the freeman followed. The colony had been bound, as has been stated, to maintain the church of England. Its civil authorities consisted, first of the English crown and Parliament, then of the English council, then of the English company, by which, according to the various charters, the local officers were appointed. These were, in the beginning, a council, with a president; but in a year or two from the beginning, a governor and suite, at first with-

* The Indian wars are related in Part II. Chapter IV.

† A Dutch man of war brought the first negro slaves, in 1619.

out and afterwards with a council. At length, under the government of Sir George Yeardley, the freemen of the colony, representing eleven corporations or plantations, were called, as burgesses, to a General Assembly, to take the matter of taxes, besides other affairs of importance, into their own hands, (1619.) This was the system of the colonial constitution granted by the company two years afterwards, (1621.) In other words, the executive authority was in the hands of a governor, the judicial in those of a governor and a council, with an appeal to an Assembly, and the legislative in that of a governor, a council, and an Assembly, all subject to the company, which, of course, was subject to the laws and the authorities of England.

An infant colony. We are apt to exaggerate the importance of the English settlements, in comparison with those of the French or the Spanish, or any other nation in our country. The truth is, that Virginia, like most of the settlements which we shall find in the north, was but an infant colony, unable to regulate its trade or its education, its habits of life or of thought, except in submission to external authorities. One or two examples, occurring under the company's jurisdiction, illustrate the dependence of the colony during the entire period of which we are now treating. A design of a college for native as well as English youth, started in England with large subscriptions, found no fulfilment in Virginia, (1619–21.) Even the want of wives was met, not by individual devotion, but by a company speculation; a large number of young women of good character being transported to be sold for a hundred and twenty, or even a hundred and fifty pounds of tobacco (at three shillings a pound) to the lonely settlers, (1620–21.)

Fall of the company. Nothing, however, marks the utter dependence of the colony so plainly as its inactivity during the troubles in which the company became involved.

Dissensions amongst the members, and jealousies amongst those who were not members, led to the royal interference; the result being the fall of the company, with all its expenditures* heavy on its head, (1624.) The colony at this time numbered about two thousand, the relics of nine thousand who had been sent out. Yet for all the two thousand did to prove their existence or their independence, the colony might have been supposed to be the company's shadow, too unsubstantial to support or to oppose the power to which it owed its being.

Virginia a royal province. Virginia became a royal province. The governor and the council received their appointment from the king, the freemen continuing to elect their Assembly. It was a national government, instead of a corporation system, and as such it seemed to relieve the Virginians. At any rate, they grew so much in spirit as to make a stand against the royal grant of what they considered their territory to the proprietor of Maryland. Their governor, John Harvey, not taking part with them as they wished, they deposed him, and sent him virtually a prisoner to England, (1635.) The king, of course, restored the governor, but without reducing the colony to silence or to retribution, (1636-37.) The spirit of dependence, however, lingered.

Growth of the colony. But the principles of growth and of independence were at work. Among the earliest settlers were men of culture and of earnestness, men who, like Alexander Whitaker, "a scholar, a graduate, and a preacher," devoted themselves to the elevation of the colony. Among the earliest governors were Lord De la Ware, (1611,) and Sir George Yeardley, (1619-21,) both of strong character and of strong influence. Around such individuals as these there would naturally gather an in-

* From £100,000 to £150,000.

creasing number and a higher stamp of colonists. The interest of the mother country in the colony would naturally be extended when the dissolution of the company opened the way to general emigration and general enterprise. The development of Virginia seemed sure.

THE PLYMOUTH COMPANY.

Members. Among the members of the Plymouth Company were many personages of distinction. The lord chief justice of England, Sir John Popham, the governor of Plymouth, Sir Ferdinando Gorges, and two Gilberts, kinsmen and successors of Sir Humphrey Gilbert and Sir Walter Raleigh, all engaged in the enterprise. The higher the rank, however, of individual members in any association, the more likely, in most cases, are clashing pretensions and menacing divisions. The Plymouth Company never held together in such a way as to carry out any effective operations.

Colonization attempted. A few members made the first move by sending out a colony of forty-five persons, who encamped for one brief year upon an island at the mouth of the Kennebec, (1607–8.) Some time elapsed before any new expedition was undertaken. Nor would any, it is probable, have been undertaken then, but for the active agency of John Smith, who, four or five years after his return from Virginia, entered the service of the Plymouth Company. A careful voyage from the Penobscot to Cape Cod impressed him so favorably, that he gave the country the name of New England, obtaining for himself the title of its admiral, (1614.) But his persevering exertions to discharge his office and to colonize his chosen land were in vain; nor was any thing more attempted by the company until it was transformed by a new charter into the

Council of Plymouth for New England, with the right to all the territory from the latitude of Philadelphia to that of Chaleur Bay, (1620.)

Various proprietors and companies.

Even then, the Council for New England set on foot no colonization of its own. Its energies seemed to be spent in making grants to individuals, — some of them its members, — or to associations, by whom the settlement of New England was to be accomplished. Singular enough, considering that it was New England, a large proportion of these subordinate agencies was directed to the establishment of what may be called a number of lordly domains upon the soil. In following this succession of proprietors and of companies, we lose sight of the Council for New England.

Settlement of Plymouth.

One settlement, originally made without a grant from the council, was by much the most important for many years. It was on no large scale. One hundred and two passengers in the Mayflower landed at a place already called New Plymouth, (December 11, 1620.) They were a band of Puritans, whose extreme principles had led to their exile, first from England to Holland, (1608,) and then from Holland to America. Obtaining a grant from the London Company, they set sail for Virginia, but landed to the north of that province, in the limits of New England. The year following, they procured a patent from the Council for New England, (1621.) But not in their own name; the grant being made to one of a company of London merchants, with whom they had formed a partnership before sailing to the west. The Londoners, holding their title under the council, thus constituted a sort of company within a company. Nor was it until after six years, marked by many troubles and by many injuries, that the colonists extricated themselves from this twofold dependence by the payment of a large sum to the London merchants, (1626.) The difficulties with the merchants had been the least of the trials of the Plymouth settlers. Half of the one hundred and two of the Mayflower died within a year from the landing. "In the time of most distress," says the historian of the settlement, Governor Bradford, "there were but six or seven sound persons." After disease came want; "all their victuals were spent, and they were only to rest on God's providence; at night not many times knowing where to have a bit of any thing the next day." When a ship load of fresh immigrants arrived nearly two years after, "the best dish they," the earlier comers, "could present their friends with, was a lobster or a piece of fish, without bread or any thing else but a cup of fair spring water." Nevertheless the Pilgrims, as they were called, sustained and extended their settlements. A second patent from the council was obtained for the country near the mouth of the Kennebec, where a trading post was presently established, (1628.) The whole extent of settlements, both at Plymouth and on the Kennebec, was included in a third patent, two years afterwards, (1630.)

Its distinction in history.

One who reads the history of these times without personal or national prepossessions will not find any thing of a very extraordinary character in the settlement of Plymouth. They who came thither, braving the perils of the unknown sea and the unknown shore, were but doing what had been done by their countrymen in Virginia, and by others in other settlements in America. Solemnity is certainly imparted to their enterprise by the reflection that they came to maintain the doctrines and laws which their consciences approved, but which the authorities of England proscribed. Yet the Huguenots of Carolina had done the same thing more than half a century before. The true distinction of the Puritans of Plymouth is this, that they relied upon themselves, that they adopted their own institutions and developed their own resources, of course in a feeble, but not the less in a manly manner. Before they landed, they "covenant and combine themselves together into a civil body politic, to enact such just and equal laws as shall be thought most convenient for the general good of the colony." The state thus founded was continued in entire independence of external authority, except in so far as its territory was held by grants from the Council for New England.

Political forms. The political forms of Plymouth were singularly simple. Every settler admitted to the privileges of the colony, and not an apprentice or a servant, was a freeman, a member of the body by which all affairs were administered or directed. An assembly of a representative character was not held for nearly twenty years, (1639.) Out of the freemen a smaller body was taken to exercise the every-day functions of government. It was composed merely of the governor and his assistants, or council, of which he was simply the presiding officer with a double vote. The first governor was John Carver; the second was William Bradford, who retained the post, with a few interruptions, for thirty-six years. It marks the simplicity, not to say the distastefulness, of these offices, that there should have been a law subjecting a man not having served the preceding year, and yet refusing to be governor, to a fine of twenty pounds, equivalent to a much larger amount in our day. A military body was headed by Miles Standish, the hero of the settlement.

Spirit. But the spirit beneath these forms is of more importance than the forms themselves. The earnest faith of the Puritans was at once the source from which the colony sprang, and the strength by which it grew. But it was also the principle of harsh and arbitrary measures. It transformed the exiles into persecutors, many of whose companions found themselves again exiles, escaping from the mother country only to be thrust out from the sandy coasts and chilly hovels of the colony.

Grants. Attempt at general government. Chaos.

Meantime New England was portioned out under various names. The secretary of the council, John Mason, called his grant Mariana, stretching from Salem River to the head of the Merrimac, (1621.) The lands between the Merrimac and the Kennebec were conveyed under the name of Maine, in a grant to Mason in company with Sir Ferdinando Gorges, (1622.) The first settlement, however, in that neighborhood was made by some fishermen on the shore near Monhegan Island, beyond the Kennebec, and therefore independently of Mason and Gorges, (1622.) The next year the sites of the later Portsmouth and Dover were occupied, each under a separate association, to which the two proprietors had partially transferred their claims, (1623.) Meanwhile the Council for New England had been attempting great things, commissioning Captain Francis West as "Admiral of New England," Captain Robert Gorges as "Governor General," and the Rev. William Morrell as "Overseer of Churches." The last named was a clergyman of the English church. "He had," says Governor Bradford, "I know not what power and authority of superintendency over other churches granted him, and sundry instructions for that end, but he never showed it or made any use of it." "It should seem," says the stout Puritan, "he saw it was in vain; he only spoke of it to some here at his going away." The governor general and the admiral cut no better figure. The council, as if disgusted by the fate of their general officers, surrendered their domains to chaos. New grants, within as well as without the limits of those already made, were issued by the council, or by members of the council; the whole coast from Plymouth to the Penobscot being cut up with dividing and intersecting lines.

New Hampshire and New Somersetshire.

Order began to be evolved. The partnership between Mason and Ferdinando Gorges being dissolved, (1629,) each obtained a new grant for himself. Mason gave the name of New Hampshire to the tract between the Merrimac (afterwards between the Salem) and the Piscataqua Rivers. The district between the Piscataqua and the Kennebec was called New Somersetshire by Gorges, who donned the title of Governor General of New England. "There was a consultation had," writes an Englishman at the time, "to send him thither with a thousand soldiers." The scheme of a general government was not yet abandoned, (1634.)

Cape Ann and Salem.

A company of Puritans in England had some time before acquired a fishing station of the Plymouth colony at Cape Ann, (1624.) Thither a few settlers were sent; Roger Conant being soon after invited to be the governor, (1625.) He was a man of great spirit, who had found it prudent to leave Plymouth in consequence of his too liberal Puritanism, and who now sustained the puny colony on the cape by his courage and his judgment. Perceiving a much better position at Naumkeag, he removed thither, (1626,) and there held the ground with a few dispirited adherents until, in accordance with his recommendation, nearly a hundred settlers arrived from England under the conduct of John Endicott, (1628.) Endicott took the direction of the colony as the agent of a new company, by which a grant of the tract between the Charles and the Merrimac Rivers had been procured from the Council for New England. The name of Naumkeag was changed to Salem in the ensuing year, (1629.)

Company of Massachusetts Bay.

New associates having joined the enterprise, — John Winthrop, Isaac Johnson, and others of note from Boston, — a royal charter was procured for "The Governor and Company of the Massachusetts Bay in New England." A governor, deputy governor, and eighteen assistants or councillors, were appointed to hold monthly courts and to conduct the affairs of administration. The members at large were to be convened from time to time in general courts, by which officers were to be chosen and laws enacted, subject only to the condition of conforming to the laws of England. No mention of religion or of religious liberty was made, it being out of the question for the Puritans to obtain the formal recognition of their own faith. Thus going behind the grant of the Council for New England, the Massachusetts association obtained an independent position, in the same character that belonged to the council itself, as an English corporation. But four months after the date of the charter, it was decided, on the proposal of the governor, Matthew Cradock, "to transfer the government of the plantation to those that shall inhabit there," (July 28, 1629.) This at once changed the corporation from an English to a colonial one.

Boston.

Reënforcements had been sent out to the colony at Salem, (1629.) But the accessions to the list were now so great as to suggest the increase of settlements. The appointment of John Winthrop as governor, under the transfer of the charter to the colony, was followed by "the great emigration," so called, of about one thousand, who, after tarrying at Salem and the neighboring Charlestown, voted "that Trimountain shall be called Boston," (September 7, 1630,) and there took up their position at the centre of Massachusetts Bay. The first General Court was held soon after, (October 19,) and from that time Boston took the lead of Massachusetts and of New England. It was entitled to do so in Massachusetts by the rank, the education, and the devotion of its settlers. It was entitled to do so in New England as the chief place in Massachusetts, then, and for many years after, the most important of all the English settlements.

Increase and independence.

The new colony grew apace. All around Boston there sprang up towns, some on spots previously occupied by individuals or by parties, but many in districts hitherto unvisited. Each new settlement contributed to the increase and the independence of the colony. So independent in some respects did its position become, that the Council for New England, sometimes as a body and sometimes through its individual members, began to dread and to resist the rising power. There was full enough in the attitude of the Massachusetts colonists to warrant the suspicion of Sir Ferdinando Gorges, "that they would in short time wholly shake off the royal jurisdiction of the sovereign magistrate."

Charter government.

No colony certainly had ever been endowed with similar powers. Charter government had hitherto been confined to companies in England. It was first inspired with all its vitality in Massachusetts. As the government, not merely of a corporation, but of a state, it invested its holders with an authority independent of all besides a mere allegiance to the crown and the law of the mother land. The officers elsewhere, as in the royal province of Virginia, appointed in England, were here elected on the spot, and by those over whom they were to preside. Governor, council, and assembly, all belonged to and proceeded from the freemen. With them resided every form of authority, save only the distant and the indefinite shapes of royal and parliamentary supremacy.

Puritan principles. It by no means followed that the government was a liberal one. Whatever it might appear to be in the abstract, its operation was rigidly controlled by Puritan principles. These narrowed its sphere and stiffened its action. An early vote declared no one a freeman under the charter who was not a church member, (1631.) As but a small proportion of the inhabitants were church members, there were less freemen than non-freemen. The privileges of the charter being thus restricted to the pale of the church, the church and the state became virtually one. The elders of the church, clerical and lay, were as much magistrates as the magistrates themselves.

External relations. Such a system favored the independence of the colony in its relations with the mother country; indeed, in all external relations. It made the colony strong in itself, relying upon its own resources, providing for its own wants. The villages of Massachusetts were hardly begun, its fields were hardly turned up by the plough, when the General Court "agree to give four hundred pounds towards a school or college," (1636.) This was subsequently located at Cambridge, and named after its first private benefactor, John Harvard, a clergyman of Charlestown, (1638.) The same year of the grant from the court, when such a sacrifice for the future must have strained the entire colony, the offer of certain noblemen to join the settlers, on condition of preserving their hereditary honors, was rejected, (1636.) All the while the colony was contending against the machinations of its adversaries in and out of the Council for New England. The charter, threatened again and again, was at length demanded back; but the men of Massachusetts stood firm, and it was spared, (1634–38.)

Internal relations. The internal relations of the colonists were by no means equally secure. The system that cut down the charter itself was not likely to respect the development of the individual. The very members of the ruling class were under the most rigid restraint. John Eliot, afterwards the missionary to the Indians, was obliged to retract the censures which he passed upon the magistrates for making an Indian treaty without consulting the freemen, (1634.) Israel Stoughton, a deputy, who ventured to write against the pretensions of the magistrates to a negative upon the General Court, was forced to ask that his manuscript "be burned as weak and offensive," and was then excluded from office for three years, (1635.) Roger Williams, denying the power of the magistrates to compel attendance upon their form of service, or to bind the conscience by human laws, was driven into exile, (1635.) It marks the spirit of the place, that even Roger Williams, the professed advocate of religious liberty, should have transgressed the very principle which he advocated, by forbidding his wife to pray with him because she would not join his scission from the church at Salem. These were all individual instances. There presently arose a party in opposition to the dominant system. It was led by a woman, Anne Hutchinson; but many of the principal men united with her in setting up what they termed a "covenant of grace" against the "covenant of works" upheld by the Puritan rulers. The leaders of the party were all banished, (1638.) One cannot wonder that William Blackstone, an early settler, who first invited the Massachusetts emigrants to settle at Boston, should retire before them, exclaiming, "I left England because I liked not the lord bishops, and now I like not the lord brethren."

Connecticut.

The Massachusetts people were already emigrating. A neighboring territory, conveyed by the Council for New England to the Earl of Warwick, passed into the hands of Lord Say and Seal, Lord Brook, and others,

(1632.) Upon their domain, a party from Plymouth established a trading post, (1633,) while another and a larger company from Massachusetts founded actual settlements at Windsor and Hartford, together called the Connecticut colony, (1635.) John Winthrop, son of the Massachusetts governor, and afterwards governor of Connecticut, led the first expedition on the part of the proprietors, and began a settlement at Saybrook, (1635.) A third colony was begun, a year or two later, by emigrants from England under the lead of John Davenport and Theophilus Eaton, who, intending to settle in Massachusetts, were driven by the dissensions of that colony to New Haven, (1638.)

Providence and Rhode Island. Connecticut was not the only colony to profit by the strifes in Massachusetts. Roger Williams, the exile, began the plantation of Providence, (1636.) As the founder of a colony, with the consent of the natives, to whom, as well as to his persecuting countrymen, he was a faithful friend, Williams deserves a far higher fame than he would ever have won as an agitator. He was followed by some of the Hutchinson exiles, who began a second colony on the northern shore of the island since called Rhode Island, (1638.) They, like Williams, obtained their lands from the natives.

Dissolution of the council. The Council for New England, with or without whose patents so many settlements had been made, was now no more. Opposed by the advocates of a free fishery and a free trade, it had lately met with fresh assaults from those who regarded the churches of Plymouth and of Massachusetts as the offspring of schism and of sin. The council was weary of itself. Its efforts after a general government of the colonies had miscarried. Its grants had ceased to be in demand; indeed, in an honest point of view, there were no more to be made. Its members, however, thought differently, and having once more parcelled out the territory of New England amongst themselves, they surrendered their patent to the crown, (1635.)

End of companies. Thus ended the companies created by the patent of Virginia. One, lasting but eighteen years, began the single colony of Virginia. The other, continuing eleven years more, did not found a solitary settlement. It saw, however, quite a number of settlements made by others under its grants or upon its lands. The only office that either company had fulfilled, was to clear the way for individual enterprise. This done, both fell, and without a regret from any side.

Position of New England. When the Virginia Company came to an end, its colony was declared a royal province. No such change ensued upon the dissolution of the Council for New England. Massachusetts, the chief settlement in the territory, was already provided with a royal charter. The other settlements were too insignificant to attract legislation, even if they attracted attention from England. Many of them, like Plymouth, were able to govern themselves. The rest would be provided for in time.

Thomas Morton. It was plain, however, that the New England colonies needed some other system than they had to establish their relations amongst themselves. An instance in point occurs in the case of Thomas Morton "of Clifford's Inn, gentleman," as he called himself. Taking the lead of a few settlers encamped at Mount Wollaston, near Boston, he gave the hill the name of Mare-Mount, of which he styled himself "Mine Host," (1626.) The use of the church liturgy and the confidence of the Indians, whom he employed as his huntsmen, gave great umbrage to the neighboring colonists, the more so that he led a free and easy, perhaps a sensual, life upon his mount, and thus attracted numbers from the surrounding settlements. A sort of crusade was started by "the chief of the straggling plantations," as Governor Bradford of Plymouth describes them; Plymouth, at their request, assuming the lead, and sending a party under Miles Standish to take Morton prisoner. He was sent to England, (1628.) As he had the audacity to return, he was apprehended by the authorities of the infant colony of Massachusetts Bay, whose charter covered his territory. The court ordered him to "be set in the bilboes, and after sent prisoner to England," his goods being seized and his house burned for wrongs, it was alleged, that had been done to the Indians, (1630.) After appealing to the privy council by petition, and to the English nation in a work called "New English Canaan," Morton returned again to encounter fine and imprisonment, (1643,) and to die in poverty, (1646.) Whatever were his faults, whether "the lord of misrule," as his adversaries represented him, or not, Thomas Morton was certainly handled by his fellow-colonists in a way the most opposed to justice and to peace.

Section III. — *Proprietors.* 1630 *to* 1638.

Grant of Maryland. A new form of grant appears. Hitherto, the individual obtaining possession of territory procured it, like Mason or like Gorges, from a company to whose authority the acquisition was subject. It was by a patent from the crown that Sir George Calvert, Lord Baltimore, was made "lord and proprietor" of a tract between the Potomac River and the latitude of Philadelphia, (1632.) To this he gave the name of Maryland, and thither, to a settlement named St. Mary's, his son, after the father's death, led a band of two hundred, (1634.)

Thus was constituted a proprietary government. The

A proprietary government. proprietor held an authority that was supreme, save in its subordination to the sovereign from whom it emanated. He directed the administration and the legislation of the colony, appointing the executive officers, the governor, especially, as his representative, and controlling the proceedings of the colonists in their assemblies. To him likewise belonged the quitrents, or taxes upon occupied lands, in addition to the general taxes for the support of the government. The colonists, on their part, — that is, "the freemen of the province," — were to have their assembly, in which their "advice, consent, and approbation" might be given or withheld in relation to the course of the proprietor.

Religious liberty. As with other settlements, so with Maryland, there are exaggerations in some of the histories. A vast deal of fine writing has been devoted to the magnanimity with which the Maryland charter provided for religious liberty. The instrument makes no mention of the subject, or of the establishment of religion, except to leave the matter to the proprietor, subject on this point, as on others, to the laws of England. The Calvert family, being Roman Catholic, could not make their own faith paramount, nor would they, perhaps, have done so, even if they could. They wanted settlers of all creeds, whose numbers and whose energies alone could give real value to their domains. It was simply a matter of policy, therefore, with the proprietary family, to let the question of religion rest exactly where it was left by the charter. We may hope that they were not merely politic enough, but generous enough, even in an age which knew little of generosity, to throw open their province to Christians, without any limitation in favor of one branch or of another.

Troubles. The colony, young as it was, fell into troubles. Its assembly began to make laws without waiting for the proprietor's legal initiative. At the same time, both proprietor and assembly were involved in disturbances excited by a member of the Virginia council, William Clayborne. Virginia herself took it ill that her territory should be invaded even by royal grants. Clayborne conceived his rights to be assailed, inasmuch as he, individually, had established trading posts within the Maryland limits. Taking up arms against the colony, he was overpowered, and sent back to Virginia, (1635.)

Other proprietors.

Other proprietors, besides those of Maryland, were in the field. Sir Robert Heath, attorney general to Charles I., obtained the patent of a vast region on the south of Virginia, and as far as the Gulf of Mexico. This he called Carolana, (1630.) Another tract, called New Albion, and including the present New Jersey, was conveyed in an irregular instrument from the viceroy of Ireland to Sir Edward Plowden, as an earl palatine, (1636.) These were but grants, not settlements, yet significant of the growing pretensions of England to the soil of America.

Conclusion. English motives.

No other nation of Europe, it need hardly be suggested, had made any settlements, individual, associated, or national, at all comparable to those of the English. Nor had there been any such definite purposes of settlement, separate from mere adventure, on the part of any other race. The English settler was emphatically a settler, rather than a treasure seeker or a conqueror, a missionary or a trader. Not that he shrank from other enterprises, but that his main motive was to gain a home, and an abiding one, in the western world. Acting in harmony with this were the desire to escape from oppression or from want, the yearning after a new faith or a new life, the various impulses that have appeared, it is

4

hoped, in the preceding pages. That there were baser instincts tending to the same end has also appeared.

Institutions. The institutions of the English were favorable to their purposes as settlers. The subjects of a limited monarchy, they brought with them the habits and the laws of comparative freemen. That they might have been freer in their political principles, needs not to be suggested anew. But in their varying charters, in their varying magistrates and tribunals, even in the least liberal, the English colonists possessed privileges to which neither the Frenchman nor the Spaniard in their neighborhood had ever actually aspired.

Circumstances. Of an equally encouraging description were the circumstances of the English. The seaboard was theirs, all at least that they could immediately occupy. The portion which they possessed was partly in the north and partly in the south, provided, therefore, with the resources of both regions, at the same time that it was not exposed either to the indulgence of the extreme south or to the privation of the extreme north. Within opened an interior region rich in its streams, its fields, its forests, its mountains; without lay the broad sea, accessible at a hundred harbors. Whatever mere position could effect was promised to the English settlers.

English names. As yet they had but begun the work before them. Their humble towns on the coast, their humbler villages and hamlets in the country, gave small token of their destinies. But the names of their territories were full of strength and of grandeur. There was New Albion on the Pacific, New Albion on the Atlantic. There was the land of Queen Elizabeth — Virginia; there was the land of the nation — New England.

CHAPTER V.

Dutch Settlements.

Group of traders.

A later group of settlers comes forward. It is composed not so much of settlers, however, as of traders, who, to carry out their commercial operations, lay the foundations of a state, and give it the name of their nation.

Spirit in Holland.

The spirit of the preceding half century in Holland had been that of a people rescuing themselves from a foreign dominion and building up a power of their own. Europe has nothing so brilliant upon its records at the time as the war of independence which the Netherlands waged, and waged successfully, against Spain. It might have been argued that such a nation would have surpassed all others in America.

Dwindled in America.

But it was not so. The Dutch came late upon the scene. They came, moreover, not with the spirit or the law of their nation so much as with those of the commercial companies by which they were sent out or controlled. The story of their settlements is therefore an anomaly in the history of American colonization. The fire of the mother-land languishes in the colony. It is because the colony is not a national, but a corporate settlement, from its beginning to its end.

Hudson's voyage.

The very year in which Holland became independent, (1609,) Henry Hudson, an Englishman in Dutch employ, sailed in search of a northern passage to the Pacific. Shut out by the ice from his projected course, he steered westward, and reaching the coast of Maine, cruised southward as far as Virginia, giving to Cape Cod, on the way, the name of New Holland. As he returned towards the north, he discovered Delaware Bay, and entered the River of the Mountains, as he called the stream since known by his own name. These waters, first visited, perhaps, by Cabot in the English, (1498,) then by Verrazzano in the French, (1524,) and then by Gomez in the Spanish (1525) service, were now more thoroughly explored by Hudson. As their discoverer, he returned to Holland, and as their possessors, the Dutch sent out various vessels to trade with the natives and to claim the shores, (1610–13.)

Company of New Netherland.

The earliest of the Dutch posts was on the Island of Manhattan, (1613.) There the first craft of European construction was built and launched by Adrian Block, whose ship had been destroyed by fire. In his Manhattan vessel, appropriately called the Restless, Block went through Long Island Sound as far as Cape Cod, then, leaving his name for Block Island, he returned home, (1614.) The prospects of the new country looking well, the association of Amsterdam and Hoorn merchants, by whom Block and other explorers had been employed, gave it the name of New Netherland, and applied to the States General for protection in their enterprise. This was obtained, in the shape of an exclusive right for three years "to visit and penetrate the said lands lying in America between New France and Virginia, whereof the coasts extend from the fortieth to the forty-fifth degrees of latitude;" that is, from Delaware to Passamaquoddy Bay. The association, taking the name of the United New Netherland Company, set themselves to work, (1614.) A fort was built at Manhattan; a fortified trading post was established up the river, near the present Albany, (1615.)

Meanwhile the little Restless, commanded by Cornelius Hendricksen, was exploring the coast to the southward, and ascending the Delaware, then called the South River, to distinguish it from the North, or Prince Maurice's River, as the Hudson was variously styled.

Proposals of the Plymouth Puritans.

The monopoly of the New Netherland Company expiring without their being able to obtain its renewal, other parties entered into the trading operations of which the colony was the centre. But the old company, or rather a portion of its members, retained a sort of vantage ground. To them, accordingly, the Puritan exiles in Holland — the same who settled Plymouth — addressed their proposals of emigrating to New Netherland. The party to whom the application was made petitioned the States General that the Puritans might be taken under the national protection, in which case the petition asserts "upwards of four hundred families" "from this country and from England" would settle in the Dutch colony, (February, 1620.) The prayer of the petitioners was refused.

West India Company.

The New Netherland Company had ceased to be a body in which the nation confided. An old project of a West India Company was revived, and a corporation of that name established, with power, not only over New Netherland, but the entire American coast, (1621.) It was some time before the company began its operations; but when it did begin, it was evidently in earnest, (1623.)

Walloon colony.

Ten years had elapsed since the trading post on Manhattan had been occupied, and there were still none but trading posts in all New Netherland. Not a colony worthy of the name as yet existed. The only plan that had ever been formed of establishing one came from the Plymouth Puritans. It is a singular coincidence that

4*

the first colony to be actually established was one of refugees, like the Puritans, from persecution. These were a band of Protestant Walloons, from the Spanish Netherlands, who, after applying unsuccessfully to the London Company of England, enlisted as colonists under the West India Company of Holland. Sent out in the first expedition of the company, they settled at Waal-bogt, or Walloons' Bay, on the western shore of Long Island, (1623–24.) Their settlement stands out amidst the surrounding trading posts as the one spot of home life in New Netherland. But it was a feeble settlement, and feeble it continued, although recruited by fresh fugitives from beyond the sea.

New Amsterdam. The company was by no means absorbed in its Walloons. On the contrary, it was erecting forts, one on the North River, another on the South, and presently, the chief of all on Manhattan Island, (1626.) Purchasing the entire island from the natives for no less than twenty-four of our dollars, Peter Minuit, the company's director, commenced the erection of a fort, with some surrounding dwellings, to which the name of New Amsterdam was subsequently applied. This settlement was to New Netherland the same principal place that it has since become as New York to the United States. Other forts were gradually raised; that of Good Hope upon the Connecticut, and that of Beversrede upon the Schuylkill, (1633.) The dominion of the company was in force upon the soil not only of New York, but of Connecticut, New Jersey, Pennsylvania, and Delaware, and all within ten years of its first operations.

Patroons. But upon this vast surface the company's settlements were as dots. Several of them, indeed, had been obliterated, and of those that remained, hardly one besides New Amsterdam was any thing more than a station for trade. New Amsterdam itself was only a commercial settlement. Other posts of the same character had been begun, but the colony, as a whole, was in a languishing condition; the company, of course, being disappointed in their expectations of rich returns. To advance their interests, they offered a slice of territory and the title of patroon to any one who, within a given period, would settle a given number of colonists upon lands bought of the natives, (1629.) This regard for the Indians was not the only proof of liberality in the patroon system, as it may be styled. The support of a clergyman and a schoolmaster, with that of a "comforter for the sick," was especially enjoined as one of the conditions to be fulfilled by the patroons. But mixed up with the more generous provisions were others of a very opposite nature. The fur trade, the great attraction of New Netherland, was reserved exclusively to the company. Pain of banishment was to deter the colonists from "making woollen, linen, or cotton cloths." "As many negroes as can be conveniently provided" were promised to the Dutch settlers. All the while, the patroons were constituted a class of feudal lords, as threatening to their superiors in the company as to their inferiors in the colony. Large purchases were made by individuals, (1629–31,) and some settlements were attempted, the chief being those of Rensselaerswyck, near Albany, Pavonia, opposite Manhattan Island, and Swaanendael, on the Delaware. Some of these reverted to the company; some disappeared.

English claims. Spain and France, as we have read, had their pretensions to the soil of New Netherland. But the only power to dispute the Dutch possession was England. Tradition asserts that the same Captain Argal who destroyed the French settlement in Maine visited the huts on Manhattan Island, as he was returning to Virginia, and compelled the few Dutchmen whom he found there to acknowledge the English supremacy, (1613.) This is uncertain; but it is certain that when the New Netherland Company appealed to the States General in behalf of the Plymouth Puritans, they represented the danger of the colony's being surprised by an expedition sent to support the claims of England, (1620.) The Council for New England was soon engaged in appealing to the Privy Council against what they deemed to be an invasion of their territory. The appeal was received, and an order of inquiry into the circumstances went to the British ambassador in Holland. He replied that there was as yet no Dutch colony upon the soil, (1621.) But as time passed, and colonies were founded, the suspicions of the English, both in England and in America, were revived. A correspondence, opened by Peter Minuit, director of New Amsterdam, with William Bradford, governor of New Plymouth, stirred the Englishman to ask that the Dutch should trade no more in his neighborhood; and further, that they should clear their title to trade or to settle in any part of the country at all. No wonder that Minuit applied to the company in Holland for forty soldiers, (1627.) On his voyage home, a few years later, Minuit and his ship were detained on touching at Plymouth in England, and to the remonstrance of the Dutch embassy, the British ministry formally opposed the title of Great Britain to New Netherland, (1632.) It was soon after that the English settlements in Connecticut began to crowd upon the fort of the Dutch, (1633–38,) while a direct invasion of Delaware was made from Virginia, (1635.) This was repelled; but the soil of Connecticut could not be retained.

Trade of the colony.

The colony was still a colony of traders. No generous views, no manly energies, were as yet excited amongst its inhabitants or its rulers. From the slave to the colonist, from the colonist to the patroon, from the patroon to the director, and even from the director to the company, there was little besides struggling for pecuniary advantages. It was esteemed a great era in the colony when, after various dissensions, its trade was nominally thrown open. But the percentages to the company were such as to prevent any really free trade, (1638.)

CHAPTER VI.

SWEDISH SETTLEMENTS.

Idea of Gustavus Adolphus.

LAST of all to claim a share as a nation in our territory were the Swedes. Their far-sighted and large-hearted king, Gustavus Adolphus, the champion of the Protestant cause in Europe, caught up the idea of supporting the same cause in America. "It is the jewel of my kingdom," he wrote just before he died, concerning the settlement that was yet to be, (1632.)

Oxenstiern calls in Germany.

The jewel of Gustavus received its setting from the regent of his infant daughter Christina, the Chancellor Oxenstiern. With the same loftiness of view, — preparing a state that was to be of benefit to "all Christendom," — Oxenstiern invited and obtained the coöperation of Protestant Germany, (1634.) The Swedish West India Company was to be the instrument by which the north of Europe, as well as Sweden, was to be linked to America. It was a design of greater ends and of broader motives than had as yet been formed for the new world.

Results.

But the results bore no proportion to the plans. It was not to be expected that such colonists as could be found in Sweden would embrace the same wide objects as their regent or their king. They would enlist only in an enterprise that promised personal as well as national returns. Some years passed before any settlement was attempted, and then a colony of only twenty-four, and these chiefly transported convicts, was established at Fort Christina, near the present Wilmington in Delaware, (1638.) The territory, which was purchased of the Indians, extended on either side of the fort, along the western shore of Delaware Bay, and up the Delaware River as far as Trenton, under the name of New Sweden.

Opposing claims. To this the Swedes had been guided by Peter Minuit, lately of New Netherland. His recommendation of lands previously purchased and occupied, though just at this time unoccupied, by his countrymen, involved the Swedish colony in immediate difficulties. A remonstrance from the governor of New Netherland against the invasion of his province was supported in Holland by the seizure of a Swedish vessel touching at a Dutch port on its way home. The English had their pretensions likewise to the lands appropriated by the new colony. On each side were conflicting claims. With feeble numbers and with scanty supplies, the Swedes would find it difficult to keep their New Sweden.

CHAPTER VII.

INDIAN RACES.

European races. THE roll of European races establishing themselves independently upon our soil was filled up by Spain, France, England, Holland, Sweden, and, with Sweden, Germany. After the Swedish colony of 1638, no national settlement was made by any nation not already upon the scene.

Indian races. It is time, therefore, to take an account of the races that occupied the country before any of those from Europe entered upon their possessions. The share of the Indians in our history endures, though their share in our territory wastes away.

Names and numbers. The idea of Columbus that he had merely rediscovered India gave the name of Indians to the existing inhabitants of the continent. Within the limits of our country they were divided into four grand divisions, as the Algonquins, the Iroquois, the Mobilians, and the Dahcotas. The last name includes the tribes west of the Mississippi, of which, in the early period, the number could not have been at all considerable. Neither were the three divisions lying east of the Mississippi by any means numerous. The entire number is estimated to have been under three hundred thousand, and perhaps not above two hundred thousand, at the time of the first European settlements. Take from the whole the large part which had little or no connection with any of the European races, and the Indian population dwindles to small proportions. It seems strange that so few, and these few savages, should have exercised so great an influence upon so many, and these many civilized. But it will be accounted for by a rapid survey of the Indian divisions and the Indian resources.

Algonquins. First of the Algonquins. The central tribe of this vast race was the Lenni-Lenape, which, occupying the shores of the Delaware, went by the name of Delawares amongst the English. The name of Lenni-Lenape, meaning Aborigines, is supposed to mark them as the parent stock of the Algonquins. The shoots of the race were enormously spread. Starting far up in the north, they stretch through New England, as the Abenakis, the Pawtuckets, the Massachusetts, the Pokanokets, the Narragansets, the Pequots, and the Mohegans. Thence they may be traced as the Manhattans of New York, the Susquehannas and the Nanticokes of Pennsylvania and Maryland, the Powhatans of Virginia, and the Pamlicos of South Carolina. Towards the west they appear as the Ottawas of Michigan, the Miamis of Ohio and Indiana, the Illinois of Illinois, and the Shawanoes of Kentucky. Long as this list is, it embraces but a portion of the names to be found in any full record of the Algonquins.

Iroquois. Next of the Iroquois. The centre of this division was among the lakes of Western New York, where the Five Nations of the Mohawks, the Oneidas, the Onondagas, the Cayugas, and the Senecas established their confederacy. To the west and north-west of the Five Nations lay their conquests of after years, the lands of the Eries, of the Hurons, and of other tribes. The prowess or the intrigue of the Iroquois had already subdued the great tribe of the Algonquins, the Lenni-Lenape. Far to the south, partly in Virginia and partly in Carolina, were the Tuscaroras, who, at a later period, migrated to unite with their brethren in the north, making six nations of the five.

Mobilians.

Lastly, of the Mobilian division. It was broken up amongst the Yamassees of Georgia; the Muskhogees or Creeks of Georgia, Alabama, and Florida; the Seminoles of Florida, with the inland tribes of Catawbas in South Carolina, Cherokees in Georgia and Alabama, Choctaws, Natchez, and Chickasaws in Alabama and Mississippi.

Customs and institutions.

There was but one line of wide distinction amongst these various tribes. It separated those who lived by the chase alone from those who lived not only by the chase, but by agriculture. The former class, of course, was the ruder of the two; yet the customs and the institutions of both were much the same. The Indian was every where a hunter, every where a warrior. If he was any thing else, if he attempted agriculture or trade, he seemed to be out of his element. The habits of civilized life were a burden, sometimes a destruction to him. This is true of all the tribes upon our soil; the only customs to which they took, and by which they held, were those of the wilderness, or, at the best, of the field. Their institutions were comparatively advanced. Gathered with his kinsmen in a totem or clan, then with other clans in a tribe, then perhaps with other tribes in a confederacy, the Indian was as much a member of a nation as the European. Above him were his chiefs, the hereditary sachems of peace, and the chosen leaders of war. Their sway and his rights rested together on laws, unwritten, but not undetermined. The devotion shown to these relations and to these institutions was that of true patriots, as well as true savages. It sustained the Indians through trials under which more civilized nations have much sooner succumbed. Had it been united with a civilization, or rather a religion, by which the different tribes could have been blended in one, beneath better statutes and holier influences, the Indian race would have left no space for the European.

Influence upon the European.

We can now appreciate the influence of the Indian upon the European. Though far from being disciplined, though still farther from being concentrated, the natives of our soil would not encounter an invader without leaving an abiding mark upon him and upon his destiny. If not numerous in proportion to the vast regions over which they were spread, they were multitudinous in proportion to the scanty settlements of the stranger. He, moreover, was in an untried land, they in one which they had occupied from infancy.

Counter influence upon the Indian.

Had there been nothing else to make the Indians formidable, the treatment which they received would have been sufficient. The white men came, if not to drag the red man into captivity, or to ransack his stores, at any rate to occupy his lands. This was done, sometimes with and sometimes without the show of justice. If any nation deserves credit above another, it is not the English, not their Puritan or their Quaker branches, as frequently boasted, but the Dutch of New Netherland. Nowhere, however, do we find more than the pretence of even dealing with the natives. The intercourse thus opened was continued in much the same fashion. The Spaniards and the French had greater numbers, proportionally, of missionaries amongst the Indians; the French, whether missionaries or not, were on comparatively good terms with many of the tribes about them. But there are no exceptions to the general course of the Indian from the time that he encountered the European. Scorn, treachery, degradation, were his portion; fury and savage warfare were his revenge. Of the Indian wars we shall take notice hereafter.

African race. As the Indian drooped beneath the blight of the stranger, and became a dependant where his fathers had been free and powerful, he came in contact with another race also in dependence upon the European. This was the African, introduced into Virginia in the thirteenth year of the colony, and into all the other colonies in after years. Of little or no account in the eyes of the early settlers, the slaves of later generations became the most exciting element in the population.

The country. And here, as we have completed the enumeration of the races in the country, it behooves us to give a glance at the country itself, varied and wide enough, as it must have seemed, for many colonies, or many nations. Although as yet the seaboard alone was occupied, the vast reaches of the interior, the stretching plains, the penetrating rivers, were descried. Most of the early dreams concerning wealth and splendor had vanished; but the reality was still full of promise. Fertile and beautiful, a land of plenty and of grandeur, it drew increasing numbers to its shores, and they who came generally remained through life. As far as the future could be secured through physical attractions or material resources, it appeared to be secure.

PART II.

THE ENGLISH DOMINION.

1638–1763.

CHAPTER I.

THE THIRTEEN COLONIES.

Old and new colonies. WE left various colonies from England scattered over the Atlantic coast. Of these, the three principal, Virginia, Massachusetts, and Maryland, were portrayed with comparative detail. Besides these three, several were mentioned as existing in New England, while others were projected in New Jersey and Carolina. It is the purpose of this chapter to show how the older colonies were concentrated, while new colonies were founded and extended.

Plymouth annexed. The oldest colony in New England — that of Plymouth — maintained its independence for seventy years. It was then annexed to Massachusetts, (1691.)

Maine annexed. The name of New Somersetshire was changed to Maine at the same time that Sir Ferdinando Gorges was constituted lord palatine of the province, (1639.) His deputy presently appeared to hold a general court at Saco, (1640.) The grant to Gorges covered the district from the Piscataqua to the Kennebec; but within a very few years one of the numerous patents, previously mentioned as conveying the same soil to different parties, was revived, and the land between the Kennebec and the Saco became a distinct territory, as Ligonia, (1643.) Some time later the two divisions were both annexed to Massachusetts, (1652–58,) then separated, (1665,) then reannexed, (1668,) and at length bought of the Gorges heirs by the colony of Massachusetts Bay, (1677.) East of the Kennebec, as far as Pemaquid Point, there lay a tract belonging to the province of New York, (1664,) but afterwards united with Massachusetts, to which the territory beyond Pemaquid, previously occupied by one or two French posts, was also attached, (1691.) This eastern region was afterwards detached by French conquest, (1696,) but was ultimately reunited to Massachusetts by treaty with France, (1713.)

New Hampshire.

Not quite so various were the fortunes of the New Hampshire settlements. Those at Dover, Portsmouth, and Exeter,* surrendering themselves to Massachusetts, (1641-42,) left nothing but unsettled lands to bear the name of New Hampshire. But on the revival of the Mason claims to the territory east of the Merrimac, New Hampshire was declared in England to be a royal province, (1677-79.) The new government had been in operation but a short and a troubled period, when the people again united themselves to Massachusetts, (1690-92;) and, though again disunited, they were once more rejoined to that colony, at least so far as to be under one and the same governor for nearly half a century, (1698-1741.) Annexation did not prevent disturbance. New Hampshire was still the object of suits and controversies on both sides of the ocean, while the course of affairs amongst the inhabitants themselves was far from being peaceful. It finally became a separate province, (1741.)

Massachusetts.

Massachusetts Bay was the thriving sister, as we see, amongst the New England family. Her large immigrations and her increasing resources gave her the stability and the unity which her neighbors lacked. She did not go without her trials. At the very time that Plymouth and Maine were added to her domains, her independence of

* Founded by Wheelwright, one of the Hutchinson exiles, in 1638.

government was reduced by a change in her charter, (1691,) of which we shall take notice hereafter. The colony continued, however, to thrive.

Connecticut. Of the three settlements in Connecticut, two, namely, Saybrook and Connecticut, were early united under the latter name, (1644.) For this colony a royal charter was afterwards procured by John Winthrop, the early governor, (1662.) The charter included the colony of New Haven; but to this community the provisions of the instrument were so unacceptable that the union was not consummated for two years, nor would it have been so soon but for external circumstances, (1665.) While the Connecticut territory was thus rounded off, it was cut into by the grant of Long Island to the province of New York, for which, likewise, the main land was claimed as far as the Connecticut River. But this claim was repelled.

Rhode Island. The settlements of Providence and Rhode Island were united under a single charter procured by their founder, Roger Williams, from the crown, (1644.) He went a second time to England to obtain its confirmation during the commonwealth, (1651–52,) being elected president of the colony on his return, (1654.) Suspended at a later time, the charter was renewed by the royal government, (1663.) A portion of the territory supposed to be covered by the charter, and lying to the west of the Narraganset waters, was for a long period separated from the colony, under the name of the King's Province, (1665–1727.)

Four colonies in New England. Thus were the various colonies of New England reduced to four — New Hampshire, Massachusetts, Rhode Island, and Connecticut. A fifth colony, the later State of Vermont, was prepared by the Massachusetts Fort Dummer, on the site of Brattleboro', (1724,) and by the New Hampshire grants of townships, Bennington being the earliest, (1749.) But the four elder colonies were all that enter into the list of the thirteen.

Virginia. Virginia, the oldest of the colonies, was still the most extensive in its limits. On the north, a bound seemed to be set by the grant of Maryland. But on the west and the south, Virginia stretched indefinitely, the grant of Carolana existing only upon paper. The government of the colony was frequently altered. Under the English commonwealth, the governors were chosen by the colonial assembly, (1652–60.) An earlier grant of the lands between the Potomac and the Rappahannoc to Lord Culpepper and his associates, (1649,) was afterwards revived, and extended to a lease of the entire colony for thirty-one years, (1673.) In vain did the Virginia assembly protest against the proceeding; in vain did it demand a charter to protect it against similar aggressions. Culpepper, buying out his associates and obtaining the appointment of governor for life, (1675,) sported his authority in England for several years before he made his appearance in Virginia, (1680.) His own disappointment being quite as great as the discontentment of his subjects, his authority over them was surrendered, and the provincial government was restored, (1684.) But, twenty years later, (1704,) a somewhat similar system was established by the appointment of one English nobleman after another to be governor; he, in his turn, sending out his lieutenant governor to administer the colony in his name. All the while the colony was increasing. On the south, indeed, its territories were restricted by the creation of new colonies; but on the west its settlers were crossing the mountains and clearing the farther valleys.

Maryland. The adjoining colony of Maryland underwent few territorial changes. Its vicissitudes, like those of Virginia, consisted in its passing and repassing into new hands. As Virginia changed from a province to a proprietary colony, so Maryland changed from a proprietary colony to a province. After various disturbances, in none of which, however, had the proprietor's power been actually cast off, a convention of the Protestant settlers deposed the proprietary officers, (1689,) and transferred the capital of the colony from the Catholic St. Mary's to the Protestant Annapolis, (1694.) As the Protestant fervor in England was just then at its height, the proceedings of the colony were confirmed by the crown. But the head of the proprietary family in the next generation, Benedict Leonard, Lord Baltimore, becoming an English churchman, recovered the possession of Maryland, (1715.)

Carolina. The first of the new colonies amongst the thirteen was Carolina. This was the territory included first in the limits of Virginia, and then in those of Carolana by royal patent. The patentee of Carolana had made no settlement or grant; but Virginia had granted at least a portion of the territory by act of assembly, (1643.) Another portion was occupied by a Massachusetts party settled near the mouth of Cape Fear River, on land purchased from the Indians, (1660.) Without regard to any of these claims, eight persons of the highest rank, amongst them the Earl of Clarendon, then prime minister, obtained a royal patent for all the territory between Albemarle Sound and the St. John's River, (1663.) A second charter extended the northern boundary to Chowan River, and the southern to below the Spanish St. Augustine, (1665,) while a third charter annexed the Bahama Islands to the swollen province, (1667.)

North and South. It was swollen only on the map. In reality, it had but one or two shrivelled settlements. The nucleus of North Carolina was a Virginian settlement, not included in Carolina until the second charter, (1665.) The Massachusetts colony formed the nucleus of South Carolina. Meeting with trials and desertions, this colony was absorbed in, rather than strengthened by, a band from Barbadoes. Other parties came from England, from New England, and from New York; with Presbyterians from Scotland and Ireland, and Huguenots from France, (1671–86.) Of the various settlements that arose, Charleston took the lead, (1680.) Both North and South Carolina were organized as proprietary governments. Such, however, were the troubles ensuing beneath these forms, that the Assembly of South Carolina, many years later, declared the proprietors to have forfeited their dominion. Following up a successful insurrection against the proprietary officials by an appeal to England, the South Carolinians obtained a provisional royal government, (1719–21.) Some time after, the crown, by act of Parliament, bought out seven of the eight proprietors, the eighth retaining his property, but not his sovereignty, (1729.) A governor was then appointed by the crown for North Carolina, both divisions being organized as royal provinces. Thenceforward, the two pursued their destinies separately.

New York. The next year after the grant of Carolina, a new grant was made in peculiar circumstances. New Netherland, though still occupied by the Dutch, was, as the province of a nation at war with England, conveyed by Charles II. to his brother James, Duke of York and Albany, as proprietor; the limits of the province being extended from the Connecticut to, and presently beyond, the Delaware, (1664.) In addition, the grant covered the eastern part of Maine and the islands to the south and west of Cape Cod, which the duke had obtained by transfer to him of early grants from the Council for New England.* These portions, however, of his domain fell at a later time

* To Sir William Alexander, afterwards Earl of Stirling, in 1621–35.

beneath the jurisdiction of Massachusetts, as has been observed; while much of the main province went to Connecticut, New Jersey, Pennsylvania, and Delaware. The seizure of the province from the Dutch will be told in another chapter. It continued under a proprietary form of government until the accession of the proprietor to the throne of England. It then became a royal province; though, while James II. ruled, it was more immediately dependent upon the royal authority than was customary with the provinces in general, (1685–88).

New Jersey. Hardly had the Duke of York obtained the grant of his province, when he conveyed that portion of it between the Hudson and Delaware Rivers to Sir George Carteret and Lord Berkeley, both amongst the proprietors of Carolina, (1664.) A few hamlets of Dutch and English, who had crossed from Long Island, were already sprinkled upon the territory, when the first town under the new proprietors was founded, and called Elizabethtown, (1665.) The province was named New Jersey. As in Maryland and Carolina, so in New Jersey, there soon arose dissensions between the colonists and the proprietors. The proprietors were changed. Berkeley sold out his half to certain Quakers, who made a settlement at Salem, (1675.) In the following year, a formal separation of the province took place, the settlement at Salem being situate in West, and that at Elizabethtown in East New Jersey; the latter division remaining with Carteret. A treaty with the Indians, under the auspices of the Quakers, confirmed the rights of the proprietors, (1678.) Soon after, a company, of which some, but not all, the members were Quakers, made the purchase of East New Jersey, (1682.) A large Presbyterian emigration from Scotland then took place, (1685.) But the growth of the province, as well as that of its western sister, was greatly impeded, partly by domestic disputes between the proprietors and the settlers, and partly by contentions with the officials of New York, who pretended to continued jurisdiction over the lands which had been separated from that province. The Jerseys were finally surrendered by their proprietors to the crown, (1702.) They were then reunited as a royal province, for many years, (until 1738,) under the same governor as New York.

Pennsylvania. A Quaker, interested in both the Jerseys during the Quaker possession, obtained the grant of the adjoining territory on the west. A royal charter constituted William Penn proprietor of a district whose extent, though uncertain, might have been described in general as lying between New York, New Jersey, and Maryland. To this the name of Pennsylvania was given by the crown, (1681.) A grant from the Duke of York conveyed the territories on the lower shore of the Delaware to the same proprietor, (1682.) Of this wide domain, a variety of settlers, Dutch, Swedes, and English, were partially in occupation. To take them beneath his rule, the proprietor sent out an agent with conciliatory assurances, while, to introduce fresh bodies of inhabitants, especially of his own persuasion, he formed an association in England. The first fruits were two colonies, one led by three commissioners, in the year of the charter, (1681,) the other conducted by Penn himself in the following year, (1682.) A convention of the different settlers, new and old, presently accepted the proprietor's organization of the province, including the territories of both the royal and the ducal grants, with their previous inhabitants. Next followed a treaty with the natives, a peaceful and a feeble tribe of Indians, whose acquiescence in his plans might have been disregarded by Penn without any danger, had he not preferred to be just. The town of Philadelphia was then begun, and there the first Assembly of Pennsylvania was soon convened, (1683.) With all

Penn's care, and all his frames of government, of which there was a goodly number, the course of his proprietorship did not run smooth. Troubles within the colony were accompanied by troubles without; the province being at one time taken from him by the English authorities, (1692–94.) Even after his restoration, he found matters so difficult to manage, that he at length proposed to cede his sovereignty to the crown, (1710.) He retained it, however, and transmitted it to his sons, to be much the same source of struggle to them that it had been to him.

Delaware.

The territories, so styled, of Delaware, originally a Swedish, afterwards a Dutch, possession, then an appendage of New York, and then again annexed to Pennsylvania, became so far separate from the latter province as to obtain a distinct assembly, though continuing to have the same governor, (1702.)

Georgia.

Last of the thirteen was the colony of Georgia, in founding which there were mingled purposes of resistance to the Spaniards and the French in the south, as well as of relief to the suffering in England. A member of the House of Commons, James Edward Oglethorpe, had been active in proposing and carrying out an inquiry into the state of the prisons in Great Britain. The idea of rescuing some of the prisoners from a state of degradation even greater than they could have fallen into by themselves, and of settling them in a colony, occurred to Oglethorpe, as a philanthropist, while, as an officer in the royal army, he was also sensitive on the point of defending the colonial boundaries against the encroachments of other powers in America. The purchase of the Carolinas by the crown (1729) opened the way to the foundation of a colony to the south of the settlements already made; and for this a grant was obtained of the territory between the Savannah and Altamaha Rivers, under the royal name of

Georgia, (1732.) The charter conveyed the land and the dominion over it, not to colonists, nor yet to proprietors, but to twenty-one trustees, who, though subject to the royal oversight, and to the obligations of the English law, were otherwise clothed with full power for twenty-one years. A common council of thirty-four members, fifteen of whom were named in the charter, and the rest appointed by the trustees, were to act as a board of administration merely. The colonial lands, it was further provided, were to be held by feudal tenure; that is, only by male heirs. A universal interest was excited by this novel scheme of colonization. General subscriptions poured in to aid the trustees in their half-benevolent, half-patriotic plans, while Parliament made a national grant of ten thousand pounds. First to enlist personally, was a party of more than one hundred, whom Oglethorpe himself led to the settlement, which he named Savannah, (1733.) Every thing seemed to bid fair; the Indians were conciliated, the colonists were satisfied, the nation was all alive with sympathy. Immigrants came from afar; Moravians from Germany; Presbyterians from the northern mountains of Scotland; the earnest and the careless, the peasant and the prisoner, united in one people, (1734-36.) To the generous project of saving the convicts of Britain was added the devoted hope of the Moravians that the natives of America might be converted. But there was a dark side to the scene from the first. The character of the colonists, that is, of the main body from England, was helpless enough, not to say corrupted enough, to cause great difficulties both to themselves and to their trustees. It will be seen hereafter that the military service expected from the colony was pretty much a failure. The colony soon became a royal province, (1754-55.)

Such were the thirteen colonies of England. Spread out with indefinite borders and indefinite resources, they lay

Aspect of the thirteen.

like misty points along the Atlantic shore. The eye that saw them, separate and indistinct, as they rose at the beginning, could catch no vision of the broad fields and the fruitful vales that were to expand and blend together in the future. As we look back ourselves, we see few promises of development or of unity in the early days of the thirteen colonies.

CHAPTER II.

Colonial Relations.

Races. THE thirteen colonies were the colonies of England. But they were far from being settled exclusively by Englishmen. The west, the centre, and the south of Europe all sent forth emigrants in greater or less numbers to people the American shore. Nor did these come to the settlements of other nations, to those of the Spaniards, the French, the Dutch, or the Swedes, alone, but rather to the English colonies, whose praise it is to have thus attracted and provided for the stranger.

Classes. As there were different races, so there were different classes. First came the gentleman, peculiarly so styled, of various look and of various spirit, according to the respective colonies, but every where classified as of "the better sort." This order was perpetuated by the law of primogeniture, the eldest son receiving at least a double, if not more than a double, share of his father's estate. Next were the people of "the poorer sort" — the lower orders, as their name denotes. But by no means the lowest; as there were others beneath them in the scale. The indented servants, or apprentices, constituted a class of temporary bondmen. Sometimes exactly what their name suggests, too young or too shiftless to be their own masters, the indented were often men of a higher grade, the adherents, in many instances, of a defeated party or of a persecuted creed, who, falling into the hands of their opponents, were sold for transportation to a market where they could be re-sold at a profit. Such were the English royalists, taken captive by the parliamentary forces; such the Roman Catholics, conquered while fighting for their faith in Ireland. Such, too, were many of the exiles from the continent. So great were the numbers imported as to amount — and in time of peace — to fifteen hundred a year in the single province of Virginia. The little consideration that there was for the class appears in the colonial codes.* Lower still, however, were the slaves. The first of this class were Indians, captured in wars or taken in snares, sometimes bought of their parents, even of themselves. Then came the negroes from Africa. These poor creatures found little mercy in the colonial statutes. The English law recognizing slavery declared the children of a free father to be free. But the Virginian code declared a child to follow the lot of the mother, (1662.) The law of England pronounced it felony to kill a slave. The law of Virginia decided it to be none, (1667.)†

Of the old world. These classes were confined to no colony, and to no division of colonies. They existed amongst the rigid settlers of the north as well as amongst the freer

* Maimed by a master, the servant is to be set free, (Mass. 1641; N. Y. 1665;) but any resistance on the servant's part entails an additional year of servitude, (Va. 1705.) Such as escape from their bonds are to be given up to their masters, or else their value is to be made up by those who harbor them, (Va. 1661.) Poorly as the class was rated, there was that about them, in their anger, which prompted the Virginians to make a "perpetual holiday" of the day on which a conspiracy, detected amongst their servants, was to have been executed, (1663.)

† The Virginia laws make it allowable to kill a fugitive, (1672,) forbid the slave at any time to carry arms, (1682,) cut him off from trial by jury, (1692,) and prohibit his manumission, except he is transported out of the province, (1692,) or except the governor and council deem him worthy of his liberty, (1724.) Other codes take much the same tone, without always entering into the same details. The most rigid laws were those of South Carolina, (1712–50.)

and easier planters of the south. But they were not of colonial creation. They came from the old world, transplanted from its ancient lands to the virgin soil of America. If they did not die, it was inevitable that they would take root and grow up with renewed luxuriance.

Institutions belong to the freemen. The sketch that goes before shows us that the colonial institutions were not the institutions of all. They belonged to the freemen, so styled, "the better sort," with but a portion of "the poorer sort" thrown in. Indented servants and slaves, of course, had no part in the political or the social privileges of their superiors. But besides the bondmen proper, there was a large number not bondmen, and yet not freemen by the laws of the colonies. "The people," says an early writer on the Massachusetts system, "begin to complain they are ruled like slaves." Actual restlessness was showing itself. "It is feared," says the same writer, "that elections cannot be safe there long, either in church or commonwealth, so that some melancholy men think it a great deal safer to be in the midst of troubles in a settled commonwealth, or in hope easily to be settled,* than in mutinies there, so far off from succors," (1641.)

English law. The institutions of the freemen sprang from the English law. How far this extended over the colonies was a vexed question. One class of jurists or of statesmen in England maintained that America was a conquered country, a country wrested from the native or the European races whom the English found in possession of it. The deduction from this view was, that the institutions of the country were at the pleasure of the crown or of the Parliament of England. But another class held opposite ground, asserting that the colonists were entitled, without

* Referring to the disturbances in England.

any consent or dissent on the part of England, to all the rights of Englishmen, inasmuch as the country was a discovered, not a conquered one. Some persons held an intermediate opinion, denying the notion of conquest, and yet denying the inherent claim of the colonists to English privileges, making their rights depend on actual grants from the sovereign power. So when the habeas corpus act, providing for the issue of a writ to produce the body of a prisoner, was passed, (1679,) it was said not to extend to the colonies, because they were not specially mentioned in the bill. A similar act, adopted by the Massachusetts General Court, was annulled by the crown, (1692.) But the privilege was afterwards tacitly, if not explicitly, allowed. The liberal system of interpretation slowly prevailing, the English law was almost universally recognized to be the birthright of the colonies as truly as of the mother-land.

Colonial governments.

The governments of the colonies were variously organized. Those under charters were altogether in the hands of the colonists. The charter of Massachusetts, indeed, was so far altered in 1691 as to transfer the appointment of the governor, lieutenant governor, and secretary to the crown, and even to prescribe the conditions on which the inhabitants should be admitted as freemen. The charters of Connecticut (1662) and Rhode Island (1644–63) left the entire administration to the colonists. The seven colonies originally under proprietary government — Maryland, the Carolinas, New York, New Jersey, Pennsylvania, and Delaware — were of course subject to the authority of their proprietors, but with many restrictions upon it in favor of the colonists. The Carolinas, under the model of John Locke,* and New York, under

* John Locke, the great philosopher, was employed by the Carolinian proprietors to embody their ideas — one cannot but think — rather than his own, in what was called " the grand model," or " the fundamental con-

the arbitrary rule of its ducal proprietor, who allowed no Assembly till 1683, were not so favorably situated. Pennsylvania was subjected to claims asserted nowhere else, as well as deprived of rights denied nowhere else, by two peculiarities in the charter to William Penn; one, the assertion of the power of Parliament to tax the colony, the other, the omission of the title of the colonists to the rights of Englishmen. The record that four of the proprietary governments were changed to royal governments, — the Carolinas, New York, and New Jersey, — and all at the desire of the colonists, bears witness against the institutions of which proprietors were the chiefs. The royal provinces, however, were organized on the same terms as the proprietary colonies, except that, the king being at the head of affairs, the institutions of the provinces were more uniform. The number of provinces was seven: the four just mentioned, with the older Virginia and New Hampshire and the younger Georgia.

Towns.

In some of the colonies, especially those in the north, the towns were at the centre of their organization. These were the primary bodies in which the colonists

stitutions." Of the system thus concocted, the primary element was property, the scale of colonial dignities being graduated according to the possessions of the colonist. Seigniories for the proprietors, baronies for landgraves and caciques, colonies for lords of manors, or freeholders, were the divisions of the soil. Authority was parcelled out amongst palatine and other courts for the proprietors, a grand council for them and their nobility, and a Parliament for the proprietors, the nobility, and the lords of manors. As for those not wealthy enough for either of these classes, they were hereditary tenants, or else slaves. The church of the colony was to be the church of England, with a certain amount of toleration for other creeds. This extraordinary mass of titles and of powers held together for just twenty-three years, (1669–1693,) but without ever getting into actual operation. It was relinquished by the proprietors at the universal desire of the colonists, who naturally preferred the simpler and the freer institutions originally reared under the charter.

were grouped and trained as freemen. Their workings, where they existed, are written on every page of the colonial and the national annals. Where they did not exist, their places were but poorly supplied by plantations or vestries. An instinct, as it may be called, after the establishment of towns, led the early legislators of Virginia into curious expedients. At one time, the resources of the colony were to be brought to bear on making Jamestown a city worthy of the name, (1662;) at another, each county was directed to lay out a town of its own, (1680.) At length a new capital was founded at Williamsburg, (1698.)

Assemblies. Next to the town or its substitute, under every form of government as ultimately established, there was one and the same body. This was the assembly, the same cherished institution to the colony that Parliament was to the mother land. At first, in some places, composed of all the freemen, then placed upon a representative basis, and then divided into two houses, one of councillors or assistants, the other of representatives or burgesses, the assembly exercised all the functions of a legislature, subject, of course, to the law and the sovereign of England. The House of Representatives, or of Burgesses, as the case might be in the different colonies, constituted the popular branch, so entirely in some instances as to go by the name of the assembly, leaving the councillors or assistants to appear, what they generally were, the officers of the crown. But the assembly was by no means popular, according to modern notions. A large amount of property, real or personal, was usually essential as a qualification of membership, the very voters being under some conditions of the same nature. The sessions were often few and far between; in some colonies, and at some periods, not more frequent than once in three years, or even more than three. An assembly, moreover, would sometimes hold over beyond its lawful term, becoming as much of a burden to the colony as it was intended to be an assistance. But when once convened, at the proper season and in the proper spirit, the assembly was a tower of strength to its people.

Churches.

That which was most variable, not to say most ineffective, in the colonies, was the very thing that should have been most stable and most powerful. The church of Christ was rent with factions. The blessings that might have issued from a common church, had it been pure and true, have no place in our history. The church of England was established in Virginia, Maryland, the Carolinas, and Georgia. The Quakers and the Presbyterians prevailed in the central colonies; in the northern, the Puritans carried all before them. Such divisions would not merely prevent unity; they would break up liberty.

Persecution in Massachusetts. Child.

Amongst the harshest provisions of the Massachusetts system was that excluding all but church members from the rights of freemen. Against this, chiefly, was directed the petition of Dr. Robert Child, and six others, some of them of the highest station, church membership excepted, in the colony, (1646.) Child was a young man, recently arrived in the country with the purpose of making some scientific inquiry into its mineral resources. At the time of his petition, he was on the point of returning to England, but with the idea, apparently, of coming back to Massachusetts, could he be received on equal terms with the freemen of the colony. Be this as it may, he and his fellow-petitioners asked for admission to the privileges of Massachusetts, instead of which they found themselves charged with "contemptuous and seditious expressions," for which they were arraigned and heavily fined. Thus treated, they set about preparing a memorial, which Child was to convey to Parliament, and in support of which, another document, praying "for liberty of conscience, and for a general governor" from England, was hastily got up amongst several of the non-freemen of Boston and its neighborhood. Only a few signatures to this paper were obtained, probably on account of the risk which the signers ran; one of the most active of their number being put in irons, on the discovery of the affair by the magistrates. Child himself, and some of his fellow-memorialists, were also seized; their papers were examined, and their persons detained in custody until after the ship in which they intended to take passage for England had departed. A copy of their memorial reached London, but was never acted upon.

Baptists.

"I have done too much of that work already," John Winthrop, the governor for many years, is reported to have said in his last hours, when urged to sign an order of banishment against a believer in a different church than his own, (1649.) But he left others to carry out the austerities from which the approach of death might well recall a human spirit. Within two years, John Clarke, a minister amongst the Baptist exiles of Rhode Island, was arrested while preaching in a house at Lynn, (1651.) "They more uncivilly disturbed us," said he, "than the pursuivants of the old English bishops were wont to do." Imprisoned with some of his fellow-Baptists in Boston, Clarke did not give way, but demanded the opportunity of proving, prisoner as he was, "that no servant of Jesus Christ hath any authority to restrain any fellow-servant in his worship, where no injury is offered to others." The answer of the magistrates was, "Fined twenty pounds, or to be well whipped." One of his comrades escaped with a smaller fine, but another was whipped, while two persons who showed compassion upon him were themselves arrested and fined. Clarke, after paying his fine, would have sailed to England. But not allowed even to do this, he made his way to New Amsterdam, where he met with humaner treatment, and found the means of crossing the sea. Arrived in England, he published his "Ill News from New England," "wherein is declared, that while old England is becoming new,* New England is becoming old." "The authority there established," he says, "cannot permit men, though of never so civil, sober, and peaceable a spirit and life, freely to enjoy their understandings and consciences, nor yet to live or come among them, unless they can do as they do, and say as they say, or else say nothing; and so may a man live at Rome also," (1652.)

Saltonstall's remonstrance.

Clarke's case appears to have excited attention, notwithstanding the late indifference in relation to Child and his fellow-petitioners. Such as were opposed to the Puritans did not stand alone in condemning their intolerance. One of their own number, an early and a distinguished member of the Massachusetts Company, wrote to the elders, Wilson and Cotton, in terms of sorrowful remonstrance. "It doth not a little grieve my spirit to hear what sad things are reported daily of your tyranny and persecution in New England, as that you fine, whip, and imprison men for their consciences. . . . These rigid ways have laid you low in the hearts of the saints." Thus wrote Sir Richard Saltonstall, a Puritan, but not a persecutor, a lover of other men's liberty, as well as of his own.

Dunster of Harvard College.

His letter was unheeded. Within a very brief period, the first president of Harvard College, Henry Dunster, a clergyman, a scholar, and a true man, was tried, convicted, and obliged to resign his office, on the charge of being a Baptist, (1654.) "The whole transaction of this business," wrote he. "is

* In the time of the commonwealth.

such, which in process of time, when all things come to mature consideration, may very probably create grief on all sides; yours subsequent, as mine antecedent. I am not the man you take me to be." In the following year, (1655,) the corporation of the college appealed to the General Court to pay the amount still due to the deposed president, as well as to allow him something additional, "in consideration of his extraordinary pains." But so intemperate was the disposition of the authorities, as to refuse not only the additional grant, but even the actual balance of the president's account. The spirit of wisdom had not yet descended either upon Harvard College or upon the community by which it had been founded.

Quakers.

A new class of victims appeared. A few unhappy Quakers — the more unhappy, if guilty of the fanatical excesses with which they were charged — came to Boston, some of them to brave, all of them to encounter, persecution, (1656.) Brought immediately before the magistrates, they were first confined, and then sent away beyond the limits of the colony. Laws were at once passed, inflicting a fine of one hundred pounds upon any master of a vessel who brought a Quaker with him, and ordering imprisonment and scourging for any Quaker that might appear. This not being deemed enough, a new batch of statutes was prepared within the next two years, (1657–58,) fining the spectator or the worshipper at a Quaker meeting, the host of a Quaker, and threatening the Quaker himself with loss of ears, mutilation of tongue, and, finally, if he returned after being banished, with death. In these horrible enactments, almost all New England, except Rhode Island, coincided. They did not remain dead letters. One of the oldest freemen of the colony, Nicholas Upsall, accused merely of kindness to the persecuted, was banished for three years, and, on his return, was thrown into a two years' imprisonment, (1656-59.) Nor was this the only case of the kind. As for the persecuted themselves, they were fined, imprisoned, scourged, and at length hanged, (1659-60.) Had it not been for the royal commands that these outrages should cease, (1660,) there is no saying how far they might have been carried. As it was, the persecution continued at intervals, until a fresh order came from the king, requiring liberty of faith for all Protestants, (1679.)

Witches. The saddest deeds of oppression in Massachusetts are yet to be told. It is explicable that the Puritan authorities should be bitter upon those who opposed their institutions or their creeds. But that they should raise a hue and cry against those who had no thought of opposing them, those against whom no charge could be substantiated but that of feebleness, of age, or of deformity, seems inexplicable. An English law of older date than any existing English colony, (1603,) by which witchcraft was declared a capital crime, found a place amongst the so-called liberties of Massachusetts, (1641.) Some years elapsed before it was enforced, (1656;) nor did it then seem to set so well upon the consciences of the rulers as to make them desirous of keeping it in operation. A later attempt at the same sort of thing in Pennsylvania resulted in the acquittal of the unfortunate object of ill will, (1684.) When all was quiet, and the troubles of witchcraft appeared to have subsided forever, there was a sudden swell. A witch, so styled and so condemned, was executed at Boston, (1688.) One victim not being enough, others were soon demanded, and found at Salem village, now Danvers. The magistrates of the colony had thrown a hundred persons into prison, when the governor, Sir William Phips, arrived from England to head the persecution. The lieutenant governor, William Stoughton, presided at the judicial tribunals.

Behind these official personages, several of the elders or ministers, led by Increase and Cotton Mather, father and son, urged on the ferocious pursuit. It lasted eight long months, devouring twenty victims, torturing many others, and threatening a still larger number, when the work of blood was arrested, partly by interference from England, and partly by accusations directed against some of the persecutors themselves, (1693.) "The Lord be merciful to the country," exclaimed Chief Justice Stoughton, on finding that he could sentence no more as guilty of witchcraft. Years later, the letters of Robert Calef, a merchant of Boston, who wrote against the fierce delusion of his neighbors, were burned in the yard of Harvard College by order of the president, Increase Mather, (1700.)

Persecution elsewhere.

We have lingered long in Massachusetts. It is there that we find the most striking traces of that persecuting spirit of which almost every colony had its share. New England, with one exception, occupied the same ground as its principal colony. New York ordered every Roman Catholic priest voluntarily entering the province to be hanged, (1700.) Protestants were likewise visited with penalties or with restrictions, unless they submitted to the church of England, (1704.) Maryland began by an act which proclaimed death to all who denied the Trinity, and fine, scourging, imprisonment, and banishment, to all who denied "the blessed Virgin Mary or the holy apostles or evangelists," (1649.) Long after, the Roman Catholics becoming, as has been mentioned, the objects of persecution, their public services were forbidden, and their offices as teachers, both private and public, were suspended, (1704.) Of all the colonies, however, none kept nearer to Massachusetts in the race of persecution than Virginia, the colony of the English, as Massachusetts was that of the Puritan church. A few Puritans, who had found a corner in Virginia, invited some ministers from Massachusetts and New Haven. Three came, but were almost immediately warned by the government "to depart the colony with all conveniency," (1642-43.) Another Puritan clergyman, with many of his persuasion, was banished a few years later, (1648-49.) The Puritans being disposed of, the Quakers came in for attention. A law inflicted a hundred pounds' fine upon the shipmaster who introduced, and upon the colonist who entertained, a Quaker, the Quaker himself being imprisoned until he gave security that he would leave the colony never to return, (1660-63.) Baptists were provided for in another law, subjecting them to a fine, (1662.) Thus the prey upon which the Puritan magistrates pounced in the north was assailed by the church of England authorities in the south. The same spirit, suspicious and oppressive, was at work throughout the land.

Save in Rhode Island.

Save in one nook, where liberality and confidence prevailed. In Rhode Island, the colony whose people were twofold exiles, — exiles from England, and exiles from New England, — persecution found no place. The assembly, gathered under the charter of 1644, established freedom of faith by legislative enactment, (1647.) In petitioning for the charter of 1663, the Rhode Islanders urged their "lively experiment that a most flourishing civil state may stand and best be maintained with a full liberty of religious concernments." Time and maturing wisdom had taught Roger Williams to practise what he preached in favor of liberty of conscience. Even the Quakers, whose doctrines he much disliked and opposed, found refuge amongst his people, and so securely, that Rhode Island refused to insist upon the oath of allegiance to the crown, on account of the Quaker scruples to taking oaths of any kind. "The first liberty," wrote Williams, "is of our spirits, which neither Old nor New England knows the like, nor no part of the world a greater." He died, (1683;) but so directly did his better spirit descend to those coming after him, that with one exception bearing upon Roman Catholics, then excluded from the privileges of all the colonies, the laws of Rhode Island continued to bear and to forbear for generation after generation.

Inter-colonial difficulties.

The relations between one class and another within the colony being such as have been described, it may be inferred how uncertain were the relations between colony and colony. Differences of origin and of situation, enhanced by differences of creed, of policy, and of interest, brought about divisions and hostilities. Nor were these confined to colonies that were far remote from one another in position or in character. On the contrary, the instances to be mentioned are those of quarrels among neighbors; nay, even among allies.

Shawomet and Massachusetts.

Samuel Gorton, a clothier from London, who found no welcome in Boston, Plymouth, or even in the Rhode Island settlements, purchased, in the last-named vicinity, some land from the Indians, and began the little colony of Shawomet. He seems to have been a sort of spiritualist, much given to rhapsody, if not blasphemy, but harmless, disposed to force his views upon none, and ready to fly rather than to fight amidst the warring parties of New England. But when pursued by his old opponents of Massachusetts, on the ground that the land which his colony occupied was theirs by virtue of subsequent negotiations with the Indians, Gorton resolved to make a stand, (1643.) It was in vain. The dozen men whom he had with him could make no effectual defence against the forty who came, with commissioners at their head, from Massachusetts. A few of the Shawomet party escaped; but Gorton, with nine others, was transported as a captive to Boston. There he was put upon trial, partly for rejecting the dominion, and partly for rejecting the creed of his conquerors. Convicted, of course, he was set to work in irons, most of his companions meeting the same fate. But as they proved troublesome, especially by instilling their doctrines into those around them, they were set free, "no more to come into the colony, upon pain of death," (1644.) Gorton at once repaired to England, where, from the Earl of Warwick, then "governor-in-chief and lord high admiral of all those islands and plantations within the bounds and upon the coasts of America," he obtained a patent for his colony as a part of the Providence Plantations, the name of Shawomet being changed to that of its protector — Warwick, (1647.) Not long after, Massachusetts attempted to get up another onslaught upon the Warwick settlement, but was prevented, (1651.)

United colonies of New England.

Massachusetts was at the head of a confederacy, the story of which will be found to throw much light upon the relations of colony to colony. It had been proposed, at an early date, (1637,) to form a league amongst the New England settlements; but the project fell through, on account of the resistance of Connecticut to the demands of Massachusetts. Circumstances induced Connecticut to give way, some time afterwards, when a confederacy was formed, under the name of "The United Colonies of New England," (1643.) Each colony was to appoint two commissioners, who must be church members, to conduct all matters of administration, to decide upon questions of peace or war, to regulate the demand and surrender of fugitive servants, slaves, or criminals; but all acts of the commissioners required ratification by the people. In case of war, a certain number of troops was to be furnished by the different members of the league. Massachusetts, furnishing a double proportion, obtained the honor of having the commissioners' annual session held twice as often at Boston as at any other place of meeting. Indeed, Massachusetts was the head and front of the whole confederacy.

Treatment of Rhode Island. The spirit of the league soon came out. Massachusetts (then including New Hampshire), Plymouth, and the two Connecticut colonies being united, there remained Maine and Rhode Island. Maine was too scantily settled, as well as too remotely situated, to be taken into account; but Rhode Island, begirt by the confederates, had some claims to consideration. At all events, it asked admission to the union. The demand was refused, except on condition that the colony would submit itself as a dependent to Plymouth. One cannot but wonder that, with such a temper, the league refrained from blotting its independent neighbor out of existence.

Disagreements. Things went by no means smoothly amongst the confederates themselves. At one time, Connecticut imposed a tax on river navigation, which acted adversely to the interests of the town of Springfield, (1647.) Massachusetts, at first remonstrating, soon broke out with an impost upon goods imported from the other three colonies of the league, (1649.) Nor was this repealed until after a grave protest from the commissioners, (1650.) A year or two later, Connecticut desired war to be declared against the Dutch and Indians. Perhaps it was a hasty project; but it found support from Plymouth. Massachusetts, however, refused to enter into it, and by so doing, nearly broke up the confederacy, (1653.) When the confederates agreed, it was often about such measures as those of persecution, to which reference has been made, or those of warfare, to which we shall arrive ere long. In fact, the United Colonies were united chiefly in deeds of violence. In works of justice or of generosity, they generally broke asunder. When their union came to an end, after a feeble existence of half a century, it was regretted by none.

Dissensions elsewhere.

The New England colonies were not alone in these disturbed relations. New York was long at variance with Connecticut on one side, and with New Jersey on the other. Pennsylvania had her complaints against Virginia; Delaware hers against Pennsylvania. Wherever there was a view from one colony to another, it seemed to open as frequently upon scenes of controversy as upon those of peace.

Penn and Baltimore

Leaving the colonies themselves, and turning to their proprietors, where they had any, we discover the same disposition to strife. When William Penn obtained the grant of his domain of Pennsylvania, he knew that it encroached upon the claims of the Baltimore family of Maryland. Their title to the territory, as far north as the fortieth degree of latitude, had been infringed upon, but by foreigners — by the Dutch and by the Swedes. It was reserved for a fellow-countryman to appropriate it to himself. Soon after the arrival of Penn in America, he met Lord Baltimore at Newcastle, but without being able to come to any agreement. This did not prevent the Quaker from founding his City of Brotherly Love upon the land claimed by the rival proprietor, (1682.) At another meeting, in the following year, Penn consented to recognize the Baltimore claim, but only on condition that a price should be fixed for a portion bordering upon the Delaware, of which he naturally wished to retain the sovereignty. But as this offer was refused, while another mode of settlement, proposed by Baltimore, was refused in turn by Penn, the two proprietors again separated in anger. When Baltimore renewed his demands, a few months after, Penn threw himself upon the Dutch title, to which he claimed succession through the Duke of York, (1683.) After such a plea as this, there was no hope of justice from Penn. Appeal was made to England, where sentence was rendered against Baltimore, without being actually executed, (1685.) It was three quarters of a century before the boundary between Pennsylvania and Maryland was definitely determined.

Relations to the mother country.

The relations of the colonies to the mother country, that is, to England, so far as they depended upon general principles, were brought forward in an earlier part of the chapter. It is time to take them up with reference to the actual course of events.

The crown.

Allegiance to the crown was one of the inborn principles of the English colonist. It extended from him to those who had come from other lands than England. The King of England was the head of the church and the head of the state — the supreme civil and military power, to whom all the magistrates, all the tribunals, all the laws, all the proceedings of the colonies, were subject. Even in the charter governments, the most independent of all, the royal supremacy was universally recognized. At the same time, the exact limits between the sovereignty of the king and the independence of the colony were nowhere defined. In the royal provinces, where the dependence upon the crown was the greatest, the rights of the popular bodies were often most pertinaciously asserted.

Charles II. and Massachusetts.

As striking an exhibition as any other of the relations of the colonies with royalty is to be found in the twenty-five years' controversy between Charles II. and Massachusetts. When the restoration of that monarch occurred, nearly a year was allowed to elapse, after the certain intelligence of the event, without any proclamation of the royal authority in Massachusetts. There was a good deal, in fact, for the colony to do, in order to make the proclamation satisfactory to all concerned. In the first place, she had to renounce all such theories as John Eliot had propounded in his Christian Commonwealth, concerning the superiority of the Mosaic over the English institutions. In the next place, she had "to reject, as an infringement of right, any parliamentary or royal imposition prejudicial to the country." So that, between her own republicans on the one side, and the monarchists of England on the other, there was some difficulty in steering a course. At length, the king being proclaimed, John Norton and Simon Bradstreet were sent as agents, with letters and instructions half servile and half defiant, to seek the royal presence and obtain a confirmation of the colonial institutions, (1662.) The king confirmed the charter, but added requisitions that were likely to set the whole colony in an uproar. All laws, he said, against the royal authority, must be repealed; the oath of allegiance to the crown must be exacted; the Book of Common Prayer must be tolerated, and the sacraments administered to "all of honest lives;" nay, the freeholders of the colony, if of suitable estate and character, must be admitted as its freemen. Such was the spite of Massachusetts men, in relation to the royal demands, even against their own helpless agents, that the minister Norton sank, it is said, under the general displeasure, (1663.) The arrival of four royal commissioners, in the following year, was followed by a celebration of the church service, and by a law from the assembly, declaring freeholders, on certain conditions, to be freemen, (1664.) The next proceedings of the commissioners resulted in the temporary toleration of churchmen and Quakers, (1665.) It must have seemed as if the very foundations of Massachusetts had been thrown down.

Long years of controversy between the colony and the king ensued. The departure of the commissioners was followed by the almost immediate arrest of the changes

Loss of the Massachusetts and other charters.

which they had introduced. A summons from the king, calling upon the colony to send representatives to answer the charges against it, was disobeyed, (1666.) Yet five years were allowed to elapse before the contumacy of the Massachusetts people was noticed, and then they were virtually passed over as "almost on the brink of renouncing any dependence on the crown," (1671.) Quite a considerable interval succeeded, in which agents after agents upheld the colony against its adversaries in England. Even bribes were resorted to, the Province of Maine and two thousand guineas being offered to the king himself. But it was too late. The royal will was roused; the warrant went forth that the colony must submit, if it would have any charter at all. The magistrates were for yielding; the representatives — that is, the mass of the colonists — were for resisting; and while they clung to their charter, it was declared to be forfeited, (1684.) The king immediately appointed a governor for Massachusetts, Plymouth, Maine, and New Hampshire; but Charles dying, another official was sent out by James II., bearing the title of president of the same colonies, with the addition of the King's Province in Rhode Island, (1685.) The same year, the Rhode Island and Connecticut charters were put in abeyance.

Parliament.

Next to the crown was the Parliament of the mother country. But this was by no means so fully acknowledged in the colonies. "We have not admitted appeals to your authority," says the Massachusetts General Court to Parliament, "being assured they cannot stand with the liberty and power granted us by our charter," (1646,) — a declaration which was followed up by Edward Winslow, then the agent for Massachusetts in England. "If the Parliament of England," he says, "should impose laws upon us, having no burgesses in their

House of Commons nor capable of a summons by reason of the vast distance, we should lose the liberty and freedom of English indeed." It was on these very grounds that the sway claimed for Parliament was again and again resisted. It was, however, again and again obeyed.

Navigation acts. Parliament asserted its powers at an early day. During the commonwealth, when it ruled supreme over England, it stretched forth its sceptre over America by an act requiring all colonial exports to England to be shipped only in American or English vessels, (1651.) This was extended by Parliament and the crown together, after the restoration of royalty, in a second act, ordering that most of the exports from the colonies should be shipped only to England, or to an English colony, and in American or English vessels, as before, (1660.) Two or three years afterwards, it was enacted that almost all imports into the colonies should be shipped only from England or from an English colony, and in American or English vessels, as by the preceding statutes, (1663.) These were the famous navigation acts, the first assertions of parliamentary authority over the commerce of the colonies. How grievous to these such restrictions were needs not to be dwelt upon.

Duties. They were followed up, at no long interval, by duties upon the export and import of certain "enumerated articles" from one colony to another, (1672.) This was interfering, not only with the trade, but with the very constitution of the colonies. It required a new body of officials in the shape of revenue officers, appointed, of course, by the crown. Royal custom houses were also needed. It was soon proposed to demand an oath from the governors of New England — where trade was busiest, and discontent rifest — that they would enforce the commercial restrictions. But John Leverett, governor of Massachusetts, refused, and the General Court of the same colony soon passed a resolution "that the acts of navigation are an invasion of the rights and privileges of the subjects of his majesty in this colony, they not being represented in the Parliament," (1676–79.) A notice of the appointment of a collector of the royal customs for New England was torn down in Boston by order of the colonial magistrates, (1680.) But it was in vain, as we shall soon find. Parliament had adopted the principle of regulating the colonial trade, and was not likely to yield to the ebullitions of Boston, or of any other place in the colonies.

Royal governors. The authority of the mother country, whether royal or parliamentary, was represented by a constantly increasing number of officials in the colonies. Of these none were so prominent as the royal governors, to whom we now arrive in pursuing the account of the colonial relations.

Berkeley in Virginia. Nowhere did things go worse than in Virginia, of which Sir William Berkeley, a loyal cavalier, had been governor for more than twenty years.* Under his influence, the very assembly of the province became a burden, protracting its sessions and extending its prerogatives, providing a perpetual (so termed) instead of an annual revenue for the royal officials, and appointing county courts to levy certain imposts which were within its own province alone. To these difficulties were added others arising from the hostile bearing of the Indians, with whom the governor was disposed to temporize far more than suited the ardent Virginians, (1676.)

Bacon's rebellion. All at once, the province rose. One of the council, Nathaniel Bacon, being refused a commission against the Indians, declared that he would take out a commission of his own; at which the governor unseated him

* From 1641 to 1652, and again from 1660.

and declared him a rebel. But he was not the only one to be put down. William Drummond, the first governor of North Carolina, and Richard Lawrence, both men of energy and of culture, came out at Jamestown on Bacon's side. At their demand, supported by other colonists of influence, the assembly by which the governor had been blindly supported was dissolved. Bacon, elected to a new assembly, carried various measures of reform, besides obtaining a commission of commanding officer against the Indians. Again declared a rebel, he called a convention, who promised to stand by him while he proceeded against the foe upon the frontier. But on the governor's taking the field with armed servants and Indians, supported by some English men-of-war, Bacon and his party returned to meet him. Berkeley retreated, Bacon fired Jamestown, and soon after died. The cause which he had staked his all to support soon fell to pieces, and his chief adherents, Drummond amongst them, were hanged. Lawrence disappeared. "That old fool," said the good natured Charles II., on hearing of his governor's revenge, "has hanged more men in that naked colony than I did here for the murder of my father." Berkeley died of shame, it is said, in England. He left Virginia crushed and desolate.

Andros in New England. New England, consolidated into one province, was given over to Sir Edmund Andros, formerly governor of New York, (1686.) He made his appearance with troops, overthrowing the colonial assemblies, if there were any left to overthrow, declaring the town organizations at an end, prohibiting the printing press, and threatening even the property of the colonists by requiring them to take out new deeds of their estates from him. It was a part of his commission to procure toleration, especially for the church of England. To do this in Boston, he saw fit to seize upon one of the Puritan churches to celebrate the church service. Resistance was not attempted, and Andros and his council ruled supreme; nor only over New England, but likewise over New York and New Jersey, both of which were attached to his government, (1688.) In fact, he was on the high road to dominion over all the colonies. The charters of the Carolinas and of Maryland — that is, of every other colony which had a charter, save Pennsylvania alone — were menaced, (1686–88.) A waste of despotism seemed to be opening wherever freedom had found a foothold.

Revolution. Just then came the news of the revolution in England, (1689.) It was welcomed by a revolution in America. Boston rose against Andros, deposing him, and declaring Simon Bradstreet governor. The reaction was by no means gentle. The churchmen, whom Andros had favored, and who supported him, sent an address to King William, bewailing the peril to them from the returning "anarchy and confusion of government under which this country hath so long groaned." Rhode Island and Connecticut went farther than Massachusetts, and resumed their treasured charters. New York took up arms under Jacob Leisler and a committee of safety. The other colonies, less sorely oppressed than those of New England and New York, received the news in comparative tranquillity. A party in Maryland rose, but not against oppression so much as for the sake of sedition. The proprietary government fell, as has been told.

But not liberty. It soon appeared, however, that the English revolution was not intended to be interpreted as setting the colonies free. The charter of 1691 proved it in Massachusetts. The execution of Jacob Leisler and his son-in-law, Milbourne, in New York, by orders, however, of the new governor, Colonel Sloughter, rather than by those of the king, was equally conclusive, (1691.)

The appointment of Andros — the same Sir Edmund who had trampled upon both Massachusetts and New York — to the government of Virginia* was a still more stunning demonstration, (1692.)

Fletcher in New York.

A new attempt at colonial consolidation soon occurred. Colonel Benjamin Fletcher, a man of far less character than Andros, was made governor of New York and Pennsylvania, including Delaware; the proprietary government in the latter colonies being then suspended, (1692.) He was also declared commander-in-chief of the Connecticut and the New Jersey militia. Soon after taking possession of New York and Pennsylvania, Fletcher proceeded to Connecticut to take command of the militia. They assembled at his orders; but instead of listening to his commission, the senior officer, Captain Wadsworth, cried, "Beat the drums!" On Fletcher's attempting to persevere, Wadsworth exclaimed, "If I am interrupted again, I'll make the sun shine through you in a moment," (1693.) Thus baffled in his military functions, the governor returned to his civil powers in New York and Pennsylvania. The latter province, after resisting his demands for a grant of money, yielded only on condition that it should be disbursed by the provincial treasurer — a condition which Fletcher would not, and, if obedient to his instructions, could not allow, (1694.) New York itself was restive under his control. A tax for the support of ministers and the erection of churches had led to a debate between the council and the assembly; the council proposing that the governor should nominate the new clergy, but the assembly opposing. "You take it upon you," declared Fletcher to the assembly, "as if you were dictators;" but the assem-

* He proved, however, to be a comparatively good governor there

bly stood fast, and soon carried their point, "that the vestry and the churchwardens have a power to call their own minister," a dissenter, if so they pleased, although the governor was strong for the church of England, (1695.) It had been proposed by a clergyman of this church to combine New York, New Jersey, Connecticut, and Rhode Island in a single province, with a bishop, residing at New York, for its civil as well as ecclesiastical head. But this, more naturally even than Governor Fletcher's designs, came to nought. Fletcher himself, falling into disgrace at home, was recalled, leaving his attempts at consolidation an utter failure, (1698.)

General strictness.

The troubles implied in the various colonial relations account for much that has been ascribed to other causes. It has been so common to consider the Puritan severity as a thing apart, that one does not immediately seize upon the fact of the almost universal strictness that prevailed. Virginia, for instance, gave no harbor to Puritanism. Yet the Virginia code thunders against "mercenary attorneys," (1643,) burgesses "disguised with over much drink," (1659,) tippling houses, (1676,) and Sunday travelling, (1692.) Maryland declares with as much solemnity as Massachusetts against profanity, (1642.) Nor were precautions of a different nature neglected. Both Maryland (1642–1715) and New York (1665) make it necessary to procure a passport before traversing or leaving the colonial precincts. It was from a similar impulse that the "handicraftsmen" of Boston petitioned the General Court of Massachusetts to be protected against "strangers from all parts" who were interfering with their trade, not to say their influence in the community, (1677.) All over the colonies, there reigned a spirit of watchfulness, perhaps more grim, but certainly not more resolute, in one place than in another.

It might be increased or diminished by the social or the religious temper of the colonists; the New Englander was likely to be more upon his guard than the Virginian. But the spirit was the common growth of the new country, whose depths were still hid in the wilderness, whose borders were still bristling with the arrow or the steel.

Perils of the frontier.

The perils of the frontier are yet to be described. All around the colonists, there extended a line, or rather a series of lines, one after another, of suspected neighbors or of open foes. The Indian lay in ambush on this side; on that, the European, Swede, Dutchman, Spaniard, or Frenchman, stood in threatening attitude. Nor was the land alone overspread with enemies; the waters swarmed with pirates and with buccaneers; nay, the very air seemed to be filled with ghostly shapes and with appalling sounds. The world of spirits, as the colonists believed, was agitated by the wars amongst the races of America.

CHAPTER III.

INDIAN WARS.

Spirit of the Indians. TROUBLE between the European and the Indian was inevitable. It did not generally originate with the Indian, for he was disposed to welcome the stranger, and to help him in his trials. One of the very earliest visitors of the Plymouth settlers, as their first winter of suffering drew to an end, was Squanto, who had been kidnapped by an English vessel, seven years before, sold to slavery in Spain, released by Spaniards, and restored to his native country. Instead of revenging himself upon the English, he caught fish for them, and showed them how to plant and dress their corn. Indeed, there are few passages in history more honorable to human nature than those which recall the trustful and generous spirit of the red men towards the white men on these shores.

Spirit of the Europeans. It was far from being always, or even habitually, requited. From the other side of the ocean, men looked upon the American natives with a magnanimous kindliness, which on this side was too often transformed into distrust and hostility. A European thought himself bound by no obligations to an Indian. His treaties were to his own advantage, his bargains to his own profit, his efforts to his own supremacy. The noblest of the English missionaries to the Indians, John Eliot, called them "the dregs of mankind." Only from a distance that lent enchantment to the view could a gentler estimate be formed. "Concerning the killing of those poor Indians," wrote John Robinson, the Puritan minister, from Holland to his brethren at Plymouth, in relation to the slaughter of several natives suspected of conspiring against that settlement, "O, how happy a thing had it been if you had converted some before you had killed any! Besides, where blood is once begun to be shed, it is seldom stanched of a long time after. . . . It is also a thing more glorious in men's eyes than pleasing in God's, or convenient for Christians, to be a terror to poor barbarous people," (1623.)

Missionary labors.

It was the idea of King James of England, in issuing the patent of Virginia, to civilize and convert the natives of the country which he was giving to his companies. The London Company, accordingly, in conjunction with individuals both in England and in America, made some exertion to carry out the royal design. A school for natives was planned, as has been mentioned, but without being established. The colony of Plymouth, listening to Robinson's appeal, recognized the possibility of brotherhood with the Indians. Laws were formally enacted to provide for the conversion of the natives to the Christian faith, (1636.) Massachusetts framed what may be called a code of "necessary and wholesome laws to reduce them to civility of life," (November 4, 1646.)

The Mayhews and Eliot.

Obtaining an English grant of Martha's Vineyard, and then confirming his title by purchase from the natives, Thomas Mayhew began almost immediately to teach those who remained with him upon the island, (1643.) A more active missionary, however, was his son Thomas, who, after ten years' exertions, perished on a voyage to England, whither he was going for aid to his mission, (1657.) His father, and afterwards his son, continued the work to which he had sacrificed himself. Meanwhile John Eliot had begun his labors on the Massachusetts mainland. Preparing himself by the study of the Indian tongue, of which he afterwards composed a grammar, he met a party of Indians, for the first time as their preacher, at Nonantum. "Upon October 28, 1646," he writes with touching simplicity, "four of us (having sought God) went unto the Indians inhabiting our bounds, with desire to make known the things of their peace to them." Thenceforward Eliot went on founding and rearing Indian churches, now travelling from the Merrimac to Cape Cod, and now laboring at the translation of the Catechism, and even of the Bible, into the language of his converts, (1661–63.)

Supports. Both Eliot and the Mayhews, as well as other missionaries to the Indians, received their chief encouragement from a Society "for Promoting and Propagating the Gospel of Jesus Christ in New England," incorporated by act of Parliament, (1649.) Large collections aided the labors and provided for the expenses of those who engaged in the holy enterprise. "Right honorable nursing fathers," is the address which Eliot uses in giving the society an account of his labors. He writes to Robert Boyle, apparently the life and soul of the society, as his "right honorable, right charitable, and indefatigable nursing father." New England itself did comparatively little. Massachusetts granted lands to the converted Indians, but without much sympathy with them or with their teachers. The work, as a colonial one, languished.

Results. The results were therefore inconsiderable. What the Indians, or many of them, thought of the missions may be gathered from the answer of a Narraganset sachem to the missionary Mayhew applying for permission to preach among the tribe. "Go make the English good first." What many of the English thought of the missions may be gathered from the declaration of Daniel Gookin, superintendent of the converts, — "a pillar," says Eliot, "in our Indian work," — that he was "afraid to be seen in the streets," at the time of much ill will against the natives. Thirty years after the missionary enterprise began, there were nominally upwards of three thousand converts, (1673.) But the first church which Eliot founded — that at Natick — was, a few years subsequent to his death, but "a small church of seven men and three women; their pastor, Daniel Tohkohwampait," (1698.) Even before Eliot departed, he had seen his work declining. Endeavoring to get out a new edition of his version of the Scriptures, he wrote, "I am deep in years, and sundry say, if I do not procure it printed while I live, it is not within the prospect of human reason whether ever, or when, or how it may be accomplished." Things must have been low indeed, when the mere reprint of the Bible was so difficult. But "his charity," to use Eliot's deathbed words, "held out still," and all that he could do was done when he died, (1690.)

Wars in Virginia and Maryland. The wars with the Indians were more effective. Earliest of these was the war of Opechancanough Powhatan's successor, against the colony of Virginia. Provoked by the murder of one of their warriors, the Indians suddenly fell upon the English settlements, which, it seems, they would have utterly annihilated, but for the warning given by a converted countryman of theirs to a Jamestown settler, (1622.) Hostilities, continued at intervals for many years, were revived by a second surprise of the colony by the Indians, (1642.) Opechancanough being taken prisoner and slain, his confederates made peace, giving up all the land between the York and James Rivers, (1646.) In this latter war, Maryland had been involved. Thirty years later, the two colonies were again united in repelling the Susquehannas, with some other tribes, (1675–77.)

Pequot war. Meanwhile, more dangerous conflicts had arisen in New England. The first actual war with the Indians there occurred in consequence of some murders by the Pequots and the Narragansets; the latter tribe extending along the western shore of Narraganset Bay, the former stretching from the Thames to the Connecticut Rivers. The Narraganset chief, Canonicus, making amends for his followers, the expedition which Massachusetts equipped to avenge the murdered was directed chiefly against the Pequots, with the result, however, of exciting rather than punishing them, (1636.) They were on the point of persuading the Narragansets to make common cause with them, when Roger Williams, at the peril of his life, sought the wigwam of Canonicus, in order to avert an alliance which would have threatened Massachusetts, not to say New England, with desolation. It was the return which the exile made for the persecution from which he had but just escaped. Instead of joining the Pequots, the Narragansets sent their young sachem Miantonimoh to make friends with the people at Boston. At about the same time, the alliance of the Mohegans, a tribe of Northern Connecticut, under Uncas, was secured by the Connecticut colonists. As the spring opened, the colonial forces, amounting in all to little more than one hundred, with two or three hundred Indian allies, took the field, and in four months swept the unhappy Pequots from the face of the earth. Nearly a thousand of them were slain; the rest, whether men or women, old or young, being reduced to captivity and slavery. Their territory was divided between Massachusetts and Connecticut, (1637.)

Narragansets. Notwithstanding the alliance with Miantonimoh and the Narragansets, they were soon treated as foes. Defeated by the Mohegans, with whom they went to war, the Narragansets saw their chieftain a prisoner. He was saved by the interposition of his friend Gorton, the founder of Warwick, only to be given up again by the commissioners of the United Colonies to the Mohegan Uncas, by whose brother he was despatched. To shield Uncas from the revenge of the Narragansets, the colonies furnished him with a body guard, and even took up arms, when Pessacus, the brother and successor of Miantonimoh, began war against his Mohegan enemies. Nor did Pessacus avert the storm thus conjured up, but by submitting to make amends to both the Mohegans and the United Colonies, (1645.) The tribute which he then consented to pay was afterwards wrenched from him by violence, (1650.)

King Philip. A quarter of a century later, and the ill-treated tribe of Miantonimoh and Pessacus were drawn into the great war that goes by the name of King Philip's. He was Metacomet, the son and successor of Massasoit, with whom the Plymouth colonists had made an early treaty, the chief of the Pokanokets or Wampanoags, a tribe on the eastern shore of Narraganset Bay. Suspected and assailed by the people of Plymouth, whose authorities claimed jurisdiction over him, Philip (to call him by his familiar name) was at length accused of hatching a general conspiracy amongst the Indians. The accuser, a native of bad character, although professedly converted, was slain by some of Philip's men, three of whom were presently hanged, without any actual proof of their being the murderers, by orders of the court at Plymouth. Philip wept, it is said, at the idea of warfare with the English. But he could not keep peace with them; and so began a war, by far the most deadly of all between the English and the Indians, (1675.)

Driven almost immediately from his domains about Mount Hope, and soon afterwards from his retreats in

War throughout New England.

the Rhode Island swamps, Philip led his few warriors into the heart of Massachusetts, where the Indians had already risen in arms. Thence the circle of hostilities spread on all sides, to the tribes of the Connecticut valley in the west, to those of the Merrimac valley in the east, and farther still, to the Abenakis of Maine — the latter, however, being engaged in warfare of their own, unconnected with Philip and his allies. Against these was arrayed the whole of New England. Rhode Island, it is true, rather suffered than fought; nor were Maine and New Hampshire, then the dependencies of Massachusetts, able to take any active part. But the United Colonies were all in arms. A few hundred combatants were the most that could be mustered in any single battle; yet the strife was more than proportioned to the numbers or the resources on either side. Month after month witnessed scenes of ambush, assault, devastation, and butchery. The work of blood was as savagely done by the English as by the Indians.

Destruction of the Narragansets.

As winter drew nigh, the suspicions of the colonies were excited by Uncas, the Mohegan, against his old foes, the Narragansets. They had given pledges of peace at the beginning of the war; nor were there now any signs of hostility on their part, except the shelter which they were charged with giving to the broken Pokanokets. But the commissioners of the United Colonies, the successors of those who had given up Miantonimoh and humbled Pessacus, declared war against the Narragansets and their chief, Canonchet. It took but a few days to overrun the Narraganset territory, and to defeat the tribe in a fearful fight which cost the colonial forces dear. Driven from their forests and their fastnesses, the Narragansets spread over the adjoining lands, and even as far as within eighteen miles of Boston. "We will die to the last man," exclaimed Canonchet, when taken in the spring, "but not be slaves to the Englishman." He was slain, and his nation laid low forever.

Of Philip. The fall of the Narragansets was accompanied by that of the tribes within the limits of Massachusetts. Most of the survivors turned their backs upon their ancient hunting grounds in search of freedom in the north and west. Philip, who had mourned over the beginning of the war, was too strong in heart to outlive its close. He sought the home of his fathers, and there, after losing his wife, his child, and most of his few remaining warriors, he was shot by a renegade Pokanoket. His boy, the last of his line, was sold into slavery in Bermuda. His race was given over to the executioner and the slave dealer; his territory went to Plymouth, and, half a century afterwards, to Rhode Island. But it was no bloodless victory that the colonies had won. "The towns are so drained of men," wrote Leverett, governor of Massachusetts, in the thick of the contest, "we are not able to send out any more." Six hundred of the best colonists had perished; ten times that number, and more, had suffered from the losses and the agonies which befall even the survivors of a war. Six hundred dwellings were burned; many a town was partially, many a one totally destroyed. The mere expenses of the war amounted to something enormous in comparison with the actual means of the colonies. It is pleasant to meet with the record of a contribution of five hundred pounds, collected by an elder brother of Increase Mather, a Puritan minister in Dublin. The war had lasted a little more than a year, (1676.)

Peace. There still remained a few Indian war parties to deal with in the Connecticut valley, as well as the Abenaki tribes in Maine. The former were soon driven off; but the latter kept to their arms until peace was literally bought of them by Sir Edmund Andros, the governor of New York, to which province, it may be remembered, the eastern part of Maine then belonged, (1678.)

Abenakis in arms.

The Abenakis were soon in arms again. Enlisted on the side of the French in the wars to be related by and by, the eastern tribes repeatedly laid waste the English settlements. A quarter of a century (1689–1713) did not still the passions thus excited. At a time of peace between England and France, the colonists of the former nation attacked the allies, nay, the very missionaries of the latter. Sebastian Rasles, the patriarch of a Norridgewock village on the Kennebec, where he dwelt alone amidst his savage converts, became the object of especial jealousy to the government of Massachusetts. An armed expedition failed in making him captive, (1722.) But a renewed assault was more successful, the venerable priest being slain, his chapel sacked, his village destroyed, (1724.) All the tribes of the east entered into the war. The only ally of Massachusetts was Connecticut; the efforts to obtain support from the Mohawks being answered by the advice that Massachusetts should do justice to her foes, (1722.) Peace was made, after a five years' conflict. It was broken more than once in the later French wars, (1744, 1754.) But the Abenakis submitted at last, (1760.)

Peace in the centre and south.

The central and southern colonies were for many years undisturbed by Indian wars. Treaties with the Five Nations — the more easily made and kept as these tribes were continually at enmity with the French of Canada — protected the frontiers of the colonies of the centre. Those of the south, for some time unassailed, were at length overrun.

War in North Carolina.

North Carolina, after frequent aggressions on the part of her settlers, was swept by the Tuscaroras, (1711.) The aid of South Carolina, with that of her Indian allies, was called in, before peace could be restored, even for a brief period. Soon breaking out again, in consequence of the continued injuries inflicted upon the Indians, the war grew so threatening as to require the interposition of Virginia as well as of South Carolina. The three colonies together forced the Tuscaroras to fly to their kindred, the Five Nations of New York, by whom, as was formerly mentioned, they were received as a sixth tribe of the confederacy, (1713.)

In South Carolina.

South Carolina, some time before involved in strife with the Indian allies of the Spaniards in Florida, was presently threatened with a more serious war. The tribes of the south, especially the Yamassees, aggrieved by the treatment which they received from the colonists, dashed upon their plantations, and, with revenge and slaughter, pressed northward towards Charleston. So great was the peril, that the governor armed the slaves of the province, besides obtaining a law from the assembly authorizing the conscription of freemen. These means, backed by the resources of North Carolina and Virginia, averted the ruin that appeared to be approaching. The Yamassees, driven back with their confederates, were forced to seek refuge in Florida, (1715.)

With Cherokees.

Nearly half a century elapsed before the Indians took up the hatchet in the south. The Cherokees, invaded first by the forces of the Carolinas and Virginia, and then by the royal troops, at that time carrying on the last French war, retorted with sword and fire, (1759-60.) But the English and the colonial soldiery together proved too much for the Cherokees, who were soon reduced to humiliating terms of peace, (1761.)

With western tribes.

Meantime, the western settlements had begun to bear the brunt of Indian warfare. Pennsylvania was attacked, just as the final contest with the French began, (1755,) by the Delawares and Shawanoes, the former of whom had been infamously driven from their land by the Pennsylvanians, or their proprietors, many years before. Other tribes, joining with these, spread havoc along all the western borders of the colonies, until peace was conquered, (1758.)

Pontiac's war. The French war over, (1763,) the same tribes, with others of varied name and race, united under the great Ottawa chieftain, Pontiac, in one simultaneous attempt to clear the western country of the English invaders. Such an onslaught, occurring at an earlier period, might have driven the English, not only from the west but from the east. But made against them when they had just prevailed against the hosts of France, the attacks of the Indians, though at first successful, were met and decisively subdued, (1764.) *

Indians in Pennsylvania. Some sad and strange events, in connection with the war thus closed, must be mentioned, for the sake of the illustration which they offer of the passions so long dividing the English and the Indians. A number of Pennsylvanians, opposed to their own authorities, and excited with suspicion and hatred against all of Indian blood, made such demonstrations against the Indian converts of the Moravian missionaries, for some time at work in Pennsylvania, that the assembly ordered the Indians to be removed to Philadelphia. Hardly was this done, when the settlers of Paxton, a frontier town, put to death a handful of Indians lingering at Conestoga, pursuing and slaying some who, for safety's sake, had been lodged in the Lancaster jail. A force of from five to fifteen hundred borderers then set out on a march against Philadelphia, where they intended to seize the Indians transported thither, if not to make themselves masters of the city and the province altogether

* The extreme western tribes remained in arms till 1765.

They were not without their sympathizers in Philadelphia; but those who were prepared to resist them took so determined a course as to avert the dangers of the insurrection. The show of force in the city persuaded the borderers to retire, (1763–64.)

Other wars, but the issue decided.

The tomahawk was not yet buried in the west or in the south. Year after year some party or some tribe of Indians broke loose upon the frontiers. But the question had long been decided as to the hands into which victory was to fall. The scattered tribes, ill provided with arms or stores, with discipline or skill, had fallen away, from the first, before the concentrated numbers and accumulated resources of the colonists. Whatever individual bravery could do, whatever the undying independence of any single tribe could achieve, was all in vain, before the resistless advance of the English. Nay, not of the English alone, but of the Indians themselves, allied with the conquerors of their countrymen. But for such as joined the stranger, the conquest would have been slower, although none the less sure.

Later missions.

The Indian wars form by no means a bright chapter in our history. But, as we found something to light up the early, so we find something to light up the later relations of the Indians and the English. The missions, begun by the Mayhews and by Eliot, had never been abandoned in Massachusetts. As time passed, and the native race grew thinner upon its former soil, new stations were taken, to reach the remoter tribes. A mission at Stockbridge, at first in the charge of John Sergeant, afterwards obtained no less a superintendent than Jonathan Edwards, (1737–50.) A more radiant name is that of David Brainerd, of Connecticut, who, after laboring between Stockbridge and Albany, turned southwards to Pennsylvania and New Jersey, (1744.) The exertions of a few years so enfeebled him that he returned to the Connecticut valley only to die, (1747.) His place was taken in Pennsylvania by Moravian missionaries, (1748,) whose labors, protracted to a much later period, came to such sad results as have just been described. The missionary would convert the Indians; the colonist would hunt them to death. Alas, that so little was wrought by the friend and the teacher, in comparison with the vast achievements of the foe and the destroyer!

CHAPTER IV.

DUTCH WARS.

Wars with Indians.

RETURNING to trace the fortunes of the Dutch settlement of New Netherland, we immediately find it, like its English neighbors, at war with the Indians, whom we may call Manhattans of the Algonquin race. Vexed by the traders, oppressed by the officials of the colony, the Manhattans had provocation enough to take up arms at an early period. But the vicinity of their dreaded foes, the Mohawks of the Five Nations, who were disposed to be friends with the Dutch, kept them at peace until peace was impossible. The incursions of the Indians into the Dutch settlements, and the horrid massacres inflicted by the Dutch in return, were of the same nature as the hostilities already described, (1640–43.) A temporary truce was instantly broken by a general war, spreading from the main land to the islands, and devastating almost the whole of the colony. But for a company of English settlers, just fresh from encounters with the Indians, it would have gone hard with New Netherland. As it was, the exhaustion of the colony was as great as that of its foes, when a treaty terminated the war, (1643–45.) Thrice, however, within the next twenty years, the Indians rose against the still oppressive Dutchmen, (1655, 1658, 1663.)

The increase of New Netherland was arrested by

Effect upon New Netherland. these repeated wars. A contemporary document* (1644) dwells upon the favorable prospects of the colony after the fur trade was thrown open, (1638,) as previously mentioned. "At which time," we are told, "the inhabitants there resident not only spread themselves far and wide, but new colonists came thither from fatherland, and the neighboring English, as well from Virginia as from New England, removed under us." The hopes thus inspired are expressly stated to have been blasted by the Indian wars.

Internal restrictions. Had the wars never occurred, the colony would have had no rapid progress. In itself it was divided by what may be called castes. The patroons, for instance, were an order by themselves, not necessarily hostile to the authorities or unfriendly to the colonists, yet often proving to be one or both. Then the colony lay at the mercy of the company and its director, whose supremacy was shared by none but a few officials and councillors. The attempts at representation on the part of the more substantial colonists, were of no avail. Boards of twelve, eight, and nine men were successively established, with the director's consent, but without any power to restrain him or to elevate themselves. It was at length resolved by the nine men to draw up a statement of their grievances to be laid before the government of the mother country. But the member charged with preparing the document, Adrian Van der Donck, was robbed of his papers, thrown into prison, and expelled from the board of the nine men as well as from the director's council, in which he had a seat, (1649.) Liberated from his imprisonment, Van der Donck set sail for Holland, with other representatives of the cause for which he had suffered. His exertions there brought about

* In O'Callaghan's History of New Netherland, Appendix E.

a provincial order from the States General, by which the West India Company was directed to make some concessions to the colony, (1650.) Two years elapse, and we find Van der Donck still appealing to the States General for justice, (1652.) The most that he procured was a municipal government for the city (as it was styled) of New Amsterdam, the first city of the United States. It was organized in the following year, (1653,) with sheriff, burgomasters, and judges, but all appointed by the director, Peter Stuyvesant, who had carried on for several years a downright war in defence of his prerogatives. In resentment against him personally much of the vigor belonging to the liberal party had been expended. He carried the day, it must be confessed, notwithstanding the city charter, notwithstanding also the remonstrances of a convention of eight towns held the same year.

Religious persecution.

The measure of arbitrary government was not yet full. At the instance of two clergymen of the Dutch church, a proclamation from the director appeared, threatening fines upon all preachers and hearers of unlicensed congregations, (1656.) The first to suffer were Lutherans, who were not merely fined, but imprisoned; then some Baptists, who were not merely fined, but banished. Soon after, a few Quakers fell into the hands of the persecutors, one of them being subjected to tortures as horrid as any inflicted in the English colonies, (1657.) A few years afterwards, the remonstrance of a Quaker, John Bowne, who had been transported to Holland as a criminal, brought upon Director Stuyvesant the censure of the company for his oppression, (1662–63.)

Subjection of New Sweden.

Despite all these drawbacks upon its strength, New Netherland was strong enough, with help from the company, to subdue its neighbor of New Sweden. That colony, though reënforced at times, continued in a precarious state, with few settlers and uncertain resources. Protested against by the Dutch as interloping within their territory, it had nevertheless invited Dutch emigrants amongst its own settlers, (1640.) But the New Netherland authorities were on the alert. Partly in opposition to a Connecticut settlement attempted on the Delaware, but chiefly in resistance to the advances of the Swedes, Stuyvesant built his Fort Casimir at the present Newcastle, (1651.) A new governor, Rysingh, coming to the Swedish colony, got possession of the fort without difficulty, (1654.) It cost him dear; for Stuyvesant, with a force of several hundred, principally sent from Holland for the purpose, not only recovered Fort Casimir, but conquered Fort Christina and the whole of New Sweden, (1655.) A few Swedes swore allegiance to the Dutch; the rest went home or emigrated to the English colonies. The Swedish government protested against the conquest of its colony; but it had too much upon its hands in Europe to recover its possessions in America. So New Sweden came to an end; and the dream of the generous Gustavus Adolphus that he was to found a place of refuge from persecution and from corruption vanished forever.

New Amstel. The victorious West India Company hardly knew what to do with its conquest. It found a purchaser, however, in the city of Amsterdam, which became the mistress of what had been New Sweden, — portions of our Delaware and Pennsylvania, — under the name of New Amstel, (1656.) This was enlarged by a subsequent purchase so as to embrace the Dutch possessions on both banks of the Delaware; in other words, New Jersey, Pennsylvania, and Delaware, (1663.)

English aggressions. But the dominions of the Dutch, whether West India Company or Amsterdam city, were passing into other hands. The claims of England to the territory had been asserted, as mentioned in a former chapter, from a very early period. They lost nothing, it may be believed, of their force, as colonies multiplied and lands were in continually increasing demand. An old grant from the Council for New England * was made to cover Long Island. Connecticut and Massachusetts pushed on towards the Hudson. On the south, parties from Connecticut and from Maryland threatened the domains upon the Delaware, (1639–63.) Year after year, during a quarter of a century, brought some fresh invasion of the English, exciting some fresh remonstrance from the Dutch. "Those of Hartford," runs one of the Dutch records, "have not only usurped and taken in the lands of Connecticut, but have also beaten the servants of their high mightinesses the honored company with sticks and plough staves, laming them," (1640.) It is the tone of all the records, querulous and feeble, the wail of a colony never numbering more than ten thousand against its far more numerous neighbors. Nor were its neighbors its only foes. Amongst its own people was a large number of Englishmen, emigrants from hostile colonies, who naturally became hostile settlers. At one time, some English villages of Long Island proclaimed "the commonwealth of England and his highness the lord protector," (1655.) At another, the towns at the west end of the island proclaimed the English king, (1663.) Finally, the danger was so great that Peter Stuyvesant, the foe of all liberal institutions, called a convention of his province. It appears how far the English had pushed their aggressions on scanning the meagre list of the towns or settlements that were represented. New Amsterdam and Rensselaerswyck head the roll of twelve. The convention favored peace with the Indians; as for the English, why, the English in New Netherland alone were "six to one," (1664.)

* To the Earl of Stirling, (1635.)

War; loss of the province.

Long as the dissensions between the English and the Dutch had lasted, neither the colonies nor the mother countries had gone to war about them. A war of two years (1652–54) between the Dutch and the English under Cromwell did not involve their American settlements. When England came under Charles II., another war with Holland was resolved upon, partly from commercial and partly from political motives, the chief of the latter being the intimate connection at that time between the Dutch and the French. Before war was formally declared, New Netherland was surprised by an English fleet. It did not come as a national, but as an individual expedition. Charles II. had made a grant, as has been narrated, of New Netherland to the Duke of York and Albany. It had been the work of a few months only for the duke to buy up other English claims, and collect commissioners and troops to take possession of his new realms. Accompanied by John Winthrop, governor of Connecticut, who, though amiable and disinterested in most respects, was full of determination against the Dutch, the commissioners, headed by Colonel Nichols, obtained possession of the province without battle. The terms of the surrender promised to the conquered their religion, their law of inheritance, and their trade and intercourse with Holland, (1664.) The transaction, at first professedly discountenanced by England, was afterwards sustained by her, and finally submitted to by Holland in the treaty of Breda, (1667.)

Recovery and final loss.

On the outbreak of fresh hostilities between the same countries, a few years later, (1672,) New York, as New Amsterdam was now called, received the summons to capitulate to a Dutch squadron, (1673.) It did so, and was held by the Dutch for upwards of a year, when it was once more, and for the last time, surrendered by them, (1674.) Thus were the Dutch, and with them the Swedes, brought beneath the English dominion.

CHAPTER V.

SPANISH WARS.

Spanish race. THERE were other races, rivals of the English, less easily to be reduced than the Dutch or the Swedes. One upon the southern border bore the flag of Spain, rent and dim indeed, but still the flag of a great nation.

Its colony. Yet the colony of the Spaniards was far from being a great one. St. Augustine, eldest of the permanent settlements upon United States soil, was amongst the least active of them all. Half garrison, half mission in its character, it formed a post where a few troops and a few priests kept up the Spanish claim upon Florida. A century after its foundation, it was nearly annihilated by one of the buccaneering expeditions that were wont to ravage the American coast. It rallied, however, especially when a treaty between Spain and England put a stop to the English commissions with which the buccaneers of the time were generally provided, (1670.)

Collisions with the English. But there was no good will to speak of between Spain and England, or amongst their colonies. A force from Florida was soon marching against the newly-organized Carolina, a more flagrant incursion, in Spanish eyes, upon the territory still claimed by Spain, than any of the northern colonies had made. The expedition was met and turned back by the resolute Carolinians, (1672.) Some years after, another invasion of the Spaniards effected the destruction of a Scotch settlement just made near the Spanish border, (1686.) These were not wars so much as the chastisements inflicted or attempted by Florida against its English trespassers.

Effect on the colony.

If there was any effect, it was not to dislodge the intruders, but rather to stimulate the intruded upon. Florida took a fresh start. St. Augustine awoke from its slumber, brushed up its means of offence and defence, and assumed a new attitude. The surrounding country, still in the hands of the Indians, was dotted over with forts and chapels, with soldiers and missionaries. On the other side of the peninsula, upon the Gulf of Mexico, Pensacola was reared with fortress and dwellings, (1696.) It seemed as if Spain was at last to occupy our soil with a colony worthy of bearing her great name.

War. Attacks on St. Augustine and Charleston.

Presently war broke out between England with various allies on one side, and on the other Spain and France, (1702.) It was but just heard of in South Carolina, when Governor Moore obtained the consent of the assembly to an attack upon St. Augustine. With twelve hundred men, half of them Indians, Moore was able to take the town, but not the fort, from which he precipitately retreated on the arrival of some Spanish men-of-war from Havana, (1702.) Poorly as his expedition turned out, Moore, no longer governor, headed a second, composed almost entirely of Indians, with whom he made a foray amongst the missionary villages of Northern Florida without any effective results, (1705.) The next year, a naval attack by both French and Spaniards upon Charleston was beaten off with great loss, three hundred out of eight hundred assailants being killed or captured, (1706.) This was the last event of the war, so far as the colonies were concerned, although peace was not made until seven years later by the treaty of Utrecht, (1713.)

Treaty of Utrecht.

This treaty is of moment in United States history. The war, of which it was the conclusion, arose from the attempt of Louis XIV. to seat a prince of his own house upon the Spanish throne; in other words, to combine Spain and France in one vast kingdom. So menacing was the attempt to Europe, that not England alone, but Holland, Germany, both the Empire and Prussia, Portugal and Savoy armed themselves against it. The treaty of Utrecht decided that France and Spain must remain separate. Had they been joined, the English colonies upon our shores would have found it difficult to withstand their united foes.

Second war. Descents on Florida.

Five years after, France was on the side of England in a war with Spain, (1718.) It was caused principally by the refusal of Spain to fulfil the Utrecht treaty so far as related to the empire of Germany, with which power France and England, and then Holland, all allied themselves. Afterwards, Spain and the Empire made peace together, while France, England, and Holland formed a league against them, (1725.) Little was done either in Europe or in America. Pensacola was taken and retaken by the French, then in their Louisiana settlements, (1719.) It was soon restored, (1721.) A force of three hundred, partly Indians, made a sally from Carolina upon the Spanish and Indian villages of Florida, (1725.) But the war was without interest or effect, and peace returned with the treaty of Seville, (1729.)

Third war. Georgia and Florida.

Then followed the settlement of Georgia, already described as intended to be an outpost against the Spaniards, (1733.) Whatever they thought of this fresh aggression upon their realm, they seem to have said or done nothing for some time; then General Oglethorpe, the head of the Georgian colony, was summoned to evacuate the territory, (1736.) War being declared by England against Spain, chiefly in consequence of Spanish depredations upon English commerce, Oglethorpe received orders to invade Florida, (1739.) He did so, with a force of twelve hundred men from both the Carolinas and Virginia, as well as from his own province, besides an equal number of Indians. With these, and with trains and ships, he laid siege to St. Augustine; but being deserted by most of his Indians, and by many of his volunteers, he was obliged to abandon the enterprise, (1740.) A large expedition from England, reënforced, first and last, by upwards of four thousand colonial troops, was equally unsuccessful against the Spanish strongholds in the West Indies, (1740–41.) But the Spaniards themselves did no better in their invasion of Georgia, from which they were repelled, partly by battle and partly by fraud, Oglethorpe being still there, (1741.) After this, the Spanish war subsided, nor did the French share in the hostilities begin for three years to come, (1744.) Four years later, the treaty of Aix-la-Chapelle restored things to their state before the war, (1748.)

Fourth war. Cession of Florida.

Just as the last colonial war with France was ending, the fourth and last colonial war with Spain began. This power came into the contest as the ally of France, in America even more than in Europe, the object being to prevent the English expelling the French from their American possessions, and then turning against the Spaniards, as was apprehended, and expelling them from theirs. But the French were already driven out; and nothing interfered with a vigorous onset of the English upon the Spaniards. New England and New York contributed to the capture of Havana in the opening year of the war, (1762.) The treaty of Paris, begun upon in the same, though not formally completed till the following year, restored Havana to Spain. But it gave an immense accession of territory to England and her colonies. What France surrendered will appear hereafter. Spain ceded Florida, once the whole of North America, but now little more than a peninsula of the southern coast, (1763.) A royal proclamation of the same year gave names and boundaries to East and West Florida, the latter province embracing the French cessions east of the Mississippi. Twenty years after, the Floridas reverted to Spain, to be again separated from it at a later period.

Spain in Louisiana and California.

To make some amends to Spain for her losses in attempting the rescue of France, the latter kingdom gave up her colony of Louisiana. To this we shall revert. At nearly the same time that the Spaniards took possession of their acquisition in the east, they extended their settlements in the west by establishing missions at San Diego and Monterey, California, (1769.)

Character of the Spanish wars.

But the Spanish wars, so far as our country was concerned, were over. They had never arisen, except in the case of the last brief war, from any consideration of American interests. Nor had they called forth any development of American energies either in crowded battles or extended campaigns. But they had continued, if we date from the first encounters, for nearly a century.

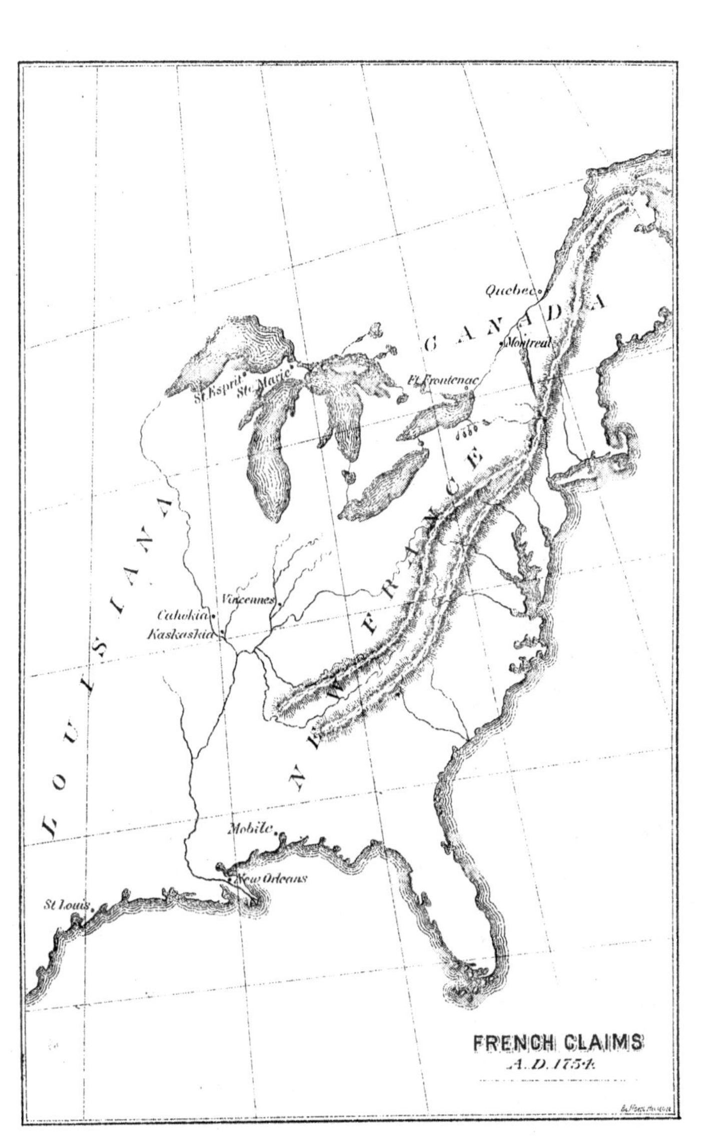
Quebec
C A N A D A
Montreal
Ft Frontenac
St Esprit
Ste Marie
L O U I S I A N A
N E W F R A N C E
Vincennes
Cahokia
Kaskaskia
Mobile
New Orleans
St Louis
FRENCH CLAIMS
A. D. 1754.

CHAPTER VI.

FRENCH POSSESSIONS.

French race. THE great rival of the English race upon our soil reappears. It is time to turn back beyond Spanish, Dutch, and Indian wars, nay, beyond the growth of the English colonies, to trace the progress of the French in America. No other nation, it will be found, not even the English, asserted claims or projected achievements of equal vastness.

New France. We left the French the masters of New France — a name of vague extension originally, but subsequently confined, as will be remembered, to Acadie and Canada. Acadie being itself shorn of its original dimensions, the province of Canada remained the chief division of New France.

System of government. The French, like the English colonies, were not always under the immediate government of the mother country. An intermediate authority, vested in the Company of New France, prevailed for thirty-five years, (1627–62.) For twelve years more, a French West India Company was commissioned to administer the affairs of the colony, (1663–75.) But with these bodies were associated some officers of royal appointment, so that there was no time when the colony was wholly removed from the oversight of the sovereign. Nor was the season during which the two companies lasted by any means so long or so decisive as the periods of the royal government. New

France, like Old France, was essentially a monarchy, and a monarchy in which the monarch was growing out of all proportion to the people. Its institutions were of the past. A governor general, representing the monarch, with an intendant for a prime minister, a council of notables for a nobility, and a host of ecclesiastics, with a bishop at their head, (from 1659,) constituted the authorities of the colony. The ruling class amongst the people was that of the seigneurs, or lords of the manor; their tenants, called habitans, holding land of them by feudal tenure. No press was allowed; no learning of a liberal nature was encouraged. The education of the province was in the hands of the religious orders, whose names and numbers were almost as manifold as in the mother-land. Under these influences, the colony could not but be greatly restricted. The main body of the people were necessarily dependent, unable to act for themselves or for their country, the few alone having the will and the power to urge on the work of colonization and of dominion.

Relations with Indians and English.

Such were the internal drawbacks upon the progress of New France. Of those which we may call external, the chief were the relations of the French with the Indians and the English. Those with the Indians were of two kinds — with the friendly and with the unfriendly tribes. Now it may seem that the amicable intercourse of the French with the large proportion of the natives around them must have been entirely conducive to their prosperity. But it did not prove to be so, on account, principally, of the tendency of the French settlers to sink to the level of their Indian allies, rather than to raise these to themselves. The Frenchman, whether missionary or soldier, explorer or trader, appeared to find a fascination in savage life which he could not resist; and yet it was the vices rather than the virtues of the

Indian character which he admired and imitated. He became indolent, treacherous, morosely cruel, in many instances far more of a savage than any Indian. As to the hostile tribes, it is enough, at the present moment, to name the Five Nations, with whom, as will appear hereafter, the French were at war for a century. As to the English, it must be left to the next chapter to set forth the obstacles which they presented to French advancement. It is sufficient to observe that these hinderances from without, joined to those from within, formed a bristling barricade over which all the ardor and all the discipline of the French character would find it difficult to mount. The stronger must have been the impulses to have extended the limits of New France so far as we shall now find them.

Acadie, including Maine.

The boundaries of Acadie stretched from the northern coasts, through all the east of Maine, as far as the Kennebec, the French asserted; as far as the Penobscot, the English allowed. With the portions of the province in the north we have no further concern than to observe that they included all now called Nova Scotia, New Brunswick, and Cape Breton, together with indefinite regions beyond. Maine was but feebly held by the French. Missions at the mouth of the Penobscot and on the Kennebec, with a post or two for trade, comprised all that could be called settlements. But for the towns and forts of the neighboring parts of Acadie, the east as well as the west of Maine would have fallen into English hands.

Canada, including New York, Wisconsin, Michigan.

Passing over the cities and fortresses of Central Canada, as foreign to our soil, but not without remembering their importance, let us pursue the Canadian settlements that were made or attempted upon actual United States territory. The first to advance was, as usual, a missionary, Le Moyne, who, with a few associates, labored amongst the Five Nations, then at peace. A colony was founded in Western New York, but only to be abandoned on account of renewed warfare between the French and Indians, (1656-58.) A few years later, Allouez, another missionary, led the way up the lakes, and founded the mission of St. Esprit, on the southern shore of Superior, in the present Wisconsin, (1666.) Two years after, Dablon and Marquette established a mission at Sault Ste. Marie, in the present Michigan, (1668.) Other missions arose in the adjoining forests and on the contiguous shores. After the missionary came the trader, and after the trader generally the soldier; so that to the mission house there were added dwellings, barracks, and, in time, a fort, whose sounding title frequently drowned the peaceful name of the mission. Thus was Canada extended beyond the St. Lawrence and its tributaries, beyond all neighborhood of the English colonies, into the valleys and the wildernesses of the west.

The Mississippi. Illinois.

Still more distant realms were reached. Father Marquette, of the Michigan mission, hearing of a great river towards the setting sun, resolved to find and to explore it. Before he started, his brethren, Allouez and Dablon, penetrated into the interior of Wisconsin and Illinois, (1672.) Marquette, with a few companions, found the Mississippi, as he had been directed by the natives, and sailed upon its waters as far down as Arkansas, (1673.) On his return, he established a new mission near the present Chicago in Illinois.

Louisiana.

The tidings from the Mississippi kindled new plans of trade, new visions of dominion. To begin upon them, there soon appeared a Frenchman, La Salle,— in youth a Jesuit, in manhood a trader and an adventurer of the highest stamp amongst the colonists of New France. Repairing to the French court, he obtained a commission to complete the discovery of the great western river, in consideration of which the monopoly of the fur trade was to be his own, (1677.) He soon engaged in his enterprise; but four years of exertion and of disappointment passed over him, before he descended the Mississippi to its mouth and to the adjacent coasts. It did not matter that the Spaniard De Soto had been the discoverer of the river a century and a half before the French. They hailed themselves possessors of the waters and of the shores, under the name of Louisiana, (1682.)

French dominion. Thus was New France extended from north to south, and from east to west. While the Swedes and the Dutch had yielded their hold upon our soil, while the Spaniards had contracted theirs to the single corner of Florida, while the English had only their New England, New York, New Jersey, Maryland, Virginia, and Carolina, the whole together forming not much more than a broken beach upon the Atlantic, the French dominion stretched from the Gulf of St. Lawrence, over vale, and prairie, and mountain, far round by the western waters, to the Gulf of Mexico. It still needed time, vigor, wisdom, to make this mighty empire a reality as well as a name.

Colony in Texas. No time was lost in sending La Salle, who had gone to France to tell his adventurous story, with a colony of two hundred, to make a settlement in Louisiana. Missing the mouth of the Mississippi, the party were landed on what is now the Texan shore, near the present Matagorda, where they built a fort with the name of St. Louis, (1685.) But things went hard with them, and when they were reduced to less than a fifth of their original number, La Salle found it time to seek relief in Canada. On his way thither, with half of his surviving comrades, he was foully murdered by one of them, (1687.) The colony of St. Louis soon vanished from the earth.

Twelve years passed before another trial to colonize Louisiana. A twofold attempt was then made, one by the

Colony in Missis-sippi. English and one by the French. The old grant of Carolana having been bought up by one of the later New Jersey proprietors, Coxe, he sent, under permission of his sovereign, a small squadron to take possession of the Mississippi. One of the vessels, sailing up the river, was met by a band of Frenchmen, who, by assuring the Englishmen that they were in a part of Canada, and not in Louisiana, prevailed upon them to turn about at a bend still called the English Turn — Détour aux Anglais. So the English retired, and the French held their own. They were a party of two hundred in number, under Lemoine D'Iberville, a Canadian of greater gallantry than prudence, who, intent upon mines and treasures rather than upon the substantial resources of a colony, chose the sands of Biloxi, in what is now Mississippi, for the site of his fort, (1699.) The next year, an expedition in search of mines travelled up the river as far as the Falls of St. Anthony, first visited by some of La Salle's companions twenty years before.

Colony in Alabama. The mines receded; the sands of Biloxi remained. D'Iberville, returning from France, whither he went twice in quest of supplies, transferred the main body of the settlers to Mobile, in the present Alabama, (1702.) But D'Iberville, who, like La Salle, was the life and the soul of his company, died, (1706,) and left the colony in a very precarious condition. "Nothing," says the French chronicler, "was more feeble." The truth was, that France was at this time too much occupied in Europe, to say nothing of the north of America, to rear a great colony in the wilderness of Louisiana.

Grant to Crozat. At length the province, extending from the mouth of the Mississippi to Lake Michigan, and from the English Carolina and the Spanish Florida to the New Mexico of Spain, was made over, for the term of fifteen years, to Antoine Crozat, a French merchant prince. He was to receive a large sum every year from the royal treasury towards the expenses of the colonial government, besides the monopoly of trade to and from the colony. In return, he was to send a certain number of vessels and settlers, year by year, in order to keep up and to increase the colonial settlements, (1712.) A faint flush of vigor seemed to overspread the struggling colony.

Western settlements. Indiana.

Meanwhile the settlements in the north-west had been extended. The missions of Kaskaskia, (about 1695,) and Cahokia, (about 1700,) in our Illinois, and the settlement of Vincennes, in our Indiana, (about 1705,) had confirmed the occupation of that region. A military post was planted at Detroit, the central point in the great arc now formed by the French possessions, (1701.)

Loss of Acadie.

But we have reached a period when the French possessions were beginning to be contracted. The war in the north, to which we must recur, had ended with the surrender, according to the treaty of Utrecht, of Acadie to England, (1713.) What was thus cut off at the end of the line was more than equal, in point of population and of settlement, to all that had been added to the middle or to the lower end.

Forts: Pennsylvania and Ohio.

Nor was there any reaction to compensate for the loss. Canada, it is true, roused herself, building forts upon New York territory, at Niagara, (1726,) and Crown Point, (1731.) Western Pennsylvania was dotted with fortifications, at the same time that others were raised through the Ohio valley, (1753.) But the most to be gained by these posts was a communication with the valley of the Mississippi and with Louisiana, where there was little to make the communication of any sensible importance.

Louisiana, soon resigned by Antoine Crozat, had passed under the control of the Company of the West, otherwise

Mississippi Company: New Orleans. known as the Mississippi Company, (1717.) During the frenzy of its speculations, both the colony and the mother country were inflated, merely to collapse with disappointment and disaster. Otherwise, the only office rendered by the company to the colony was the establishment of its capital at New Orleans, (1718–23.) The company soon returned the colony upon the royal hands, (1730.)

Missouri: the thirteen of France. Our narrative ends with the final outbreak of hostilities between the French and the English in America, (1754.) Forty years had passed since the treaty of Utrecht began the rupture of the French possessions; but how much was there still left! Beyond the limits of the United States the domains of the French were far more valuable, within the same limits they were far more extensive, than those of England. Over and above the colonies and posts that have been mentioned, the first essays were made, at the epoch in question, towards the occupation of our Missouri. Counting by the states of a later period, we have thirteen of French* to match with the thirteen of English parentage.

Vastness and weakness. Enough has been said, however, to explain how easily the French possessions were extended by adventure, and yet how slightly they were either held or developed by actual settlement. The French dominion was as weak as it was vast. It spread over America like a cloud brilliant with the morning sunshine; but, unsubstantial as a cloud, it was swept by the breeze and rent asunder by the storm.

* Three of each division were the same. The French list comprised Maine, New York, and Pennsylvania, with Wisconsin, Michigan, Illinois, Louisiana, Texas, Mississippi, Alabama, Indiana, Ohio, and Missouri.

CHAPTER VII.

French Wars.

Wars with Indians in the north.

THE earliest wars in which the colonies of France engaged were those with the Indians. They were also the longest. From the time when Champlain headed a war party of Algonquins against the Five Nations of New York, (1609,) this great confederacy was at war with the French, some intervals of peace excepted, for more than a century. To describe the descents upon the Canadian settlements, the wild cries and the wilder deeds of battles, the waste and the agony of homes, would be but to repeat our previous sketches of Indian warfare. Not until the treaty of Utrecht restored peace for a time between France and England did the Five Nations, then the allies of the English, bury the tomahawk that had so long gleamed above the heads of the French, (1713.)

In the south.

Later wars with Indians broke out in the south. The Natchez were beaten, (1729–30,) but the Chickasaws could not be subdued, (1736–40.) These conflicts, however, were of moment chiefly to Louisiana. They did not affect the destinies of the French possessions generally.

Strife between the French and the English.

Except the brief contest with the Spaniards of Florida, described in the last chapter but one, the French had no wars to conduct against any European race besides the English in America. This, it is true, was enough for the French to contend with. Enemies for ages past in Europe, these nations turned to America in rivalry and contention. It was to outvie each other, in a great degree, that they made their settlements; claiming the same lands at the beginning, and extending themselves in the same directions as time went on. The strife between the two great combatants began at an early period, as long ago related, when England, or rather England's colony of Virginia, destroyed the French settlement of St. Sauveur, (1613.) Continued by England herself, (1628–30,) war produced no effect; her conquests, as was mentioned, being surrendered, (1632.)

Indecisive wars. The wars of the next half century were not a whit more decisive. One, during the English commonwealth, (1652–56,) reduced Acadie for a time beneath the sway of England. Another, after the restoration, (1666–67,) brought about nothing except a proposal to the New England colonies that they should conquer Canada. Peace restored Acadie, as far as the Penobscot, to France, leaving once more no results from the passion and the hostility that had been aroused.

King William's war. Acts of violence did not cease on either side. An English trader on Lake Huron was seized, as a trespasser, by the French, (1687.) At the other extremity of New France, the governor of New England, Sir Edmund Andros, made an assault upon the trading post of a Frenchman on the Penobscot, (1688.) Each race was determined to hold, and, if possible, to increase its own. A fresh trial of their strength — the fourth in all, but the first in which the colonies of either nation took an active part — began with the war called King William's by the English colonists, (1689.) As far as concerned England, then under William III., the chief cause of the war was the support given by Louis XIV. to the lately dethroned James II. But Louis had excited in one way or another the greater part of Europe. England was supported by the German Empire, Holland, Spain, and Savoy. From Europe the strife extended to Asia, as well as to America.

Its character and course.

The difference between the contending parties in America soon appeared. On one side was the mother country rather than the colony, the strength of France rather than the weakness of Canada and Acadie. On the other side was the increasing vigor of New England and New York, supported at one time by grants from Maryland and Virginia, and thus presenting an array of colonies, rather than a single mother-land. Both sides were alike in the allies gathered from the forest and the prairie; the Indians of Canada, Acadie, and Maine following the French, while the English were assisted by the forays of the Five Nations along the Canadian lines. Indeed, the war was more of an Indian than of a European one in character. It began with the descents of French and Indian war parties upon Schenectady in New York, Salmon Falls and Casco in New England, (1690.) An expedition from Massachusetts against Acadie, and another, partly from New England and partly from New York, against Canada, were more regular operations, (1690.) The latter scheme was prepared in a convention of delegates from Massachusetts, Plymouth, Connecticut, and New York, held in the last-named colony; and although Canada was not invaded, the plans all failing, the colonies were united, at least for a season, by new bonds. The Massachusetts force, under Sir William Phips, succeeded in ravaging Acadie, and even in seizing the eastern part of Maine, where a fort was presently constructed at Pemaquid, (1692;) but this was retaken in a few years by the French under D'Iberville, (1696,) the same who appeared in the south at a later time. Peace being made between the French and the Five Nations, — who were really far more formidable enemies than the English, — while the Abenakis of Maine still swept the frontiers of New England, a general invasion of the northern colonies was planned by the French, (1696-97.) But the apprehensions of the English were happily relieved by the treaty of Ryswick between the mother countries, (1697.) The war, though lasting eight years, had produced no sensible effect upon the relative strength of the parties engaged in it, nor had it decided any of the differences that had led to it, or that would lead to fresh strife in the future.

Religious differences.

One of these differences has not yet been brought out as it should be. Between the French and the English there existed the widest and the deepest gulf that ever opens between man and man or between nation and nation. It was the chasm between opposing creeds. Both professed to be Christians; but the French were Catholic, the English Protestant. To the former the latter were heretics, the rightful objects of human enmity as of divine. To the English Protestant, on the contrary, the French Catholic was the minister of a superstition and an oppression as hateful to God as to man. It may be conceived how much these feelings contributed to whet the swords and to blunt the sensibilities of the warriors on either side. Sad, indeed, is the grouping of the two nations upon the American page, staining it with the passions of the old world, the more hateful in the new, because allied with the savage and the heathen.

Queen Anne's war.

No marvel, then, that warfare was soon renewed. Four years after the peace of Ryswick, Queen Anne's war began, on account, as has been related, of the designs of Louis XIV. upon the Spanish crown,

(1702.) In America, the same Indian alliances were formed, the same Indian hostilities were excited, as in the preceding contest, except that the Five Nations did not take up the hatchet against the French until the war was two thirds over, (1709.) There were also the same attacks upon the border settlements; Deerfield (1704) and Haverhill (1708) being both wasted by the French, while the French territory about the Penobscot was scoured by the English, (1704.) But the war, as a whole, was characterized by greater and more decisive operations. Two expeditions were directed from New England against Port Royal; the first laying waste the adjoining country, (1707,) the second capturing the town; the very name of which disappeared in that of Annapolis, (1710.) The first permanent settlement of the French, it was also the first permanent conquest from them by the English. Two expeditions, likewise, were planned by New England, New York, and New Jersey, against Canada; the first being merely planned, (1709,) and the second, though attempted, failing through the inefficiency of the admiral conducting the English force in aid of the enterprise, (1711.) As in the last war, so in this, the northern colonies of England were arrayed against France rather than her colonies. The English colonies of the centre were inactive; those of the south were occupied at this period, as must be remembered, with Spanish and Indian hostilities. Twelve years having passed in warfare, peace was made at Utrecht, and France surrendered Acadie to England, (1713.) The war was the first of the five between the two nations to make any change in their American possessions.

Collision in the west.

New points of collision were appearing in the west. As early as the beginning of the last war, a treaty with members of the Five Nations was made the basis of an English claim to vast territories,

(1701.) To explain the claim on any principles is not very easy. It not only made out the Five Nations to be the masters of the west, far beyond their own borders, but also made out the English king to be the master of the Five Nations. A quarter of a century afterwards, a new treaty with the same tribes actually transferred to the English a portion of the country claimed by them, (1726.) Meanwhile the pretensions of the English to the entire interior, from the coast on which their colonies were planted to the Pacific, had never been abandoned. It was their right, they alleged, to possess the western, if they occupied the eastern shores. To aid the English advance towards the west, a trading post had been established at Oswego. It now became a fort, (1727.) But where it stood, and where its range, so to speak, was meant to extend, the French claimed the sovereignty.

And in the east. There were also difficulties, both old and new, arising in the east. The war between the English and the Abenakis, in which French missions were assailed, and a French missionary was murdered, threatened fresh hostilities, (1724.) The French, on their side, exasperated, perhaps, by the loss of Acadie, were inclined to infringe upon English rights. Acadie, they argued, was only the peninsula, or what is now called Nova Scotia. But the English replied with reason, that it was not only the peninsula, but the adjoining mainland, and even the surrounding islands. Yet to these the French held fast, especially to Cape Breton, where stood their stronghold of Louisburg, by far more important in their eyes, and in those of their adversaries, than any of the inconsiderable posts upon the territory that had been surrendered.

King George's war. At length, after a third of a century of nominal peace, war was renewed, (1744.) It was called King George's by the English colonists, from

George II. His interposition in favor of Austria and Sardinia, then combined against France and Spain with other powers, led to a French declaration of war; Spain, as may be recollected, being already at war with England. France was now under Louis XV. The French being at peace with the Five, now the Six Nations, and the Indians within the English limits being much diminished in numbers and in spirits, the European races fought their battles more by themselves. An expedition, proposed by Massachusetts, and supported by men from Connecticut, New Hampshire, and subsequently Rhode Island, as well as by supplies from New York, New Jersey, and Pennsylvania, all under the command of William Pepperell, of Maine, and all accompanied by a fleet from England, accomplished the reduction of Louisburg in less than two months, (1745.) A still more extensive campaign was projected for the following year, when New England, New York, New Jersey, Maryland, and Virginia, with a grant from Pennsylvania, and an armament from England, were to invade Canada; but the English force did not appear, and rumors of a French descent upon New England broke up the colonial ranks, (1746.) France did little of any kind. Her troops at Crown Point made some incursions into Massachusetts and New York, but the meditated invasion of New England was an utter failure. The treaty of Aix-la-Chapelle closed the war, four years after its outbreak, restoring Cape Breton and Louisburg to France, (1748.)

Blood shed in Nova Scotia.

Peace was soon broken. An attack upon the French at Chignecto, on the Isthmus of Nova Scotia, caused the first blood to be shed, (1750.) Forts rising in various places betokened additional conflicts. It was evident that the troubles in the east were far from being allayed.

Nor was the prospect calmer in the west. At the expi-

The Ohio Company. ration of the last war, a number of individuals, partly Englishmen and partly colonists, associated as the Ohio Company, obtained a grant of half a million of acres on the eastern bank of the Ohio River, (1749.) Virginia, whose governor was interested in the enterprise, took the lead in the treaties with the Indians and the negotiations with the French required by the plans of the company. But the French were not to be made friends of on that ground. They attacked an Indian settlement where some English traders had found refuge, and seized them as prisoners, (1752.) They then assailed the troops of the Ohio Company. A Virginia party, sent to construct a fort at the head of the Ohio, was driven back by a French force, who completed the fortification, and called it Fort Du Quesne, (1753–54.)

Blood shed in Pennsylvania. George Washington. A larger band, already on the march from Virginia to the disputed territory, was soon engaged in battle with the French upon Pennsylvanian soil. The first encounter between detachments from both sides resulted in the defeat of the French; but the second, between the main bodies at the Great Meadows, ended in the retreat of the Virginians. They had been bravely led, their leader being George Washington. An envoy of peace to the French before he thus appeared as an officer in war, he was the same in character, if not in experience, that he showed himself to be in after years. He was now but twenty-two.

The final struggle. It was the final struggle that had thus begun on the shores of Nova Scotia and in the forests of Pennsylvania. The mother countries came into collision in the following year, (1755.) Then the English fleet took some French transports off Newfoundland, and followed up the attack by scouring the seas. The land forces were equally active. One army, partly of colonial and partly of English troops, marched under General Braddock to defeat near Fort Du Quesne. Another, exclusively colonial, first under General Lyman, and then under Sir William Johnson, with Mohawks in the train, routed the French under Baron Dieskau at Lake George, and built Fort William Henry. But they made no attempt at the reduction of Ticonderoga and Crown Point, against which they had originally started on their march. Another colonial force under the English General Shirley, setting out to reduce Fort Niagara, ventured no farther than Oswego. The only expedition to succeed was one that even the victors might afterwards wish to have failed. Not content with forcing the French troops to evacuate their forts on the Isthmus of Nova Scotia, which was done by a force from Massachusetts, aided by a few hundred English soldiers, the conquerors decided to drive the entire population of the territory into exile. Seven thousand miserable creatures, separated from their families, and bereft of their possessions, were thrown upon the charity of the English colonies, where every association, religious and social, national and individual, was against them. Thus opened the war, (1755.) It was formally declared in the spring of the following year, (1756.)

Extent. Like the last of the Spanish wars, which broke out in connection with this, the last French war sprang from American causes, at least to a great degree. Actual hostilities occurred in America near six years sooner than in Europe. But Europe did not sit looking across the seas. She armed herself for her Seven Years' War, as it was styled. Prussia was on the side of England, Austria on that of France. Russia and Sweden took part against Prussia, rather than for England. After Spain came in on the French side, Portugal declared in favor of the English. Germany was the chief scene of action in Europe. Asia and Africa also furnished battle grounds.

Losses of the English.

American operations were for some time yet more adverse to the English than those already described. Niagara, Crown Point, and Du Quesne continued the objects of attack and of defence; but far from being able to take them, the English were unable to defend their own posts. The fort at Oswego yielded to the Marquis of Montcalm the same year that war was declared, (1756.) The next year, (1757,) Montcalm was the master of Fort William Henry. Thus, after four campaigns, (1754–57,) the English were retiring before the French. Yet the resources of the English had been infinitely greater than those of their foes. Canada, which bore the brunt of war, did not contain more than twenty thousand effective troops; and even these were in danger of becoming ineffective by their isolation from the mother country, on which the French colonists were ever wont to rely.

Their subsequent victories.

It was not surprising, therefore, that the renewed exertions of England, and above all of her colonies, by which alone twenty thousand men were now raised, should repair the losses of the preceding years. Louisburg was the first prize, the whole Gulf of St. Lawrence being taken possession of immediately. Fort Frontenac, on the northern shore of Ontario, and Fort Du Quesne were found deserted. Amongst those who marched against the latter fortress, only to see it in ruins, was Washington, then at the head of the Virginian forces. There, where he had fought his first battles, where he had been twice obliged to retreat, once in command and once in Braddock's staff, he now made his last appearance in the war. His strength was reserved for a greater conflict. All these acquisitions of the English were made in one year, (1758.) The next brought the abandonment of

Ticonderoga, Crown Point, and Niagara, and more momentous still, the surrender of Quebec, after the great Montcalm's defeat by the troops whom the greater Wolfe had led to amazing victory, (1759.) The two years, together, decided the war.

Conclusion of the war.

But it continued a year or two to come. An attempt of the French to regain Quebec being repulsed, Montreal soon after capitulated to the English, who were acknowledged conquerors of Canada, (1760.) All but a few posts in the farther west were surrendered to them within the following year, (1761.) Meanwhile operations, previously commenced, were renewed against the French West Indies by an armament composed in part of colonial troops; the islands of the Caribbean group being all captured, (1759–62.) There was no such thing as fighting against reverses like these. After twelve years of actual warfare, the French made peace; the treaty of Paris ceding to England all east of the Mississippi save three little islands, St. Pierre and the Miquelons, in the north, and New Orleans in the south; this last, with all west of the same river, being transferred to Spain, whose part in the war has been previously described, (1763.)

The French retire.

The French colonists were loath to give up the territory which their mother country had surrendered. Such of the western posts as were not not already in possession of the English did not come under their new masters for a year or two, (1765.) Indeed, it was some months after the treaty that a French party under Pierre Laclède established a new settlement at St. Louis, in our Missouri, upon the lands ceded to Spain. (1764.) Several years more passed before the Spaniards installed themselves in Western Louisiana, (1768.) But the French nation had played its part as a power on United

States territory. Not the less lasting, however, were the influences that had arisen from its possessions and its wars while they endured.

French and English compared.

The issue of the French wars needs little comment after what has gone before. The English, in their compact colonies, resembled a man in full armor, in contending with whom, the French, scattered over their disjointed settlements, were like a knight protected by nothing but fragments of his coat of mail. The Englishman, moreover, stood strong in himself, strong in his colony even more than in his mother land; but the Frenchman leaned upon the distant France, with all his enterprise a dependent colonist, with all his gallantry a submissive subject. So much for the causes and contrasts that were at work in America. If we return to Europe, we shall find France too much engaged in ambition and in battle there to put forth her strength for the defence of colonies as languishing in fact as they were magnificent in form.

CHAPTER VIII.

Colonial Development.

Development of territory. The English territory was immensely increased by the successful wars that have been described. Nor were its limits extended solely at the expense of neighboring domains. Within the boundaries already belonging to the colonies of England, there had been a large accession to the lands formerly occupied. New fields were brought into cultivation; new towns were formed; new means of communication were opened between the old habitations and the new.

Of occupation. The development of territory arose chiefly from the development of occupation. As the numbers and wants of the colonists multiplied with time, they found fresh ways of employing and of enriching themselves. The seaboard was lined with merchants and traders; the interior was filled with farmers and planters; while around them all were clustered the artisans and the laborers whose services were needed to complete the circle of toil. Few men, or even women, in the early period, were without some laborious pursuit; few, as wealth increased and individuals grew to be above the necessity of labor, laid aside industry altogether. In one light, the entire people is seen exerting itself to improve the soil, to build up the dwelling, to enlarge the limits of commerce, of trade, and of manufacture. How successful these exertions were, appears from the steady growth of the colonies in resources and in possessions.

Of habits of life. The habits of the colonists were long of the simplest nature. Little space for liberality or for luxury could be found in a new land crowded with its ever-recurring demands for sobriety and for self-denial. Wherever men lived, in the little knot of cottages that was called a town, in the scattered villages of the country, in the isolated posts of the frontier, they had a narrow life before them. Afterwards things changed, and in many a spacious enclosure there arose dwellings of greater comfort and of greater pretension. As the strict rules of the primitive period were loosened, there was also more frequent and more genial intercourse amongst men and amongst women. Without falling into extravagance, the wealthy found new objects of expenditure. Without yielding to idleness, the poorer classes found new means of relaxation. The change was for the better, physically and mentally. It relieved the nerves that had been tightly strung. It enlarged the interests that had been closely confined. If it did away with the primitive simplicity, it also did away with the primitive ruggedness of life. Time was gained for thought, for culture, for expansion.

Of education. The sources of education had been opened at an early period. The first laws of Massachusetts provided for the schoolmaster and the school, each township of fifty families being bound to maintain a teacher of reading and writing, while each of a hundred families was called upon to set up a grammar school, (1645-47.) The example was generally imitated throughout New England. Some of the central colonies were equally on the alert, Pennsylvania, especially, making provision from the first for public schools, (1685-89.) Maryland was much later in the field, proposing schools long before she established them, and laying them, when established, under the restriction of being taught only by members of the church of England,

(1723.) The southern colonies were mostly behindhand in the matter of education. South Carolina was amongst the earliest to organize public schools, (1721;) but these, like the schools of almost all the country, were of a very limited design. Private instruction being preferred by the richer colonists, the schools were left to the middle and lower classes, whose interest was not strong enough to support them.

Colleges. The patronage of the upper classes turned to the colleges which began with Harvard, in Massachusetts. Virginia, after depending upon a Latin school at New Amsterdam, bestirred herself to have a seminary of her own. At the instance of the Bishop of London's commissary, — the ecclesiastical head of the province, — James Blair, the long-sleeping project of a college was revived. The aid of the king was invoked; and he granted a charter, with donations in money and lands, to create a corporation, whose chief charge it should be to provide instruction for such as proposed to take orders in the established church. A department was also to be organized for the education of Indians. The royal names of William and Mary, then king and queen, were bestowed upon the rising institution, (1691.) Connecticut soon had her Yale College, (1700;) New Jersey her College of New Jersey, (1738–46;) New York her King's College, (1754;) and Pennsylvania her Academy, (1750,) afterwards the University of Pennsylvania. These institutions became the centres of quite an amount of intellectual activity.

Of the press. The printing press had long been at work. The first to be set up was at Cambridge in Massachusetts, (1639.) But it was under so much restraint that it can hardly be said to have exerted any general influence. The importation of books was under similar hinderances, certain volumes being absolutely prohibited, (1654.) Notwithstanding, the trade seemed to flourish, there soon being as many as four bookstores in Boston, while libraries were gathering on a small scale, (1686.) The first newspaper of the colonies was a diminutive sheet, issued once a week, under the title of the Boston News Letter, (1704.) No other press kept pace with that of Massachusetts. The royal governor of Virginia, Sir William Berkeley, made it a boast that under him "there are no free schools nor printing." "God keep us," he profanely added, "from both!" (1671.) Not many years after, the owner of a press introduced into the colony was bound over to make no use of it until the royal pleasure could be consulted. The royal pleasure turned out to be, that the press and its proprietor should leave Virginia, (1682–83.)

Official interference. The increasing activity of the press is proved by nothing more clearly than the continued interference to which it was subject from the colonial officials. In time, the governors of the royal provinces were regularly instructed to allow no printing without their special license, (1702.) It was virtually the same in all the colonies. In Pennsylvania, a printer was called to account for one of his publications in such a way as to suggest a retreat to New York, (1692.) Thirty years subsequently, the publisher of the Philadelphia Mercury, the only newspaper out of Boston, was obliged to apologize for an article displeasing to the governor and the council, (1722.) "I'll have no printing of your address," says Governor Shute of Massachusetts to the House of Representatives, on their remonstrating against his proceedings; "the press is under my control." But he did not succeed in preventing the printing, or even in bringing the printers to trial, (1719.) It was not because the Massachusetts press was free. On the contrary, within a very few years, Benjamin Franklin, then a boy of seventeen, was admonished by a joint committee of the council and the house for certain articles of his in his brother James's paper, the New England Courant; James himself having been thrown into jail for a month in consequence of publishing animadversions upon the colonial administration, (1723.) Cosby, governor of New York, went farther than Shute against the freedom of the press. His council, with whom he was having a violent dispute, took to a newspaper, the Weekly Journal, of which John Peter Zenger was the publisher. The governor, although he had his organ in the New York Gazette, determined that the council should be deprived of theirs, and that Zenger should be punished. After an imprisonment of eight months, Zenger was tried for libel, and escaped condemnation only by the exertions of his counsel, Andrew Hamilton, of Pennsylvania. The little sympathy that there was with Zenger on the score of a free press may be conceived from the fact that, though acquitted, he was left to bear the losses of his imprisonment, (1732–33.)

Editions of the Bible.

It was a striking proof of advancing energies that the Boston press gave in issuing an edition of the Bible, the privilege of printing the English version being a monopoly of the Universities of Oxford and Cambridge. The Boston edition bore the imprint of the king's printer in London, (about 1752.) A German Bible had been already printed in Germantown, Pennsylvania, (1743.)

Intellectual development: in action.

The intellectual development of the colonies was altogether of a grave cast. To trace it in action, we are obliged to follow the men of the time into circumstances where exertion, anxiety, and devouring care exclude all lighter aspects. We seldom find the graceful mind or the sportive spirit; it is all solemn deliberation, weighty argument, the natural methods of dealing with subjects so serious and relations so momentous as those in which the colonists were involved.

In literature. Pass from men of action to men of contemplation, and the same signs appear. The primitive writings treat of matters of life and death to their authors. Whether it is the chronicler, like Governor Bradford, of Plymouth, or the traveller, like John Lederer, in Virginia, each wears a sober countenance and tells a sober story. If we penetrate into the mazes of witchcraft literature, as much of the early New England writings may be styled, we find that what look to us like the wildest hallucinations then appeared the sternest facts. Imagination, it is true, had much to do with them; but it was imagination excited to that degree in which the unreal seems more true than the real. At a later time, the colonial literature assumed lighter forms. There were writers of travels, of essays, even of poems, to some of which we shall presently advert. But the chief men of letters were still of grave mien; indeed, there was hardly one out of the clerical ranks. The influence of clergymen upon literature as upon life was very sensible for many years beyond the period of which we treat. At the head, perhaps, of the colonial writers, was the theologian and the metaphysician Jonathan Edwards, a native of Connecticut and a minister of Western Massachusetts, whose treatise on the Freedom of the Will reads like a plea for all the gravity of learning as well as for all the severity of dogma then vanishing away.

In science. Science found its earnest votaries. There was one, indeed, whose inquiries were so resolute and so brilliant as to throw lustre over the whole country. Benjamin Franklin, a student and a writer from his early youth, at the same time that he was a hard-working printer, solved the mysteries of the thunder cloud, into which, frequently as it appeared, science had not then actually penetrated, (1752.) Nor were his electrical discoveries the only results of his scientific attainments. A sometime neighbor of

Franklin, John Bartram, of Pennsylvania, whom the great Linnæus called "the first natural botanist in the world," was the creator of a botanic garden near Philadelphia, and at the same time the explorer of the whole country from Canada to Florida, (1751–66.) His son, William Bartram, continued the work begun by the father, leaving an account of his own journeyings as full of freshness as the forests and the plains which he explored. Another branch of science was nobly cultivated by John Winthrop, a descendant of the Massachusetts governor, who occupied the chair of mathematics and natural philosophy at Harvard College. His astronomical observations, continued for many years, (1740–79,) enlarged the sphere of knowledge in Europe as well as in America.

In art. Art, even in its lower forms, was hardly recognized. The dramatic exhibitions, attempted at a late day in Boston, were instantly interrupted by the Puritan authorities, (1749.) In the towns and colonies more tolerant of amusement, there was nothing better than a strolling company, which was obliged to wander in turn from Newport to Williamsburg, (1752.) The first dramatic composition of the country was the Prince of Parthia, (1759,) a tragedy by Thomas Godfrey, a native of Philadelphia, whose poetic aspirations were much more successful than those of his countrymen before him. A few musical instruments, a piece or two of ordinary sculpture, a larger proportion of paintings, might be found in the more refined mansions. The first organ for a church encountered so great opposition in Boston that it remained unpacked for several months after its arrival from England, (1713.) Thirty years afterwards, an organ of considerable excellence was constructed in Boston itself by Edward Bromfield, (1745.) The musical publications of the period, beginning with "The Cantus or Trebles of twenty-eight Psalms," under the supervision of Rev. John Tufts, of Newbury, (1710,) were chiefly confined to psalmody. Portrait painters were making their appearance; the first two, Watson and Smybert, being both from Scotland. John Singleton Copley, a native of Boston, and Benjamin West, a native of Springfield, in Pennsylvania, gave better promise of the art that was yet to walk in beauty through the nation.

Influences from abroad. The intellectual progress of the colonies was sensibly affected by influences from abroad. Not merely that the literature, the science and the art of other countries were within the reach of the new people, but that they were actually brought to its door, so to speak, by sojourners from beyond the sea. An English naturalist, Mark Catesby, was a visitor to Virginia and South Carolina, (1712-22.) A Swedish man of letters, Peter Kalm, travelled through all the central colonies, (1748-51.) His name still dwells amongst us in the *kalmia*, a genus of plants embracing our beautiful mountain laurel. A group of clerical visitors came at about the same time. George Berkeley, afterwards Bishop of Cloyne, spent some years (1729-31) at Newport, spreading around him the influences of a cultivated and a devout spirit. He tarried there on the way to the Bermudas, where he hoped in vain to found a college for the youth, Indian and English, of America. Georgia was visited by the Wesleys, John and Charles, (1736-37,) then just entering upon their efforts as reformers in the English church. George Whitefield, at first the churchman and then the sectary, traversed the whole land from north to south; his appeals to the people resulting in revivals, as the phrase went, which were repeated until the charm began to lose its power, but not before it had greatly loosened the hold of ancient doctrines, (1738-70.)

Liberality in religion. Of all the progress that we have to notice, no point is more remarkable than the increasing liberality in religion. It was beginning to be seen that men might be fellow-Christians without being fellow-churchmen or fellow-Puritans. Dissenters found toleration in the church-province of Virginia, (1698.) On the other hand, the Puritan churches made peace with their antagonists. Cotton Mather, preaching at the ordination of a Baptist, expresses "our dislike of every thing which looked like persecution in the days that have passed over us," (1718.) Churchmen in Massachusetts were released from Puritan tithes, (1727.) Baptists and Quakers were both released from the same tithes in Massachusetts, (1728,) New Hampshire, (1729,) and Connecticut, (1729,) the last colony, however, continuing the restrictions upon separate places of worship. Even the Roman Catholics had their crumb of toleration. On their celebrating mass in Philadelphia, the governor proposed to enforce the penalties of the English, not the Pennsylvanian, law against them; but the council opposed the proceeding, on the ground that the Roman Catholics were protected in the charter of the colony, (1734.) The air seems to grow freer as we meet with such a record. But it was not yet purified. Charles Carroll, a Roman Catholic of Maryland, found himself so hemmed in by illiberality, that he petitioned the French government for a grant in Louisiana, (1751.)

Church of England. The church of England — the moderate church of the reformation — was the mean, as formerly described, between the extremes of the Roman and the Protestant sides. But, as the Roman church was hardly represented in the colonies, the church of England appeared to occupy, not so much a mean as an extreme position, the opposite to the extreme of Puritanism. It was, therefore, the great foe of Puritanism, just as Puritanism was its great foe. Both the churchman and the Puritan found it hard to bear and to forbear with each other, the more so as the church of England increased, and assumed the lead. John Checkley, preparing to be a church missionary, threw the Puritan clergy of Boston into quite an excitement, by taking upon himself to say that there could be "no Christian minister without episcopal ordination," (1724.) So, when the Massachusetts ministers, headed by Cotton Mather, petitioned the General Court that a synod of their churches might be convened, as in former days, the church clergy appealed to England for the suppression of the proposed assembly, (1725.) It was not merely ill will that these proceedings kindled; it was apprehension of oppression.

Project of bishops. Dissenters generally, but with the Puritans still in the van, stood arrayed against a project in which the church of England was deeply interested. As early as the reign of Charles II., a bishop for Virginia had been nominated at the instigation of the prime minister Clarendon, (1672.) It proved merely a nomination. Thirty years passed, when the Society for Propagating the Gospel in Foreign Parts (1701) took up the matter, partly in consequence of applications from the churchmen of the colonies, (1703.) It was twelve years more before the society, after petitions to and answers from Queen Anne, undertook "a draught of a bill, proper to be offered to the Parliament, for establishing bishops and bishoprics in America," (1715.) The queen's death interfering with the execution of these projects, they were laid aside, resumed, and then laid aside again until some of the English prelates, members of the society still, espoused the cause so full of interest to them and to their church. Their plan, drawn up by Bishop Butler, of Durham, was not one, it would seem, to provoke opposition. It suggested the limitation of the episcopal power to the clergy in orders, declaring, at the same time, that "no bishops are intended to be settled in places where the government is in the hands of dissenters, as in New

England," &c. Such, however, were the difficulties attending the scheme, even in this modified form, that it failed, (1750.) Its advocates, joined or succeeded by others, did not give up the hope of carrying their point at a future time. But the passions of the colonists, as well from political as from religious causes, ran too high to admit of further provocation. Nor were dissenters only arrayed against the plan of the episcopate. Churchmen were almost equally earnest, on account, chiefly, of the jealousy entertained in relation to the mother country. So that when, at a later time, the Bishop of London's commissary for Virginia called a convention of his clergy, to discuss an address to the king, "upon an American episcopate," certain clergymen, who protested against the proposal, received the thanks of the House of Burgesses for their course, (1771.) The clergy of Virginia, however, and the Burgesses had long been on poor terms, in consequence of certain acts passed by the latter to the detriment of clerical revenues, indeed, to the violation of clerical rights, (1755–58.) The church of England, it must be confessed, was far from being a church of peace in the colonies.

Classes: the slaves. The classes in the colonies remained the same as heretofore. But the relations between them were varying with their members and their numbers. Amongst the echoes from those distant years we catch the sounds of sympathy for the enslaved. Some German, not English, Quakers of Pennsylvania began by declaring against the whole system of slavery, (1688.) An English Quaker of the same colony was stirred to make the same declaration; but his remonstrance was mingled with fanaticism and sedition, (1692.) A few years later, Pennsylvania pronounced against the importation of Indian bondmen, (1705.) Massachusetts passed a similar prohibition, (1712.) But when Pennsylvania, or a portion of its people, petitioned for the general emancipation of the slaves in the province, the assembly rejected the proposal, (1712.) The slaves did not every where sit still while the masters legislated. New York was thrown into terror by a negro plot to fire the city, (1712.) South Carolina was twice threatened by a negro massacre, (1730, 1738.) It was not to be expected, with all the advantages or all the alleviations of slavery in the English colonies, that the system was to escape the dangers and the wrongs to which it had led in every land and in every age of its history. One earnest voice was lifted up against it in the colonies by John Woolman, of New Jersey, a Quaker of singular refinement as well as singular simplicity, who published Some Considerations on the Keeping of Negroes, towards the close of the period, (1753.) Woolman's Journal of his life and his devotions should be mentioned as one of the most attractive works in our early literature.

Colonies: union. Between colony and colony there were new bands of union. Suggestions of combining them in some common organization had appeared from time to time. The first project of the sort, on the part of the colonies, was of William Penn's proposal. He urged a congress of twenty members, to be elected by the colonial assemblies, with a president appointed by the king. This body was to keep the peace amongst the colonies, to regulate their commerce, and to secure their defence, (1697.) A quarter of a century later, Daniel Coxe, of New Jersey, brought forward a plan of much the same nature, (1722.) Thirty years later, the deputies of seven colonies — the four of New England, New York, Pennsylvania, and Maryland — met at Albany on the recommendation of the secretary of state in England, (1754.) The subjects before this assembly were the relations of the colonies with the Indians and with one another, referring chiefly to the war then opening between England and France. It was to promote the military rather than the civil union of the colonies, that Benjamin Franklin, a deputy from Pennsylvania, laid his proposals before the convention. He suggested a council of forty-eight, apportioned to the contributions of each colony, who were to conduct the affairs of war, and, to a certain extent, the affairs of peace; the members, chosen for three years, by the colonial assemblies, to elect their own speaker, but to be under a president, or governor general, nominated by the crown. This system suited neither those who favored nor those who opposed the interests of the colonies, the appointing power and the veto, with which the president was armed, being deemed as unfavorable to colonial liberty as the rights of the council were to royal prerogative. It was at the same time that the king commanded one of his ministers, the Earl of Halifax, to prepare a plan of colonial union. Each colony was to elect, by common consent of assembly, council, and governor, a single commissioner to a federal body, by which a revenue was to be raised and the general defence assured. A commander-in-chief was to be placed at the head of the government, which, as we see, was a merely military organization. Union was not to be achieved by a fluctuating succession of projects like these.

Contributions to Boston.

The sympathy existing amongst the colonies appears on another record than that of systems or assemblies. A great fire, breaking out in Boston, caused immense loss and immense distress, (1760.) What Boston itself could do was promptly done; its people were not in the habit of giving up, however severe the trial. But there came a large sum from New York, another from Pennsylvania, besides one from Nova Scotia, and various subscriptions from England. The colonial contributions to Boston proved that there were bonds, if not yet drawn together, still capable of being tightened, closely and lastingly, amongst the colonies.

CHAPTER IX.

The Mother Country.

Views of the mother country.

As the colonies passed through the struggles of infancy into the promises of manhood, they wore a new look in the sight of the mother country. Something more than had been anticipated was to be hoped, something more also was to be feared from them. It seemed as if they might be able to contribute largely to the resources of Great Britain; and yet it seemed as if they might think themselves able to withhold as well as to contribute. Strange symptoms of insubordination had appeared. The crown, the parliament, and the officials by which both were represented, had been confronted, here and there, with amazing boldness. It was high time, so thought the English rulers, to take the colonies in hand, to tighten the reins of government, and to confine them to the course marked out, as it was thought, by the interests of the mother country.

Board of trade.

Chief of the agencies put in operation was the board of trade, consisting of a president and seven members, entitled the Lords Commissioners for Trade and Plantations, (1696.) To this body were committed the functions hitherto exercised by committees of the privy council, but now magnified into large powers of administration. It was intrusted with the execution of the navigation acts, to which were at this time appended fresh and oppressive provisions of colonial Courts of Admiralty. It was also empowered to carry out the new acts by which not merely the trade but the administration of the colonies was to be brought under stricter control. The royal approval of all colonial governors, and the conformity of all colonial laws to the statutes of Parliament, were amongst the first steps to be taken. The board entered heartily into its mission. It proposed the appointment of a captain general with absolute power to levy and to organize an army without reference to any colonial authority, (1697.) It laid a prohibition upon the exportation of colonial woollens, even from one colony to another, (1698.) It actually went so far as to recommend the resumption of the charters that remained to some of the colonies, (1701.) Time and again, a bill was brought into Parliament to declare the charters void; but, for one reason or another, the design was postponed. The board of trade, approving itself by its zeal, became a sort of ministerial body on being attached to a secretary of state as its chief, (1714.) Its course, however, was not improved. The secretary longest in office (1724–48) — the Duke of Newcastle — supposed New England to be an island. The board of trade acted as if they thought all the colonies a broken cluster off the British coast.

African Company. About the same time that the board of trade was organized, the Royal African Company, previously a monopoly, was so enlarged as to allow general participation in its operations. What these were appears from its name. But the name gives no indication of the near connection of the company with the American colonies, of their restiveness, and of its oppressiveness. "Give due encouragement," say the royal instructions of Queen Anne to the governor of New York and New Jersey, "to merchants, and, in particular, to the Royal African Company," (1702.) "The slave trade," reëchoes Parliament, half a century afterwards, in making the trade independent of the African Company, "is very advantageous to Great Britain,"

(1750.) It was, in fact, a cardinal point in the treaties of England with the European powers. The treaty of Utrecht contained a contract on the part of Spain that her colonies should be provided with slaves by Great Britain alone, (1713.) The treaty of Aix-la-Chapelle was followed by a convention indemnifying Great Britain, to the amount of a hundred thousand pounds, for relinquishing the monopoly of the slave trade with the Spanish colonies, (1750.) The closer was the gripe upon the English colonies. Vainly did Virginia and South Carolina, for instance, lay a prohibitory duty upon the importation of slaves; their acts were annulled by the royal command. And by what reasoning, it will be asked, were the advantages of the traffic upheld in the mother country? The answer is simple. In the first place, the profits of the African Company and of the private slave traders were enormous. In the second place, the dependence of the colonists in agriculture, manufacture, and trade, as well as in government, was assured, so long as they were kept to slave labor. This was openly avowed in England; so that, resist as they would, the colonies were at the mercy of the Royal African Company as long as it endured.

Colonial governors.

The boards and companies of the mother country found congenial instruments in the governors of the various colonies. All but those whom the colonists were able to elect for themselves, as in Connecticut and Rhode Island, may be said, as a general remark, to have been the main stays of the policy pursued by the English authorities. A needier, greedier set of men was never sent forth to rule than the spendthrift courtiers, the broken-down officials, and the cringing colonists, who successively appeared in the scramble after colonial spoils.

An illustration offers itself in the career of Edward Hyde, Lord Cornbury, grandson of the great Earl of Clar-

Cornbury in New York.

endon, and cousin to Queen Anne, by whom he was appointed governor of New York, (1702.) His arrival was greeted with delight by a faction then suffering from the reaction consequent upon Leisler's cruel fate, ten years before. The party opposed to Leisler and his adherents, now getting the upper hand, voted an enthusiastic grant to his lordship the governor, and doubled his salary besides. He was not contented; but, on the vote of a large sum, in the ensuing year, for the fortification of the Narrows, he appropriated it to himself without leave or license. This drove the assembly to insist upon having a treasurer of its own — a demand that was afterwards allowed by the queen, (1705.) Cornbury became more and more odious to those who had welcomed him with rapturous obedience. One assembly after another was dissolved for not meeting his multiplied requisitions. Two Presbyterian missionaries from England were prosecuted by him on no other charge than their creed, but were triumphantly acquitted by the jury, (1707.) His course was much the same in New Jersey, then under the New York governor, where, after violent assaults upon the political and religious privileges of the colony, he was met face to face in the assembly by charges of oppression and corruption, (1707.) Such proceedings as Cornbury's were too wanton to be tolerated even in England. He was recalled, but without any other amends besides the recall, for the indignities from which New York and New Jersey had suffered during seven bitter years, (1709.)

Burnet and Belcher in Massachusetts.

Some years pass, and the then governor of New York, Colonel Cosby, complains to the board of trade of "the example of the Boston people," (1732.) With his views and with the views of the board there was ample motive for complaint. William Burnet, formerly governor of New York, now of Massachusetts, had made it a point, from his first entrance upon his new government, to obtain a permanent salary, (1728.) The House of Representatives would not hear of such a thing, much preferring their usual mode of a yearly vote. This the governor scorned, and hinted at the loss of the charter in case he was denied his will. A town meeting of the Bostonians sustained the house with so much effect that Burnet held the next General Court at Salem. Boston is the proper place for our sessions, declared the sturdy representatives. "Then meet in Cambridge the next time," rejoined the governor, (1729.) Burnet dying, one of the agents sent to complain of him in England, Jonathan Belcher, was appointed his successor. But the colonist was soon involved in the same disputes as the Englishman, both, in the present case, obeying instructions rather than following their own desires. After a two years' controversy, Belcher obtained leave from England to accept a salary for the year, (1731.) Even this was cut off, on his opposing, as he was instructed to do, the further issue of paper money, already a sore subject in Massachusetts. Belcher wrote to the board of trade that a crisis was at hand. The house, on the other side, wrote to request the king to recall the governor's instructions, (1732.) On the king's refusal, the agents of the house made the same request to Parliament. "This is a high insult," replied that body, "upon his majesty's government, and tending to shake off the dependency of the colonies," (1733.) The House of Representatives restored the salaries which it had suspended; but some fresh disputes arising, the removal of Belcher was asked for and obtained, (1740.)

Clinton's appeal. A few years later, and Governor Clinton of New York, failing to obtain a grant for five years, appealed to the secretary at the head of the board of trade "to make a good example for all America," (1748.) What his idea was, appeared more clearly when he begged that Parliament would impose certain taxes to provide "the civil list," (1750.) It was the natural result of the exactions and the clamors of the previous half century. But even before the half century began, Clinton's appeal had been anticipated by a scheme of parliamentary taxation, brought forward at the time when the board of trade was entering upon its career, (1696.)

Parliamentary interference.

Meantime Parliament had not left the administration of the colonies entirely in other hands. It extended the post office of Great Britain to America, (1710.) It regulated the system of naturalization, until then different in the different colonies, by requiring a probation of seven years, and an oath of allegiance, together with the profession of some form of Protestantism, (1740.) It interfered with questions of currency and of banking,* in which, indeed, the colonies had got far beyond their depth, (1740–51.)

Commercial rule.

All the while, Parliament maintained its authority over the colonial trade. Never, in truth, had it gone so far as when it passed what was called the "molasses act," laying duties on molasses, sugar, and rum imported from any but the British West India Islands, (1733.) "It is divesting the colonists," said the agent of New York in England, "of their rights as the king's natural born subjects and Englishmen, in levying subsidies upon them against their consent." Parliament was also extending its interference with manufactures in the colonies. It crowned its acts on this score by prohibiting the exportation of hats, (1732,) and the erection of mills for slitting or rolling iron, and of furnaces for making steel, (1750.) The commer-

* It was the way with most of the colonies, beginning with South Carolina, (1712,) to issue bills which were loaned to individuals as a borrowed capital.

cial rule, commenced by the navigation acts of a century before, was thus approaching its completion.

Military rule.

Another rule was beginning to appear. The wars in which the colonies were involved led to their subordination beneath the military and naval commanders of the mother country. It was inevitable that the English officers should assume a superiority which would be felt, not merely in the field, but in the town — not merely amongst the soldiers, but amongst the citizens of the colonies.

Impressment at Boston.

Wild work was that which Commodore Knowles made in undertaking to fill up his fleet by the impressment of Bostonians. The people seized his officers who happened to be on shore, and, retaining them as hostages, took such an attitude of fury and of strength, that Governor Shirley withdrew to the Castle in the harbor. Knowles threatened the bombardment of the town. The upper classes, through their representatives in the house, and in a town meeting of their own, abjured all connection with the so-called populace. But they who had risen for the sake of saving their brothers and their neighbors from outrage, though wholly deserted, were not wholly unsuccessful. The greater part of the men who had been pressed were surrendered by the commodore, and peace ensued. Yet there was more parade at the return of the governor than at the rescue of the artisans and the sailors of the town from their captivity, (1747.)

A commander-in-chief of the colonies.

Clouds were gathering heavy with menace and with ruin. An order went forth from the board of trade to the colonial governors, directing them to raise a fund for the general expenses of the colonies, then driving, with the mother country, into the fiercest of the wars with France. At the same time, the mutiny act, providing for the discipline and the quarters of the English army, was extended to the colonies, (1754.) The next year (1755) brought over the Earl of Loudoun, governor of Virginia, and commander-in-chief of the whole thirteen. As the general fund to support his authority did not appear, Parliament addressed the colonial assemblies with the assertion that "the claim of right in an assembly to raise and apply public money by its own act alone is derogatory to the crown and to the rights of the people of Great Britain," (1757.) Both the property and the freedom of the colonists were thus involved in the establishment of a military rule.

Judicial tenure. The signs were dark in all directions. Most of the colonial judges had long been appointed by the crown, or by its representatives the governors; but once appointed, they were independent, as they held office during good behavior. But Chief Justice Pratt, of New York, received a commission to continue only "at the king's pleasure." In vain he remonstrated with the governor of the province; in vain the governor supported the remonstrance in an appeal to the board of trade. "Your good behavior," answered the board, "is a pernicious proposition." So the secretary at the head of the board maintained, in instructing the colonial governors to issue no commissions "but during pleasure." All this was stranger and more threatening than any previous act of the powers in England. New York showed its sense of the danger by refusing any salary to the chief justice. He, however, procured from the board of trade a grant, to be paid out of the royal quitrents of the province, (1761–62.)

Writs of assistance. With all the game now in view, the authorities still stuck to their "acts of trade." Francis Bernard, lately governor of New Jersey, and at present of Massachusetts, had but just assured the latter colony of the "blessings from their subjection to Great Britain," when they were thrown into alarm by an application of the custom house officials to the Superior Court for writs of assistance, authorizing search after merchandise imported in defiance of the acts of trade. The hearing came on before Chief Justice Hutchinson, who was also the lieutenant governor. All that legal skill, as well as official influence, could do to obtain the writs, was done; but the counsel whom the Boston merchants had retained stood out to the last — Oxenbridge Thacher, "soft and cool;" James Otis, "a flame of fire." "Every man," says one who was present, "of an immense crowded audience appeared to me to go away as I did, ready to take up arms against writs of assistance." Of course, the writs were granted, but they were little used, (1761.) The same spirit that had resisted them broke out against the schemes of taxation with which the acts of trade were now connected. "Government," argued James Otis, "must not raise taxes on the property of the people without the consent of them or their deputies." It was not the plea of the politician alone. "I do not say," exclaimed the Boston clergyman Jonathan Mayhew, "our invaluable rights have been struck at; but if they have, they are not wrested from us," (1762.)

English dominion. It was amidst these controversies that the French were conquered, and the English dominion rose to its height in America. In the north, it extended over the three provinces of St. John's, or Newfoundland, Nova Scotia, and Quebec, the new name for Canada. In the centre, it embraced the thirteen colonies, in which had lain the germ of its present growth. In the south, it comprehended the two provinces of East and West Florida, together with a large portion of the West Indies. So vast an empire overtopped all other dominions in the western world.

Effects on the colonies.

And now, to mark the effects of the victories upon the victors. First, upon the colonists. They had passed through agonizing times, when losses of friends and of resources weighed upon almost every household, when alternations of grief and of revenge racked almost every breast. As a community, likewise, each colony had met its trials and its reverses. Notwithstanding the reimbursements received from England, the colonies were in debt to the amount of more than ten million dollars, one quarter of which stood against Massachusetts alone, at the expiration of the last war with France. Debts, however, were nothing compared to the diminution of the means of paying them, or of gathering new resources. The sacrifices of warfare are not to be measured by any single schedule; roll after roll must be inscribed with losses, and even then the losses of the future, if they can be calculated, remain to be appended. On the other hand, the colonists were not without their compensations. They had rid themselves of an enemy whose neighborhood had been a constant source of peril, both from French and from Indian warfare, for a century and a half, (1613–1763.) They had proved their strength in repeated efforts and repeated successes. Better still, they had proved their union amongst themselves, especially in the final conflict which brought every colony of the thirteen shoulder to shoulder. Best of all, they had proved their patriotism, their love of their own land, hitherto overpowered by the affections that bound them to the other side of the sea, but now rising in solemn strength from out the battles and the agonies by which they had defended their country, and made it the first object of their devotion.

Upon the mother country.

Next, to trace the effects of victory upon the mother country. Here we find the marks of sorrow and of calamity, but they are lost in the blaze of glory which seemed to have been kindled. "England," the king is said to have exclaimed, "never signed such a peace before." The king was George III., then in the third year of his reign. The aristocracy, still in power, thought with the king. They were dazzled by their success. It made them believe that their sway was irresistible, that their colonies were to be ruled, burdened, and crushed as they pleased. Only a few, of keener vision and of truer principle, saw that the conquest of the French colonies, if resulting in the issues to which it seemed to be leading, would entail the loss of the English colonies.

Temporary unity. But for the moment, the English of England and the English of America were one. The exultation of triumph over a common foe, the assurance of prosperity under a common king, just risen in his youth to the throne, blended with the ties of a common law, a common literature, and a common ancestry. New hopes for both were appearing in the west. The Indian humbled, every race from Europe conquered, the English were the undisputed possessors of the far-stretching, the rich-promising land.

PART III.

INDEPENDENCE.

1763–1797.

CHAPTER I.

PROVOCATIONS.

Old troubles extended.

THE old troubles between the mother country and the colonies remained. They were now extended. To enforce the commercial rule of Great Britain, her fleet upon the American coast was turned into a revenue squadron. To keep up the military rule, the colonies were organized in divisions, with British commander-in-chief, British officers, and British troops, in short, a standing army. To maintain the whole system, commercial and military, the authorities of the mother country soon lent themselves to graver measures.

Parties in the mother country.

The great majority of the British people regarded the American colonists as countrymen, who could not suffer without their suffering, or prosper without their prospering. But the majority of the people was powerless, or comparatively so. The dominion over the mother country, as well as over her colonies, was with the aristocracy, with men who, whether liberal or not, — according to the phrase, — whether whig or tory, were of almost one and the same mind in regarding the colonists as their subjects. So thought the king, at this time the head of the aristocracy rather than the sovereign of the nation. So thought the Parliament, at this time the representative assembly of the aristocracy rather than of the nation. So thought the successive ministries, the common representatives of the king and of the Parliament, to whom attached the credit or the discredit of any general course or of any particular measure that might be adopted in the councils of Great Britain. Thus it was but a portion of the nation — and this the smaller, although the more powerful portion — which was prepared to deal rigorously with the colonies.

Views of the colonies. So the colonies perceived. If they had thanks to offer for occasional acts of liberality, they gave them to the nation, knowing that in any liberal measures the nation must be united. But if there were complaints to make, if there were outcries of indignation and agony to utter, the object of them was not the nation. The colonies knew that the nation, as a whole, was on their side, and that it was the king, the Parliament, or the ministry who alone, as a general rule, deserved reproach. Hence the emphasis upon the word *ministerial* in relation to the system upheld in Britain, and opposed in America.

Parties in the colonies. The colonies themselves were not a unit. Even the old thirteen, with which we are concerned, presented by no means an unbroken front. The very number of their inhabitants — near two millions (1763) — implied differences and separations. A considerable part consisted of slaves and of servants scattered in varying proportions amongst the various colonies. Of the freemen themselves, a very considerable proportion was more accustomed to subjection than to independence. There were certainly many who were wholly unfit to defend their liberty, many more who were wholly unfit to raise it to a position of security. Happily there was a large and an increasing body of men, women, and children, whose natures and whose principles were of a higher stamp. On these the colonies relied as much against the weaknesses that were within, as against the oppressions that were without. The same class was prominent in the preceding period; here, more than ever, is it in the foreground.

The two sides. Thus, then, in the story of the provocations dividing the mother country and the colonies, we have not England, not Great Britain, pitted against America, but the ruling class in the mother country opposed to the better class in the colonies. The distinction is important. Nothing else could explain the amount of blundering on one side, or the amount of wisdom, comparatively speaking, on the other. Nor could any thing else so clearly indicate the difference between the principles at stake — the principles of an old aristocracy on the one hand, and on the other those of a young commonalty, all fervent with vigor and with hope.

Ministries of the period. The ministers representing the British side may be noted in this place. The Earl of Bute, prime minister at the beginning of the period, (1763,) was succeeded by George Grenville in the same year; then by the Marquis of Rockingham, (1765;) then by William Pitt, made Earl of Chatham, (1766;) then by the Duke of Grafton, (1768;) and then by Lord North, (1770.) The Rockingham and Chatham ministries alone were comparatively liberal, not even these being liberal in the true sense of the term.

Point of taxation. England was laboring under the increased debts occasioned by the late war with France. It was not her part, argued the aristocracy, to bear them alone; they had been incurred, in a great degree, on account of the colonies, and the colonies should bear their share. The argument proceeded upon a strange forgetfulness of the fact that the colonies were already bearing their share, and more than their share, of debts and difficulties in consequence of the war. Not the less determined to increase the burdens of America, the authorities in England cast about for the means of accomplishing their purpose. There was but one, and this taxation. Now, taxation of a certain sort was nothing new to the colonies. They had long borne with taxes for the so-called regulation of trade. But the ministry and their supporters, not content with the old taxes, were for raising new ones — taxes for revenue as well as for regulation of trade. Substantially, there was no difference; taxes were taxes, whether laid upon imports or upon any thing else; but the colonies were persuaded at the time, and for some time after, that there was a difference, and a vital one.

Discussion. When, therefore, Parliament voted, in the beginning of the year, (1764,) that it had "a right to tax the colonies," implying in any way whatever, the colonies took alarm. The Massachusetts House of Representatives ordered a committee of correspondence with the other colonies. James Otis, in a pamphlet on the Rights of the British Colonies, exclaimed, "that by this [the British] constitution, every man in the dominions is a free man; that no part of his majesty's dominions can be taxed without their consent." "The book," said Lord Mansfield, chief justice of the King's Bench, "is full of wildness." But it did not satisfy many of the colonists, and wilder still, as the chief justice would have said, became their assertions of independence. It was not long before the right of Parliament to lay any taxes whatsoever was discussed and denied.

Sugar act. But for the moment, the colonies were willing to bear with taxation under one name, provided it was not levied under another. The ministry, however, adopted the very style which the colonies disliked, and passed an act laying duties upon sugar and other articles of colonial import, with the expressed understanding that "it is just and necessary that a revenue be raised in America for defraying the expenses of defending, protecting, and securing the same." In other words, both the commercial and the military sway over the colonies was to be supported and carried out by a course of taxation. Thus decided George Grenville and his party by the sugar act of 1764. It was a momentous decision.

Stamp act. The earnest remonstrances of the colonies, especially of New York and Rhode Island, produced no effect, except to precipitate measures in England. Ten months after the sugar act, a series of acts far more decisive was passed. A stamp act, proposed some time before, was enacted without any other serious opposition than that of English merchants in the American trade. By this act, all business papers and certificates, as well as newspapers, required a stamp, similar to that already used in Great Britain. At the same time, the jurisdiction of the Admiralty Court was extended, to the exclusion, therefore, of juries in many cases previously brought before them. Together with these new burdens upon the colonies, an old one was revived in the quartering act, by which quarters and various supplies were demanded from the colonies for the British troops amongst them. But neither the provisions for the troops nor those for the admiralty had any significance to be compared with the stamp duties, so unwonted and so unbearable, (1765.)

Resistance. They roused the colonies with a general start. "This unconstitutional method of taxation," was the comment of George Washington, who, for the last six years, had been a burgess of Virginia. "That parliamentary procedure," was the subsequent language of Jonathan Mayhew, of Boston, "which threatened us and our posterity with perpetual bondage and slavery." Virginia was the first to speak out, as a colony, in resolutions proposed by Patrick Henry. "Those Virginians," responded Oxenbridge Thacher, of Massachusetts, the associate of Otis in opposing the writs of assistance, — "those Virginians are men." The response of Massachusetts, as a colony, was the vote of her representatives, on the proposal of James Otis, that the colonies should be invited to send committees of their representatives or burgesses to meet at New York. South Carolina, led by Christopher Gadsden, was the first to appoint a committee to the proposed assembly.

Congress. The first congress of the colonies met on the 7th of October, 1765. South Carolina, Massachusetts, Rhode Island, Connecticut, Pennsylvania, and Maryland sent committees of their respective assemblies, according to the original plan; the committees of New York, New Jersey, and Delaware being otherwise appointed. New Hampshire and Georgia, without sending committees, promised to adhere to the decisions of the congress. Virginia and North Carolina were absent and silent, but not from want of sympathy. Timothy Ruggles, of Massachusetts, an officer in the late war with France, was chosen president; amongst the members were James Otis and Christopher Gadsden, the two prime movers in the creation of the congress. Otis, like the other Massachusetts members, came instructed by the House of Representatives "to insist upon an exclusive right in the colony to all acts of taxation." This instruction sounds like the key note of the congress.

Declaration of rights and liberties. All other doings of the body, whether petition to king or addresses to Lords and Commons of Great Britain, sink into comparative insignificance by the side of a declaration of rights and liberties. This document, acknowledging the allegiance due by the colonies to the crown, dwells with peculiar emphasis upon their claim "to all the inherent rights and liberties of natural born subjects within the kingdom of Great Britain."

The rights especially demanded by the colonies are those of taxation by their own assemblies, and of trial by their own juries; the two, as will be remembered, assailed by the stamp act. The injustice and impolicy of the recent proceedings in the mother country are pointed out, with an earnest demand that all the obnoxious statutes should be at once repealed. The importance of the declaration must be evident. Preferring no claim to independence, it preferred claims to privileges which, in the existing relations between the colonies and the mother country, could not be secured without independence. The Declaration of Rights, dated the 19th of October, 1765, foretells the birth of the new nation as near at hand.*

* With the exception of a few lines in the preamble, here follows in full the

DECLARATION OF RIGHTS AND LIBERTIES.

The members of this congress esteem it our indispensable duty to make the following declaration of our humble opinion respecting the most essential rights and liberties of the colonists, and of the grievances under which they labor by reason of several late acts of Parliament.

I. That his majesty's subjects in these colonies owe the same allegiance to the crown of Great Britain that is owing from his subjects born within the realm, and all due subordination to that august body, the Parliament of Great Britain.

II. That his majesty's liege subjects in these colonies are entitled to all the inherent rights and liberties of his natural born subjects within the kingdom of Great Britain.

III. That it is inseparably essential to the freedom of a people, and the undoubted right of Englishmen, that no taxes be imposed on them but with their own consent, given personally or by their representatives.

IV. That the people of these colonies are not, and, from their local circumstances, cannot be represented in the House of Commons in Great Britain.

V. That the only representatives of the people of these colonies are persons chosen therein by themselves, and that no taxes ever have been or can be constitutionally imposed on them but by their respective legislatures.

VI. That all supplies to the crown being free gifts of the people, it is

Effect. The declaration was not made by every colony. But though signed by the representatives of only six colonies,* it was virtually the act of all but two, Virginia and North Carolina; and as such, it went forth to convince the mother country, nay, the colonies themselves,

unreasonable and inconsistent with the principles and spirit of the British constitution for the people of Great Britain to grant to his majesty the property of the colonists.

VII. That trial by jury is the inherent and invaluable right of every British subject in these colonies.

VIII. That the late act of Parliament entitled "An act for granting and applying certain stamp duties and other duties in the British colonies and plantations in America," &c., by imposing taxes on the inhabitants of these colonies, and the said act, and several other acts, by extending the jurisdiction of the Courts of Admiralty beyond its ancient limits, have a manifest tendency to subvert the rights and liberties of the colonists.

IX. That the duties imposed by several late acts of Parliament, from the peculiar circumstances of these colonies, will be extremely burdensome and grievous, and, from the scarcity of specie, the payment of them absolutely impracticable.

X. That as the profits of the trade of these colonies ultimately centre in Great Britain, to pay for the manufactures which they are obliged to take from thence, they eventually contribute very largely to all supplies granted there to the crown.

XI. That the restrictions imposed by several late acts of Parliament on the trade of these colonies will render them unable to purchase the manufactures of Great Britain.

XII. That the increase, prosperity, and happiness of these colonies depend on the full and free enjoyments of their rights and liberties, and an intercourse with Great Britain mutually affectionate and advantageous.

XIII. That it is the right of the British subjects in these colonies to petition the king or either House of Parliament.

Lastly. That it is the indispensable duty of these colonies, to the best of sovereigns, to the mother country, and to themselves, to endeavor by a loyal and dutiful address to his majesty, and humble applications to both Houses of Parliament, to procure the repeal of the act for granting and applying certain stamp duties, of all clauses of any other acts of Parliament whereby the jurisdiction of the admiralty is extended as aforesaid, and of the other late acts for the restriction of American commerce.

---

* Massachusetts, Rhode Island, Pennsylvania, Maryland, New Jersey, and Delaware.

that they were no longer separate settlements, but a single country. So bold was the whole course of the congress, so startling the effect, in English eyes, that the Lord Chancellor Northington exclaimed, "I declare as a lawyer, they have forfeited all their charters." It was all done in a three weeks' session.

Riots.

Thus far the colonies appear to have met their provocations with all the composure of men who knew the right to be upon their side. But it was not always so. When one of the New Jersey representatives, who had declined signing the acts of the congress, returned home, he was hanged and burned in effigy by his constituents. The mob spirit had shown itself, months before, in Boston and in Providence, where effigies were paraded and houses sacked amidst violence the most abhorrent to all the better class of the townspeople. When the stamp act went into operation, just after the close of the congress, a great riot broke out in New York, although there, as elsewhere, not a stamp officer remained to execute the provisions of the act. It is wiser to pass by such things with regret than to pause over their details as if they were the deeds of heroes. They sprang from strong feelings, we must allow, but not from strong principles; and so far from aiding the colonies in obtaining justice, did more than any thing besides to increase the oppressiveness of the mother country. Bitterly, therefore, were they deplored by men like those who met in the congress or approved its acts of magnanimity. But such is ever the effect of oppression. It overturns the reason of the feeble; it overthrows the influence of the strong.

Non-importation and non-consumption.

The outbreak in New York led to one result of value. An agreement to suspend importations from Great Britain was fortified by the resolution to encourage manufactures at home, even by such means as eating no lamb or mutton, so that there might be wool enough for the country. All this being communicated by a committee of correspondence to the other colonies, there ensued a general, though not a universal, abstinence from British goods. Non-importation and non-consumption became the watchwords of the colonies; and though broken again and again, they were again and again renewed during the ensuing years. The great change that resulted in the outward looks of society harmonized with the transformation of feelings which was going on every where.

Repeal of stamp act.

Meanwhile the want of stamp officers, and the indisposition of the colonial authorities to enforce the stamp act by themselves, had left it in a lifeless condition. Demands that it should be put out of existence altogether came, not from the colonies alone, but from a large number of merchants in England. Pitt and Burke, the greatest of English statesmen at the time, took up the opposition; and as the act had but augmented the expenditures of the kingdom without increasing its revenues,* the ministry, then professing to be a liberal one, listened to the general clamor for repeal. Amidst the throngs of tradesmen and merchants, politicians and statesmen, discussing the question, we see the colonial agents all alive to the interests with which they were charged. Foremost stood Benjamin Franklin, for several years † the agent of Pennsylvania, and now called before the House of Commons, where he assured his questioners that the colonies would never submit to the stamp act, nor to any similar statute, however much they might yield upon the point of duties to regulate commerce. The repeal was carried, accom-

* It had cost the treasury £12,000, of which but little more than a twelfth part was returned from duties levied in Newfoundland, Nova Scotia, Quebec, Florida, and the West Indies.

† Since 1757, but with an interval.

panied, however, by a declaratory act, "for the better securing the dependency of his majesty's dominions in America upon the crown and Parliament of Great Britain in all cases whatsoever." This was the answer of England to the congress of America; the stamp act was laid aside; but the power of taxation was more tightly grasped than ever.

American rejoicings.

It was now the spring of 1766. And never had that season been so full of bloom as in the gladness which it now brought to the colonies. The fact that their rejoicings over the repeal of the stamp act were unmingled with any apparent misgivings as to the purpose of the declaratory act, shows the warmth of their attachment to the mother country. Statues to Pitt and to the king, with indemnities to those who had suffered from the riots of the preceding year, were voted amidst a turbulence of congratulation such as no event had ever occasioned in America.

New acts.

Forebodings returned with the following year. The Parliament of 1767 created a board of revenue commissioners for America; passed a tea act, by which duties were imposed upon tea and other imports into the colonies, for the purpose not only of providing for troops as before, but of securing fixed salaries for the royal governors and the royal judges; then pronounced the New York assembly incapable of legislation until the quartering act of 1765 was obeyed by that body, hitherto resisting its execution. Here were three measures more comprehensive and more oppressive than any parliamentary legislation had as yet been.

Resistance again.

They were met as might have been expected. "Let us complain to our parent," wrote John Dickinson, a native of Maryland, and a representative of Pennsylvania, in his Letters from a Farmer, "but let our complaints speak at the same time the language of affliction and veneration," (1767.) The beginning of the next year (1768) brought out the sterner voice of Massachusetts through her representatives, inveighing against all the enactments of Parliament, and calling upon the colonies to join in one firm front of resistance. This measure the next house was called upon to rescind, and by no less an authority than that of the ministry; but in vain. The same spirit showed itself in all classes. The students of Harvard College declared the proceedings of their tutors unconstitutional, and called a tree by the name of Liberty. The Boston Cadets — a volunteer guard of the governor — refused to appear if the revenue commissioners, who had their head quarters at Boston, were invited to join a procession. The commissioners were soon flying from a riot occasioned by the seizure of John Hancock's sloop for a fraudulent entry at the custom house. Such was the prevailing confusion, that British troops were ordered to the town, (1768.)

Massachusetts convention.

This was too much for Boston. A town meeting called upon the governor to convene the General Court. On his refusal, the meeting advised the people to get their arms ready, on account, it was said, "of an approaching war with France;" then summoned a convention from all Massachusetts. This gathered, and again requested the governor to summon the legislature. He again refused, and hinted at treason in the convention, with reason, indeed, considering the entire novelty of such a body to him and to the colony. The convention, not very full of fire, deprecated the displeasure of the governor, and addressed a petition to the king. Just as the convention was separating, the troops arrived, but without finding the quarters that were demanded for them from Boston, sturdier as a town than Massachusetts as a colony. "O my countrymen!" exclaimed Josiah Quincy, Jr., one of the truest-hearted young men of Boston; "what will our children say when they read the history of these times, should they find we tamely gave away, without one noble struggle, the most invaluable of earthly blessings?" This was no appeal to violence. "To banish folly and luxury," continued the Christian patriot, "correct vice and immorality, and stand immovable in the freedom in which we are free indeed, is eminently the duty of each individual at this day," (1768.)

Act concerning trials in England.

The new year (1769) began with a new provocation, in the shape of an act directing that all cases of treason, whether occurring in the colonies or not, should be tried in the mother country. This was worse than any taxation, worse than any extension of admiralty courts, any demand for quarters, any creation of revenue commissioners, any suspension of assemblies; it struck a blow at the safety of the person as well as the freedom of the subject. The planter at Mount Vernon, hitherto calm, exclaims with indignation that "our lordly masters in Great Britain will be satisfied with nothing less than the deprivation of American freedom." "That no man," he writes, "should scruple or hesitate a moment to use arms in defence of so valuable a blessing, is clearly my opinion. Yet arms, I would beg leave to add, should be the last resource." The Virginia assembly, of which Washington was still a member, passed resolutions of kindred spirit. Massachusetts was more than ready to follow. The Suffolk grand jury indicted the governor of Massachusetts, the commander-in-chief of the colonies in general, with the revenue commissioners and officers of the customs, for libelling the province to the ministry. Joseph Hawley, representative from Northampton, declared in the house that he knew not "how Parliament could have acquired a right of legislation over the colonies." Thus for every fresh provocation was there a fresh resistance, denying more and more of the power that was more and more oppressive.

Colonial divisions.

The New York assembly now made its submission to the quartering act. In doing so it gave great offence to many of the people, one of whom was thrown into prison for his violent denunciation of the assembly. Neither he nor the assembly showed much wisdom in thus contending at a time when union was so much required. But there were parties amongst the colonists, just as there had been, indeed, from the beginning, but now more distinctly marked and more widely separated. No less than five divisions existed, the central and the most substantial being that of the class already mentioned as chief in the colonies. This was flanked, on one side, by two orders more or less inclined to submit to the mother country, and on the other side by two orders more or less inclined to defy the mother country. To begin with the royalists, their name explaining itself; then came the neutrals, as they may be styled, neither precisely royalist nor precisely colonist; next the colonists proper, in their close and resolute ranks — the men on whom the issue depended more than on any others; and after them the more excited parties, first of the Sons of Liberty, as they called themselves,* and second of the rioters. Thus, with royalists and neutrals on one wing, and with Sons of Liberty and rioters on the other, the main body of the colonists had but a weary and an anxious march.

Boston massacre.

The difficulties of the case were nowhere more apparent than in Boston. A constant tendency to riot on the part of a portion of the townspeople required as much energy on the part of the better class as any provocations from abroad against which they were contending. While the wiser Bostonians were endeavoring to procure

* From the words of Barré's famous speech of 1765. Many of the original Sons of Liberty were of the class described as the better one of the time; but, at the present period, the order was made up of the more turbulent spirits, yet not the most turbulent of all.

the withdrawal of the troops quartered amongst them, a party of men and boys involved themselves in a quarrel with the soldiers, the end of which was blood. This Boston Massacre, as it was called, did but add to the burden of the moderate and the effective citizens. The soldiers who had fired upon the people required to be defended upon a charge of murder; the authorities in England required to be convinced that the violence of the populace was as much deplored as the musketry of the soldiery. It marks the increasing passions of the times, that the two advocates retained by the English officer in command on the night of the affray, though they were no less tried patriots than John Adams and Josiah Quincy, Jr., should have fallen under censure for undertaking the defence. Happily for the fame of Boston, they secured the safety of the accused, only two out of nine being brought in guilty, and those of manslaughter alone, for which they were branded in the hand and then discharged, (1770.)

Other disturbances.

Boston was not alone in these disturbances. North Carolina saw a large portion of her interior settlers banded together as Regulators* against the colonial government; nor were they brought to reason without a battle, in which they were defeated by a volunteer force from the orderly portion of the colony, (1771.) In the north, again, the burning of storehouses at Portsmouth, and the destruction of the revenue schooner Gaspe in Narraganset Bay, kept up the flames of rashness and of outrage, (1772.) The Gaspe, or its officers, however, had done all that was possible to provoke its doom.

The mother country had been pursuing a comparatively gentle course. The repeal of the duty upon many arti-

* A name first applied in South Carolina to a party undertaking to execute the laws for themselves; in modern phrase, Lynch-law men.

Additional act concerning trials.

cles imported into the colonies showed a disposition to conciliate, (1770.) Two years passed before any act appeared in relation to the colonies; nor could that then enacted be called a provocation. In consequence of the occurrence at Portsmouth, a bill passed Parliament to secure the trial in England of any incendiaries of the royal stores or ships in America, (1772.) It did not please the colonists, not even the great party of moderation, to think that they had brought this sentence upon themselves. The truth was, that the less moderate the course of things, the fewer moderate men there were to bring things back to moderation. What was done only by the violent was upheld in many instances by the prudent; a common sympathy was fast fusing all parties. So Boston now held its town meeting, and put forth its memorial not only against the acts of which it had to complain, but against those which it seemed to have to apprehend.

Tea destroyed in Boston.

The next year showed how fast the colonies were driving on. It began with resolutions from Virginia, where a committee was appointed to correspond with the other colonies. To the closer union thus proposed, Rhode Island was the first to adhere, but without immediate results. Yet, as the year advanced, the colonists found themselves the better prepared to combine in resistance to the introduction of large quantities of tea, still subject to duty. It was the plan partly of the East India Company and partly of the ministry; the former hoping to dispose of their swollen stock, the latter to obtain some of the taxes that appeared to have been levied in vain upon the colonies. Philadelphia was the first to take the field by town meeting against tea and taxation. Boston soon followed; and when the proceedings of town meetings, both ordinary and extraordinary, came to nought, as the governor stood fast for the East India Company and the ministry, the three vessels that had come in with tea were boarded, and their cargoes thrown into the dock. It was a sad event for many even of the more resolute citizens; but the majority, under the lead of Samuel Adams, was now composed of the rash as well as the resolute; a party from the country having been most active in the destruction of the tea, (December, 1773.) A few weeks later, a smaller quantity of tea, imported to private order, was also destroyed at Boston, (February, 1774.)

And elsewhere. The same thing happened at New York and Annapolis. But the larger portion of the tea received at New York, and all received at Philadelphia, was swiftly returned to England. This returning the tea, or the storing it where it would soon lose its virtue, as in Charleston, was a far wiser course than destroying it. The process of destruction was also the less bold. It was effected by men disguised, or else so maddened as to scorn disguise.

Slave trade. It has already appeared how small a part of the provocations to the colonies consisted in mere measures of taxation. A signal instance of the comprehensive inflictions from the mother country came up in the midst of the transactions lately occurred. The repugnance of the colonies to the slave trade, reviving in these times of struggle, brought out renewed expressions of opposition and abhorrence. Virginia attempted by her assembly to lay restrictions on the traffic; but the royal governor was at once directed by the authorities at home to consent to no laws affecting the interests of the slave dealers, (1770.) The efforts of other colonies met with similar obstacles. Bills of assemblies, petitions to the king, called forth by the startling development of the trade,* were alike ineffect-

* In less than nine months, 6431 slaves were imported into the single colony of South Carolina, from Africa and the West Indies.

ual. "It is the opinion of this meeting,"—thus ran the resolves of the county of Fairfax, George Washington chairman,—"that during our present difficulties and distress, no slaves ought to be imported into any of the British colonies on this continent; and we take this opportunity of declaring our most earnest wishes to see an entire stop forever put to such a wicked, cruel, and unnatural trade," (1774.)

Chastisement of Massachusetts and Boston.

Provocations were gathering heavily and rapidly. Massachusetts and Boston, foremost in the tea troubles, and, soon after, in the disturbances occasioned by royal salaries to the governors and judges of the colonies, were singled out for peculiar chastisement. The Boston port bill closed the harbor of that town to all importation and exportation. Then General Gage, commander-in-chief of the British forces in the colonies, was appointed governor of Massachusetts. Not content with creating this state of siege, the ministry brought in a bill for the better regulating the government of Massachusetts Bay, by which the colony was virtually deprived of its charter. The councillors and superior judges were all to be appointed by the crown; the inferior judges and other officers being left to the nomination of the governor, who was invested with a sort of absolute authority. No town meetings were to be held, except for elections, unless the governor saw fit to make any further exceptions. No juries were to be summoned, except by the sheriffs, that is, by the officers of the governor. To crown the whole, a third bill provided that persons charged with murder in sustaining the government, should be sent to another colony or to England for trial—a shrewd precaution, considering the certainty of collision between the people and the government under the system about to be enforced. Such were the measures by which Massachusetts was to be crushed and her sister colonies overawed. The crisis had come with the spring and summer of 1774.

Quebec act.

Another proceeding of the same period was intended to separate the thirteen colonies from their neighbors on the continent. The French settlers in the west had shown some signs of sympathy with the English colonies, not, indeed, by any direct coöperation, or even intercourse, but by the same irrepressible instincts after liberty. When their petition for a form of government in which they could have some share was met by a system in which none but the royal officials had any part, the French in the Illinois country protested against it with all the fervor of their nature, (1773.) To keep such spirits down, especially to keep them from combining with the kindred spirits of the English colonies, seems to have been the main object of the Quebec act, by which that province, extended from the Gulf of St. Lawrence to the Mississippi, was placed under a government mostly of royal officials. At the same time, the French were conciliated by the restoration of their law and of their church, (1774.)

Conventions and Provincial Congress in Massachusetts.

Thus cut off from their northern and western neighbors, the inhabitants of the thirteen colonies gathered together against the mother-land. A circular from Boston to the towns of Massachusetts called upon them to make common resistance to the recent acts. Several of the towns, or rather counties, met by delegates in convention at Boston to resolve upon measures of defence, amongst which "the military art" and "a Provincial Congress" were prominent. A convention of Middlesex county at Concord resolved that "to obey them," that is, the acts of Parliament, "would be to annihilate the last vestiges of liberty in this province," (August.) Ten days after, (September,) a convention of Suffolk county at Milton recommended that the detested acts "should be rejected as the attempts of a wicked administration to enslave America." The next month, (October,) the House of Representatives voted itself a Provincial Congress. This was decisive. But that it was done, must be ascribed not merely to the inherent independence of Massachusetts, but to the pervading sympathy of the sister colonies.

National spirit.

"Has not this," wrote Washington, nearly three months before, in relation to the acts of Parliament and the proceedings of Governor General Gage,—"has not this exhibited an unexampled testimony of the most despotic system of tyranny that was ever practised in a free government? . . . Shall we supinely sit, and see one province after another fall a sacrifice to despotism? . . . My nature recoils at the thought of submitting to measures which I think subversive of every thing that I ought to hold dear and valuable." Such was the tone of every true voice, the feeling of every true heart. A national spirit was aroused.

Continental Congress.

More than a year previously, Benjamin Franklin —now agent not only for Pennsylvania, but for Massachusetts, New Jersey, and Georgia—wrote officially to the Massachusetts House of Representatives, recommending a General Congress, (1773.) But it was not until ten months afterwards that the project was taken up, and then not in Massachusetts, but in Rhode Island. Virginia followed close, recommending that the Congress should be annual, and voting that "an attack upon one colony was an attack upon all British America," (May, 1774.) Rhode Island was the first to appoint delegates; Massachusetts doing the same almost immediately, and the other colonies, Georgia excepted, imitating these examples. The method of appointment varied from choice by the assembly, or by a convention of the whole colony, to choice by committees, county and town, or by a single committee. It was a noble body that met at Philadelphia on the 5th of September,

1774. Samuel Adams and John Adams were there from Massachusetts; John Jay from New York; John Dickinson from Pennsylvania; George Washington, Patrick Henry, and Richard Henry Lee, from Virginia; Christopher Gadsden and John Rutledge from South Carolina. "If you speak of eloquence," said Patrick Henry, on being asked about the greatest man in Congress, "Mr. Rutledge is by far the greatest orator; but if you speak of solid information and sound judgment, Colonel Washington is unquestionably the greatest man on that floor." It needed all that the leaders, all that the members as a body, could command, to meet the exigencies of the time. The Congress that met to reject the stamp act, nine years before, had but child's play to go through, compared with the work of the present Congress — the Continental Congress, as it was called.

Its work. Taxation had been the substance of three acts of Parliament, or, at the most, of four.* There were twice or thrice that number † upon other points to be opposed. Against all these provocations the Continental Congress put forth their declaration of colonial rights. In this, much the same ground as to the allegiance and the general rights of the colonies was taken as had been held by the earlier Congress. It is therefore a document of secondary importance in the progress of our history.

American Association. Not so the American Association. This was a body of articles, by which a stop was to be put, after certain dates, to all importation from or exportation

* The sugar, the stamp, and the tea acts, with the act creating revenue commissioners.

† The quartering acts, the act suspending the New York assembly, the acts concerning trials for treason and incendiarism, the three acts against Massachusetts, the Quebec act, besides those portions of the stamp and tea acts relating to Admiralty Courts and royal salaries.

to Great Britain and its dependencies, so long as the oppressive acts of Parliament were not repealed. "We will neither import nor purchase any slaves imported after the first day of December next," was one of the articles; "after which time we will neither be concerned in it ourselves, nor will we hire our vessels, nor sell our commodities or manufactures, to those who are concerned in it." Thus humane as well as bold, considerate for their inferiors as well as resolute towards their superiors, or those claiming to be such, the members of the Continental Congress signed the American Association. The date was October 20, 1774. It was the birthday of the nation.

Petition and addresses.

Together with the Association and the declaration, there came from Congress a petition to the king and addresses to the people of Great Britain, British America, and Canada, besides letters to Newfoundland, Nova Scotia, and the two Floridas. These various documents being adopted, and the debates on all the stirring questions of the time being concluded, not altogether with unanimity, Congress separated, (October 26,) having provided that another Congress should be convened, if necessary, in the ensuing spring.

Peace or war.

"More blood," wrote Washington, during the session of Congress, "will be spilled on this occasion, if the ministry are determined to push matters to extremity, than history has ever yet furnished instances of in the annals of North America." "After all," wrote Joseph Hawley from Massachusetts to John Adams in Congress, — "after all, we must fight." Adams read the letter to his colleague from Virginia, the fervid Patrick Henry, who burst out with the exclamation, "I am of that man's mind!" It was not the opinion of every one. Richard Henry Lee parted from Adams with the assurance that "all the offensive acts will be repealed. . . . Britain will give up her foolish project."

Preparation. Come peace or come war, the Americans, as they are hereafter to be called, were prepared. Not, it is true, with armies or fortresses, not with the material resources which they seemed to require, but with the spirit that was of far greater importance, the source of all outward strength and success. This spirit was not without its supports, intellectual or physical. The struggles with the mother country had called out orators and statesmen, whose minds were daily making some fresh contribution to the thought and the power of humanity. Physically, the Americans were increasing their stores and extending their domains. The road to the great west was opened with the first settlement made in the present Tennessee, (1768.) If old weaknesses lingered, if the disputes between colony and colony continued, now on a question of boundary, now on one of doctrine, they were lost in the union that had been achieved, in the nation that had been born.

CHAPTER II.

WAR.

Arming of Massachusetts.

THE very day that the Continental Congress separated, — October 26, 1774, — the Provincial Congress of Massachusetts took a step decisive of war. This was the organization of the militia, consisting of all the able-bodied men of the colony, one fourth of them being constituted minute men, bound to take up arms at a minute's warning. Soon afterwards, provision was made for supplying the equipments and munitions of an army. The whole was placed under the direction of a committee of safety, with John Hancock for a chairman.

Not unprovoked or unanticipated.

The arming of the colony had not been unprovoked. Two months before, General Gage, the commander-in-chief and the governor, had begun to fortify the land approach to Boston. He had also seized upon some stores of powder belonging to the province at Charlestown. Such was the temper excited against him, that Christopher Gadsden, the representative of South Carolina in the Continental Congress, proposed an immediate attack upon the British head quarters in Boston. Neither was the arming of Massachusetts altogether unanticipated. No colony, indeed, had gone so far; but many a town, many a band of individuals, was prepared for conflict. A rumor that Boston was bombarded by the British brought out numbers of the Connecticut militia to the rescue of their countrymen. Years before, when the stamp

Quebec
Ticonderoga
Saratoga
Lexington
Salem
Boston
West Point
New York
Newport
Trenton
Philadelphia
Yorktown
Kings Mt.
Camden
Eutaw Springs
Charleston
Savannah
REVOLUTION
1775-81.
Bufford Boston

act was rousing the land to resistance, some ardent New Yorkers had voted "to march with all despatch . . . to the relief of those who should or might be in danger from the stamp act or its abettors," (1765.) The juncture thus prepared for arrived when Massachusetts armed herself. From that day, war was inevitable. The British authorities would never sit by while such things were going on, nor could they attempt any measures of repression without arousing the colonists to use the weapons which they had assumed.

Arming of other colonies.

The example of Massachusetts was soon followed. Far and near, the colonies, by act of assembly, or of convention, or of individual resolution, took up the posture of defence. All the while, the national spirit was sustained by the American Association, and by the committees appointed to enforce it. Though not universally prevalent, the Association had extended itself more widely and more deeply than any previous bond of union amongst the colonies. Earnest to maintain their ties and their rights, the Americans drew out their lines. It was no great show in a military point of view. In point of courage, of sacrifice, it was sublime.

Course of Parliament.

The year was closing in England with a new Parliament, in which the majorities for the ministry were irresistible. Amongst the members was a native of New York, Henry Cruger, who, having settled as a merchant at Bristol, was elected mayor, and returned to Parliament. In the prime of manhood, flushed with generous emotion for the country of his birth, although opposed to its revolutionary courses, he rose to make his maiden speech against the severities with which the ministry was threatening America. "Can it be believed," he cries, "that Americans will be dragooned into a conviction of this right of parliamentary taxation?" The plea was taken up by men of greater influence. As the new year (1775) opened, Chatham and Burke devoted themselves to obtaining justice for America. In vain; the petition of the Continental Congress to the king was refused a hearing; rebellion was declared to exist in Massachusetts, and to be abetted by other colonies. The "New England restraining act" cut off the New England colonies from the fishery and from all trade, save to Great Britain, Ireland, and the British West Indies. The prohibition was soon extended to the other colonies; New York, North Carolina, and Georgia being spared on account of their expected submission. At the same time, Lord North, the prime minister, brought out what he called a conciliatory proposition, to the effect that the colonies should not be taxed by Parliament, if they would tax themselves, and therewith raise the sums which Parliament should deem necessary. "They complain," was the decisive reply of Edmund Burke, "that they are taxed without their consent; you answer that you will fix the sum at which they shall be taxed. That is, you give them the very grievance for the remedy." The proposition, thus clearly seen through by an Englishman, was not likely to blind Americans. Out of Parliament, there were few to take any active part in relation to America. We should not, however, pass over the suggestion of Dr. Tucker, Dean of Gloucester, that Parliament should declare the colonies separated from the mother country until they humbled themselves to ask for forgiveness and for restoration. Had the dean's idea been adopted, how much wrong, how much blood, might have been saved!

First collision.

But the Americans and the British were now to meet in arms. A party of one hundred and fifty troops, sent from Boston to seize some cannon at Salem, not finding it there, marched on towards Danvers. On their way, they came to a bridge, occupied at first by a few country people, but presently by a company of militia under Colonel Pickering. As the draw was up, the British attempted to cross the stream in boats, and in doing so, used their bayonets freely enough to wound the men who kept the boats from them. A serious conflict would have ensued but for the mediation of Mr. Barnard, a clergyman of Salem, who prevailed on the British officer, Lieutenant Colonel Leslie, to return in case the troops were allowed to cross the bridge. This was agreed to on the American side; the troops crossed, advanced a few rods, then faced about, and retired without the cannon of which they had come in search. The date was February 26, 1775.

Its significance. The collision is memorable as the first of the war. It is also to be remarked as strikingly significant of the collisions that followed. The same paucity of numbers, the same restriction of movements, the same ineffectiveness of results, characterize the whole strife between Great Britain and America. We must be prepared for operations on a small scale, and with a small effect, each taken alone. Taken together, however, the operations of the war bear a nearer proportion to the greatness of the stakes at issue.

Lexington and Concord. The next encounter was more serious. It took place in the early morning of April 19. A force of eight hundred troops, marching from Boston to Concord, for the purpose of destroying the military stores collected in that place, met not quite a hundred minute men at Lexington. The British fired; the minute men returned the fire, but, of course, retreated, leaving a few of their number killed and wounded. The men of Concord retired before the troops without attempting resistance; but from the surrounding towns there came other minute men so numerous and so spirited as to engage with the British, and compel them to retreat. The retreat became a flight;

nor would the fugitives have escaped but for the reënforcements which met them at Lexington. The number of the Americans being also on the increase, the retreat, resumed at Lexington, proved very difficult. Had it been protracted, the arrival of fresh parties of minute men would have cut it off altogether. As it was, the British, out of seventeen hundred troops, lost nearly three hundred in killed, wounded, and prisoners. The Americans, amounting in all to several hundred, lost less than one hundred.

Effect. Mecklenburg declaration.

"An inhuman soldiery," wrote Joseph Warren, president of the Provincial Congress, to the committees of safety throughout Massachusetts, "enraged at being repulsed from the field of slaughter, will, without the least doubt, take the first opportunity in their power to ravage this devoted country with fire and sword. We conjure you, therefore, that you give all assistance possible in forming an army." Massachusetts voted that at least thirty thousand men ought to be raised by New England, herself furnishing nearly half the number. Rhode Island, Connecticut, and New Hampshire soon responded, but not quite so liberally as the sister colony had desired. Out of New England, the agitation was the same. "The once happy and peaceful plains of America," wrote Washington from Philadelphia, "are either to be drenched with blood or inhabited by slaves. Sad alternative! But can a virtuous man hesitate in his choice?" The news, travelling slowly, reached the town of Charlotte, Mecklenburg county, North Carolina, where a county convention was in session. It lent resolution to the delegates, who adopted some resolves, which have been called a declaration of independence, but which, in their more authentic form, simply declare the colonial constitution, as it had been, to be suspended, and the legislative and executive power to be vested for the time in the Provincial and Continental Congresses, (May.) This declaration of

Mecklenburg county was communicated to the Provincial Congress of the colony, without, however, obtaining the sympathy of that assembly. It was also forwarded to the North Carolina representatives in the Continental Congress; but so little did it move them, that they did not even lay it before their colleagues.

War in Massachusetts. The troops of New England were gathering about Boston. The people of Massachusetts sent an address to the people of Great Britain. "Appealing to Heaven," they declared, "for the justice of our cause, we determine to die or to be free." Repelling a Connecticut offer of mediation between herself and her governor, General Gage, Massachusetts voted him "an unnatural and inveterate enemy" — a compliment which he afterwards returned by pronouncing the Massachusetts people "rebels and traitors." The breach yawned wide, and wider still, as the passions and the outrages of war poured in.

Ticonderoga and Crown Point. So far the Americans had acted on the defensive. But now a band of volunteers from Connecticut and the Green Mountains, led by Ethan Allen and Seth Warner, with whom went Benedict Arnold, under a Massachusetts commission, surprised the small garrisons at Ticonderoga and Crown Point, (May 10–12.) Descending thence against various places on Lake Champlain, the adventurous band secured a large booty, and then separated, leaving a considerable portion of their number in possession of the Point and Ticonderoga.

Proceedings in Congress. The spirit aroused in action appeared in deliberation likewise. When the new Congress assembled at Philadelphia in the spring, (May 10,) it began upon measures more determined by far than those of the former body. The members were mostly the same; but the circumstances in which they met were as different as peace and war. Massachusetts opened the way to new resolutions, by recommending the creation of an American army, and by asking instruction as to the form of government under which she should place herself. Congress answered the request by advising the election of a council and an assembly, who should administer the colony by themselves, until a governor should appear to take his part according to the charter of 1691. Soon afterwards, the Provincial Congress of Massachusetts gave way to a General Court or assembly. The recommendation of an army was followed by Congress in adopting the troops before Boston as the American continental army. To this were also summoned a few companies of riflemen from the southern colonies.

Washington appointed commander-in-chief.

The creation of an army required the creation of a commander. No act of Congress could be more important, none proved more successful, than the appointment of Colonel George Washington, representative from Virginia. "We, the delegates of the United Colonies," — thus runs the commission of Washington, — "reposing special trust and confidence in your patriotism, conduct, and fidelity, do by these presents constitute and appoint you to be general and commander-in-chief of the army of the United Colonies. . . . And you are hereby vested with full power and authority to act as you shall think for the good and welfare of the service." Rapid as these outlines of events must be, they will bear repeated testimony to the unequalled, indeed the hitherto unconceived devotion of Washington to the cause of his country. His acceptance of the commission. itself the greatest act of sacrifice that he could make, was accompanied by the refusal of all pecuniary compensation for his services. It was a memorable day when this devoted career began — June 15, 1775.

Bunker Hill.

As if to do honor to the general thus given them, the New England troops, just declared the continental army, furnished a detachment of one thousand, under Colonel Prescott, to take possession of Bunker's Hill, a point of great importance to the lines around Boston. He, through a mistake assisted by the ardor of his character, threw up his redoubt upon Breed's Hill, an eminence considerably nearer to the town. Reënforced by a thousand men, the party completed their fortifications in time to receive the three thousand British troops assailing them from Boston. Twice was the advance of the enemy repelled; but the failure of ammunition obliged the Americans to retreat, leaving one of their most heroic hearts, President and Major General Joseph Warren, dead upon the field. Four hundred and fifty of them in all were killed or wounded; the British losing more than twice that number. The battle of Bunker Hill, as it was afterwards called, has been greatly magnified beyond the importance attached to it at the time. But there can be no question of its having done much to mortify the British, who had always boasted that the Americans would fly before them, as well as much to elate the Americans, although they had always boasted that they would resist their foes, (June 17.)

Washington at the head of the army

Washington heard of the battle at New York, on his way to the army. Hastening his journey, he arrived at Cambridge, which was to be his head quarters, and assumed the command. On the next day, July 4, he issued an order to the forces. "The Continental Congress," he proclaimed, "having now taken all the troops of the several colonies, which have been raised or which may be hereafter raised for the support and defence of the liberties of America, into their pay and service, they are now the troops of the United Provinces of North America; and it is hoped that all distinctions of colonies will be laid aside, so that one and the same spirit may animate the whole. . . . The general requires and expects of all officers, not engaged on actual duty, a punctual attendance on divine service, to implore the blessings of Heaven upon the means used for our safety and defence." Thus appealing to the love of country and to the fear of God, Washington called upon his countrymen to do their duty in the war.

Difficulties. Not every one was disposed to hear him. Indeed, there were but few who came up to the standard of their chief, either as soldiers or as men. When we read of their deficiencies and of his embarrassments, we must remember that he and those like him were the representatives of the better class of Americans, already described as most prominent and most wise during the struggles of the preceding years. They, on the other hand, who fell short of the demands upon them, were of the other classes, the rash or the timid, the too presumptuous or the too submissive.

Siege of Boston. Washington at once determined to lay regular siege to Boston. His first object was merely to shut up the British in the town, (July.) Presently, he tried to bring on an attack from the enemy against the American lines, (August.) This failing, he formed the purpose of attacking the British in their own lines, (September.) He deferred to the objections of his officers, and put off the assault, without, however, abandoning his designs. All the while, he had no arms, no ammunition, no pay for his troops from Congress; no general support from his officers or men; no obedience even, at times, from the soldiers or from the crews of the armed vessels acting in concert with the army. It was very difficult to fill the ranks to any degree at all proportioned to the operations of the siege. "There must be some other stimulus," he writes to the president of Congress, "besides love for their country, to make men fond of the service." "Such a dearth of public spirit," he laments to a personal friend, "and such want of virtue, such stockjobbing and fertility to obtain advantages of one kind and another, I never saw before, and pray God's mercy that I may never be witness to again. . . . I tremble at the prospect. . . . Could I have foreseen what I have experienced and am likely to experience, no consideration upon earth should have induced me to accept this command." Such were the circumstances, and such the feelings, in which the commander-in-chief found himself conducting the great operation of the year.

General government.

By this time there was not only an army, but a government of America. The Continental Congress, declaring themselves to be acting "in defence of the freedom that is our birthright," took all the measures, military, financial, and diplomatic, which the cause appeared to require. The organization of the army was continued; that of the militia was attempted. A naval committee was appointed, and a navy — if the name can be used on so small a scale — was called into existence. Hospitals were provided. Several millions of continental currency were issued, and a treasury department created. A post office was also organized. Several of the colonies who had applied for advice upon the point were recommended to frame governments for themselves. The Indian relations were reduced to system. A last petition to the king, with addresses to Great Britain and London, Ireland and Jamaica, was adopted. More significant than all else was the appointment of a committee of secret correspondence with Europe. In short, the functions of a general government were assumed by Congress and recognized throughout the colonies.

At the beginning of August, Georgia signified her acces-

The thirteen complete.

sion to the other colonies, thus completing the thirteen. A fourteenth offered itself in Transylvania, the present Kentucky, where one or two small settlements had just been made. But Congress could not admit the delegate of a territory which Virginia claimed as under her jurisdiction. The nation and the government remained as the Thirteen United Colonies.

Military operations.

Military operations, apart from the siege of Boston, were numerous, if not extensive. The landing of a British party at Gloucester was repelled. The fort near Charleston was seized by the Americans, who also drove the British ships out of the harbor. Norfolk, for some time in the hands of the British, was recovered after a gallant action. On the other hand, Stonington, Bristol, and Falmouth were not saved from bombardment, Falmouth (now Portland) being nearly annihilated. The Americans, in return, sent out their privateers; those commissioned by Washington, especially his "famous Manly," as he called one of his captains, doing great execution in Massachusetts Bay. Offensive operations were pursued on land. A projected expedition against Nova Scotia was given up, chiefly on account of the friendly feeling of that province. But a twofold force, partly from the New York and partly from the Maine side, marched against Canada. St. John's and Montreal were taken by the Americans under General Montgomery, who fell in an assault on Quebec the last day of the year. Arnold, the same who had gone against Crown Point and Ticonderoga, kept up the show of besieging Quebec through the winter, but in the spring the Americans retreated within their own borders. One of the most successful operations of the period was towards the close of winter, when fifteen hundred Highlanders and Regulators, who had enlisted under the royal banner in North Carolina, were defeated by two thirds their number of

Americans, under Colonel Moore. It saved the province to the country.

Loyalists.

The mention of those enlisted in the royal cause suggests the increasing divisions amongst the Americans. A large number, who had looked on or even joined in the proceedings of former days, drew off, if they did not take a hostile position, in these days of war. Companies and regiments of royal or loyal Americans began to abound. Some of these loyalists, as they were styled, were roughly handled by their indignant neighbors, who spared neither person nor property. One of the New York Sons of Liberty, Isaac Sears, impatient at the moderate course pursued by the committee of safety, brought in an armed band from Connecticut, to destroy the press of Rivington's Gazetteer, a journal in the British interest. Such doings were more likely to introduce dissensions amongst the patriots than to subdue the loyalists. But when did riot fail to go hand in hand with war?

Great Britain determined.

Great Britain, on her part, was united. Few and faint were the voices raised in defence of the Americans, since the news of Lexington and Bunker Hill. Edmund Burke and one or two of the same spirit continued to plead for the American cause, but all unavailingly. The last petition of Congress to the king was rejected. A bill of confiscation, as it may be called, was passed against the trade, the merchandise, and the shipping of the colonies; whatever crews might be captured were to be impressed into the British navy. The army in America was augmented to forty thousand, partly by British and partly by German troops. In fine, the reduction of the colonies was the one great object with the larger part of the people, as with the rulers of Great Britain.

All the while, Washington was before Boston. But his attention was not wholly concentrated there. On the con-

Washington before Boston.

trary, his voice was to be heard in all directions, on the march to Canada, in the posts of New York, on board the national cruisers, at the meetings of committees and assemblies, in the provincial legislatures, within Congress itself, every where pointing out what was to be done, and the spirit in which it was to be done. They who doubt his military ability or his intellectual greatness will do well to follow him through these first months of the war; if they do it faithfully, they will doubt no more. The activity, the judgment, the executive power, and above all the moral power of the great general and the great man are nowhere in history more conspicuous than in those rude lines before Boston.

Recovery of the town.

To add to the difficulties of the siege, the army went through a complete process of disbanding and recruiting, on account of the general unwillingness to serve for any length of time. Without men and without munitions, Washington sublimely kept his post, until, after months of disappointment, he obtained the means to take possession of Dorchester Heights, whence the town was completely commanded. The enemy, under General Howe, had long meditated the evacuation of the place; and they now the more readily agreed to leave it on condition that they should be unmolested. The 17th of March, 1776, eight months and a half from the time that Washington undertook the siege, his generalship and his constancy were rewarded with success.

The victory.

It was certainly an amazing victory. "I have been here months together," he wrote to his brother, "with what will scarcely be believed, not thirty rounds of musket cartridges to a man. . . . We have maintained our ground against the enemy under this want of powder, and we have disbanded one army, and recruited another, within musket shot of two and twenty regiments, the flower of the British army, whilst our force has been but little, if any, superior to theirs; and, at last, have beaten them into a shameful and precipitate retreat out of a place the strongest by nature on this continent, and strengthened and fortified at an enormous expense." Such being the result of the only operation in which the Americans and the British met each other as actual armies, there was reason for Washington and his true-hearted countrymen to exult and to hope.

Increasing perils. But the country was in danger. An attack was feared at New York; another at Charleston: the whole coast, indeed, lay open and defenceless. The year of warfare ended in greater apprehensions and in greater perils than those in which it began.

CHAPTER III.

DECLARATION OF INDEPENDENCE.

Transformation of colonies to states.

THE colonies were fighting at a disadvantage. Not only were their resources, in a military point of view, inferior to those of their great antagonist; this was but a minor consideration with them. They were taxed with rebellion; they were branded with the name of rebels by their enemies, nay, by those of their own people who opposed the war. On many, these epithets made no impression; they were rather acceptable than otherwise to the more ardent and the more violent. But to the moderate and to the calm, it was intolerable to be charged with mere sedition. They to whom the nation owed all that was prudent, as well as valiant in its present situation, were men of law and order in a peculiar degree. The earliest care with those of Massachusetts, after the affair of Lexington, had been to prove that the British troops were the first to fire; in other words, that the people were defending, and not transgressing, their rights. So now it became a matter of the highest interest to set the war in its true light, by raising the Americans from the position of subjects to that of a nation. There was but one way, and this the transformation of the colonies into states.

Idea of independence.

The idea of independence, however, was of slow growth. The Mecklenburg declaration, as we have read, found no favor. The general, if not the universal, sentiment was still in favor of reconciliation. "During the course of my life," said John Jay in later years, "and until after the second petition of Congress in 1775, I never heard an American of any class or of any description express a wish for the independence of the colonies." But when that petition of Congress to the king was rejected, when the English government, in consequence, pledged itself to continue its system of oppression, then the resolution of the colonies rose, all the more determined for having been delayed.

North Carolina and Virginia.

Nearly a year had elapsed since the North Carolinians of Mecklenburg county made their declaration, when the North Carolinians of the entire colony united in authorizing their delegates in Congress to concur with those of the other colonies in declaring independence, (April 23, 1776.) A few weeks afterwards, (May 15,) the Virginians instructed their delegates to propose a declaration of independence to Congress.

Congress.

Congress had already committed itself. Its recommendations of the year previous to some of the colonies, that they should set up governments for themselves, had just been extended to all. It had also voted "that the exercise of every kind of authority under the crown should be totally suppressed," (May 15.) What else was this than to pronounce the colonies independent states? Subsequent resolutions and declarations were but the carrying out of the decision already made.

Hesitation.

But as it had not been made, so it was not carried out without hesitation. More than one earnest mind, bent upon independence in the end, considered the course of things thitherward to be much too hurried. "My countrymen," wrote Washington, (April 1,) "from their form of government, and their steady attachment heretofore to royalty, will come reluctantly into the idea of independence; but time and persecution bring many wonderful things to pass." He was right; the spirits and numbers of those resolved upon immediate independence increased apace

Lee's resolution. The instructions of Virginia were soon obeyed. Upon the journals of Congress, under date of June 7, there occurs an affecting entry of "certain resolutions respecting independency being moved and seconded." No names are mentioned, no words of the resolutions are recorded. It is as if Congress had felt its own feebleness in comparison with the solemnity of the cause, and so deeply, as to hold its breath and give no sign of what was passing. The mover was Richard Henry Lee, of Virginia, the seconder John Adams, of Massachusetts; and the resolution was, "That these United Colonies are, and of right ought to be, free and independent states; that they are absolved from all allegiance to the British crown; and that all political connection between them and the state of Great Britain is, and ought to be, totally dissolved."

Debate. Opposition was immediate and resolute. At its head stood John Dickinson, of Pennsylvania, whose ten years' championship of colonial rights was assurance of his present faithfulness. The ground common to him and to the other opponents of the resolution was simply the prematureness of the measure. Nor does it seem that they were altogether mistaken. Whatever was urged by the advocates of the resolution, there were but seven colonies, the barest possible majority, to unite in favor of a proceeding so decisive, (June 10.) Instead of pressing their views, the party in favor of the resolution were wise enough to postpone its final disposition for several weeks. On the other side, the opposing party, so far from exciting the country against the resolution, appear to have decided that it should have a fair consideration, and that if the colonies rejecting it could be brought to favor it, they would be satisfied by the delay that had been interposed for deliberation

Committee on declaration.

At the same time, a committee was appointed to prepare a declaration according to the tenor of the resolution. Thomas Jefferson, of Virginia, John Adams, Benjamin Franklin, of Pennsylvania, Roger Sherman, of Connecticut, and Robert R. Livingston, of New York, constituting the committee, united upon a draught by Jefferson. "Whether I had gathered my ideas," he said at a later time, "from reading or reflection, I do not know. I know only that I turned to neither book nor pamphlet while writing it. I did not consider it as any part of my charge to invent new ideas altogether, and to offer no sentiment which had never been expressed before." Truth to be told, there was neither originality nor novelty in the production. Its facts, so far as they related to the course of Britain or of the British king, were peculiar to the cause at issue. But the principles of human and of colonial rights were substantially such as Englishman after Englishman, as well as American after American, had asserted. The merit of the document was its appropriateness, its harmony with the ideas of a people who had risen to defend their birthright, rather than to win any thing not already theirs. The committee reported the declaration to Congress, (June 28.)

Resolution adopted.

Its adoption depended upon the adoption of the resolution of which it was but the expression. The resolution was therefore called up, (July 1.) A day's debate ensued; nor was the decision unanimous. Four delegations hung back; one, New York, because it had received no instructions to vote upon so grave a question; the other three, Pennsylvania, Delaware, and South Carolina, on account of their own reluctance. The South

Carolinians asked the postponement of a definitive vote until the next morning. When the morning came, they withdrew their opposition. The Pennsylvanian and Delaware delegates — some members retiring and others coming in — gave their voices likewise to the resolution. It thus received the unanimous vote of all the colonies, New York excepted, and she only for a few days, until her delegates could be instructed to concur with their colleagues, (July 9–15.) It was the 2d of July, 1776, the true date of American independence.*

And the declaration. The declaration followed as a matter of course. It was delayed only to receive a few amendments, when it was adopted by the same vote as the resolution, (July 4.)

The United States. Thus were the colonies of Great Britain transformed into the United States of America. "As free and independent states," were the words of the declaration, "they have full power to levy war, conclude peace, contract alliances, establish commerce, and to do all other acts and things which independent states may of right do." No longer the subjects of Great Britain, but an equally independent nation, the United States were no longer open to imputations upon their course from abroad, or to doubts of it amongst themselves. When Admiral Lord Howe, and his brother, the general, commander-in-chief of the British army, offered amnesty in the king's name to all Americans who would return to their allegiance, the offer was regarded as a national insult by Congress. What had Great Britain to forgive, or who had asked for forgiveness?

The day after a committee had been appointed to draw

* As the utmost discrepancy exists amongst the later histories as to these votes and dates, it seems advisable to state that Jefferson and Adams are the authorities followed in the text.

Plan of confederation. up the declaration, another, and a larger one, received the charge of preparing a plan of confederation, (June 12.) This was reported a week after the adoption of the declaration, but no action was taken upon it, (July 12.) Circumstances postponed any decision; nor were the Articles of Confederation and Perpetual Union, as they were styled, actually adopted by Congress until more than a year later, (November 15–17, 1777,) when they were recommended to the states for adoption. A long time elapsed before all the states complied.

Unity in Congress. Meanwhile Congress continued to be the uniting as well as the governing authority. Its members, renewed from time to time by their respective constituencies, met together as the representatives, not merely of the different states, but of the common nation. It was imperfectly, as we shall perceive, that Congress served the purpose of a central power. Its treaties, its laws, its finances, its armaments, all depended upon the consent and the coöperation of the states. But it continued to be the body in which the states were blended together, however variously, in one.

State constitutions. The states were every where forming governments of their own. Massachusetts took the lead, as was observed, in the early summer of 1775. Six or seven months afterwards, New Hampshire organized her assembly and council, with a president of the latter body, (1776.) The same year brought about the establishment of state authorities in New Jersey, Pennsylvania, Delaware, Maryland, Virginia, North and South Carolina. Of the other states, Rhode Island and Connecticut were naturally content with the liberal governments which already existed under their ancient charters. New York and Georgia set up their governments a year subsequently, (1777.) But the original forms underwent numerous and repeated modifications; each state amending its constitution or constructing a new one, according to its exigencies. As a general thing, each had a governor, with or without a council, for an executive; a council, or Senate, and a House of Representatives, for a legislature; and one or more judicial bodies for a judiciary. Indeed, the states were much more thoroughly organized than the nation.

Divisions amongst the people.

Both constitutions and declarations had arisen amidst the most distracting divisions. The differences in Congress, or amongst the leading class throughout the country, were trifling in comparison with the factions of the people as a whole. On this side were flaming patriots, who thought nothing done unless outcry and force were employed; on that were selfish and abject spirits, thinking that nothing should be done at all. Tories, or loyalists, abounded in one place; in another, rioters and marauders; every where dark plots were laid, dark deeds perpetrated. The greater was the work of those, the few, the wise, and the devoted, who led the nation through its strifes to independence.

CHAPTER IV.

WAR, CONTINUED.

SECOND PERIOD.

Three periods. THE war of independence naturally divides itself into three periods. Of these, the first has been described in a preceding chapter, as beginning with the arming of Massachusetts, in October, 1774, and extending to the recovery of Boston, in March, 1776—a period of a year and a half, of which something less than a year, dating from the affrays at Lexington and Concord, was actually a period of war. We are now to go through the second and third periods.

Characteristics of the second period. The second period is of little more than two years—from April, 1776, to July, 1778. The chief points to characterize it are these, namely, that the main operations were in the north, and that the Americans fought their battles without allies.

Reception of the Declaration. The Declaration of Independence was transmitted to the commander-in-chief, with the request of Congress to "have it proclaimed at the head of the army." It was what both commander and army had been waiting for. "The general hopes"—thus ran the order of the day—"that this important event will serve as a fresh incentive to every officer and soldier to act with fidelity and courage, as knowing that now the peace and safety of his country depend, under God, solely on the success of our arms, and that he is now in the service of a state possessed of sufficient power to reward his merit and advance him to the highest honors of a free country," (July 9.) On the same day, Washington wrote to the president of Congress: "I caused the Declaration to be proclaimed before all the army under my immediate command, and have the pleasure to inform Congress that the measure seemed to have their most hearty assent; the expressions and behavior, both of officers and men, testifying their warmest approbation of it." The adhesion of the army was one thing; their obedience to the inspiration which their commander suggested was another. But, for the moment, a new impulse seemed to be felt by all.

Defence of Charleston.

A brilliant feat of arms had preceded the declaration. The anticipated descent upon the southern coast was made off Charleston, by a British force, partly land and partly naval, under the command of General Clinton and Admiral Parker. The Americans, chiefly militia, were under General Lee. Fort Sullivan,* a few miles below Charleston, became the object of attack. It was so gallantly defended, the fort itself by Colonel Moultrie, and an adjoining battery by Colonel Thomson, that the British were obliged to abandon their expedition and retire to the north, (June 28.) A long time passed before the enemy reappeared in the south.

Loss of New York.

Meanwhile Washington had transferred his quarters from Boston to New York, (April 13,) which he was busy in fortifying against the expected foe. Troops from Halifax, under General Howe, joined by British and Hessians under Admiral Howe, and by the discomfited forces of the southern expedition, landed at various times on Staten Island, to the number of between twenty

* Afterwards Fort Moultrie.

and thirty thousand. The number of the Americans was considerably less. After long delays, the enemy crossed to Long Island, and routed the American detachments under General Putnam, (August 27.) A speedy retreat to New York Island alone saved the Americans from a surrender. A fortnight after, the British crossed in pursuit, the advanced posts of the Americans actually flying before them, (September 15.) The city of New York was at once evacuated by Washington, who led his forces towards the north. "We are now encamped," he writes, "with the main body of the army on the Heights of Haerlem, where I should hope the enemy would meet with a defeat in case of an attack, if the generality of our troops would behave with tolerable bravery. But experience, to my extreme affliction, has convinced me that this is rather to be wished for than expected." He did not write thus without good reason. Little besides incompetency and desertion on the part of his men had attended his vain attempt to save New York.

Loss of Lake Champlain and the lower Hudson.

Loss succeeded loss. Two defeats on Lake Champlain drove the Americans, under Benedict Arnold, not only from the lake, but from the fortress of Crown Point, (October 11–14.) In the neighborhood of New York, Washington was obliged to abandon one position after another; the defeat of White Plains (October 28) making still farther retreat necessary. The forts upon the Hudson were presently lost; Fort Washington being taken with its garrison, (November 16,) and Fort Lee being evacuated, (November 20.) With a diminishing army, in which, moreover, he had lost his confidence, the commander-in-chief decided to fall back from the banks of the Hudson into New Jersey.

Loss of Newport.

At the same time that the Americans were retreating from New York, another of their chief towns upon the seaboard was captured. A large detachment from the British army took possession of Newport without a blow, (December 8.) The island was overrun, and Providence blockaded.

Defence of New Jersey. Losses increased defections. "Between you and me," writes Washington on his retreat, "I think our affairs are in a very bad condition, — not so much from the apprehension of General Howe's army, as from the defection of New York, the Jerseys, and Pennsylvania. In short, the conduct of the Jerseys has been most infamous. . . . If every nerve is not strained, . . . I think the game is pretty nearly up," (December 18.) Disheartening as were the circumstances, he called around him his more faithful officers, and with them planned an achievement which seemed to require all the encouragements of prosperity and of sympathy. Followed by his handful of twenty-four hundred, while other detachments failed to keep up with him, he crossed the Delaware amid the ice and the cold of Christmas night, and on the following morning took a thousand Hessian prisoners at Trenton. The British immediately advanced against him. He could not meet them; for it would be destruction to his inferior numbers. He would not retreat before them; for it would be despair to his gallant adherents. To avoid either alternative, he marched, after a slight engagement, upon the rear of the hostile army at Princeton, (January 3.) Three hundred prisoners, the safety and the increased animation of his soldiers and his countrymen, were his reward. The only drawback was the loss of many brave spirits, amongst whom none was braver than General Mercer. Had Washington had but a few hundred fresh troops, he would have pushed on to Brunswick and destroyed the entire stores of the enemy. As it was, the rising of the militia, and the continued activity of Washington, even in his winter quarters, cleared the state of the invaders, excepting at Brunswick and Amboy. Six months after, it was totally evacuated, (June 30, 1777.)

Organization of army.

All the time that Washington was thus retreating and advancing, he was enforcing the lesson of his experiences upon the government. He could do comparatively little, as he repeatedly informed Congress, for want of no less essential an instrument than an army. The American forces, during the campaign, had consisted in part of continental, or regular, and in part of militia troops, all raised on different terms, — that is, by different bounties and under different appointments, — by the different states. What Washington wanted, what the country needed, was an army recruited, officered, equipped, and paid upon a national system. Nor was Congress insensible to the necessity. Before the declaration of independence, a board of war and of ordnance had been chosen from the members of Congress, to direct the military affairs of the nation. Afterwards, when the calamities of the autumn were weighing heavily, Congress ordered the formation of a continental army. But the wants, thus attempted to be supplied, continued. It was left entirely to the states to raise the troops and to appoint all but the general officers, while the pay and the term of enlistment proposed by Congress were wholly inadequate to the emergencies on which Washington insisted. "The measure was not commenced," wrote he to his brother, "till it was too late to be effected, and then in such a manner as to bid adieu to every hope of getting an army from which any services are to be expected." "The unhappy policy of short enlistments," the need of "some greater encouragement" in pay, "the different states' nominating such officers as are not fit to be shoeblacks," the tendency of the states to fall back from regular troops upon the militia, "a destructive, expensive, and disorderly mob," — all these complaints from the commander-in-chief show that there was still no organization of the army.

Dictatorship. Alarmed by the disasters of the time, Congress resolved, "that General Washington shall be, and he is hereby, vested with full, ample, and complete powers" to raise, officer, and equip an army. To provide for its necessities, he was authorized "to take, wherever he may be, whatever he may want for the use of the army, if the inhabitants will not sell it, allowing a reasonable price for the same." He was also commissioned "to arrest and confine persons who refuse to take the continental currency, or are otherwise disaffected to the American cause," (December 27, 1776.) This commission of a dictatorship, the last resort of the ineffective Congress, and yet one of that body's wisest deeds, was to continue six months. It was afterwards renewed in much the same terms. But the powers were too dictatorial for such a man as Washington to exercise fully; nor did the partial use which he made of them effect the object of so great importance in his eyes. The war went on without any thing that could be called an actual army on the American side.

Paper money. The want of an army sprang, to a great degree, from the want of a treasury. Congress, voting all sorts of appropriations, had no way of meeting them but by continued issues of paper money. These soon began to depreciate; the depreciation required larger amounts to be put forth; and then the larger amounts added to the depreciation. When the value of the bills had sunk very low, an attempt was made to restore the currency by recalling the old issues and sending out new ones; but these, too, depreciated fast. Then lotteries were resorted to, and loans, both at home and abroad. The states were called in, and taxes raised by them were substituted for the national bills. But the embarrassments of the finances were irreparable. Every year added to the debt and to the poverty of the nation.

Arrival of Lafayette

In the midst of trials so various and so profound, there was a thrill of hope. It was caused by the arrival of a Frenchman, not yet twenty years old, who came bearing the sympathies of the old world to the new. "It was the last combat of liberty," wrote Lafayette, as he afterwards recalled his early inspirations. While he was hastening his departure from France, the news of the defeats in New York arrived, to throw the American cause into the shade, even in the eyes of the commissioners who had been sent to seek supplies in France. They would have dissuaded the young Frenchman from his projects. "We must be of good cheer," he replied; "it is in danger that I like best to share your fortunes." Escaping the pursuit of the government, who would have prevented a man of so high a rank as the Marquis de Lafayette from compromising them with the English by joining the Americans; tearing himself from a brilliant home, and a wife as young in years as he, Lafayette crossed the sea in his own vessel, and reached the coast of Carolina in safety. He hastened to Philadelphia to offer his services to Congress, which, more and more wont to be behindhand in its mission, gave him a cold welcome through the committee of foreign affairs. "The coldness was such," he wrote, "as to amount to a rejection; but without being disconcerted by the manner of the members, I begged them to return to the hall, and to read the following note: 'After the sacrifices which I have made, I have the right to demand two favors: one is to serve at my own expense, the other to commence as a volunteer.'" Congress was touched, and appointed the generous stranger a major-general, (July 31, 1777.) He found no hesitation in the welcome which he received from Washington on their first meeting. "Make my head quarters your home," was the warm and appreciative greeting from the commander-in-chief to the young major-general.

The army and the people imitated Washington's example, and gave their confidence to the noble Frenchman, with joy that their cause had attracted such a champion.

Defeat of Burgoyne.

The spring of 1777 was marked only by some predatory excursions from the British side into Connecticut, and from the American into Long Island. The summer brought about the evacuation of New Jersey, as has been mentioned. But the British retired only to strike harder elsewhere. A well-appointed army under General Burgoyne was already on its march from Canada to Lake Champlain and the Hudson. As this descended, it was the plan of the British in New York to ascend the Hudson, meeting the other army, and cutting off the communication between New England and her sister states. It was a promising scheme, and the first movements in it were successful. Burgoyne took Ticonderoga, and swept the adjacent country, menacing Northern New York on his right, and the Green Mountain region on his left. General St. Clair, who had evacuated Ticonderoga, could make no resistance; nor was his superior officer, General Schuyler, the commander of the northern army, in any position to check the advance of the enemy. But Schuyler bore up bravely; and the officers under him did their part. A British detachment against Bennington was defeated by John Stark and his New England militia, (August 16.) Fort Schuyler was defended by continental troops, the British retiring on the approach of reënforcements under Arnold, (August 22.) Just as these reverses had checked the advance of Burgoyne, the gallant Schuyler was ousted of his command to make room for General Gates, a very inferior man, if not a very inferior general. He, profiting by the preparations of his predecessor, met the British, and defeating them in two actions near Saratoga, (September 19, October 7,) compelled them to surrender. Nearly six thousand troops laid down their arms; but more than twice that number were now collected on the American side, (October 16.)

Loss of the Hudson Highlands.

While this triumph was won, losses were still occurring elsewhere. The advance of the British from New York, after being strangely delayed, began with the capture of the forts which protected the Highlands, (October 5–6.) But on proceeding some way farther up the river, the enemy found it advisable to return to New York.

Loss of Philadelphia.

The main army of Great Britain was that which Washington had to deal with in New Jersey and the vicinity. "If General Howe can be kept at bay," wrote the commander-in-chief, "and prevented from effecting his principal purposes, the successes of General Burgoyne, whatever they may be, must be partial and temporary." After much uncertainty as to the intentions of the British general, he suddenly appeared in the Chesapeake, and landing, prepared to advance against Philadelphia, (August 25.) Washington immediately marched his entire army of about eleven thousand to stop the progress of the enemy. Notwithstanding the superior number — about seventeen thousand — opposed to him, Washington decided that battle must be given for the sake of Philadelphia. After various skirmishes, a general engagement took place by the Brandywine, resulting in the defeat of the Americans, (September 11.) But so little were they dispirited, that their commander decided upon immediately fighting a second battle, which was prevented only by a great storm. Washington then withdrew towards the interior, and Howe took possession of Philadelphia, (September 26.) Not yet willing to abandon the city, Washington attacked the main division of the British encamped at Germantown. At the very moment of victory, a panic seized the Americans, and they retreated, (October 4.) There was no help for Philadelphia; it was decidedly lost.

Washington's embarrassments.

The contrast between the defeat of Burgoyne and the loss of Philadelphia was made a matter of reproach to the commander-in-chief. Let him make his own defence. "I was left," he says, "to fight two battles, in order, if possible, to save Philadelphia, with less numbers than composed the army of my antagonist. . . . Had the same spirit pervaded the people of this and the neighboring states, . . . as the states of New York and New England, . . . we might before this time have had General Howe nearly in the situation of General Burgoyne, with this difference — that the former would never have been out of reach of his ships, whilst the latter increased his danger every step he took." More than this, Washington conducted his operations in a district where great disaffection to the American cause cut off supplies for the army, and intelligence of the enemy. To have done what he did, notwithstanding these embarrassments, was greater than a victory. It was felt to be so at the time. "Nothing," said the French minister, the Count de Vergennes, to the American commissioners in France, — "nothing has struck me so much as General Washington's attacking and giving battle to General Howe's army: to bring an army, raised within a year, to this, promises every thing."

Loss of the Delaware.

The enemy were not yet secure in Philadelphia, the Delaware below the city being still in the possession of the Americans. Nor did they give it up without a struggle. Fort Mercer, upon the Jersey shore, was gallantly defended under Lieutenant Colonel Christopher Greene against a Hessian attack, (October 22;) but when Fort Mifflin, upon an island in the river, gave way after a noble struggle, under Lieutenant Colonel Samuel Smith, (November 15,) Fort Mercer was evacuated, and the Delaware was lost, (November 20.) An attack meditated by the Americans upon Philadelphia, and one attempted by the British upon the American camp at Whitemarsh, (December 5–8,) resulted in nothing. The operations of 1777 were ended.

Wickes's cruise. One enterprise of the year is not to be passed over. Captain Wickes, of the cruiser Reprisal, after distinguishing himself in the West Indies, sailed for France in the autumn of 1776. Encouraged by his success in making prizes in the Bay of Biscay, Wickes started on a cruise round Ireland in the following summer, (1777.) Attended by the Lexington and the Dolphin, the Reprisal swept the Irish and the English seas of their merchantmen. But on the way to America, the Lexington was captured, and the Reprisal, with the gallant Wickes and all his crew, was lost on the coast of Newfoundland. It was for the navy, of which Wickes was so great an ornament, that a national flag had been adopted in the summer of his cruise, (June 14.)

Cabal against Washington. "I see plainly," wrote Lafayette to Washington, at the close of the year, "that America can defend herself, if proper measures are taken; but I begin to fear that she may be lost by herself and her own sons. When I was in Europe, I thought that here almost every man was a lover of liberty, and would rather die free than live a slave. You can conceive my astonishment, when I saw that toryism was as apparently professed as whiggism itself." "We must not," replied Washington, "in so great a contest, expect to meet with nothing but sunshine." These mournful complaints, this cheerful answer, referred to an intrigue that had been formed against Washington, for the purpose of displacing him from his command. Generals Gates and Mifflin, both members of the board of war, lately organized, with Conway, a foreign general in the service, were at the head of a cabal, which was secretly supported by some members of Congress. Had their unworthy plots prevailed, had their anonymous letters to the civil authorities, and their underhand appeals to military men, succeeded, Washington would have been superseded by Gates or by Lee, it was uncertain which, both of British birth, both of far more selfishness than magnanimity, of far more pretension than power. Gates, as we shall read hereafter, met the most utter of all the defeats, Lee conducted the most shameful of all the retreats, in which the Americans were involved. Happily for the struggling nation, these men were not its leaders. The cabal in which they were involved fell asunder; yet without crushing them beneath its ruins. They retained their offices and their honors, as well as Washington.

Army quarrels. The army was full of quarrels. Sectional jealousies were active, the northern man distrusting the southern, and the southern the northern. National jealousies were equally rife, the American officers opposing the foreign, and the foreign officers the American. More serious, because more reasonable, were the angry feelings excited in the army against Congress, now for its interference, and now for its neglect. Much ill will on both sides was excited by the question of half pay for life to the officers; it being opposed in Congress, and settled only by a compromise of half pay for seven years after the conclusion of the war. Washington contended with all the intellectual and moral strength of his nature against the jealousy which Congress unhappily entertained of the army. "The prejudices of other countries," as he says, "have only gone to them [the troops] in time of peace. . . . It is our policy to be prejudiced against them in time of war; though they are citizens, having all the ties and interests of citizens."

Army sufferings.

The experience of the past twelvemonth had given Washington more confidence in his soldiers. He had had time to learn their better points, their enthusiasm, their endurance, their devotion. The winter following the loss of Philadelphia was one of cruel sufferings, and the manner in which they were borne formed a new link between the troops and the commander. His remonstrances against the jealousies of Congress are accompanied by representations of the agonies of the army. "Without arrogance or the smallest deviation from truth, it may be said that no history now extant can furnish an instance of an army's suffering such hardships as ours has done, bearing them with the same patience and fortitude. To see men without clothes to cover their nakedness, without blankets to lie on, without shoes, (for the want of which their marches might be traced by the blood from their feet,) and almost as often without provisions as with them; marching through frost and snow, and at Christmas taking up their winter quarters within a day's march of the enemy, without a house or hut to cover them, till they could be built, and submitting without a murmur, is a proof of patience and obedience which, in my opinion, can scarce be paralleled." This story, at once so heroic and so sad, is dated from Valley Forge.

Aspect of Congress.

Congress, meanwhile, though finding time to abet the enemies of Washington, and to suspect his faithful followers, was far from active in promoting the interests of the nation. Great changes had taken place in the composition of the assembly. Many of the earlier members had retired, some to the offices of their respective states, some to the field, some to diplomacy, some to private life. But a very small number attended the sessions; twenty-five or thirty making what was now considered quite a full Congress. "America once had a representation," wrote Alexander Hamilton, one of Washington's aids, from head quarters, "that would do honor to any age or nation. The present falling off is very alarming and dangerous."

Treaty with France.

The question of foreign alliances had been started at an early date. It met with very considerable opposition. The more earnest spirits thought it humiliating to court the protection of the European powers. They also thought it more likely to increase the dangers than the resources of the country to be drawn into the interests and the intrigues of the old world. But as time passed, and the difficulties of the war increased, the tendency to foreign connections grew stronger. Before the declaration of independence, Silas Deane was sent to France, as an agent, with hints of an alliance. Ere he reached his destination, a secret subsidy had been promised to the Americans. Meanwhile a committee of Congress was appointed "to prepare a plan of treaties to be proposed to foreign powers," (June, 1776.) Their plan being adopted, Deane, Benjamin Franklin, and Arthur Lee, of Virginia, were appointed commissioners to France, (September;) others being sent to Spain, Prussia, Austria, and Tuscany, (December.) The French envoys, amongst whom Deane gave place to John Adams, devoted quite as much attention to their own disputes as to the negotiations with which they were intrusted. But the disposition of France against her old enemy of England was too decided to require much diplomacy on the part of America. After a year's delay, a treaty between the French king, Louis XVI., and the United States was made, (January 30, February 6, 1778,) and ratified, (May 5.)

British conciliation.

The news of the treaty broke like a thunderbolt upon the British ministry. Three years had their armies, superior both in discipline and in number, contended against the so-called rebels; and what had been gained? A few towns on the seaboard, New York, Newport, Philadelphia, the islands near New York, the island on which Newport stands, the lower banks of the Hudson and of the Delaware. This was all. Nothing had been, nothing, it must have almost seemed, could be, gained except upon the coast; the interior was untenable, if not unconquerable. And what had been lost? Twenty thousand troops, hundreds of vessels, millions of treasure; to say nothing of the colonial commerce, once so precious, and now so worthless. It might well strike the ministry, that they must win back their colonies by some other means than war, especially if the French were to be parties in the strife. Accordingly, Lord North laid before Parliament a bill renouncing the purpose of taxing America, and another providing for commissioners to bring about a reconciliation, (February 17.) The bills were passed, and three commissioners were appointed to act with the military and the naval commanders in procuring the submission of the United States. To their proposals Congress returned an answer on the anniversary of Bunker Hill, refusing to enter into any negotiations until the independence of the nation was recognized. The commissioners appealed from Congress to the states; but in vain. Their mission was fruitless, except in proving that the United States would never relapse into British colonies.

Recovery of Philadelphia.

Desirous of concentrating his forces before the French appeared in the field, Sir Henry Clinton, now the British commander-in-chief, evacuated Philadelphia, (June 18.) Washington instantly set out in pursuit of the enemy. Coming up with them in a few days, he ordered General Lee, commanding the van of the army, to begin the attack in the morning. Lee began it by making a retreat, notwithstanding the remonstrances of Lafayette, who had held the command until within a few hours. But for Washington's coming up in time to arrest the flight of the troops under Lee, and to protect the advance of his own soldiers, the army would have been lost. As it was, he formed his line and drove the British from the field of Monmouth, (June 28.) They stole away in the night, and reached New York with still more loss from desertion than from battle.

Possession of Illinois.

At about the same time, a Virginia expedition, under the command of Major Clarke, surprised the British garrison at Kaskaskia, (July 4,) and took possession of the surrounding villages. The more important post of Vincennes was afterwards secured by the aid of its French inhabitants.* The country was organized as a part of Virginia, under the name of Illinois county.

End of the period.

Thus the end of the period finds the Americans conquerors as well as the British. If the latter have New York and Newport, with their neighborhoods, the former are in possession of Illinois. The main forces on either side are again where they were at the beginning of the period, save that the British are now in New York, and the Americans waiting their opportunity to retake the city. "It is not a little pleasing, nor less wonderful to contemplate," wrote Washington from his camp at White Plains, "that after two years' manœuvring, and undergoing the strangest vicissitudes that perhaps ever attended any one contest since the creation, both armies are brought back to the very point they set out from, and that the offending party at the beginning is now reduced to the use of the spade and pickaxe for defence. The hand of Providence has been so conspicuous in all this, that he need be worse than an infidel that lacks faith, and more than wicked that has not gratitude enough to acknowledge his obligations."

* It was subsequently surprised by a British party, but recovered by Clarke in the beginning of the following year.

CHAPTER V.

WAR, CONTINUED.

THIRD PERIOD.

Charac-teristics. THE third and last period of the war extends from July, 1778, to January, 1784, five years and a half. Its characteristics are, the alliance of the French with the Americans, and the concentration of the more important operations in the Southern States. These points, it is to be noted, are precisely the opposite of those which characterized the preceding period.

Failure to recover Newport. The first minister of France to the United States, M. Gérard, came accompanied by a fleet and army, under D'Estaing, (July.) "Unforeseen and unfavorable circumstances," as Washington wrote, "lessened the importance of the French services in a great degree." In the first place, the arrival was just late enough to miss the opportunity of surprising the British fleet in the Delaware, not to mention the British army on its retreat to New York. In the next place, the French vessels proved to be of too great draught to penetrate the channel and coöperate in an attack upon New York. Thus disappointing and disappointed, D'Estaing engaged in an enterprise against Newport, still in British hands. It proved another failure. But not through the French alone; the American troops that were to enter the island at the north being greatly behindhand. The same day that they took their place, under

Sullivan, Greene, and Lafayette, the French left theirs at the lower end of the island in order to meet the British fleet arriving from New York, (August 10.) A severe storm prevented more than a partial engagement; but D'Estaing returned to Newport only to plead the injuries received in the gale as compelling his retirement to Boston for repairs. The orders of the French government had been peremptory that in case of any damage to the fleet it should put into port at once. So far was D'Estaing from avoiding action on personal grounds, that when Lafayette hurried to Boston to persuade his countrymen to return, the commander offered to serve as a volunteer until the fleet should be refitted. The Americans, however, talked of desertion and of inefficiency, — so freely, indeed, as to affront their faithful Lafayette. At the same time, large numbers of them imitated the very course which they censured, by deserting their own army. The remaining forces retreated from their lines to the northern end of the island, and, after an engagement, withdrew to the mainland, (August 30.) It required all the good offices of Lafayette, of Washington, and of Congress, to keep the peace between the Americans and their allies. D'Estaing, soothed by the language of those whom he most respected, was provoked, on the other hand, by the hostility of the masses, both in the army and amongst the people. Collisions between his men and the Bostonians kept up his disgust; and, when his fleet was repaired, he sailed for the West Indies, (November.)

British and Indian ravages.

The summer and autumn passed away without any further exertions of moment upon the American side. On the part of the British, there was nothing attempted that would not have been far better unattempted. Marauding parties from Newport went against New Bedford and Fairhaven. Others from New York went against Little Egg Harbor. Tories and Indians —

"a collection of banditti," as they were rightly styled by Washington, descended from the northern country to wreak massacre at Wyoming and at Cherry Valley. The war seemed to be assuming a new character: it was one of ravages unworthy of any cause, and most unworthy of such a cause as the British professed to be.

Decline of American affairs. Affairs were at a low state amongst the Americans. "The common interests of America," wrote Washington at the close of 1778, "are mouldering and sinking into irretrievable ruin." Was he who had never despaired at length despairing? There was reason to do so. "If I were to be called upon," he said, "to draw a picture of the times and of men, from what I have seen, heard, and in part know, I should in one word say that idleness, dissipation, and extravagance seem to have laid fast hold upon most of them; that speculation, peculation, and an insatiable thirst for riches seem to have got the better of every other consideration, and almost of every order of men; that party disputes and personal quarrels are the great business of the day; whilst the momentous concerns of an empire, a great and accumulating debt, ruined finances, depreciated money, and want of credit, which, in its consequences, is the want of every thing, are but secondary considerations, and postponed from day to day, from week to week, as if our affairs wore the most promising aspect. After drawing this picture, which from my soul I believe to be a true one, I need not repeat to you that I am alarmed, and wish to see my countrymen roused." This gloomy sketch is of the government — Congress and the various officials at Philadelphia. What was true of the government was true of the people, save only the diminishing rather than increasing class to which we have frequently referred, as constituting the strength of the nation.

A border warfare had been carried on during two suc-

Loss of Georgia.

cessive summers, (1777-78,) between East Florida and Georgia. The British authorities sent parties from their garrisons, on one side, and on the other, the Americans, chiefly Georgians and Carolinians, mustered their militia. Nothing, however, but alarm and bloodshed had been accomplished, when, at the close of 1778, a serious invasion of Georgia was planned by the British commander. Twenty-five hundred troops from New York, under the command of Lieutenant Colonel Campbell, landed near Savannah. Hardly nine hundred Americans, under General Howe, were there to oppose them; and, after a short encounter, the town was taken, (December 29.) A few days later, the only other strong place upon the seaboard, Sunbury, surrendered to a force of two thousand British, advancing, under General Prevost, from Florida. Prevost, taking command of the united forces of the British, sent Colonel Campbell against Augusta. The expedition, successful at first, was soon so threatened by the operations of various partisans, and by those of General Lincoln, the commander of the continental troops, that Campbell evacuated Augusta after a fortnight's possession. Prevost then advanced from Savannah. An American force, under General Ashe, was routed at Brier Creek, and Georgia was lost, (March 4, 1779.) A few months later, Sir James Wright, the royal governor at the beginning of the war, returned and set up the provincial government once more.

Defence of Charleston.

The conqueror of Georgia aspired to become the conqueror of Carolina. With chosen troops, and a numerous body of Indians, Prevost set out against Charleston. He was met before that town by the legion under Count Pulaski, a Pole who had been in the American service for nearly two years; but Pulaski's men were scattered, and Prevost pressed on. The militia, assembled for the defence of the place, were under the orders of Governor

Rutledge; the continental troops under those of Charleston's earlier defender, Moultrie. But the disparity of forces was fearful, and proposals for surrender were under consideration, when the approach of General Lincoln with his army compelled the British to retire, (May 12.) It was more than a month, however, before they left the adjacent country. They then withdrew to Savannah and St. Augustine.

Failure to recover Savannah. The Americans were by no means disposed to acquiesce in the loss of Georgia. On the reappearance of the French fleet, under D'Estaing, after a successful cruise in the West Indies, he consented to join General Lincoln in an attack on Savannah, (September.) But he was too apprehensive of being surprised by the British fleet, as well as too desirous of getting back to the larger operations in the West Indies, to be a useful ally. The impatience of D'Estaing precipitated an assault upon the town, in which Pulaski fell, and both the French and the Americans suffered great loss, (October 9.) The French sailed southward; the Americans retired to the interior, leaving Savannah to the enemy.

Invasion of Virginia. Previously to the events last described, Virginia had been invaded. An expedition from New York, landing at Portsmouth, plundered that town and all the neighboring country. Not a blow was struck against the foe. But booty rather than conquest being their object, they withdrew, (May.)

Operations in the north. The operations in the north during the year were of altogether inferior importance. As the main body of the British continued at New York, Washington kept his small army in that vicinity. But he had no plans of decisive action. On making his preparations at the beginning of the year, he resolved upon an offensive course towards the Indians of Western New York, whose repeated hostilities, in conjunction with the British, were chastised by an American expedition under General Sullivan, (August and September.) In relation to the British, Washington could hold only a defensive attitude. Yet, when Stony Point and Verplanck Point were taken, to the great peril of the Highland fortifications, as well as to the great interruption of intercourse with New England, Washington decided upon striking a blow. A gallant party, under the gallant Wayne, surprised the strong works which the British had constructed at Stony Point, (July 15,) and, though obliged to evacuate them, destroyed them, and recovered the Hudson, that is, the part which had been recently taken from the Americans. The fortification of West Point was undertaken, as an additional safeguard. In other directions, beyond the immediate reach of Washington, although never beyond his interest and his influence, the movements of the year were still less effective. Connecticut was invaded by a British force from New York, and great was the devastation, yet not without resistance, (July.) At the same period, a force from Massachusetts assailed a post which the British had taken on the Penobscot, but with great loss. Some months later, apprehensions of the French fleet induced the British commander to draw in his outposts on the Hudson and to evacuate Newport, (October.) These movements, effected without loss, or even collision, were the only ones of any strong bearing upon the issue of the war.

Jones's cruises.

Far away, upon the coasts of Great Britain itself, the war was now extended. Following in the track of the brave Wickes, John Paul Jones sailed in the Ranger from France to the coast of England and Scotland, entering Whitehaven, where he took the fortifications and fired the shipping of the fort. This was in the spring of 1778. In the spring of the following year, Jones being then in France, it was proposed that he should take the naval command of an expedition in which Lafayette was to be the general-in-chief, the object being nothing less than the invasion of England. This project failing, Jones got to sea in summer, with a squadron of seven sail, from a French port. Although much embarrassed by the insubordinate conduct of one of his chief officers, Jones pursued his cruise with great success along the Scotch coast. Thence descending on the eastern side of England, he encountered a fleet of merchantmen, under convoy of two vessels of war. The two were at once engaged — the larger, the Serapis, by Jones's Bonhomme Richard, and the smaller, the Countess of Scarborough, by the Pallas, under Captain Cottineau. It was a fearful and a remarkable action. Jones was exposed not only to the fire of his antagonist, but to that of one of his own vessels, from the treachery or the incompetency of its commander; and so completely battered was his ship, the Bonhomme Richard, that it went down sixteen hours after the surrender of the Serapis. The other British vessel also surrendered, (September 23, 1779.) The brave victor made his way safely to Holland.*

Spain in the war.

The war was gathering fresh combatants. Spain, after vainly offering her mediation between Great Britain and France, entered into the lists on the side of the latter power, (June, 1779.) There was no thought of the United States in the transaction. John Jay, hastily appointed minister to Spain, (September,) could not obtain a recognition of American independence. But the United States hailed the entrance of a new nation into the arena. It was so much against their enemy, however little it was for themselves.

The beginning of 1780 beheld large detachments from the British at New York, under Clinton, the commander-in-

* He did not return to America till the beginning of 1781.

Loss of South Carolina.

chief himself, on their way southward. Charleston, twice already assailed in vain, was the first object. The siege began with five thousand British against fifteen hundred Americans, (April 11;) the numbers afterwards increasing to eight thousand on the British side and three thousand on the American. The naval forces of the attack and the defence were still more unequal. Lincoln, yet in command of the southern army, made a brave resistance, but was of course overpowered. The loss of Charleston (May 12) was followed by the loss of the state, or the greater part of it. Three expeditions, the chief under Lord Cornwallis, penetrated into the interior without meeting any repulse. So complete was the prostration of South Carolina, that Clinton returned to New York, leaving Cornwallis to retain and to extend the conquest which had been made, (June.)

Failure to recover it.

All was not yet lost. The partisans of South Carolina, like those of Georgia, held out in the upper country, whence they made frequent descents upon the British posts. The names of Thomas Sumter and Francis Marion recall many a chivalrous enterprise. Continental troops and militia were marching from the north under De Kalb, the companion of Lafayette in his voyage, and under Gates, who assumed the command in North Carolina, (July.) Thence entering South Carolina in the hope of recovering it from its conquerors, Gates encountered Cornwallis near Camden, and, although much superior in numbers, was routed, — the militia of North Carolina and Virginia leaving the few continental troops to bear the brunt of the battle in vain. The brave De Kalb fell a sacrifice upon the field, (August 16.) Two days afterwards, Sumter was surprised by the British cavalry under Lieutenant Colonel Tarleton, and his party scattered. Marion was at the same time driven into North Carolina.

Abandonment of the south.

It seemed as if the south were given up to the foe. So little exertion to defend it was made in the other portions of the country, that a rumor gained ground of an intention to abandon South Carolina and Georgia altogether. The French minister, De La Luzerne, wrote home of still greater sacrifices in contemplation. He mentions the possibility of a proposal from the British that the other states should be acknowledged to be independent if the Carolinas, both North and South, and Georgia, were surrendered. Such a proposition was never made; but it must have been thought of and talked about. Such, too, were the sectional divisions in and out of Congress, that there were some to whom the abandonment of the south wore no look of horror or of wrong.

Its defence.

Fortunately there were others, and a far greater number, who never hesitated at the necessity of defending their southern brothers. Washington, still on the watch about New York, turned anxious glances to the operations at the south. "The affairs of the Southern States," he wrote to the president of Congress, "seem to be so exceedingly disordered, and their resources so much exhausted, that whatever may be undertaken there must chiefly depend on the means carried from hence. If these fail, we shall be condemned to a disgraceful and fatal inactivity." When Gates proved incompetent to the work, Washington appointed his best officer, Major General Greene, to save the invaded states and to keep the country whole, (October.)

Darkness in the north.

It was a dark time, even in the north. Washington had looked forward, at the opening of the year, to an active campaign; but the hopes of his heart died out one by one. Lafayette, returning from a year's absence in France, where he had been unwearied in upholding the interests of America, announced the coming of an armament, both land and naval, from his country. This arrived at Newport, (July,) and there it remained during the rest of the year, blockaded by a British fleet. Washington's plans of an attack with the French upon New York fell through, to his great disappointment. What the French thought of the state of things may be gathered from a despatch of their commander, the Count de Rochambeau, to the government. "Upon our arrival here," he writes, "the country was in consternation. The paper money had fallen to sixty for one. . . . I landed with my staff without troops; nobody appeared in the streets; those at the windows looked sad and depressed. . . . Send us troops, ships, and money, but do not depend upon this people or upon their means." * It was soon afterwards that Washington wrote, "If either the temper or the resources of the country will not admit of an alteration, we may expect soon to be reduced to the humiliating condition of seeing the cause of America in America upheld by foreign arms." "But I give it as my opinion," he wrote again, "that a foreign loan is indispensably necessary to the continuance of the war." The autumn came, and Benedict Arnold, one of the officers upon whom the military fortunes of the nation had most depended, all but succeeded in betraying West Point to the enemy, (September.) He escaped, leaving Major André, with whom he had been treating, to die the death of a spy. A descent, partly of British, partly of loyalist Americans, and partly of Indians, surprised the fortresses and devastated the fields of Northern New York, (October.) Disaster was succeeding disaster, when Congress, listening to the exhortations of the commander-in-chief, again addressed itself to the organization of an army. It proposed enlistments of soldiers to continue

* Mr. Sparks's translation, in Washington's Writings, vol. vii. pp. 504-506.

during the war, and half pay of officers to continue afterwards and for life; but it was only a proposal. More effective were the exertions of the women of Pennsylvania, under the guidance of Mrs. Reed, the wife of the Pennsylvanian president, and those of New Jersey, led by Mrs. Dickinson, who raised generous subscriptions * to meet the necessities of the American army. "The spirit that animated the members of your association," wrote Washington to the ladies of Philadelphia on the death of Mrs. Reed, "entitles them to an equal place with any who have preceded them in the walk of female patriotism. It embellishes the American character with a new trait."

Light in the south.

Cornwallis, conqueror of South Carolina, prepared to march upon North Carolina. To secure the upper country, he detached a trusted officer, Major Ferguson, with a small band of regular troops and loyalists, in addition to whom large accessions were soon obtained from the tory part of the population. These recruits, like all of the same stamp, were full of hatred towards their countrymen on the American side; and fierce were the ravages of the party as Ferguson marched on. Aroused by the agony of the country, a considerable number of volunteers gathered, under various officers — Colonel Campbell, of Virginia, Colonels Cleaveland, Sevier, and Shelby, of North Carolina, and others. Nine hundred chosen men hastened to overtake the enemy, whom they found encamped in security on King's Mountain, near the frontier of South Carolina. The Americans never fought more resolutely. Ferguson was killed, and his surviving men surrendered at discretion, (October 7.) The march of Cornwallis was instantly checked; instead of advancing, he fell back. Nay,

* In paper money, upwards of $300,000; but in specie from $5000 to $7000.

more; a force which had been sent from New York to establish itself in Virginia was summoned by Cornwallis to his aid.

Holland in the war.

The year had been marked by important movements in Europe. The Empress Catharine of Russia put forth a declaration of independence, as it may be styled, in behalf of the neutral states, by proclaiming their right to carry on their commerce in time of war exactly as in time of peace, provided they conveyed no contraband articles. This doctrine was wholly at variance with the rights of search and of blockade, as asserted by England in relation to neutral nations. But it prevailed; and a league, by the name of the Armed Neutrality, soon comprehended nearly the whole of Europe. Little, however, was effected by it; the Empress of Russia herself called it her Armed Nullity. Yet the circle of hostility against England went on widening. On the accession of Holland to the Armed Neutrality, Great Britain, having just before captured a minister to the Dutch from the United States, — Henry Laurens, of South Carolina, — declared war at the close of 1780. But Holland no more became an ally of the United States than Spain had done.

Final adoption of the Confederation.

The "Articles of Confederation and Perpetual Union between the States," adopted by Congress towards the end of 1777, were still in abeyance. The states to whom they were sent for approval had found many objections to the plan of union. Some of the larger states disliked the right of the smaller states to an equal vote with themselves in Congress. The smaller opposed the claims of the larger to the unoccupied lands of the country, alleging that what was won by common exertion should be turned to common advantage. One state — New Jersey — had the wisdom to object that Congress, or the general government, was not endowed with sufficient power especially on the matter of regulating the trade of the coun try. These and other difficulties were but slowly surmounted. When all the rest had been removed, the question of the unoccupied lands was still a point upon which the articles hung motionless. The magnanimity with which this last obstacle was removed is a bright episode in the history of the times. New Jersey was the first of the smaller states to come into the Confederacy, relying upon the justice of her more powerful sisters, (November 20, 1778.) First of the landed states to cede her claims for the general welfare was New York, (February 19, 1780.) Her generosity, and the confidence of such states as New Jersey, induced the hitherto reluctant Maryland to waive her objections and sign the Articles. The thirteen were then complete, (March 1, 1781.)

Its inefficiency. Congratulations were general, and well founded, so far as they related to the closer union of the states. But nothing had been gained on the score of a national government. On the contrary, something had been lost; the powers of Congress being rather diminished than increased under the Articles of Confederation. Before their adoption, a majority of states decided a question; now, nine out of the thirteen must be united to carry any measure. The half pay for life, for instance, that had been voted to the officers of the army, was reconsidered and refused by the Congress of the Confederation, for want of nine states to vote for its fulfilment. All this had been foreboded and lamented. "A nominal head, which at present is but another name for Congress, will no longer do," — thus wrote Washington. His aide-de-camp, Hamilton, wrote that Congress must be clothed with proper authority, "by resuming and exercising the discretionary powers originally vested in them," or "by calling immediately a convention of all the states, with full authority to conclude finally upon a general confederation," (1780.) Just before the adoption of the Articles, the legislature of New York presented a formal memorial to Congress, saying, "We shall not presume to give our opinion on the question whether Congress has adequate powers or not. But we will without hesitation declare that, if they have not, they ought to have them, and that we stand ready on our part to confer them." If all these things could be said before the ratification of the Confederation, they could of course be repeated with even greater truth afterwards. A specimen of the inefficiency of the government occurs in relation to a proposal of import duties to be laid by Congress. Rhode Island refused to grant the necessary power to the government, and Virginia, after granting it, retracted it, (December, 1782.)

Defence of the Carolinas.

In the mean time events were hastening to a crisis in the field. General Greene, taking command of the southern army, with several American officers and the Pole Kosciuszko in his train, determined to save the Carolinas. He was confirmed in his purpose by his brigadier, General Morgan, who, distinguished in various actions, won a decisive victory over Tarleton at the Cowpens, in South Carolina, (January 17.) Two months later, Greene and Morgan having retreated in the interval, the main bodies of the armies, British and American, met at Guilford, in North Carolina, (March 15.) Both retired from the field; the Americans first, but the British with the greater loss. Cornwallis withdrew towards Wilmington, pursued by Greene, who presently dashed into South Carolina. There he was opposed by Lord Rawdon, who at once defeated him in an engagement at Hobkirk's Hill, near Camden, (April 25.) This was a cruel blow to Greene's hopes of surprising South Carolina. "This distressed country," he wrote, "cannot struggle much longer without more effectual support." But it was not in Greene's nature to despair. While he advanced against the stronghold of

Ninety-Six, in South Carolina, he detached a body of troops under Lieutenant Colonel Lee to join a band of Carolinians and Georgians who were besieging Augusta. The result was the surrender of that town, (June 5.) But the fort at Ninety-Six held out against repeated assaults, and Greene was obliged to retire before the superior force which Rawdon was leading to raise the siege, (June 19.) For a time, the war subsided; then Greene reappeared, and fought the action of Eutaw Springs. He lost the field of battle, (September 8;) but the British, under Colonel Stuart, were so much weakened as to give way, and retreat precipitately towards Charleston. Thus from defeat to defeat, without the intermission of a single victory, in the common sense, Greene had now marched, now retreated, in such a brave and brilliant way, as to force the enemy back upon the seaboard. The successes of the militia and of the partisan corps had been equally effective. All the upper country, not only of the Carolinas, but of Georgia, was once more in the American possession.

The central states in danger.

At the time when things were darkest at the south, greater perils arose at the centre of the country. Virginia was invaded in the first days of 1781 by a formidable force, chiefly of loyalists under the traitor Arnold. He took Richmond, but only to leave it and retire to Portsmouth, where he bade defiance both to the American militia and the French vessels from Newport, (January.) Soon after, two thousand British troops were sent from New York, under General Phillips, with directions to march up the Chesapeake against Maryland and Pennsylvania, (March.) This plan embraced the twofold idea of cutting off the Carolinas from all assistance, and of laying the central states equally prostrate. At about the same time, Cornwallis, baffled by Greene in North Carolina, set out to join the forces assembled in Virginia.

They, meanwhile, had penetrated the interior, swept the plantations and the towns, and taken Petersburg, (April.) The arrival of Cornwallis completed the array of the enemy, (May.) The very heart of the country was in danger.

Crisis.

"Our affairs," wrote Washington before the concentration of the enemy in Virginia, "are brought to an awful crisis." "Why need I run into details," he wrote again, "when it may be declared in a word, that we are at the end of our tether, and that now or never our deliverance must come?" "But we must not despair," he urged, as dangers accumulated; "the game is yet in our own hands; to play it well is all we have to do, and I trust the experience of error will enable us to act better in future. A cloud may yet pass over us, individuals may be ruined, and the country at large, or particular states, undergo temporary distress; but certain I am that it is in our power to bring the war to a happy conclusion."

American preparations.

The nation was far from being up to the emergency. A spirit of weariness and selfishness was prevailing among the people. The army, ill disciplined and ill paid, was exceedingly restless. Troops of the Pennsylvania and New Jersey lines had broken out into actual revolt at the beginning of the year. The government was still ineffective, the Confederation feeble, Congress inert, not to say broken down. When one reads that this body stood ready to give up the Mississippi to Spain, nay, to waive the express acknowledgment of American independence as an indispensable preliminary to negotiations with Great Britain, — when one reads these things, he may well wonder that there were any preparations to meet the exigencies of the times. The German Baron de Steuben, collecting troops in Virginia at the time of the invasion, was afterwards joined by Lafayette, whose troops had been clad on their march at his expense. By sea, the French fleet was engaged in defending the coasts against the invader. It seemed as if the stranger were the only defender of Virginia and of America. But on the southern border was Greene, with his troops and his partisan allies. At the north was Washington, planning, acting, summoning troops from the states, and the French from Newport, to aid him in an attack upon New York, as the stronghold of the foe, until, convinced of the impossibility of securing the force required for such an enterprise, he resolved upon taking the command in Virginia, (August 14.) Thither he at once directed the greater part of his scanty troops, as well as of the French. The allied army was to be strengthened by the French fleet, and not merely by that of Newport, but by another and a larger fleet from the West Indies.

Defeat of Cornwallis.

The British under Cornwallis were now within fortified lines at Yorktown and Gloucester, (August 1–22.) There they had retired under orders from the commander-in-chief at New York, who thought both that post and the Virginian conquests in danger from the increasing activity of the Americans, and especially the French. Little had been done in the field by Cornwallis. He had been most gallantly watched, and even pursued by Lafayette, whose praises for skill, as well as heroism, rang far and wide. Washington and the French General Rochambeau joined Lafayette at Williamsburg, (September 14.) A great fleet under Count de Grasse was already in the Chesapeake. As soon as the land forces arrived, the siege of Yorktown was begun, (September 28.) The result was certain. Washington had contrived to leave Sir Henry Clinton impressed with the idea that New York was still the main object. Sir Henry, therefore, thought of no reënforcements for Cornwallis, until they were too late, until, indeed, they were out of the question in consequence of the naval superiority of the French. In fact, an expedition to lay waste the eastern part of Connecticut was occupying Clinton's mind. He placed the loyalists and the Hessians despatched for the purpose under the traitor Arnold, who succeeded in destroying New London, (September.) Thus there were but seven thousand five hundred British at Yorktown to resist nine thousand Americans and seven thousand French, besides the numerous fleet. In less than three weeks, Cornwallis asked for terms, (October 17,) and two days afterwards surrendered.

Effect. The blow was decisive. The United States were transported. Government, army, people were for once united, for once elevated to the altitude of those noble spirits, who, like Washington, had sustained the nation until the moment of victory. "The play is over," wrote Lafayette, "and the fifth act is just finished." "O God!" exclaimed the English prime minister, on hearing of the event. "It is all over — all over!"

Prospects. It was Washington's earnest desire to avail of the French fleet in an attack on Charleston. De Grasse refused. Then Washington urged him to transport troops to Wilmington. But De Grasse alleged his engagements in the West Indies, and sailed thither. The French under Rochambeau went into winter quarters at Williamsburg, while the Americans marched, a part to reënforce the southern army, and a part to the various posts in the north. Prospects were uncertain. It was evident that the war was approaching its close, but none could tell how nearly. Washington implored his countrymen to be on the alert. Again and again he rebuked the inaction into which they were falling, as if their work was done. The British still held their post by the Penobscot. They were still strong at New York. Wilmington was evacuated by them; but

Charleston, the chief town of the south, and Savannah, remained in their hands. Lafayette wrote from France, whither he went at the close of the year, that "the evacuation of New York and Charleston are as far from British intentions as the evacuation of London."

Evacuation of the south.

It turned out differently. A vote of Parliament that the king be requested to bring the war to a close, (February 27, 1782,) led to a change of ministry. Determining to recognize the independence of the United States, and to concentrate hostilities against the European powers, the new ministry sent out Sir Guy Carleton as commander-in-chief, with instructions to evacuate New York, Charleston, and Savannah; in a word, the entire seaboard. Savannah was evacuated in the summer, (July 11,) Charleston in the early winter, (December 14.) It was the result of past campaigns, not of any present one. The Americans were without armies, without supplies, at least without such as were indispensable for any active operations. When the French under Rochambeau reached the American camp on the Hudson in the autumn, they passed between two lines of troops clothed and armed by subsidies from France. It was a touching tribute of gratitude, and an equally touching confession of weakness. All but a single corps of the French embarked at the close of the year. The remainder followed in the ensuing spring.

The European combatants.

Peace was then decided upon. It had been brought about by other operations besides those which have been described. The contest in America, indeed, was but an episode in the extended warfare of the period. Upon the sea, the fleets of Britain hardly encountered an American man-of-war. The opposing squadrons were those of France and Spain and Holland. By land, the French opposed the British in the East Indies, upon the coast of Africa, and in the West

Indies. They also aided the Spaniards to conquer Minorca, in the Mediterranean, and to assail, but in vain, the great stronghold of Gibraltar. The Spanish forces were also active in the Floridas. Holland, alone of the European combatants, made no stand against Great Britain. In the Indies, both East and West, and in South American Guiana, the Dutch were immense losers. What was gained from them, however, did not compensate for what was lost to others by the British. The preliminaries of peace, at first with America, (November 30,) and afterwards with the European powers, (January 20, 1783,) were signed to the general contentment of Great Britain, of Europe, and of America.

Cessation of hostilities.

Hostilities soon ceased. In America, Sir Guy Carleton proclaimed their cessation on the part of the British, (April 8.) Washington, with the consent of Congress, made proclamation to the same effect. By a singular coincidence, the day on which hostilities were stayed was the anniversary of that on which they were begun at Lexington, eight years before, (April 19.)

Release of prisoners.

Measures, already proposed by the British commander, were at once taken on both sides for the release of prisoners. The treatment and the exchange of these unfortunate men had given rise to great difficulties during the war. Even where actual cruelty did not exist, etiquette and policy were too strong for humanity. The horrors of the British jails and prison ships were bywords, and when their unhappy victims were offered in exchange for the better treated prisoners of the other side, the Americans hesitated to receive them. The troops that surrendered at Saratoga, on condition of a free passage to Great Britain, were detained, in consequence of various objections, to be freed only by desertions and slow exchanges after the lapse of years. In short, the prisoners of both armies seem to have been regarded in the light of troublesome burdens, alike by those who had captured them and those from whom they were captured. Individual benevolence alone lights up the gloomy scene. At the close of the war, we find Congress voting its thanks, on the the recommendation of Washington, to Reuben Harvey, a merchant of Cork, and on that of Franklin, to Thomas Wren, a minister of Portsmouth, for their humane succors to American prisoners.

Treaties of peace. Negotiations for peace met with many interruptions. So far as the United States were concerned, the questions of boundary, of the St. Lawrence and Newfoundland fisheries, of indemnity to British creditors, as well as to American loyalists, were all knotty points; the more so, that the four negotiators — Franklin, John Jay, John Adams, and Henry Laurens — were by no means agreed upon the principles by which to decide them. Some of the envoys, moreover, were possessed of the idea that France was disposed to betray her American allies; and so strong was this feeling that the consent of the French government, the point which had been agreed upon as the essential condition of making peace, was not even asked before the signature of the preliminaries already mentioned. It was before the preliminaries were signed that all these embarrassments appeared; and they continued afterwards. At length, however, definitive treaties were signed at Paris and at Versailles between Great Britain and her foes, (September 3.) * America obtained her independence, with all the accompanying privileges and possessions which she desired. She agreed, however, against her will, to make her debts good, and to recommend the loyalists, whose property had been confiscated, to the favor of the state governments. Spain recovered the Flor-

* The treaty with Holland was not concluded until the following spring.

idas. The other terms of the treaties — the cessions on one side and on the other — do not belong to our history. The treaty between Great Britain and the United States was formally confirmed by Congress at the beginning of the following year, (January 14, 1784.)

Evacuation of the north.

After long delays, the British withdrew from their post on the Penobscot. New York was evacuated, (November 25, 1783,) and ten days later, the remaining forces embarked from Staten Island and Long Island, (December 4–6.) A few western posts excepted, the territory of the United States was free.

Troubles in the American army.

The disposal of the American army had long been a serious question. A year before, the army had addressed Congress on the subject of the pay, then months, and even years, in arrears, (December, 1782.) Congress was powerless. The army was incensed. When, therefore, anonymous addresses to the officers were issued from the camp at Newburg, proposing the alternative of redress or of desertion,* the worst consequences appeared inevitable. The more so, that the excitement was greatest amongst the better class of soldiers, the "worthy and faithful men," as their commander described them, "who, from their early engaging in the war at moderate bounties, and from their patient continuance under innumerable distresses, have not only deserved well of their country, but have obtained an honorable distinction over those who, with shorter times, have gained large pecuniary rewards." Washington, and Washington alone, was equal to the crisis. He had repelled with unutterable disdain the offer of a crown from certain individuals in the army a year before, (May, 1782.) He now rebuked the spirit of the Newburg addresses, and by his majestic

* "If peace [comes], that nothing shall separate you from your arms but death; if war, that . . you will retire to some unsettled country."

integrity, quelled the rising passions of those around him. But he entered with all the greater fervor into the just claims of the army. His refusal at the outset of the war, renewed at the close,* to receive any compensation for his services to the country, placed him in precisely the position from which he could now appeal in behalf of his officers and soldiers to Congress and the nation. His voice was heard. The army obtained a promise of its pay, including the commutation to a fixed sum of the half pay for life formerly promised to the officers at the expiration of the war, (March, 1783.) All was not yet secure. But three months later, and a body of Pennsylvanian troops marched upon Congress itself in Philadelphia. Washington denounced the act with scorn. "These Pennsylvania levies," he says, "who have now mutinied, are recruits and soldiers of a day, who have not borne the heat and burden of the war." He at once sent a force to reduce and to chastise them, (June.)

Disbanding. "It is high time for a peace," Washington had written some months previously. The army was slowly disbanded, a small number only being left when the formal proclamation of dissolution was made, (November 3.) A few troops were still retained in arms. Of these, and of his faithful officers, the commander-in-chief took his leave at New York, (December 4.) Thence he repaired to Annapolis, where Congress was in session, and there resigned the commission which he had held, unstained and glorious, for eight years and a half, (December 23.)

Government of the nation. It seems as if he left no one behind him. The town and the state, each had its authorities; but the nation was without a government, at least with nothing more than the name of one. Yet the

* Just after resigning his commission, he declined the overtures of Pennsylvania to propose a national remuneration for his sacrifices.

need of a directing and a sustaining power had never been greater or clearer. If the war itself was over, its consequences, its burdens, its debts, its wasting influences, were but begun.

Washington's counsels.

No one saw this more plainly, no one felt it more deeply, than the retiring commander-in-chief. At no time had he been absorbed in his military duties. In his relations to Congress, to the states, even to the citizens, as well as in those to foreigners, whether allies or enemies, he had been almost as much the civil as the military head of the country. The arm that had led the nation through the field was now lifted to point out the paths that opened beyond. "According to the system of policy the states shall adopt at this moment," — thus Washington wrote to the governors of the states, on disbanding the army, — "they will stand or fall; and by their confirmation or lapse, it is yet to be decided whether the revolution must ultimately be considered as a blessing or a curse; a blessing or a curse, not to the present age alone, for with our fate will the destiny of unborn millions be involved." "There are four things," he continued, "which I humbly conceive are essential to the well being, I may even venture to say, to the existence, of the United States as an independent power.

"First. An indissoluble union of the states under one federal head.

"Second. A sacred regard to public justice.

"Third. The adoption of a proper peace establishment. And

"Fourth. The prevalence of that pacific and friendly disposition among the people of the United States which will induce them to forget their local prejudices and policies; to make those mutual concessions which are requisite to the general prosperity; and in some instances, to sacrifice their individual advantages to the interest of the community."

And prayers. "I now make it my earnest prayer," concluded the Christian hero, "that God would have you, and the state over which you preside, in His holy protection; that He would incline the hearts of the citizens to cultivate a spirit of subordination and obedience to government, to entertain a brotherly affection and love for one another, for their fellow-citizens of the United States at large, and particularly for their brethren who have served them in the field; and finally, that He would most graciously be pleased to dispose us all to do justice, to love mercy, and to demean ourselves with that charity, humility, and pacific temper of mind, which were the characteristics of the divine Author of our blessed religion, and without a humble imitation of whose example in these things we can never hope to be a happy nation."

CHAPTER VI.

THE CONSTITUTION.

Foreign sympathy.

ONE loves to dwell upon the sympathy from abroad for the infant nation. What had been repressed while the states were still claimed as the colonies of Great Britain broke forth after the claim was set aside. From all parts of Europe, from all parts of Great Britain itself, there came congratulations and applauses. Even sovereigns did homage to the republic. The King of France continued its friend. The King of Spain, recognizing its national existence, sent gifts and compliments to its great leader, Washington.

Lafayette's visit.

No proof of regard was dearer to Washington or to the nation than one which came from the friend and the champion of many years, the devoted Lafayette. He had spent two years and a half in generous exertions at home, when he crossed the seas to join in the American rejoicings at the definite establishment of independence. The whole people welcomed him. Divided on many points, they were united in the grateful affection which he had inspired. Soldiers and citizens, the wild borderers and the plodding townspeople, the inhabitants of every section, thronged together with a common desire of doing honor to Lafayette. He was feasted in all the principal places. Congress gave him a public reception. Washington crowned him with love and parental gratitude at Mount Vernon. After a six months' tour, he left America to share in the struggles of his native country, (August, 1784—January, 1785.)

Wants of America. He left the country of his adoption in the midst of struggles of its own. It was contending against manifold wants, some common to any youthful nation, others peculiar to itself, to a nation so unique in its history, and especially in the history of the last twenty years. It is to these wants, and to the manner in which they were supplied, that we are to turn.

Organization. Chief of them all, the one, indeed, in which they will be found to have been comprehended, like segments in a circle, was organization. The sharp points, the intersecting lines, the clashing forms of different districts and of different institutions, needed to be reduced to order within the curve, at once enfolding and harmonizing, of a national system. There was hardly a political principle upon which the entire country agreed. There was not one political power by which it was governed. Interests were opposed to interests, classes to classes; nay, men to men. When the officers of the army, for instance, formed into a society, under the name of the Cincinnati, for the purpose of keeping up their relations with one another, and more particularly of succoring those who might fall into distress, a general uproar was raised, because the membership of the society was to be hereditary, from father to son, or from kinsman to kinsman. It was found necessary to strike out this provision, at the first general meeting of the Cincinnati, (1784.) Even then, though there remained nothing but a charitable association, it was inveighed against as a caste, as an aristocracy; as any thing, in short, save what it really was. It is easy to say that all this is a sign of republicanism, of a devoted anxiety to preserve the institutions for which loss and sufferings had been endured. But it is a clearer sign of the suspicions and the collisions which were rending the nation asunder. There was but a single remedy. The people were to be united; the country was to be made one.

The states. Internal troubles

The states were absorbed in their own troubles. The debts of the Confederation lay heavy upon them, in addition to those contracted by themselves. Their citizens were impoverished, here and there maddened by the calamities and the burdens, private and public, which they were obliged to bear together. At Exeter, the assembly of New Hampshire was assailed by two hundred men with weapons, demanding an emission of paper money. All day, the insurgents held possession of the legislative chamber; but in the early evening, they were dispersed by a rumor that Exeter was taking up arms against them, (1786.) The same year, the courts of Massachusetts were prevented from holding their usual sessions by bodies of armed men, whose main object it was to prevent any collection of debts or taxes. So general was the sympathy with the movement, not only in Massachusetts, but in the adjoining states, that twelve or fifteen thousand were supposed to be ready to do the same. Nearly two thousand were in arms at the beginning of the following year, (1787.) The horror excited in the rest of the country was intense. Congress ordered troops to be raised, but as it had no power to interfere with the states, the pretext of Indian hostilities was set up. Massachusetts was fortunate in having James Bowdoin for a governor. Under his influence chiefly, — for the legislature was partly paralyzed and partly infected, — the danger was met. One or two thousand militia, under the command of General Lincoln, marched against the insurgents, at the head of whom was Daniel Shays, a captain in the continental army. Already driven back from Springfield, where they had attacked the arsenal, the insurgents retreated to

Petersham, and were there put to rout. Of all the prisoners, fourteen alone were tried and condemned, not one being executed. The insurrection had lasted about six months, (August, 1786—February, 1787.)

Dismemberments. Nor were such insurrections the only ones of the time. A body of settlers in Wyoming, principally emigrants from New England, held their land by grants from Connecticut, long the claimant of the territory. When Connecticut gave way to Pennsylvania, and the latter state insisted upon the necessity of new titles to the settlements of Wyoming, the settlers armed themselves, and threatened to set up a state of their own, (1782–87.) What was threatened there was actually executed elsewhere. The western counties of North Carolina, excited by being ceded to the United States, organized an independent government, as the state of Franklin or Frankland, (1784.) But the people were divided, and the governor, Colonel Sevier, of King's Mountain fame, was ultimately compelled to fly by the opponents of an independent organization, (1788.) Meanwhile old projects of independence had been revived in the Kentucky counties of Virginia. Petitions and resolutions led to acts of the Virginia legislature consenting to the independence of Kentucky on certain conditions, (1785–86.) Kentucky soon after petitioned Congress for admission to the Union, but without immediate effect, (1787–88.) All these instances of dismemberment, proposed or accomplished, relate to frontier settlements, where independence was suggested as much by the position as by the character of the settlers. But the older districts were stirred in the same way. Maine again and again strove to be detached from Massachusetts, (1786.)

Case of Vermont. The case of Vermont was one apart. It came up near the beginning of the war, when the inhabitants of that district, then known as the New Hampshire grants, declared it the State of Vermont, (January, 1777,) and asked admission to the Union, (July.) The request was denied, on account of the claims of New York to the territory. A number of towns in the valley of the Connecticut, and partly within the limits of New Hampshire, afterwards formed themselves into the State of New Connecticut, (1779.) This soon fell through, leaving its predecessor, Vermont, to be enlarged by the New Hampshire towns on the eastern banks of the Connecticut, together with the New York settlements as far as the Hudson, (1781.) Overtures were then made to the British authorities in Canada, with whom the Vermonters might well wish to be on good terms, so long as they were excluded from the Union. Congress took alarm, as Vermont expected, and proposed to grant admission, provided the recent annexations from New Hampshire and New York were surrendered. This was done; but Congress still kept Vermont at a distance, (1782.) A member of the body, James Madison, explains the reasons why a promise, so long delayed, was finally violated. The Eastern States, except New Hampshire, and the Central States, except New York, advocated the entrance of Vermont, while New York and the Southern States opposed it, as Mr. Madison relates, through "first, an habitual jealousy of a predominance of eastern interests; secondly, the opposition expected from Vermont to western claims; thirdly, the inexpediency of admitting so unimportant a state to an equal vote in deciding a peace, and all the other grand interests of the Union now depending; fourthly, the influence of the example on a premature dismemberment of the other states." So Vermont remained aloof, contented, one may believe, to be free from the troubles of the United States.

The strife exhibited in the case of Vermont was nothing new or temporary. Disputes between state and state arose,

Disputes between state and state.

as we have had occasion to observe, in the midst of war, and peace had not put them to rest. When Mr. Madison speaks of sectional interests, he alludes to the varieties of occupation and of investment which distinguished one state from another. Such things could not but lead to different systems in different parts of the country, the more so, especially in the north and in the south, that there were differences of character, and even of principle, to enhance the differences of pursuits or of possessions. The allusion to the western territory is to a subject already noticed in our pages. Partially settled at the time when the Confederation was completed, the question of the unoccupied lands was still undecided. It united the smaller states, as a general rule, against the larger ones, by whom the western regions were claimed. Besides these great divisions between north and south, and between the larger and the smaller states, there were others of more limited nature. Boundary questions came up, some to be determined, and others to be left undetermined, but none to subside immediately. Variances as to the share of the national debt, and more particularly as to the method of meeting it, endured from year to year. In short, the thirteen states, instead of being intertwined, were set against one another on almost every point of importance that arose amongst them.

General government.

The general government continued in the same feeble state that has been repeatedly observed. If there was any change, it was that the Confederation and its Congress had sunk to a still lower degree of inefficiency. There was even less attention to its wants on the part of the states; its requisitions went almost unanswered, their obligations almost unregarded. The superintendent of finance, Robert Morris, of Philadelphia, by whose personal exertions and advances the country had been forced through the last years of the war, laid down his office in despair, after a year of peace. His creation of a bank — the Bank of North America (1781) — was recommended by Congress to the states, with the request that branches should be established; but in vain. Congress renewed its petition, as it may be styled, for power to lay a duty on imports, if only for a limited period, (1783.) After long delay, a fresh appeal was made with really piteous representations of the national insolvency. New York refused to comply upon the terms proposed, and Congress was again humiliated, (1786.) During its efforts on this point, Congress had roused itself upon another, and asked for authority over foreign commerce. Such was the urgency of the interests at stake, that Congress went so far as to appoint a commission for the purpose of negotiating commercial treaties with the European powers, (1784.) * But the supplications of Congress to the states were once more denied, (1784-86.)

Organization of the north-west territory.

On one point alone was Congress worthy to be called a government. It organized the western territory, after having prevailed upon the states, or most of them, to abandon their pretensions to regions so remote from themselves. Virginia having followed the earlier example of New York, a plan was brought forward by one of her delegates, Thomas Jefferson, for the division and constitution of the western territory. The plan, at first, embraced the organization of the entire western territory, out of which seventeen states, all free, were to be formed. The proposed prohibition of slavery was at once voted down; otherwise the project was adopted,

* A treaty was made with only one of them, (Prussia,) but it contained substance enough for a score of old treaties, in prohibiting privateering, and sustaining the liberty of neutral commerce in case of war, (1785.) See the next chapter.

(April, 1784.) But the cessions of the states not yet covering the whole of the region thus apportioned, its organization was postponed until the national title to the lands could be made complete. Massachusetts (1785) and Connecticut (1786) ceded their claims, the latter state, however, with a reservation. Treaties with various tribes disposed in part of the Indian titles to the western territories, (1784–86.) * All these cessions completing the hold of the nation upon the tract north-west of the Ohio,† that country was definitely organized as the North-west Territory, by an ordinance of Congress, (July 13, 1787) This intrusted the government of the territory partly to officers appointed by Congress, and partly to an assembly to be chosen by the settlers as soon as they amounted to five thousand; the inhabitants and the authorities being alike bound to the observance of certain articles of compact between the old states and the new ones that might arise within the territory. These articles provided for religious liberty; for habeas corpus, trial by jury, and kindred privileges; for the encouragement of religion and education, and for justice towards the Indians; for the equal rights and responsibilities of the new states and the old; for the division of the territory into states; and lastly, for the prohibition of slavery. Under so liberal an organization, surveys, sales, and settlements followed fast. A colony from Massachusetts was the first to occupy Ohio, at Marietta, (1788.)

Difficulties with Spain.

Singular enough, while Congress was taking these steps to preserve the western domains, it was taking others to endanger them. Eager to secure a treaty

* It was many years before the Indian title was completely extinguished

† The south-west territory, though ceded in great part by the Indians, was not yet ceded by the states on whose borders it lay. South Carolina was the first to give up her claims, (August, 1787.)

of commerce with Spain, the Northern and Central States assented to surrender the navigation of the Mississippi to that power, (1786.) In this they had no less an authority upon their side than Washington, who appears to have attached more importance to internal communication between the west and the east alone than to that wider intercourse which the west would possess by means of its mighty river. Jefferson, then the American minister at Paris, was farther sighted. "The act," he wrote, "which abandons the navigation of the Mississippi, is an act of separation between the eastern and western country," (1787.) Suppose the right to the Mississippi waived, even for a limited period, and the probability is, that a large number of the western settlers, conceiving themselves sacrificed, would have separated from their countrymen, and gained a passage through the stream either in war or in alliance with Spain.

And Great Britain. Relations with Great Britain were still more disturbed than those with Spain. Nor were they less threatening to the west. The treaty of peace exacted the surrender of the western posts by Britain. But America was required at the same time to provide for the debts of great magnitude due to British merchants. This, however, was not done. Congress was unable, and the states were unwilling, to effect any thing; five states, indeed, continuing or commencing measures to prevent the collection of British debts. When, therefore, John Adams, the first minister to Great Britain, entered into a negotiation for the recovery of the posts which the British still held, he was met at once by the demand that the American part in the treaty should be fulfilled, (1786.) The subject of debts was not the only one on which the states were violating the treaty. But it was the chief infraction; and against it chiefly was directed a remonstrance which Congress addressed to the states, altogether in vain, (1787.)

Dark times. "The consideration felt for America by Europe," wrote Lafayette, "is diminishing to a degree truly painful; and what has been gained by the revolution is in danger of being lost little by little, at least during an interval of trial to all the friends of the nation." "I am mortified beyond expression," wrote Washington, "when I view the clouds that have spread over the brightest morn that ever dawned upon any country."

Old foundations. Amid this tottering of the national system, the old foundations stood secure. The laws that had been laid deep in the past, the institutions, political and social, that had been reared above them, remained to support the present uncertainties. Every strong principle of the mother country, every broad reform of the colonies, contributed to the strength and the development of the struggling nation.

Recent superstructures. Nor were recent superstructures wanting. The states, in forming and reforming their constitutions, set up many a great principle, undeveloped, if not unknown, in earlier times. Nothing, for instance, could be more novel, as well as more admirable, than the indemnity * voted by Pennsylvania to the proprietary family of which she had cast off the dominion. It was a recognition of rights belonging to rulers, that had never been made by subjects in a successful revolution. The law of inheritance was another point of new proportions. The claim of the eldest son to a double share of his father's property, if not to all the prerogatives of primogeniture, was gradually prohibited, Georgia taking the lead. Suffrage was extended in several states,† from holders of real

* £130,000 sterling, in addition to all the private domains of the family. Maryland made no such indemnity; but the representative of her proprietor was an illegitimate son.

† New Hampshire, Pennsylvania, Delaware, South Carolina, and, partially, North Carolina

or personal property to all tax-paying freemen. Personal liberty obtained extension and protection. The class of indented servants diminished. That of slaves disappeared altogether in some of the states. Massachusetts, declaring men free and equal by her Bill of Rights, was pronounced by her Supreme Court to have put an end to slavery within her limits, (1780–83.) Pennsylvania, New Hampshire, Rhode Island, and Connecticut forbade the importation of slaves, and the bondage of any persons thereafter born upon their soil. Other states declared against the transportation of slaves from state to state, others against the foreign slave trade; all, in fine, moving with greater or less energy in the same direction, save only South Carolina and Georgia. Societies were formed in many places to quicken the action of the authorities. In making exertions, and in maintaining principles like these, the nation was proving its title to independence.

Religious privileges. Nothing, however, was more full of promise than the religious privileges to which the states consented. Rhode Island, who, as formerly mentioned, had no disposition to change her existing institutions, made one alteration by striking out the prohibitory statute against Roman Catholics, (1784.) But Rhode Island was no longer alone in her glory. The majority of the state constitutions allowed entire religious liberty. The only real restrictions upon it were those to which the Puritan states still clung in enforcing the payment of taxes, and the attendance upon services in some church or other; the old leaven not having entirely lost its power. Particular forms of faith were here and there required, if not from the citizens, at any rate from the magistrates; Roman Catholics being excluded from office in several states of the north, the centre, and the south.

As there was no single fold into which the Christians of

Ecclesiastical organizations. the United States would enter, it was of the highest importance that their separate folds should be marked out and governed upon definite principles. Nothing else was likely to prevent collision among the more zealous, or straying away among the more lukewarm. The American branch of the church of England, deserted by the loyalists, and suspected, if not assailed, by the patriots, had but just survived the revolutionary struggle. It obtained its first bishop, Samuel Seabury, by ordination in Scotland, (1784,) his first associates, White and Provoost, being consecrated in England, (1787.) A convention of several states at New York declared their church the Protestant Episcopal church of the United States, (1784.) The Methodist Episcopal church, strongest in the centre and the south, obtained its first bishop, Thomas Coke, (1784.) Two years afterwards, the first Roman Catholic bishop, John Carroll, was appointed to the see of Baltimore, (1786.) The Presbyterians then formed their synods for the Central and the Southern States, (1788.) In the north, the Presbyterians and the Congregationalists, uniting to a certain degree, continued their ancient institutions. All over the country, ecclesiastical systems were reducing themselves to form and law.

Suggestions of a national Constitution. It was time for the nation to profit by the examples and the principles that have been enumerated, — time for it to guard against the conflicts and the perils that have been described. Alexander Hamilton, as mentioned in a former chapter, conceived the idea of a Convention for forming a national Constitution as early as 1780. Other individuals advocated the same measure, in private or in public. The legislature of New York supported it in 1782. The legislature of Massachusetts supported it in 1785.

In the spring of the same year, (1785,) a number of

Conventions at Alexandria and Annapolis.

commissioners from Maryland and Virginia assembled at Alexandria, for the purpose of regulating the navigation of the Chesapeake and the Potomac. They also met at Mount Vernon. James Madison was one of their number, and he suggested the appointment of commissioners with additional powers to act, with the assent of Congress, in organizing a tariff for the two states. This being recommended by the commission at Alexandria, the Virginia legislature enlarged the plan, by appointing commissioners to meet others, not only from Maryland, but from all the states, and "to take into consideration the trade of the United States." Five states were represented in a Convention at Annapolis in the autumn of the following year, (1786.) They were wise enough to see two things: one, that five states could not act for the whole; and the other, that the subject of trade was but a drop in the ocean of difficulties with which the nation was threatened. At the proposal of Alexander Hamilton, one of the commissioners, and the same who had urged the formation of a Constitution six years before, the Convention at Annapolis recommended a national convention at Philadelphia in the ensuing month of May, "to take into consideration the situation of the United States, to devise such further provisions as shall appear necessary to render the Constitution of the federal government adequate to the exigencies of the Union, and to report such an act for that purpose to the United States in Congress assembled, as, when agreed to by them, and afterwards confirmed by the legislature of every state, will effectually provide for the same."

Action of Virginia.

The first to act upon this proposal from Annapolis was the state so often foremost in the cause of the country. Thus spoke Virginia: "The General Assembly of this commonwealth, taking into view the actual situation of the Confederacy, . . . can no longer doubt that the crisis is arrived at which the good people of America are to decide the solemn question whether they will, by wise and magnanimous efforts, reap the just fruits of that independence which they have so gloriously acquired, and of that union which they have cemented with so much of their common blood, or whether, by giving way to unmanly jealousies and prejudices, or to partial and transitory interests, they will renounce the auspicious blessings prepared for them by the revolution. . . . The same noble and extended policy, and the same fraternal and affectionate sentiments which originally determined the citizens of this commonwealth to unite with their brethren of the other states in establishing a federal government, cannot but be felt with equal force now, as motives to lay aside every inferior consideration, and to concur in such further concessions and provisions as may be necessary to secure the great objects for which that government was instituted, and to render the United States as happy in peace as they have been glorious in war." Thereupon the legislature appointed its deputies to join with those of the other states "in devising and discussing all such alterations and provisions as may be necessary to render the Federal Constitution adequate to the exigencies of the Union."

Of other states and of Congress.

The noble example thus set was at once followed by New Jersey, Pennsylvania, North Carolina, and Delaware. By the time these states declared themselves, (February, 1787,) Congress, after many doubts as to the propriety of the course, came out with a call of its own. Instead, however, of taking the broad ground on which Virginia set herself, Congress limited its summons to a convention "for the sole and express purpose of revising the Articles of Confederation." The other states, Rhode Island excepted, went on to appoint their delegates. The credentials of some representations supported the liberal views of Virginia; those of others the narrower purpose of Congress. Only one state, Delaware, laid its representatives under a positive restriction, namely, to maintain the right of the state, the smallest but one in the Union, to an equal vote in any government that might be framed.

Opening of the Convention.

The same hall in which the Declaration of Independence had been adopted, more than eleven years before, and in which Congress had continued to sit during the greater part of the intervening period, in the State House at Philadelphia, was chosen for the sessions of the Convention. The day fixed for the opening arrived. "Such members as were in town" — runs the diary of Washington, who had consented, against his inclination, to sit in the Convention — "assembled at the State House; but only two states being represented, namely, Virginia and Pennsylvania, agreed to meet to-morrow," (May 14, 1787.) It must have been with anxious thoughts that the few who met found themselves obliged to separate day after day, without being able to make so much as a beginning in the work before them. At length, eleven days after the appointed time, the representatives of seven states — a bare majority — assembled and opened the Convention. As a matter of course, George Washington was elected president, (May 25.)

Aspect.

The United States of America never wore a more majestic aspect than in the Convention, which gradually * filled up with the delegates of every state except Rhode Island. The purpose of the assembly was sufficient to invest it with solemnity. To meet in the design of strengthening instead of enfeebling authority, of forming a

* New Hampshire was not represented till July 23.

government which should enable the nation to fulfil, instead of eluding its obligations alike to the citizen and the stranger, — to meet with these intentions was to do what the world had never witnessed. It is scarcely necessary to say that lower motives entered in; that the interests of classes and of sections, the prejudices of narrow politicians and of selfish men, obtruded themselves with ominous strength. Many of the members were altogether unequal to the national duties of the Convention. But they were surrounded by others of a nobler mould — by the venerable Franklin, lately returned from his French mission, the representative of the later colonial days; by various members of the Stamp Act Congress, of the Congress that declared independence, and of the subsequent Congresses before and during the Confederation; by several representatives of the younger class of patriots, notably by Alexander Hamilton and James Madison, who had been conspicuous in the movements preliminary to the Convention; and by many more whose names do not depend upon a volume like the present for reverential recollection.

Plans of a constitution.

The rules of the Convention ordered secrecy of debate and the right of each state to an equal vote. Governor Randolph, of Virginia, then opened the deliberations upon a constitution by offering a series of resolutions proposing a national legislature of two branches, a national executive, and a national judiciary of supreme and inferior tribunals. Charles C. Pinckney, of South Carolina, offered a sketch of government, based on the same principles as Randolph's, but developed with greater detail. Both the plans were referred to a committee of the whole; but Randolph's, or the Virginia plan, as it was rightly called, engrossed the debate. At the end of a fortnight the committee reported in favor of the Virginia system. Things had not gone so far without opposition, to the elements of which we will revert immediately. On the report of the committee, a new plan was offered by William Patterson, of New Jersey, embodying the views of Connecticut, New York, Delaware, and Maryland, as well as New Jersey delegates. This New Jersey plan, so styled, proposed a government of much more limited powers than that of the Virginia pattern. The two were referred to a committee of the whole. Soon after, Alexander Hamilton broached a plan of his own, going to the very opposite extreme of the New Jersey system. He was for taking the British constitution as "the best model the world has ever produced," and for creating a national government, of which the executive and the higher branch of the legislature, as well as the judiciary, should all be elected to serve during good behavior or life. Hamilton presented his plan as an exposition of his personal convictions rather than as a subject for debate, confessing that it was "very remote from the idea of the people." The question, therefore, lay between the Virginia and the New Jersey plans.

Question of powers. But there was another question to be previously decided, if not by formal vote, at least by the course of opinions. Doubt existed about the powers of the Convention. Some insisted that it could do no more than revise the Articles of the Confederation; in other words, that it might reform, but not displace, the existing government. These members were of course the supporters of the New Jersey plan. They called it by the name of federal, in opposition to the system, at the time styled anti-federal, of their opponents. The anti-federal — that is, the national men — maintained the necessity of a new government as sufficient to authorize the Convention to frame one, even if the power to do so had not been expressly given. They urged this the more, in that the Convention would not create the government, but simply recommend its creation to the nation. The difference between the two sides was, as we see, immense. As the one or as the other prevailed, so followed the fate not merely of the Virginia and the New Jersey plans, but of the Constitution and the nation.

A national system adopted.

It was, therefore, a turning point in the movements of the Convention, when the committee of the whole reported once more in favor of the Virginia plan. The labors of construction and of detail were all to be gone through. But the one guiding and assuring principle of a national system was gained, (June 19.)

Parties: small states and large states.

Parties were by this time but too distinctly defined. The federal side was taken, as a general rule, by the representatives of the small states, the national by those of the large. Whatever was upheld by the large states, especially Massachusetts, Pennsylvania, and, above all, Virginia, was, as if for this simple reason, opposed by the small ones. There was a constant dread of the dominion which, it was supposed, would be exercised by the superior states to the disadvantage and the disgrace of those of inferior rank. Perhaps the tone assumed by the large states was such as reasonably to inspire suspicion. Certain it is, that the breach between the two parties grew wider and wider, particularly when the committee and the Convention pronounced in favor of the national plan. Within ten days afterwards, Franklin, shocked by the altercations around him, moved that prayers should be said every morning. The motion was parried, partly, it was said, to prevent the public from surmising the divisions of the Convention.

Views of state government.

The starting point, so far as theory was concerned, of the two parties, was the government by states. In this, the federal members argued, resides the only principle of sovereignty, and to this recourse must be had for the life and breath of a government for the nation. Hence the name of federal, implying the support of a league — that is, a league between the states — as the true form of a general government. All this the national party opposed. We are not met, they reasoned, to fashion a Constitution out of the states or for the states, but to create a Constitution for the people; it is the people, not the states, who are to be governed and united; it is the people, moreover, from whom the power required for the Constitution is to emanate. At the same time, the national members, with a few exceptions, were far from denying the excellence of state governments. These, they urged, are precisely what we want to manage the local affairs of the different portions of the country; in this capacity, the states will be truly the pillars of the Union.

Votes of states. These views had entered largely into the debates already decided by the adoption of a national plan for the Constitution. They were again brought forward, and with renewed earnestness, in relation to a question now coming up for decision. Before the Confederation, and after it, the votes of the states in Congress had been equal, each state having a single vote, and no more. This was the rule, as has been mentioned, of the Convention. But when the point was reached in the constitutional debates, the national party insisted upon an entirely different system. The votes to be taken in the legislative branches of the new government are not, it was asserted, the votes of the states, but the votes of the people; let them, therefore, be given according to the numbers of the people, not of the states. Not so, replied the federal members, — and they had reason to be excited, for it was from apprehension on this very point that they had opposed the national plan, — not so, they replied, or our states, with their scanty votes, will be utterly absorbed in the larger states. One of the small states, Delaware, sent her representatives, as may be remembered, with express instructions to reserve her equal vote in the national legislature. But the federal party, already disappointed, found itself doomed to a fresh disappointment. Abandoning, or intimating that it was willing to abandon, the claim of an equal vote in both branches of the legislature, it stood the firmer for equality in one of the branches — the Senate of the Constitution. Even this more moderate demand was disregarded by the majority, intent upon unequal votes in both the branches.

Agitation. Great agitation followed. "We will sooner submit to foreign power!" cried a representative from one of the small states. But for the reference of the matter to a committee, who, at the instance of Franklin, adopted a compromise, making the votes of the states equal in the Senate, the work of the Convention would have come to a sudden close. As it was, the report of the committee hardly allayed the tumultuous passions that had been aroused. It but partly satisfied the small states, while it kindled the wrath of the large, secure as these thought themselves, upon the point which they were now required to yield. "If no compromise should take place," asked Elbridge Gerry, of Massachusetts, "what will be the consequence? A secession will take place, for some gentlemen seem decided on it." It was the federal party that talked of secession. The national party, no wiser, as a whole, spoke of the dismemberment and absorption of the smaller states, hinting at the sword. Two of the New York delegation, incensed or dejected by the triumphant course of the national members, deserted the Convention. "We were on the verge of dissolution," said Luther Martin, a member from Maryland, "scarce held together by the strength of a hair." Fortunately, peace prevailed. The compromise was accepted, and both national and federal members united in determining on an equal vote in the Senate and an unequal vote in the House that were to be.

Parties: north and south.

Another division besides that between the large and the small states had now appeared. It separated the north from the south. How many reasons there were for the separation has been remarked; but the reason of all, the one so strong as to lead men to acknowledge that the division between the north and the south was wider than any other in the Convention, — the great reason was slavery. This system, pierced, if not overthrown, in all the Northern and in some of the Central States, was still cherished in the south. The scanty numbers of the free population in the Southern States seemed to make slaves a necessity there.

Apportionment of representation.

The first struggle upon the point arose with respect to the apportionment of representation. It was to be decided how the people were to be represented, in what proportions, and in what classes. Upon this subject all other questions yielded to one, namely, whether slaves should be included with freemen, not, of course, as voting, but as making up the number entitled to representation. The extreme party of the south said that they must be, and on the same terms, being equally valuable as the free laborers of the north. On the other hand, the extreme party of the north declared that slaves should never be taken into account until they were emancipated, as they ought to be. The necessity for compromise was again evident. The moderate members of either side came together, and agreed that three fifths of the slave population should be enumerated with the whole of the white population in apportioning the representatives amongst the different states.

The slave trade.

A graver point was raised. In the draught of the Constitution now under debate, there stood a clause forbidding the general government to lay any tax or prohibition upon the migrations or the importations authorized by the states. This signified that there was to be no interference with the slave trade. "It is inconsistent," exclaimed Martin, of Maryland, "with the principles of the revolution, and dishonorable to the American character, to have such a feature in the Constitution!" "Religion and humanity," answered John Rutledge, of South Carolina, "have nothing to do with this question. Interest alone is the governing principle of nations. The true question at present is, whether the Southern States shall or shall not be parties to the Union." Charles C. Pinckney, calmer than his colleague, took broader ground. "If the states be left at liberty on this subject, South Carolina may perhaps by degrees do of herself what is wished, as Virginia and Maryland have already done." The opposition to the claims of the extreme south came from the Central States, especially from Virginia, not from the north. The north, intent upon the passage of acts protective of its large shipping interests, was quite ready to come to an understanding with the south. The consequence was that, instead of imitating the example of earlier years and declaring the slave trade at an end, the Convention protracted its existence for twenty years, (till 1808.) At the same time, the restriction upon acts relating to commerce was stricken from the Constitution. Dark as this transaction seems, it was still a compromise. To extend the slave trade for twenty years was far better than to leave it without any limit at all. It was at the close of these discussions that the draught of the clause respecting fugitive slaves was introduced, and accepted without discussion. The word *slaves*, however, was avoided here, as it had been in all the portions of the Constitution relating to slavery.

Details and discussions.

There is no occasion in this place for dwelling upon the details and the discussions of the Convention. Wherever there was a detail, there was almost invariably a discussion; but the interest in the debates generally was altogether subordinate to that excited by the questions which have been mentioned. On these, as the questions involving compromise, it was felt that the Constitution depended. "The Constitution which we now present" — thus ran the draught of a letter proposed to be addressed to Congress — "is the result of a spirit of amity and of that mutual deference and concession which the peculiarity of our political situation rendered indispensable." "I can well recollect," said James Wilson to his constituents of Pennsylvania, "the impression which on many occasions was made by the difficulties which surrounded and pressed the Convention. The great undertaking sometimes seemed to be at a stand; and other times its motions seemed to be retrograde."

Adoption of the Constitution.

At length, after nearly four months' perseverance through all the heat of summer, the Convention agreed to the Constitution, (September 15.) As soon as it could be properly engrossed, it was signed by all the delegates, save Gerry, of Massachusetts, — who hinted at civil war being about to ensue, — Randolph and George Mason, of Virginia, (September 17.) As the last members were signing, Franklin pointed to a sun painted upon the back of the president's chair, saying, "I have often and often, in the course of the session and the vicissitude of my hopes and fears as to its issue, looked at that sun behind the president, without being able to tell whether it was rising or setting; but now, at length, I have the happiness to know that it is a rising and not a setting sun."

Opposition in the nation.

The dawn was still uncertain. Presented to Congress, and thence transmitted to the states, to be by them accepted or rejected, the Constitution was received with very general murmurs. Even some members of the Convention, on reaching home, declared, like Martin, of Maryland, "I would reduce myself to indigence and poverty, . . . if on those terms only I could procure my country to reject those chains which are forged for it." The words imply the chief cause of the opposition excited throughout the nation. It was thought that the Constitution was too strong, that it exalted the powers of the government too high, and depressed the rights of the states and the people too low. This was the opinion of the anti-federalists — a name borne rather than assumed by those who had constituted, or by those who succeeded to, the federal party in the Convention. On the other side stood the federalists, the national party of the Convention, with their adherents throughout the country. But the names, like most party names, rather obscured than explained the relations of those to whom they were attached. The federalists were no advocates of a simple league between the states. Nor were the anti-federalists the opponents of such a league, but, on the contrary, its supporters. They opposed, not the union, but what they called the subjection of the states, proposed by the Constitution.

Constitutional writings.

One who acted for the Constitution at the time, and who wrote of it in after years, — Jeremy Belknap, then a clergyman of Boston, — tells a story illustrating the changing tempers of the period. A man has a new pair of small-clothes brought home to him. "It is too small here, says he, and wants to be let out; it is too big here, and wants to be taken in. I am afraid there will be a hole there, and you must put on a patch; this button is not strong enough — you must set on another." But, taking his wife's advice, he tried on the garment, and found himself satisfied. The constitutional writings, as they may be called, of the twelvemonth succeeding the Convention, were far in advance of any preceding productions of America. The greatness of the cause called forth new powers of mind, nay, new powers of heart. Washington's letters upon the subject overflow with emotions such as his calm demeanor had seldom betrayed before. Under the signature of Publius, Alexander Hamilton, James Madison, and John Jay united in the composition of the Federalist. It was a succession of essays, some profound in argument, others thrilling in appeal, and all devoted to setting forth the principles and foretelling the operations of the Constitution. Under the signature of Fabius, John Dickinson — the same whose Farmer's Letters had pleaded for liberty twenty years before — now pleaded for constitutional government. It was not merely the Constitution that was thus rendered clear and precious. The subject was as wide as the rights of man.

Adoption by the states.

So strong and so wise exertion was not in vain. State after state, beginning with Delaware, (December 7, 1787,) assented to the Constitution, some by large, some by exceedingly small majorities. In most of the bodies by which the ratification was declared, a series of amendments was framed and passed. North Carolina assented only on condition of her amendments being adopted. In one of the state Conventions, New York, the recommendation of another general Convention was pressed upon the nation. New York was the scene of more decided demonstrations. The list of what can be called riots throughout the country, at the time, begins and ends with a collision between two bands of the rival parties, at Albany, and the destruction of the type in an anti-federalist newspaper establishment at New York, (July 4–27, 1788.) The project of a second Convention found favor in Pennsylvania. It was then taken up by the assembly of Virginia, but after the Convention of that state had accepted the Constitution. In seeing these states arrayed in greater or less strength against the Constitution, one is struck by their being large states, to which the Constitution was supposed to be particularly acceptable. The other of the largest states, Massachusetts, had but a bare majority to give in favor of the Constitution. On the other hand, several of the small states were now the most earnest supporters of federalist principles. The causes of this revolution were chiefly local. But, actuated by different motives, the large states, or rather the parties in the large states, opposing the unconditional adoption of the Constitution, were unable to combine with any effect. The generous impulses and the united exertions of their opponents carried the day. Only North Carolina and Rhode Island stood aloof, and the former but partially, when Congress performed the last act preliminary to the establishment of the Constitution, by appointing days for the requisite elections and for the organization of the new government, (September 13, 1788.)

Character of the transaction.

Thus was completed the most extraordinary transaction of which merely human history bears record. A nation enfeebled, dismembered, and dispirited, broken by the losses of war, by the dissensions of peace, incapacitated for its duties to its own citizens or to foreign powers, suddenly bestirred itself and prepared to create a government. It chose its representatives without conflicts or even commotions. They came together, at first only to disagree, to threaten, and to fail. But against the spells of individual selfishness and sectional passion, the inspiration of the national cause proved potent. The representatives of the nation consented to the measures on which the common honor and the common safety depended. Then the nation itself broke out in clamors. Still there was no violence, or next to none. No sort of contention arose between state and state. Each had its own differences, its own hesitations; but when each had decided for itself, it joined the rest and proclaimed the Constitution.

Sympathy for mankind.

The work thus achieved was not merely for the nation that achieved it. In the midst of their doubts and their dangers, a few generous spirits, if no more, gathered fresh courage by looking beyond the limits of their country. Let Washington speak for them. "I conceive," says he, " under an energetic general government, such regulations might be made, and such measures taken, as would render this country the asylum of pacific and industrious characters from all parts of Europe," — "a kind of asylum," as he says in another place, "for mankind." It was not, therefore, for America alone that her sons believed themselves to have labored, but for the world.

Literature of the revolution and the Constitution.

It has already appeared that the writings of the soldiers and the statesmen of the period were, in many instances, as important as their actions. There were other writers, who stood conspicuous, solely or almost solely, on account of their literary exertions. Such was Thomas Paine, an Englishman, whose pamphlet of Common Sense (1776) had so great an effect that its author, though then but a few months in the country, pretended afterwards to have started the revolution. His later pamphlets, issued during the war under the name of the Crisis, were of equal power. Amongst the American authors were John Trumbull, of Connecticut, whose poem of McFingal (begun 1774) was a satire at once upon his countrymen and upon their foes; Francis Hopkinson, of Philadelphia, who, after various productions in prose and in rhyme relating to the war, came to the aid of the Constitution in an allegory entitled the New Roof; and Philip Freneau, of New York, whose verses upon the battles of the revolution were amongst the most popular and the most artistic compositions of the times. The influence of such a literature may be conceived. It spread the stirring spirit of the camp and of the council around the fireside and within the closet, kindling sympathy, arousing action, and thus contributing largely to the national redemption.

The music of Billings.

Nor should we forget, in this connection, the influence of the first of our composers, William Billings, a Bostonian. Such was his enthusiasm at once for his art and for his country, that, though almost uneducated as a musician, he moved many a spirit by his ardent strains. His melodies were heard on the march and on the battle field as well as in the choir; such as his Independence and his Columbia may be called psalms of the revolution and of the Constitution.

CHAPTER VII.

WASHINGTON'S ADMINISTRATION.

Washington president.

THE name of Washington was almost a part of the Constitution. "The Constitution would never have been adopted," — thus Edmund Randolph, by no means a strong adherent to Washington, wrote to him afterwards, — "but from a knowledge that you had once sanctioned it, and an expectation that you would execute it." "The Constitution," Lafayette wrote at once from Paris, "satisfies many of our desires; but I am much mistaken if there are not some points that would be perilous, had not the United States the happiness of possessing their guardian angel, who will lead them to whatever still remains to be done before reaching perfection." Such was the universal voice of the nation, and of the nation's well wishers. The presidential electors gave in their votes without a single exception in favor of Washington; and he consented to what he had reason to call "this last great sacrifice." "I bade adieu to Mount Vernon," he writes in his diary, "to private life, and to domestic felicity; and with a mind oppressed with more anxious and painful sensations than I have words to express, set out with the best disposition to render service to my country in obedience to its call, but with less hope of answering its expectations."

The two houses of Congress had been organized in New

Organization of government.

York, after a month's delay.* A day or two before Washington's arrival, John Adams took his place as vice president. The inauguration of the president, postponed a few days after he was ready for the ceremony, at length completed the organization of the government, (April 30, 1789.)

Solemnity of the work.

It was one thing for Washington to receive the homages of his countrymen, on his journey to the seat of government, and on his entrance into office there; all this was smiling to the eye, and full of promise to the ear. But it was another thing to remember the weaknesses and the divisions of the nation; to behold the present sources of peril; and to feel that the Constitution was still an untried instrument, unmoved, perhaps unmovable. Whatever has been said of the solemnity of former periods, or of former duties, must be repeated with stronger emphasis of the work now before Washington and his coadjutors. Of far greater difficulty than the formation of the Constitution was the setting it in operation. Washington knew it all. And almost the first words which broke from his lips, as president of the United States, were words of prayer. "It would be peculiarly improper," he said at the beginning of his inaugural speech, "to omit in this first official act my fervent supplications to that Almighty Being who rules over the universe, who presides in the councils of nations, and whose providential aids can supply every human defect, that His benediction may consecrate to the liberties and happiness of the people of the United States, a government instituted by themselves for these essential purposes, and may enable every instrument employed in its

* March 4 being the appointed day; and the House not having a quorum till March 30, the Senate none till April 6.

administration to execute with success the functions allotted to his charge."

Washington to his fellow-Christians.

In the same spirit Washington invoked the support of those around him, not merely as his fellow-countrymen, but as his fellow-Christians. Among all the addresses hailing his accession to the presidency, from political and industrial, from literary and scientific bodies, none seemed to please him more than those received from religious organizations. In his replies, he remarks upon his need of their sympathies and prayers. Convinced that nothing could so bind the nation together as charity amongst the different branches of Christians, he insists upon it with peculiar earnestness. In an address to his own church, the Protestant Episcopal, he expresses his joy "to see Christians of different denominations dwell together in more charity, and conduct themselves in respect to each other with a more Christian-like spirit, than ever they have done in any former age or in any other nation." To the church that had been an object of persecution through the whole colonial period, the Roman Catholic, the president wrote as follows: "I hope ever to see America among the foremost nations in examples of justice and liberality. And I presume that your fellow-citizens will not forget the patriotic part which you took in the accomplishment of their revolution, and the establishment of their government."

The nation.

These principles, so far above any of a merely political character, were to be applied to a nation now numbering nearly four millions.* This was the population of all the thirteen states. The Constitution, as will be recollected, went into operation with the assent of but

* The census of 1790 gave, whites, 3,172,464; free blacks, 59,466; slaves, 697,897: total, 3,929,827.

eleven. North Carolina acceded in eight months, (November 13;) Rhode Island in fifteen, (May 29, 1790.)

Work of Congress. The departments and the judiciary.

The great feature of the opening years of Washington's administration was the work of Congress, the body upon whose laws the government depended for movement, if not for life. The departments were organized; one of state, one of the treasury, and one of war; each being under the control of a secretary. The three secretaries, with an attorney general, constituted the cabinet of the president; the postmaster general not being a cabinet officer until a later period. Washington appointed Thomas Jefferson the first secretary of state, Alexander Hamilton the first secretary of the treasury, Henry Knox the first secretary of war, Edmund Randolph the first attorney general, and Samuel Osgood the first postmaster general, (September, 1789.) At the same time, he made his appointments for the offices of the judiciary; Congress having created a Supreme Court, with Circuit and District Courts appended. John Jay was the first chief justice of the United States.

Amendments to the Constitution.

Congress had already launched into constitutional discussions. The amendments to the Constitution, proposed by the different states, were numerous enough — fifty and upwards — to call for early attention. It was not suggested either by the states or by their congressional representatives, to make any fundamental alterations in the Constitution. The old federal, now the anti-federalist party, from whom most of the amendments came, asked for no subversion of the national system. They were contented with a few articles, declaring the states and the people in possession of all the powers and all the rights not otherwise surrendered to the general government. These articles, to the number of ten, were adopted by Congress, and accepted by the states.

Revenue.

A far more vital matter was the revenue. To this Congress addressed itself in the first weeks of the session. The result of long and difficult debates was the enactment of a tariff, intended to serve at once for revenue and for protection of domestic interests. A tonnage duty, with great advantages to American shipping, was also adopted. Some time afterwards, indeed towards the close of the first Congress, an excise was laid on domestic spirits. These measures were modified at intervals. But beneath them, in all their forms, there continued the principle, that the duties upon imports were to provide for government in the shape of a revenue, and for the nation in the shape of protection. It was no time for free trade.

Credit.

It fell to the first Congress, likewise, to provide for the public credit. The debts of the Confederation amounted to fifty-four millions of dollars, or to eighty millions if the debts of the states, incurred for general objects, were added. It was the plan of Hamilton, secretary of the treasury, that these debts should be taken as a whole to be assumed and funded by the new government. All sorts of opinions were started. Agreeing that the foreign debt should be treated in the manner proposed, the members of Congress were altogether at variance upon the subject, first, of the domestic debt due from the Confederation itself, and second, of the debt due from the separate states of the Confederation. On the first point, it was argued by a large number, that the certificates of the public debt were no longer in the hands of the original holders, and that to fund them at their par value was simply to put money into the pockets of speculators to whom the first holders had transferred them at great sacrifices. On the second point, that of assuming the state debts, the opposition was still more earnest, especially from the representatives of those states whose exertions during the war of the revolution had been comparatively limited. It was a matter, moreover, to be supported or opposed according to the various views of the state and the national governments. They who, like the proposer of the system, desired to see the national government strong, advocated its being made the centre of the public credit; while they who inclined to the rights of the states, preferred to have the debt remain in state rather than in national stocks.

Manner of decision.

The question was not decided upon any abstract grounds. It had been a bone of contention where the seat of the general government should be located, some going for one place and some for another. When the House of Representatives decided against assuming the state debts, the advocates of the assumption hit upon the plan of securing the necessary votes from some of the Virginian or Maryland members, by consenting to fix the projected capital on the Potomac.* The bait was snapped at, and a measure on which the honor of the states, if not of the nation, depended, passed by means of unconcealed intrigue. The state debts were then assumed, not in mass, but in certain proportions. This being the chief object of altercation, the funding of the domestic and foreign debt of the general government was rapidly completed, (August 4, 1790.) The transaction was by no means to the satisfaction of the entire nation. Even Virginia, whose representatives had voted for the scheme, considering their state to be amply repaid by the location of the capital on the Potomac, declared against the whole system, save only that part relating to the foreign debt. The funding of the general domestic debt was pronounced to be "dangerous to the rights, and subversive of the interests, of the people;" while that of the state debts was "repugnant to the Constitution." The opposition did not end here.

* Philadelphia to be the capital until 1800.

National bank.

The public creditors, on the other hand, were delighted. All the moneyed interests of the country, indeed, were quickened, the public bonds being so much additional capital thrown into the world of industry and of commerce. The creation of a national bank, with the design of sustaining the financial operations of government, took place in the early part of the following year, (1791.) On the opening of the subscription books, a signal proof of the confidence now placed in the national credit was given, the whole number of shares offered being taken up in two hours. At the same time, the number and the earnestness of the party averse to these movements of the government were increased by the success with which they were attended. It had been made a question in the very cabinet of the president, by Jefferson and Randolph, whether the charter of the bank was not beyond the limits of the Constitution. Washington himself had hesitated to approve the act of Congress.

Parties.

The construction of the Constitution was one of the points on which parties were now contending. It was a natural principle with the federalists that the Constitution should be interpreted freely; that is, in such a way as to give the government the full measure of its powers. On the other hand, the anti-federalists were for limiting the provisions of the Constitution, if not as far as possible, at least as far as they thought required by the independence of the states and of the people. Every subject brought before Congress excited questions of congressional powers. The organization of the government, the creation of a tariff, of a national debt, and, as just mentioned, of a bank, all were argued for or against, according to the different views of the work to be done by Congress. Party spirit, however, was by no means confined to constitutional arguments. It appeared on every occasion, charging the federalists, now the dominant class, with monarchical schemes as their ends, and with corrupt dealings as their means; while the anti-federalists, who took the name of republicans, were accused of tendencies to intrigue and to sedition. So violent was the temper on both sides, that the cry went up of separation from the Union. This, too, when the Union was but just formed.

Especially north and south.

But of all the passions so prematurely exploding, none were so threatening as those of the north and the south. The same division that had been observed to be wider than any other before the Constitution, continued wider than any still. Even the controversies between the federalists and the republicans were not so great or so absorbing as to crowd out the matters of dissension between the Southern and the Northern States. Nay, the divisions of the two portions of the country were rather enhanced by those between the two parties; for although there were many republicans in the north and many federalists in the south, yet the south, as a general rule, was republican, and the north federalist. This was inevitable. The interests of the northern industry, its shipping, its commerce, and its manufactures, called for a very different policy on the part of the government from that demanded by the southern agriculture.

Points concerning slavery.

The great line of distinction was run by slavery. The points of this thorny subject, so far from being smoothed by the compromises of the Constitution, stood up as bristling as ever. In the very first year of the new government, there came petitions from the Quakers of Pennsylvania, Delaware, and New Jersey, asking for the abolition of the slave trade. With this, as stated in the account of the Convention, Congress had no power to interfere for a period of twenty years. But the introduction of the subject brought up a storm, as it was called by a member from Georgia, which lasted for days and even weeks, until the adoption of a committee's report that Congress had no authority over the slave trade, except with foreign countries, until 1808, the date prescribed by the Constitution. At the same time, all pretensions to control the treatment or the emancipation of slaves, in the states where they existed, were expressly abjured by Congress. This did not prevent an earnest Delaware Quaker from petitioning some two or three years afterwards for the abolition of slavery. The petition was returned to the petitioner, (November, 1792.) A later memorial, (January, 1794,) from a convention of societies for the abolition of slavery, held at Philadelphia, asking Congress to take such measures as the Constitution allowed against the slave trade, resulted in an act prohibiting the trade with foreign lands. So far as related to the slave trade, there seems to have been no opposition on the part of the Southern States to its suppression. They were all moving more or less actively in the same direction.* What they opposed was the interference of Congress with slavery within the limits of the country.

As to the territories.

On this particular point the opposing theories of after years were not yet distinctly formed. But there was an evident foreboding of future divisions. It was generally agreed that Congress had no power in relation to slavery in the states. But it was generally urged on one side, and by no means generally repelled on the other, that the existence of slavery, as of any other system, in the territories, did depend upon Congress. There were the clauses of the Constitution — "The Congress shall have power to dispose of, and make all needful rules and regulations respecting, the territory or other property

* The traffic was prohibited in all the states by 1798. South Carolina, however, revived it in 1804.

belonging to the United States;" "New states may be admitted by the Congress into this Union." On these the opponents of slavery relied, as empowering Congress to exclude the system from any territories to be organized, or any states to be admitted. The great precedent of the Northwest Territory, where slavery was expressly prohibited by the Congress of the Confederation, was ratified by the first Congress under the Constitution. It claimed — so the northern men felt — to be not only ratified, but followed. That it might be followed, was distinctly amongst the apprehensions of the southerners, the more naturally from its having been proposed by one of themselves, Thomas Jefferson, as we have read, to exclude slavery from all the unsettled territories. When North Carolina ceded her western lands to the Union, she did so on the express condition "that no regulation made or to be made by Congress shall tend to the emancipation of slaves," (1789.)

Starting point of future strife.

Here was the starting point of all future strife. It was in the power of Congress to reject the proposed condition on the ground that its authority over the territories was not thus to be trammelled. Or it might have taken exactly the opposite ground, and declared that it had no right to impose any conditions upon the territories. Supposing either position to have been taken permanently, the question of slavery in the territories might have come up again. But the constitutional principle on which it could be decided as often as it recurred, would have been established. Of all this there seems to have been little or no perception. Not even Washington — he who was so fixed against all sectional divisions — exerted himself to close this prolific source of bitterness and of contention. Congress accepted the cession of North Carolina, and organized the district as the Territory South of the Ohio, (1790.)

Presidential tours.

Meanwhile the unity of the country, despite its parties and its broils, had been happily illustrated in the tours of the president. He first visited the New England States, Rhode Island excepted,* (October, November, 1789;) then Rhode Island, (August, 1790;) and, lastly, the Central and Southern States, (April–June, 1791.) No earthly potentate had ever received such homage as the republican magistrate, the revolutionary chief, the Christian man, all blended in Washington. It was a homage offered principally to the individual, but the light which shone about him was diffused over the nation of which he was the head and the representative.

Work of the states.

The states had not been idle. They were learning their new relations to the general government, and, through this, to one another. Within their own borders, much was to be done to set up the law that had been shaken and the order that had been disturbed for the ten, twenty, or even thirty years before. Many of the late Constitutions were remodelled, and some new ones were framed.

New states.

New states were presenting themselves for admission into the line of the thirteen. The consent of New York having been obtained, Vermont was admitted, (March 4, 1791.) Provision was already made for the entrance of Kentucky in the following year, (June 1, 1792.) The Territory South of the Ohio was subsequently admitted as the State of Tennessee, (June 1, 1796.)

Dependence upon Washington.

But the interest of the period was concentrated on the general government. By this, it was felt, and not by any local authorities or any local movements, the difficulties of the nation were to be met and overcome. The general government itself was concen-

* Not then a member of the Union.

trated in Washington. They who deny him power of character, acknowledging his excellence and his judiciousness, without acknowledging his inspiration of thought and his energy of action, may turn to the group gathered at Philadelphia, the capital, and see the eyes of their heroes, federalist or republican, northerner or southerner, all fixed on Washington for protection, especially as the four years of his presidency drew to a close. Jefferson, the head of the republicans, wrote to him, "The confidence of the whole Union is centred in you. Your being at the helm will be more than an answer to every argument which can be used to alarm and lead the people in any quarter into violence or secession. North and south will hang together, if they have you to hang on." "It is clear," wrote Hamilton, the leader of the federalists, "that a general and strenuous effort is making in every state to place the administration of the national government in the hands of its enemies, as if they were its safest guardians; that the period of the next House of Representatives is likely to prove the crisis of its permanent character; that, if you continue in office, nothing materially mischievous is to be apprehended — if you quit, much is to be dreaded." Randolph, the attorney general, — a sort of leader to a middle party, neither wholly federalist nor wholly republican, — was equally pressing. "The fuel," he wrote to Washington, "which has been already gathered for combustion, wants no addition. But how awfully might it be increased, were the violence which is now suspended by a universal submission to your pretensions let loose by your resignation!" Thus urged, Washington could do no less than accept the unanimous summons to another term of labor for his country. Adams was again chosen vice president, (1792–93.)

There was one thing over which Washington had no influence. The animosity of parties had spared him, but

Animosity of parties.

without being checked by him. He vainly exerted himself to keep the peace, even in his own cabinet. Jefferson and Hamilton were at swords' points, and at swords' points they remained until Jefferson retired, (1794.) In Congress, all was uproar. The slightest question sufficed to set the northerner against the southerner, the federalist against the republican. Out of Congress, the tumult was increasing. Influences to which we must revert had swelled the dissensions of the nation with "very different views," as Washington wrote, "some bad, and, if I might be allowed to use so harsh an expression, diabolical." A new party, chiefly from the republican ranks, had gathered, under the name of democrats, in societies of which the model was taken from abroad, and which, as Washington wrote, might "shake the government to its foundation."

Insurrection in Pennsylvania.

The fearful passion of the time at length broke out in insurrection. In consequence of the excise upon domestic spirits, some parts of the country where distillation was common had been greatly discontented. North Carolina and Pennsylvania, or rather the interior counties of those states, had been agitated to such a degree, that the president deemed it necessary to issue a proclamation, calling upon his fellow-citizens to support the laws, (1792.) The excitement gradually subsided, except in Pennsylvania, where, after various acts of violence, an armed convention, seven thousand strong, met at Braddock's Field, (August, 1794.) The president of this assembly was a Colonel Cook, the secretary, Albert Gallatin, a Swiss emigrant; and the commander of the troops a lawyer named Bradford. Of course, the objects of so large a body were various; some being intent merely upon suspending the collection of the excise, while others meditated the possession of the country, and separation from the Union. The president at once put forth a proclamation, "warning the insurgents to desist from their opposition to the laws." Commissioners were at the same time appointed to proceed to the scene of disturbance, and persuade the actors to return to their duty. It being found, however, that nothing but force, or the show of force, would put down the insurrection, another proclamation was published, announcing the march of fifteen thousand militia from Pennsylvania, New Jersey, Maryland, and Virginia. The president himself took the field for a few days; but finding that the insurgents had disappeared before the approach of his troops, he left his officers — General Henry Lee, governor of Virginia, being commander-in-chief — to complete the work that was no sooner begun than it was ended. A considerable number of prisoners was taken; but no executions followed, (November.) Enough had been done to decide "the contest," as Washington described it, "whether a small proportion of the United States shall dictate to the whole Union."

Indian wars. The same year (1794) witnessed the suppression of a danger, half domestic and half foreign — a long-continued Indian war. It broke out, four years before, on the attempt of various western tribes to recover the country as far as the Ohio. A thousand men, partly United States troops, and partly militia from Pennsylvania and Kentucky, were sent into the heart of the hostile region. Two detachments, under Colonel Hardin, fell into ambuscades; while the main body, under General Harmer, marched, countermarched, and at length retreated, (1790.) The next year, after several incursions of volunteers into the Indian territory, an army of some two thousand, under General St. Clair, started, late in the autumn, to reduce the enemy. Delayed by the construction of forts, the troops were advancing but slowly, when they were surprised in camp, and utterly routed by the Indians, (1791.) Two years passed in fruitless attempts at negotiation. An army of three or four thousand, slowly enlisted under the command of General Wayne, the hero of Stony Point, at length proceeded to more decisive measures. Spending the winter and the spring in camp, Wayne took the field in the following summer. Securing his rear by forts along the route which he pursued, he overtook and completely vanquished the Indians, driving them from their posts, and laying waste their fields, (1794.) A treaty made with Wayne a year afterwards (1795) renounced the claims which had led the unhappy Indians into war. There still remained upon the south-western borders the restless tribes that had taken up arms from time to time during the war with their brethren of the north-west. Peace with them was made a year later, (1796.) In both treaties, the United States took an attitude never before assumed by the whites, as a nation, towards the red man. The truth that the Indians were not the aggressors so much as the borderers, nay, the United States themselves, seems to have been tacitly recognized by the indemnities to the conquered or the pacified tribes.

Indian interests. It was equally new in the history of the Indian race, that the white men should unite nationally in supplying their wants and improving their relations. No part of Washington's administration, domestic or foreign, was more original or more benign than the policy which he constantly urged towards the Indians of the United States. To save them from the frauds of traders, a national system of trade was adopted. To protect them from the aggressions of borderers, as well as to secure them in the rights allowed them by their treaties, a number of laws were prepared. "I add with pleasure," said the president in one of his later addresses to Congress, "that the probability of their civilization is not diminished by the experiments which have been thus far made under the auspices of government. The accomplishment of this work, if practicable, will reflect undecaying lustre on our national character, and administer the most grateful consolation that virtuous minds can know," (December, 1795.)

Heckewelder, the missionary.

Among the agents employed by the administration in dealing with the Indians was a remarkable man. John Heckewelder, born in England, of German parentage, came to Pennsylvania in his youth, and there in his early manhood became a missionary of the United Brethren, or Moravians, amongst the Delawares and the Mohegans, (1771.) His life thenceforward was devoted to the Indians. He preached to them, that they might be converted to God. He wrote of them, that they might be respected of men. "I still indulge the hope," he wrote in his old age, "that this work [for the Indians] will be accomplished by a wise and benevolent government."

Tribute to Algiers.

A far more savage foe than the Indian was appeased at the same period, but with much less credit, it must be added, to the nation. This was the Dey of Algiers, who, with a number of neighbors like himself, was wont to sweep the seas with piratical craft. Singular to say, the sway of these buccaneering potentates was acknowledged by the European states, who paid an annual tribute on condition of their commerce being spared. Ten years before the present date, the freebooters of the Dey of Algiers had captured two American vessels, and thrown their crews into bondage. He now (1795) consented to release his captives, and to respect the merchantmen of the United States, on the reception of a tribute like that received from the powers of Europe. Three quarters of a million were paid down; an annual payment of full fifty thousand dollars being promised in addition. Other treaties of the same sort with Tripoli and Tunis were under way.

Foreign relations. The relations of the United States with civilized nations were hardly more satisfactory. The monarchies of Europe looked down, if they looked at all, upon the infant republic, of which many of them really knew almost nothing. What was of vast moment to a people rising out of depression and of obscurity, was a trifle in the eyes of old states, accustomed to deal with great interests and with great resources. Their relations with America were matters of little concern to them. On the other hand, the relations of America to them, or to some of them, formed the chief point of attention and of exertion with the American nation for a quarter of a century.

Commercial treaties. We must go back to days over which we have passed, in order to see how the United States presented themselves to the older nations. "Our fathers," said John Quincy Adams, himself a foreign minister under Washington, "extended the hand of friendship to every nation on the globe." Their first treaty, the one with France, in which the affairs of commerce and of peace were mingled with those of alliance and of war, was followed by one with Prussia, (1785.) "This," remarked Adams, "consecrated three fundamental principles of foreign intercourse. First, equal reciprocity and the mutual stipulation of the commercial exchanges of peace; secondly, the abolition of private war on the ocean; and thirdly, restrictions favorable to neutral commerce upon belligerent parties with regard to contraband of war and blockades. These principles were assumed as cardinal points of the policy of the Union." It was a policy, however, in perpetual collision with the usages and prerogatives of the European powers; so much so, that, though the young nation held out an open hand, it was met by contracted grasps. The state of things will appear as we go on to the negotiations of Washington's administration.

Treaty with Spain.

One of the first to come into more settled relations with the new government was Spain. That power, through its colonial authorities in Florida, had been supposed to be tampering with the southern Indians. On the other hand, it was notorious that several expeditions from the southern and western frontiers were planned against the Spanish territory. All the while, the dividing line between Florida and the United States was unsettled, and the claim to the navigation of the Mississippi undetermined. Finally, a special envoy, Thomas Pinckney, was sent to Spain. It took him nearly a year to bring about a treaty defining the Florida boundary, and opening the Mississippi to the United States, (1795.) Even then the Spaniards delayed to fulfil provisions in which they took but small interest.

Relations with Great Britain and France.

The relations with Spain were bad enough. But those with Great Britain and France were worse. We must speak of these nations together, since it was their common, rather than their separate, influences which operated to the extent that is to be described. Side by side, in the first place, were the feelings of amity to France and of animosity to Britain; the seeds were planted in war, and their growth was not checked in peace. Britain continued to wear the aspect of an antagonist, keeping her troops upon the United States territory until her demands were satisfied, while on the other side of the sea she laid one restraint after another upon commerce, as if she would have kept the Americans at a distance from her shores. France, on the contrary, was still the friend of the rising nation, and not only as its patron, but as its follower. The same year that Washington entered the presidency, the French revolution began.

Its early movements, professedly inspired by those that had taken place in America, kindled all the sympathies of American hearts. Hitherto, the bond between them and the French was one of gratitude and of dependence; now it was one of sympathy and of equality.

Parties thereupon.

But we are not to imagine our fathers to have harmonized upon these points any more than upon the others that have been noticed. The nation was by no means unanimous against Great Britain, by no means unanimous for France. Deep, indeed, but still in action, were the sentiments of former times when France was the foe, and Britain the mother-land. To these a new impulse was given by the early excesses of the revolution. With their ideas of law and order, the Americans could not go along with the French, rioters from the first, and soon destroyers and murderers, rather than freemen. Many paused, and turning with distrust from the scenes of which France was the unhappy theatre, looked with kinder emotions towards the sedater and the wiser Britain. It would be too much to say that this led to a British party; but it did lead to a neutral one, while, on the other hand, a French party, applauding the license as well as the liberty of the revolution, clapped their hands the more enthusiastically as the spectacle became wilder and bloodier. This party was the republican; its more impetuous members being the democratic republicans. Their opponents were the federalists. The new dissensions came just in time to keep up the division between the two. Mere federalist and republican questions might have waned; they were already less glowing than they had been. They were revived by the strife of the French with the anti-French party.

Few had spoken of doing more than looking on at the events in Europe. Yet there were some so excited, so maddened, as to be ready for any extremities, especially

Washington proclaims neutrality. when the France whom they worshipped declared war against the Britain whom they abhorred. More divided than ever, the nation was again close upon the breakers, when Washington — never greater, never wiser — issued his proclamation of neutrality, making it known "that the duty and interest of the United States require that they should with sincerity and good faith adopt and pursue a conduct friendly and impartial towards the belligerent powers," (April 22, 1793.) It is a memorable act in our history.

Point proposed. Its purpose is not always rightly estimated. Look at the nation tasked to its utmost, one may almost say, to subdue a few Indian tribes, obliged to pay tribute to the Algerines, unable to keep the Spaniards to their obligations, and we shall not behold a power that could enter safely into European wars. If such a thing were attempted, it would be at the hazard of the independence that had been achieved. There were two risks; one arising from the certainty that the United States must be a subordinate ally in any war to which it became a party; and the other, — a still graver one, — that the passions aroused by a foreign would find no vent but in a civil war. It was, as he said, "to keep the United States free," that Washington proclaimed neutrality.

Mission of Genet. The system was soon put to trial. France, having baptized herself a republic in the blood of her king, Louis XVI., sent a new minister to the United States in the person of citizen Genet. An enthusiastic representative of his nation, Genet excited a fresh enthusiasm in the French party of America. Feasted at Charleston, where he landed, (April, 1793,) and at all the principal places on the route northward, he was led to imagine the entire country at his feet, or at those of the French republic. He began at Charleston to send out privateers, and to order that their prizes should be tried and condemned by the French consuls in the United States. It was a part of the treaty of commerce between the two nations, that the privateers and prizes of the French should be admitted to the American ports. But Genet was soon to be checked. He had not merely a divided people to deal with, but a government; and although the government itself had its divisions, it was so far accordant as to oppose the ambassador, to whom, on his arrival at Philadelphia, it stood ready to declare that whatever the treaty provided for, it did not provide for the commission of privateers or the condemnation of prizes within American limits. This is not the place to describe the proceedings of so wild a personage as Genet. He did battle for his privateers and his courts; appealed from the executive to Congress and the people; and pursued so extreme a course as to set his supporters and his opponents bitterly at variance. The French party now went openly for war against England. "Marat, Robespierre, Brissot, and the Mountain," says Vice President Adams, "were the constant themes of panegyric and the daily toasts at table. . . . Washington's house was surrounded by an innumerable multitude from day to day, huzzaing, demanding war against England, cursing Washington, and crying, 'Success to the French patriots and virtuous republicans.' Frederic A. Muhlenberg, the speaker of the House of Representatives, toasted publicly, 'The Mountain: may it be a pyramid that shall reach the skies.'" "I had rather be in my grave," exclaimed Washington one day in great excitement, "than in my present situation." He was equal, however, and more than equal, to his duty and, supported by his cabinet, he sent to request the recall of Genet, (August.) As the party by which Genet had been commissioned had sunk to ruin, their successors readily appointed a minister of their own — citizen Fauchet.

Great Britain and France invade American neutrality.

But the troubles of the time were too complicated to be reached by a mere change of ministers. France had pronounced against the neutrality of America, — not, indeed, by direct menace or violence, but by ordering that neutral vessels, containing goods belonging to her enemies, should be captured, (May 1, 1793.) An embargo was then laid upon the shipping at Bordeaux. Both these measures were decided violations of the treaty with America. The most that France did, however, was as nothing compared with the extremes to which her chief enemy, Great Britain, resorted. France had ordered that the goods of an enemy were liable to capture. Great Britain now ordered that the goods of a neutral power, if consisting of provisions for the enemy, were to be captured or bought up, unless shipped to a friendly port, (June.) This was followed by an order that all vessels laden with the produce of a French colony, or with supplies for the same, were lawful prizes, (November;) a decree so arbitrary that it was soon modified by the nation that issued it, (January, 1794.) Worse than all, Great Britain claimed the right to impress into her service every seaman of British birth, wherever he might be found; so that the ships of the United States would be stopped, searched, and stripped of their crews, at the pleasure of the British cruisers. It often happened that American sailors, as well as British, were the victims of this impressment. A thrill of indignation and of defiance against such proceedings ran through the Americans. They would have been less than freemen, less, even, than men, to have borne with such injuries in silence.

Threatened war with Great Britain.

The course of Great Britain is easily explained. Its rulers regarded the United States merely as a commercial people who were contributing to the resources of the enemy. Did they look upon the nation in any political light, they felt sure — thus Washington was informed from London — "that there was a party so decidedly in the British sentiment that bearing and forbearing would be carried to any length." But they were mistaken. The very party most opposed to France were earnest in sustaining the necessity of preparations for war, defensive, indeed, but still war with Great Britain. A temporary embargo upon the American ports was voted by Congress, for the purpose of suspending commercial intercourse, (March, 1794.) The House of Representatives passed an act prohibiting all trade with Great Britain and her colonies, until she redressed the wrongs which she had perpetrated; the act would have passed the Senate likewise, but for the casting vote of the vice president, (April.) The partisans of the French were all alive for further action; their opponents were hardly prepared to resist it. One step on the part of the executive, one hint that Washington, the still trusted though still slandered magistrate, was in favor of arming, and the nation would have armed. With Great Britain, in all her might, for a foe, and with France, in all her blood-red despotism, for an ally, what would have been the war!

Mission of Jay. One of Washington's secretaries, Jefferson, had lately resigned his post, leaving his personal as well as political opponent, Hamilton, the head of the cabinet. To him, as the most eminent member of the administration, the president would have confided the special mission which it was proposed to send to Great Britain. But Hamilton, as an extreme federalist, was too unacceptable to the great body of Congress and of the nation to be employed upon a service which of itself was an object of general distrust and aversion. Washington therefore selected Chief Justice Jay, (April, 1794.) It was a fitting choice, far more so than that of Hamilton. The secretary would have been the representative, not of the nation alone, but of the party which acknowledged him as its leader; he was always a party man, whether in office or out of office. But the chief justice, though a federalist, was no partisan. Amongst all the prominent figures of the time, Jay's is almost, perhaps altogether, the only one that stands close to Washington's, aloof from the tarnishes and the collisions of opposing parties. No other man was so fit to join with Washington in rescuing the nation from its present perils.

His treaty. Accordingly, Jay proceeded to England, and, after some months of anxious diplomacy, obtained a treaty, (November.) It was not much to obtain. The United States agreeing to indemnify their British creditors, Great Britain consented to surrender the posts which she had so long held in the west.* She also promised indemnity to the sufferers from her system of search and of capture; yet the system itself, though partially modified, was by no means renounced. A few concessions to the claims of American commerce were also made; but the rigid policy of Britain, especially in relation to her colonial trade, was strongly maintained. In short, the treaty did not acknowledge the rights of the Americans as neutrals, or their privileges as traders; both matters of the highest importance to their commercial interests. At the same time, the earlier points of controversy were determined, and from the later ones the sting was taken away, at least in some degree. So Jay thought, so Washington, though neither considered the treaty decidedly satisfactory. It was better, at any rate, they reasoned, than war. Thus, too, reasoned the Senate, who, convened in special session, advised the ratification of the treaty, (June, 1795.)

* The surrender to take effect June 1, 1796.

Opposition. Not thus, however, the nation. If the necessity of the treaty, even as it stood, needed to be proved, the proof was the general insanity which it provoked. Meetings were held every where; harangues were made, resolutions passed; copies of the treaty were destroyed; Jay was burned in effigy. The French and the American flags waved together over these scenes; while the British ensign was dragged through the dirt and burned before the doors of the British representatives.

Ratification. All this, and more, if intended to intimidate government, had a precisely contrary effect. "I have never," wrote Washington, "since I have been in the administration of the government, seen a crisis which is pregnant with more interesting events, nor one from which more is to be apprehended." "Did the treaty with Great Britain," he asked afterwards, "surrender any right of which the United States had been in possession? Did it make any change or alteration in the law of nations, under which Great Britain had acted in defiance of all the powers of Europe? If none of these, why all this farrago?" The French party were of course the active leaders in all disturbances. Their antagonists, certainly not a British party now, kept themselves in the background at first, but presently rallied, not as a British, or even as an anti-French, so much as an American party, to the support of the president, assuring him and his government of the unabated confidence of the nation. At the same time, Jefferson's successor, Randolph, being suspected of intrigue with the French minister, resigned his office, and in the reaction thus excited against the influence and the partisanship of France, the cabinet advised the ratification of the British treaty. It was done, (August.)

Continued opposition. Opposition continued. The Virginian legislature, approving the stand of their senators against the treaty, refused to pass a vote of undiminished confidence in the president. If Virginia could thus turn away from the son to whom she had hitherto clung with all a mother's pride, the tone in other states may be conceived to have been even more expressive of disapprobation. But Virginia was strongly republican and strongly French, consequently strongly anti-British. So far did the legislature go in its wrath, as to propose an amendment of the Constitution, to the effect of requiring the assent of the House of Representatives before a treaty could be ratified, (November.) The example of Virginia was imitated even in Congress, where the phrase of "undiminished confidence" was stricken from an address of the house to the president, (December.) As the session progressed, a fierce struggle arose with respect to the bills for carrying out the British treaty. The opponents of the treaty made it their first effort to obtain the papers relating to the transaction, on the plea that it lay with the House to consent or to refuse to execute the provisions of the treaty. A three weeks' debate terminated in a call upon the president for the specified documents. He and his cabinet being alike of opinion that the House had transgressed its powers, the call was refused. The House took the denial with a better grace than might have been anticipated; the leaders of the opposition now throwing their whole weight upon the point of defeating the bills on which the execution of the treaty depended. Nor was it until after a fortnight's debate, in which Fisher Ames distinguished himself above all his colleagues in defending the treaty, that a vote, by a bare majority, determined that the House would proceed to its duty, (March, April, 1796.) By this time the frenzy out of doors had died away.

The point gained. Thus terminated the great event of Washington's administration. Its course, so far as he was concerned, followed precisely the principles with which he had entered office. In face of the parties that divided the country, in face of their feelings and their relations to Great Britain and France, Washington saw but one alternative — peace or war. And not peace or war with the stranger alone, but between citizen and citizen. Enough has been already said on the interests and the dangers involved in the decision. The proclamation of neutrality was the first decisive step, the treaty with Great Britain was the second, and, for the present, the last. The point thus gained may be called the starting point of the infant nation in its foreign relations. But hear Washington himself: "My ardent desire is, and my aim has been, to keep the United States free from political connections with every other country, to see them independent of all and under the influence of none. In a word, I want an American character, that the powers of Europe may be convinced we act for ourselves, and not for others. This, in my judgment, is the only way to be respected abroad and happy at home; and not, by becoming the partisans of Great Britain or France, create dissensions, disturb the public tranquillity, and destroy, perhaps forever, the cement which binds the Union."

Continued embarrassments: from abroad.

Things were far, however, from going smoothly. What Washington wrote a few months before was still true: "This government, in relation to France and England, may be compared to a ship between the rocks of Scylla and Charybdis." The treaty being ratified, Charybdis was avoided. But Scylla rose the more frowningly. If the French party of the United States, if the minister of the United States to France, James Monroe, were indignant at the British treaty, it was but natural that France should be the same. The French government announced to Mr. Monroe that they considered their alliance with the United States to be at an end, (February,

1796.) The chief reason was the treaty with Great Britain; but the list of grievances, then and afterwards filled out, comprehended all the measures by which American neutrality had been sustained. To prove that they were in earnest, the authorities of France, in addition to their previous orders of capture and embargo, decreed that neutral vessels were to be treated exactly as they were treated by the British; that is, stopped, searched, and seized upon the seas, (July.) This was subsequently made known to the United States by a communication from the French envoy, Adet, (October,) who improved the opportunity by appealing to the people to take part with France and against Great Britain, (November.) To restore matters, as far as possible, to a better position, Washington had sent out Charles C. Pinckney as minister to France, in the place of Monroe, (September.) But the clouds that had been dissipated on the side of Great Britain were more than replaced by the ominous signs in the direction of France.

And at home.

It was still worse at home. The parties — northern and southern, federalist and republican, anti-French and French — that racked the nation were never so much agitated. "Until within the last year or two," wrote Washington, "I had no idea that parties would, or even could, go to the length I have been witness to." Congress was a continual battle ground. The federalist party, falling into the minority in the House, and in danger of losing their majority in the Senate, fought, it may be literally said, on one side; their opponents, the republicans, animated with the hope of the superiority, being equally pugnacious on the other. Newspapers, especially those published at Philadelphia, carried the hostile notes from Congress to the nation, and echoed them back to Congress. It is difficult, without having room for extracts, to convey any idea of the virulence of political writing at the time. Statesmanship disappears in partisanship, the love of country in the hatred of countrymen. All this, while it demonstrated the wisdom of the administration or of its head, rendered the course of the administration doubtful and imperilled. In fact, both the administration and its head were objects of the fiercest assault.

Abuse of Washington. Washington wrote with natural indignation of the abuse which he, "no party man," as he truly called himself, had received, "and that, too, in such exaggerated and indecent terms as could scarcely be applied to a Nero, a notorious defaulter, or even to a common pickpocket." It was amidst these outrages that Washington sent forth his Farewell Address to the people of the United States, (September 17, 1796.) Soon afterwards, Congress came together, and showed that many of its members were violent against the retiring president. On the proposal of an address of grateful acknowledgments from the House of Representatives, a man from Washington's own state, William B. Giles, of Virginia, took exception to the more expressive passages, saying, "If I stand alone in the opinion, I will declare that I am not convinced that the administration of the government for these six years has been wise and firm. I do not regret the president's retiring from office." Giles was not alone. The same attitude was taken by a considerable number, and amongst them Andrew Jackson, of Tennessee, (December.) "Although he is soon to become a private citizen," wrote Washington of himself, (January, 1797,) "his opinions are to be knocked down, and his character reduced as low as they are capable of sinking it." Two months later, in the last hours of his administration, he said, "To the wearied traveller, who sees a resting place, and is bending his body to lean thereon, I now compare myself; but to be suffered to do this in peace, is too much to be endured by some." If Washington could thus excite animosity and wrong, what must it have been with ordinary men? The country seemed unwilling to be pacified, unwilling to be saved.

Retirement of Washington.

Washington retired. He had done even greater things at the head of the government than he had done at the head of the army. But it was beyond his power to change the character of the nation. He left it as he found it — divided and impassioned. Yet he left it as he had not found it — with a Constitution in operation, with principles and with laws in action — on the road to increase and to maturity. "I can never believe," were almost his last words as president, "that Providence, which has guided us so long, and through such a labyrinth, will withdraw its protection at this crisis." The day after writing this, he saw his successor, John Adams, inaugurated, (March 4, 1797.)

Lafayette.

One who had hailed the administration at its beginning was not amongst those to behold its close. Lafayette was a prisoner at Olmütz, under the power of Austria. But he was not forgotten. It is refreshing amidst the angry chaos of foreign controversies and of domestic struggles, to encounter Washington, not as the president, but as the American, writing his "private letter," as he termed it, to the Emperor of Germany, "to recommend Lafayette to the mediation of humanity," and "to entreat that he may be permitted to come to this country," (May, 1796.) The effect of the appeal is not known; but Lafayette was liberated not long afterwards.

PART IV.

UNION.

1797–1872.

CHAPTER I.

Party Administrations.

Parties in power. WASHINGTON'S administration was our only really national one. The administrations of his successors were those of parties rather than of presidents. With John Adams (1797) the federalists were in power; with Thomas Jefferson (1801) and James Madison (1809) the republicans. The struggles of these parties upon questions of domestic and foreign policy make up our history for the next twenty years.

Missions to France. At the outset, the relations with France occupy the foreground. Charles C. Pinckney, accredited by Washington to negotiate with the French government, was refused an audience at Paris; and not only that, but was ordered to depart the French territory, (December, 1796 — February, 1797.) Notwithstanding this, notwithstanding the rapidly following decrees against American ships and American crews, President Adams sent out a new mission, consisting of Pinckney, John Marshall, and Elbridge Gerry, with moderate instructions, which, however, availed nothing. Pinckney and Marshall, incensed by the intrigue as well as the insolence of which they were the objects, (October, 1797 — April, 1798,) shook off the dust of France from their feet, being followed in a few months by Gerry, who had undertaken to do alone what he had not been able to do with his colleagues.

Arming of the United States.

Before the withdrawal of Pinckney and Marshall, the intelligence of their treatment had thrown the United States into a great excitement. The republicans taunted their opponents with the failure which they said they had predicted for the French missions. All the more bitter were the federalists, who inveighed against the venality of the French government, some even going so far as to call for a declaration of war. The president leaned to the side of his party. He had no mind to declare war, but he recommended Congress to put the country in a state of defence, (March, 1798.) The recommendation was at once opposed by the republican leaders. According to Vice President Jefferson, indeed, the president was aiming at a dissolution of the Union or at the establishment of a monarchical government. But the federalists upheld the president, and carried a series of measures providing for the organization of a provisional army, as well as of a naval department, by which the existing navy might be more efficiently managed, (May.) Orders were issued, directing the national ships to seize all armed vessels engaged in hostile acts against American shipping; while merchantmen were authorized to arm themselves, and capture their assailants upon the seas. But to prevent hostilities, as far as possible, commercial intercourse with France and her colonies was formally prohibited, (June.) Soon after, Washington was appointed to the command of the provisional army, (July.) The United States were fairly in arms.

War.

War followed at sea. No declaration was made; the most that was done being to proclaim the treaties with France void, and then to authorize the president to send out national and to commission private vessels for the purpose of capturing any armed ships of the French, whether participating or not in hostilities, (July.) The seas were at once overrun with American ships, by which the French privateers were taken or driven from the coast. No actual engagement between national vessels, however, occurred, until the beginning of the following year, when Commander Truxtun, in the Constellation, forced the French frigate L'Insurgente to strike, (February, 1799.) Hostilities were continued chiefly by privateers, the profits to whose owners were the principal results of the war. Still it pleased the party by whom it was favored. "A glorious and triumphant war it was!" exclaimed Adams, in after years. "The proud pavilion of France was humiliated."

Strain upon the nation.

But against the deeds of battle must be set the measures of government which disclose the real strain upon the nation. To provide ways and means, stamp duties and taxes on houses and slaves were voted, besides the loans that were procured. To keep down party opposition, alien and sedition acts, as they were called, were passed. The first authorized the president to banish all aliens suspected of conspiracy against the United States. This was more of a party manœuvre than appears on the face of it; inasmuch as many of the most ardent spirits among the republicans, especially the democratic republicans, were aliens. The sedition act denounced fine and imprisonment upon all conspiracies, and even all publications, "with intent to excite any unlawful combination for opposing or resisting any law of the United States, or any lawful act of the president." It was at midsummer that party spirit rose so high as to demand and to enact these urgent laws, (June — July, 1798.) Both of them however, were to be but temporary.* The alien act was

* The alien to be in force for two years, the sedition until March 4, 1801, the end of Adams's administration.

never put in operation. But the sedition act was again and again enforced, and almost, if not altogether, invariably upon party grounds. It may safely be said that the nation was straining itself too far.

Nullification. So thought the party opposing the administration and the war. Strongest in the south and in the west, the republican leaders threw down the gauntlet to their opponents, nay, even to their rulers. The legislature of Kentucky, in resolutions drawn up for that body by no less a person than Vice President Jefferson, declared the alien and sedition laws "not law, but altogether void and of no force," (November, 1798.) The note thus sounded was taken up in the Virginia legislature, whose resolutions, draughted by James Madison, declared the obnoxious laws "palpable and alarming infractions of the Constitution," (December.) Both sets of resolutions, as they came from the hands of their framers, were stronger still. Jefferson had written, "Where powers are assumed which have not been delegated, a nullification of the act is the right remedy, and every state has a natural right, in cases not within the compact, [the Constitution,] to nullify of their own authority all assumptions of power by others within their limits." Madison, after stating "that in case of a deliberate, palpable, and dangerous exercise of other powers not granted by the compact, the states, who are the parties thereto, have the right, and are in duty bound, to interpose for correcting the progress of the evil, and for maintaining within their respective limits the authorities, rights, and liberties appertaining to them," had made his resolutions declare the acts in question "null, void, and of no force or effect." But it was an early day for nullification; and neither Kentucky nor Virginia went the length prescribed for them. They went far enough, as has been seen, to excite very general opposition from their sister states, especially those of the centre and the north, where legislature after legislature came out with strong and denunciatory denials of the right of any state to sit in judgment upon the national government.

Another mission to France. Things were in this seething state, when the president nominated as minister to France William Vans Murray, to whom he afterwards joined Oliver Ellsworth, then chief justice, and William R. Davie, as colleagues, (February, 1799.) The reason assigned for a fresh attempt at negotiation was the assurance that had been received through the minister at the Hague, of the willingness of the French government to treat with a new mission. The din upon these nominations was tremendous, particularly among the more active federalists, and even the principal members of the cabinet, Timothy Pickering and Oliver Wolcott. The president was suspected of urging the mission, in some degree, out of spite against the federalist party, by whom, or by whose extreme members, he considered himself badly used. "The British faction," he wrote afterwards, "was determined to have a war with France, and Alexander Hamilton at the head of the army, and then president of the United States. Peace with France was therefore treason." The envoys reached their destination in the beginning of the following year, (1800.) They found Napoleon Bonaparte first consul. With his government, after some difficulty, they concluded a convention, providing in part for mutual redress, but leaving many of the questions between the two nations for future settlement, (October.) When brought before the Senate of the United States, the convention was modified by cancelling the provision for additional negotiations. This was assented to in France, on condition that the claims for indemnities on either side should be abandoned. The effect was soon seen in claims for French spoliations presented to the government of the United States. But the treaty sufficed to restore peace.

Mississippi Territory: slavery under debate.

Important events had occurred at home. The Mississippi Territory was formed, including at first the lower part of the present Alabama and Mississippi, (1798.) This organization excited a debate concerning slavery, which, as the organizing act provided, was not to be prohibited in the territory. Here was no such plea as had existed in the case of the Territory South of the Ohio. No cession from a state, no conditions laid any restraint upon Congress. Yet but twelve votes were given in favor of an amendment proposed by George Thacher, of Massachusetts, prohibiting the introduction of slavery into the territory. The most that Congress would agree to, was to forbid the importation of slaves from abroad; a concession, inasmuch as the slave trade, it will be remembered, was still allowed by the Constitution. So, for the second time, and this time without its being required by terms with any state,* the decision of the national government was given in favor of slavery.

Territory of Indiana: slavery again.

But Congress took the other side, likewise. The western portion of the North-west Territory soon needed to be set off as the Territory of Indiana, embracing the present Indiana, Illinois, and Michigan, (1800.) There slavery was already prohibited. But this went against the interests of the inhabitants, as they thought, and they petitioned Congress, within three and again within seven years after the organization of the

* The part of the territory at this time organized was claimed by the United States as a portion of the old Florida domain. Georgia likewise claimed it as hers; and when she surrendered what was allowed to be hers, that is, the upper part of the present Alabama and Mississippi, she made it a condition that slavery should not be prohibited, (1802.)

territory, to be allowed to introduce slaves amongst them. Once a committee of Congress reported adversely; but twice a report was made in favor of the petition. Reports and petitions, however, were alike fruitless. Congress would not authorize slavery where it had been prohibited.

Death of Washington.

No domestic event compared in interest with the death of Washington, which occurred unexpectedly on the 14th of December, 1799. His last service had been the organization of the provisional army against France, of which one can hardly say that it was the crowning act of such a life. Party passions ran so high as to affect the serenity of his declining years, and it may not have been too soon for his peace or his fame that he was taken away. Beside his grave, his countrymen stood united for a moment, but no longer.

Fall of the federalists.

The presidential election of 1800 reduced the federalists to a hopeless minority. They had done more for the country than for themselves. During Washington's administration, they had sustained his great measures, and originated great measures of their own; but during Adams's, they had spent their strength in quarrelling with him or among themselves, and his defeat and theirs followed almost of course. Their fall was their own work, rather than that of their opponents. They had started as the more aristocratic party of the two, and every year had developed a distrust of the people which was sure to overthrow them at no distant day. The daughter of one of their most amiable and eminent leaders, Theodore Sedgwick, tells us that her father habitually spoke of the people as "Jacobins and miscreants," and he was by no means singular in his expressions. It seems strange that the party which may be said to have founded our government was not able to administer it; but the very characteristics which fitted it to do the one work may have unfitted it to do the other. As between Adams and Jefferson, personally, there is no such comparison to be made as may be drawn between their parties. Both were identified with the independence and the organization of the nation, and both were qualified in the highest degree for its chief magistracy.

Acquisition of Louisiana.

Theoretically, the federalists had gone for increasing the authority of the general government, while the republicans had made a stand to check it. But the chief measure of Jefferson's administration implied a readiness to stretch the powers of the government, and particularly of the executive branch, far beyond federalist theories. This was the acquisition of Louisiana, by which we are to understand, not the present state, but a region extending indefinitely to the west and north on the farther side of the Mississippi. Spain had acquired this territory from France in 1763; she restored it to France in 1800. Before the Spanish authorities withdrew, they excluded the citizens of the United States from New Orleans as a depot for the commerce of their western states, and France was credited with entertaining the same unfavorable designs. It was proposed in the United States Senate to seize New Orleans; but this was too extreme a course. Left to his own counsels, the president instructed the envoys to France, Robert R. Livingston and James Monroe, to purchase the part of Louisiana which included New Orleans; but finding the French government disposed to sell the whole, they bought the whole for fifteen millions of dollars, (April 30, 1803.) Jefferson allowed this to be "an act beyond the Constitution," and hinted at a constitutional amendment which should justify it. The great importance of the acquisition, securing the Mississippi to its mouth, and freeing the western territory from all possible interference from France or Spain, was a convincing argument, and the Senate confirmed the negotiation, (October 20.) The chief argument that might have been brought against it was the extension of slavery by the annexation of foreign territory containing upwards of fifty thousand slaves, and open to fifty times as many in the future; but this was hardly touched. The federalists opposed the purchase simply as a republican measure, and as the republicans themselves were divided upon it, party bitterness was intensified.

Organization of Louisiana territories.

The immense region thus acquired was divided into two portions, (1804.) The southern, in which all the settlements of any importance were included, was called the Territory of Orleans. It comprehended the present State of Louisiana, but with very indefinite boundaries on the west. North of this lay the District of Louisiana, embracing the present Arkansas and Missouri, with as much more as could be brought within its elastic limits on the north and west, its principal settlement being St. Louis. This district was made a part of the same jurisdiction with the Indiana Territory, from which, however, it was soon detached, (1805.) At the same time, the provisions for the Territory of Orleans, complained of by some of the inhabitants, were rendered more liberal. The terms of the treaty concluding the purchase had been these: "The inhabitants of the ceded territory shall be incorporated in the Union of the United States, and admitted as soon as possible, according to the principles of the federal Constitution, to the enjoyment of all the rights, advantages, and immunities of citizens of the United States; and in the mean time shall be maintained and protected in the free enjoyment of their liberty, property, and the religion which they profess." Treaties of this kind were not every-day occurrences with Napoleon. But the inhabitants for whom he required this pledge were only a part, and a small part, of the Louisianians; he did not interfere in behalf of their fifty thousand slaves.

Other territorial and state organizations.

The new State of Ohio was already admitted to the Union, (November 29, 1802.) New territories — Michigan (1805) and Illinois (1809) — were subsequently formed from out of the Indiana Territory. The signs of expansion were written every where, but nowhere so strikingly as along the western plains.

Burr's projects.

There they were such as to kindle projects of a new empire. Aaron Burr, vice president during Jefferson's first term, but displaced in the second term by George Clinton, (1805,) — branded, too, with the recent murder of Alexander Hamilton in a duel, — was generally avoided amongst his old associates. Turning his face westward, he there drew into his net various men, some of position and some of obscurity, with whose aid he seems to have intended making himself master of the Mississippi valley, or of Mexico, one or both, (1806.) Whatever his schemes were, they miscarried. A handful only of followers were gathered round him on the banks of the Mississippi, a hundred miles or more above New Orleans, when he surrendered himself to the government of the Mississippi Territory, (January, 1807.) Some months afterwards he was brought to trial for high treason before Chief Justice Marshall, of the Supreme Court, with whom sat the district judge for Virginia; the reason for trying Burr in that state being the fact that one of the places where he was charged with having organized a military expedition was within the Virginian limits. The trial, like every thing else in those days, was made a party question; the administration and its supporters going strongly against Burr, while its opponents were disposed to take his part. He was acquitted for want of proof; and for the same reason he was again acquitted when tried for undertaking to invade the Spanish territories.

Difficulties with Great Britain.

Frowning high above all these domestic dangers were those from abroad which sank in one direction only to rise the more threateningly in another. Great Britain was now extending impressment even to the American navy, whose vessels were once and again plundered of their seamen by British men-of-war. Another subject on which Great Britain set herself against the claims of the United States, was the neutral trade, of which the latter nation engrossed a large and constantly increasing share during the European wars. France was equally adverse to American commerce. If Great Britain led off by declaring the French ports, from Brest to the Elbe, closed to American as to all other shipping, (May 16, 1806,) France retorted by the Berlin decree, so called because issued from Prussia, prohibiting any commerce with Great Britain, (November 21.) That power immediately forbade the coasting trade between one port and another in the possession of her enemies, (January 7, 1807.) Not satisfied with this, she went on to forbid all trade whatsoever with France and her allies, except on payment of a tribute to Great Britain, each vessel to pay in proportion to its cargo, (November 11.) Then followed the Milan decree of Napoleon, prohibiting all trade whatsoever with Great Britain, and declaring such vessels as paid the recently demanded tribute to be lawful prizes to the French marine, (December 17.)

Affair of the Chesapeake.

The heaviest blow was struck by Great Britain. The American frigate Chesapeake, sailing from Hampton Roads, was hailed off the capes of Chesapeake Bay by the British frigate Leopard, the captain of which demanded to search the Chesapeake for deserters. Captain Barron, the commander of the Chesapeake, refused; whereupon the Leopard opened fire. As Barron and his crew were totally unprepared for action, they fired but a single gun, to save their honor; then, having lost several men, struck their flag. The British commander took those of whom he was in search, three of the four being Americans, and left the Chesapeake to make her way back dishonored, (June 22, 1807.) The president issued a proclamation, ordering British men-of-war from the waters of the United States. Instructions were sent to the American envoys at London, directing them, not merely to seek reparation for the wrong that had been done, but to obtain the renunciation of the pretensions to a right of search and of impressment, from which the wrong had sprung. The British government recognized their responsibility, by sending a special minister to settle the difficulty at Washington. It was four years, however, before the desired reparation was procured, (1811.) The desired renunciation was never made. One can scarcely credit his eyes, when he reads that the affair of the Chesapeake was made a party point. But so it was. The friends of Great Britain, the capitalists and commercial classes, generally, murmured at the course of their government, as too decided, too French, they sometimes called it; as if resistance to Great Britain were subordination to France.

The administration against war.

"In the present maniac state of Europe," wrote Jefferson, a little later, "I should not estimate the point of honor by the ordinary scale. I believe we shall, on the contrary, have credit with the world for having made the avoidance of being engaged in the present unexampled war our first object." To this end, the president hit upon the most self-denying of plans. The aggressions of the European powers were directed against the rights of owners and of crews. That these might be secured, the president recommended, and Congress adopted, an embargo upon all United States vessels, and upon all foreign vessels with cargoes shipped after the passage of the act in United States ports, (December 22, 1807). In other words, as commerce led to injuries from foreign nations, commerce was to be abandoned. France, on whose side the violent federalists declared the embargo to be, answered by a decree of Napoleon's from Bayonne, ordering the confiscation of all American vessels in French ports, (April 17, 1808.) Great Britain soon after made her response, by an order prohibiting the exportation of American produce, whether paying tribute or not, to the European continent, (December 21.) So ineffective abroad, so productive of discontent at home, even amongst the supporters of the administration, did the embargo prove, that it was repealed, (March, 1809.) But its place was taken by non-intercourse or non-importation acts as restrictive as the embargo, so far as the designated nations were concerned, but leaving free the trade with other countries. The administration, now Madison's, amused itself with suspending the restrictions, in favor first of Great Britain, (1809,) and then of France, (1810,) hoping to induce those powers to reciprocate the compliment by a suspension of their own aggressive orders. There was a show of doing so. Napoleon had recently issued a decree from Rambouillet, ordering the sale of more than a hundred American vessels as condemned prizes, (March 23, 1810.) But on the news from America, eager to involve another nation in hostilities, he intimated his readiness to retract the decrees of which the United States complained. But not, he made it known, except on one of two conditions; either the British orders must be recalled, or else, if they were not, the United States must enforce their claims. To this Great Britain replied, that when the French decrees were actually, and not conditionally, revoked, her orders should be revoked likewise. It was but a mockery on both sides; and America, mortified, but not yet enlightened, returned to her prohibitions. They were scoffed at by her own people.

Opposition. It is difficult to catch the hue and cry, on the part of the opposition, against the embargo and the subsequent acts. Whatever discontent, whatever nullification had been expressed by the republicans against the war measures of Adams, was rivalled, if not outrivalled, by the federalists against the so-called peace measures of Jefferson and Madison. Town meetings, state legislatures, even the courts in some places, declared against the constitutionality of the embargo. The federalists of Massachusetts were charged with the design of dissolving the Union. It was not their intention, but their language had warranted its being imputed to them. "Choose, then, fellow-citizens," their legislature exclaimed, "between the condition of a free state, possessing its equal weight and influence in the general government, or that of a colony, free in name, but in fact enslaved by sister states."

Indian hostilities. While affairs, domestic and foreign, were thus agitated, there came a fresh outbreak of Indian hostilities. It was under Jefferson that the plan of removing the Indians westward was begun, (1804,) but the first effect was disastrous. Two chiefs of the Shawanoes, Tecumseh and his twin brother, styled the Prophet, for some time settled on the Tippecanoe River, in the Indiana Territory, had set themselves at the head of a sort of confederacy among the western races. One great point was to secure the title of the Indians, as a whole, to the lands of which the whites were getting possession, by bargains with individuals or with individual tribes. Another was the prohibition of the ardent spirits with which the traders were destroying the Indians, body and soul. But to support these principles, the confederates, or their leaders, relied upon treachery and terror, superstition and blasphemy. The governor of Indiana Territory, William H. Harrison, marched against them with a force of a few hundred. Tecumseh was absent at the time, but his brother and his confederates were overtaken. To the last, they professed peace, then fell upon the camp of the Americans. They were expected, however, and were routed, (November 7, 1811.)

Louisiana and Florida.

The steel was glistening upon the southern frontier. An insurrection against the Spanish authority in West Florida had been followed by a presidential proclamation declaring the territory on the east bank of the Mississippi a portion of Louisiana, (October, 1810.) Soon after, (January, 1811,) Congress authorized the acquisition of the entire province of Florida, provided either that Spain consented to it, or that any other power attempted to take possession. The next year, Louisiana, with a large portion of Florida, according to the Spanish claim, was admitted a state, (April 8, 1812.) Another slice of Florida was annexed to the Mississippi Territory, while an insurrection within the remaining Florida limits was stimulated by an American functionary; a demonstration being made against St. Augustine. This was promptly disavowed by the government at Washington; but the troops were not withdrawn until the following year, nor then entirely, Mobile being retained by way of compensation for what was surrendered, (1813.)

It was plain that war was becoming popular in the United States. As for that, it had long been so; when Washington opposed it, he was abused; when Adams

Warlike preparations against Great Britain.

favored it, he was extolled; when Jefferson avoided it, he risked even his immense influence over the nation. Congress now took up the question, and voted one measure after another, preparatory to hostilities with Great Britain, (December — March 1812.) The president hesitated; he was no war leader by nature or by principle. But his party, or the more active portion of it, was all for arms; when he doubted, they urged; when he inclined to draw back, they drove him forward. It being the time when the congressional caucus was about to nominate for the presidency, Madison received a direct intimation that if he was a candidate for re-election, he must come out for war. He then sent a message to Congress, recommending an embargo of sixty days. Congress received it, according to its intention, as a preliminary to war, and voted it, though far from unanimously, for ninety days, (April 4, 1812.)

CHAPTER II.

War with Great Britain.

Declaration. Another message from the president, (June 1,) and war with Great Britain was voted by Congress, (June 18,) and then declared by the president, (June 19, 1812.)

Cause of the United States. The United States went to war for two great principles; one, the rights of neutrals, the other, the rights of seamen; both involving the honor and the independence of the nation. The former principle was at once secured; for when France unconditionally repealed her decrees, Great Britain withdrew her orders in council just as the war was declared, (June 23.) The other principle could be secured, so Great Britain insisted, if the United States would take measures to prevent British seamen from enlisting in the American service. "We must fight," cried the war party, "if it is only for what has been, for the seizure of nine hundred American vessels and six thousand American seamen, for the injuries which are beyond redress by negotiation." If the party had been frank, it would have added, "We must fight, if it is only for ourselves, and for the position which we have staked on war." The cause of the United States was, primarily, the cause of a party, nominally headed by Madison, the president, by James Monroe, the secretary of state, by Albert Gallatin, (the same who appeared in the Pennsylvania insurrection of Washington's time,) the secretary of the treasury, and by others supporting the administration ; but the real leaders were younger men, some risen to distinction, like Henry Clay, speaker of the House of Representatives, and John C. Calhoun, member of the same body, but many more aspiring to place in council or in camp, to place any where, so that it promised the fame or the game for which they yearned. As such it was opposed by the party out of power. The signal, given by a protest from the federalist members of Congress, was caught up and repeated in meetings and at hearth-stones. Even the pulpit threw open its doors to political harangues, and those not of the mildest sort. "The alternative then is," exclaimed a clergyman at Boston, "that if you do not wish to become the slaves of those who own slaves, and who are themselves the slaves of French slaves, you must either, in the language of the day, cut the connection, or so far alter the national Constitution as to secure yourselves a due share in the government. The Union has long since been virtually dissolved, and it is full time that this portion of the United States should take care of itself."

War at home. The war began at home. The office of a federalist paper, the Federal Republican, conducted by Alexander Hanson, at Baltimore, was sacked by a mob, who then went on to attack dwellings, pillage vessels, and, finally, to fire the house of an individual suspected of partialities for Great Britain, (June 22, 23.) A month later, Hanson opened another office, and prepared to defend it, with the assistance of his friends, against the assault which he felt sure his boldness would provoke. The mob came, and, after a night of horror, forced the party in the office to yield themselves prisoners on a charge of murder. The next night the prison was assailed ; Hanson and his friends, excepting some who escaped, being beaten and tortured with indescribable fury. General Henry Lee, a revolutionary hero, who had taken the lead in the measures of defence, was injured for life. Another soldier of the revolution, General Lingan, was actually slain; a fate which would have been shared by many, but for the exhaustion of the destroyers, (July 26, 27.) All this was done with nothing more than the show of interference on the part of the authorities. Even at the subsequent trial of the ringleaders in the mob, they were acquitted. Hanson kept up his paper only by removing to Georgetown.

Means for the war. Such being the passions, such the divisions internally, the nation needed more than the usual panoply to protect itself externally. But it had less. The colonies of 1775 did not go to war more unprepared than the United States of 1812. There was no army to speak of. Generals abounded, it is true, Henry Dearborn, late secretary of war, being at the head of the list; but troops were scanty, a few thousand regulars and volunteers constituting the entire force. As to the militia, there was a general distrust of it, at the same time that the power of the government to call it out was denied by some state authorities.* If the army was small, the navy was smaller, embracing only eight or ten frigates, as many more smaller vessels, and a flotilla of comparatively useless gunboats. The national finances were in a correspondingly low condition. The revenue, affected by the interruptions to commerce during the preceding years, needed all the stimulants which it could obtain, even in time of peace. It was wholly inadequate to the exigencies of war. Accordingly, resort was had to loans, then to direct taxes and licenses, (1813.) In fine, the country had

* The Constitution authorized Congress "to provide for calling forth the militia to execute the laws of the Union, suppress insurrections, and repel invasions."

hardly another resource than its numbers merely, which were now increased to six millions free.*

Position of Great Britain. Fortunate, therefore, was it that Great Britain was otherwise occupied. Her mighty struggle with Napoleon was at its height when the United States declared war, a declaration sounding much the same in British ears as the wail of a child amid the contentions of men.

The war. Losses on north-western frontier. Notwithstanding all want of means, the United States government determined to carry the war into the enemy's country. For this purpose, William Hull, general and governor of Michigan Territory, crossed from Detroit to Sandwich, in Canada, with about two thousand men, (July 12.) In a little more than a month he had not only retreated, but surrendered, without a blow, to General Brock, the governor of Lower Canada, (August 16.) The British, already in possession of the northern part of Michigan, were soon masters of the entire territory. So far from being able to recover it, General Harrison, who made the attempt in the ensuing autumn and winter, found it all he could do to save Ohio from falling with Michigan. A detachment of Kentuckians yielded to a superior force of British at Frenchtown, on the River Raisin, (January, 1813;) whereupon Harrison took post by the Maumee, at Fort Meigs, holding out there against the British and their Indian allies, (April, May.) The same fort was again assailed and again defended, General Clay being at that time in command, (July.) Fort Stevenson, on the Sandusky, was then attacked, but defended with great spirit and success by a small garrison under Major Croghan, (August.) Yet Ohio was still in danger.

* The census of 1810 gave a total of 7,239,814, of which 1,191,364 were slaves.

Perry's victory on Lake Erie.

It was rescued by different operations from those as yet described. Captain Chauncey, after gathering a little fleet on Lake Ontario, where he achieved some successes, appointed Lieutenant Oliver H. Perry to the command on Lake Erie. Perry's first duty was to provide a fleet; his next, to lead it against the British vessels under Captain Barclay. At length the squadrons met off Sandusky, the British to suffer total defeat, the Americans to win complete victory, (September 10, 1813.) It was in more than official language that the president communicated this achievement to Congress. "The conduct of Captain Perry," he said, "adroit as it was daring, and which was so well seconded by his comrades, justly entitles them to the admiration and gratitude of their country, and will fill an early page in its naval annals with a victory never surpassed in lustre, however much it may have been in magnitude." It was a victory on a small scale. Yet its importance immediately appeared. Taking on board a body of troops from Ohio and Kentucky, under Harrison, Perry transported them to the neighborhood of Sandwich, on the Canada shore, the same spot against which Hull had marched more than a twelvemonth before. The British having retired, Harrison crossed to Detroit. Recrossing, he advanced in pursuit of the much less numerous enemy, whom he defeated on two successive days, (October 4, 5.) The latter action, on the bank of the Thames, was decisive; the British General Proctor making his escape with but a small portion of his troops, while his Indian ally, Tecumseh, was slain. Ohio was thus saved, and Michigan recovered, though not entirely.

Operations on New York frontier.

On the frontier of New York the chief movement was an attack against Queenstown, on the Canada shore of the Niagara River. Advanced parties gained possession of a battery on the bank, but there they were checked, and at length obliged to surrender, for want of support from their comrades on the American side. General Van Rensselaer was the American, General Brock the British commander; the latter falling in battle, the former resigning in disgust after the battle was over, (October 13, 1812.) In the following spring, General Dearborn and the land troops, in conjunction with Chauncey and the fleet, took York, (now Toronto,) the capital of Upper Canada, burning the Parliament House, and then proceeding successfully against the forts on the Niagara River, (April, May, 1813.) At this point, however, affairs took an unfavorable turn. The British mustered strong, and, though repulsed from Sackett's Harbor by General Brown, at the head of some regular troops and volunteers, they obtained the command of the lake, making descents in various places, and reducing the American forces, both land and naval, to comparative inactivity, (June.) Months afterwards, the land forces, now under the lead of General Wilkinson, started on a long-proposed expedition against Montreal; but encountering resistance on the way down the St. Lawrence, went straight into winter quarters within the New York frontier. A body of troops under General Hampton, moving in the same direction from Lake Champlain, met with a feint of opposition, rather than opposition itself, from the British; it was sufficient, however, to induce a retreat, (November.) Both these armies far outnumbered the enemy, Wilkinson having seventy-five hundred, and Hampton forty-five hundred men under them. On the western border of New York, things went still worse. General M'Clure, left in charge of the Niagara frontier, was so weakened by the loss of men at the expiration of their terms of service, and at the same time so pressed by the enemy, as to abandon the Canada shore, leaving behind him the ruins of Fort George and the village of Newark. Parties of British and Indians, crossing the frontier at different places, took Fort Niagara, at the mouth of the river, and swept the adjacent country with fire and sword as far as Buffalo, (December.) Glutted with success, the invaders retired, save from Fort Niagara, which they held until the end of the war. In the following spring, (March, 1814,) General Wilkinson emerged from his retreat, and, with a portion of his troops, undertook to carry the approaches to Canada from the side of Lake Champlain. But on coming up with a stone mill held by British troops, he abruptly withdrew.

On Niagara frontier.

As the war, thus pitiably prosecuted, entered into its third year, (1814,) a concentration of efforts, both American and British, took place upon the Niagara frontier. General Brown, the defender of Sackett's Harbor, obtained the command, and with such supporters as General Scott and other gallant officers, resolved upon crossing to the Canada side. There, with an army of about thirty-five hundred men, he took Fort Erie, (July 2,) gained the battle of Chippewa, (July 5,) and drove the enemy, under General Riall, from the frontier, save from a single stronghold, Fort George. The British, however, on being reënforced, returned under Generals Riall and Drummond, and met the Americans at Bridgewater, within the roar of Niagara. Begun by Scott, in advance of the main body, which soon came up under Brown, the battle was continued until midnight, to the advantage of the American army, (July 25.) But they were unable to follow up or even to maintain their success, and fell back upon Fort Erie. Thither the British proceeded, and after a night assault, laid siege to the place, then under the command of General Gaines. As soon as Brown, who had withdrawn to recover from his wounds, resumed his command at the fort, he at once ordered a sortie, the result being the raising of the siege, (September 17.) He was soon after called away to defend Sackett's Harbor, the enemy having the upper hand on the lake. His successor in command on the Niagara frontier, General Izard, blew up Fort Erie, and abandoned the Canada shore, (November.)

Defence of Lake Champlain.

Meanwhile the American arms had distinguished themselves on the side of Lake Champlain. Thither descended the British General Provost with twelve thousand soldiers, lately arrived from Europe, his object being to carry the American works at Plattsburg, and to drive the American vessels from the waters. He was totally unsuccessful. Captain McDonough, after long exertions, had constructed a fleet, with which he now met and overwhelmed the British squadron. The land attack upon the few thousand regulars and militia under General Macomb was hardly begun before it was given over in consequence of the naval action, (September 11.) No engagement in the war, before or after, was more unequal in point of force, the British being greatly the superiors; yet none was more decisive.

British superiority.

The British superiority observable at Lake Champlain and elsewhere requires a word of explanation. Napoleon, fallen some months before, had left the armies and fleets of Great Britain free to act in other scenes than those to which they had been so long confined. The troops transported to America — some to Canada, as we have seen, more to other places, as we shall soon see — were superior to the Americans generally in numbers, and always in appointment and discipline. They were the men to whom France had succumbed; it must have seemed impossible that the United States should resist them.

Successes at sea. The apprehensions of the enemy, aroused by some of the operations on land, had been highly excited by some of those at sea. Before the gallant actions upon the lakes, a succession of remarkable exploits had occurred upon the ocean. It had been the policy of the republican administration to keep down the navy, which their federalist predecessors had encouraged. But the navy, or that fragment of one which remained, returned good for evil. The frigate Essex, under Captain Porter, took the sloop of war Alert off the northern coast, (August 13, 1812;) the frigate Constitution, Captain Isaac Hull, took the frigate Guerrière in the Gulf of St. Lawrence, (August 19;) the sloop of war Wasp, Captain Jones, took the brig Frolic, both, however, falling prizes to the seventy-four Poictiers, not far from the Bermudas, (October 13;) the frigate United States, Captain Decatur, took the frigate Macedonian off the Azores, (October 25;) and the Constitution again, now under Captain Bainbridge, took the frigate Java off Brazil, (December 29.) This series of triumphs was broken by but two reverses, the capture of the brig Nautilus by the British squadron, and that of the brig Vixen by the British frigate Southampton, both off the Atlantic coast. Nothing could be more striking than the effect upon both the nations that were at war. The British started at defeat, particularly on the sea; and the war assumed an aspect not before admitted on their side. The Americans were proportionately animated. "I never felt the national feeling so strongly aroused," wrote Washington Irving, "for I never before saw, in this country, so true a cause for national triumph."

Subsequent reverses. Here, however, the impulse ceased, or began to cease. The navy was too inconsiderable to continue its victories, the nation too inactive to recruit its numbers and its powers. The captures of the succeeding period of the war, though made with quite as much gallantry, were of much less importance; while one vessel after another, beginning with the frigate Chesapeake, off Boston harbor, (June 1, 1813,) was forced to strike to the enemy. Many of the larger ships were hemmed in by the British blockade, when this, commencing with the war, was extended along the entire coast. The last glimmer of naval victory for the time was the defeat of the sloop of war Avon by the Wasp, Captain Blakely, off the French coast, (September 1, 1814.) But a few weeks later, the Wasp was lost with all its crew, leaving not a single vessel of the United States navy on the seas. Every one that had escaped the perils of the ocean and of war was shut up in port behind the greatly superior squadrons of Great Britain.

Losses upon the coast.

The coast, from the first blockaded, and occasionally visited by invading parties of the British, was in an appalling state, (1814.) Eastport was taken; Castine, Belfast, and Machias were seized, with claims against the whole country east of the Penobscot Cape Cod, or some of the towns upon it, had to purchase safety; Stonington was bombarded. Fortifications were hastily thrown up wherever they could be by the Americans; the militia was called out by the states, and the general government was urged to despatch its regular troops to the menaced shores. It was officially announced by the British Admiral Cochrane that he was imperatively instructed "to destroy and lay waste all towns and districts of the United States found accessive to the attack of British armaments." This was not war, but devastation.

Capture of Washington and Alexandria.

The Chesapeake, long a favorite point for the British descents, was now occupied by a large, indeed a double fleet, under Admirals Cochrane and Cockburn, with several thousand land troops and marines under General Ross. This body, landing about fifty miles from Washington, marched against that city, while the American militia retreated hither and thither, making a stand for a few moments only at Bladensburg, (August 24.) On the evening following this rout, the British took possession of Washington, and next day proceeded to carry out the orders announced by the admiral. Stores were destroyed; a frigate and a sloop were burned; the public buildings, including the Capitol, and even the mansion of the president, were plundered and fired. Against this "unwarrantable extension of the ravages of war," as it is styled by a British writer, the United States had no right to complain, remembering the burning of the Parliament House at York, or the destruction of Newark, in the preceding year, although both these outrages had been already avenged on the New York frontier. A few hours were enough for the work of ruin at Washington, (August 25,) and the British returned to their ships. The same day (August 29) some frigates appeared off Alexandria, and extorted an enormous ransom for the town. Every thing on the American side was helplessness and submission. The president and his cabinet had reviewed the troops, which mustered to the number of several thousands; generals and officers had been thick upon the field; but there was no consistent counsel, no steadfast action, and the country lay as open to the enemy as if it had been uninhabited.

Defence of Baltimore.

It is a relief to turn to Baltimore. Fresh from their marauding victories, the British landed at North Point, some miles below that city. They were too strong for the Americans, who retired, but not until after a bravely contested battle, in which the British commander, General Ross, was slain, (September 12.) As the army advanced against the town, the next day, the fleet bombarded Fort McHenry, an inconsiderable defence just below Baltimore. But the bombardment and the advance proving ineffectual, the invaders retreated. They had been courageously met, triumphantly repelled. North Point and Fort McHenry are names which shine out, like those of Erie and Champlain, brilliant amidst encompassing darkness.

Indian foes. As if one war were not enough for a nation so hard pressed, another had broken out. The Indians on the north-west, the followers of Tecumseh, and others besides, were but the allies of the British. Independent foes, fighting altogether for themselves, uprose in the Creeks of the Mississippi Territory, where they surprised some hundreds of Americans at Fort Mimms, (August, 1813.) Numerous bodies of border volunteers at once started for the haunts of the enemy, chief amongst the number being the troops of Tennessee, under General Jackson. Penetrating into the heart of the Creek country, after various bloody encounters, Jackson at length routed the main body of the foe at a place called Tohopeka, (March 27, 1814.) A few months after, he concluded a treaty, by which the Creeks surrendered the larger part of their territory.

National straits. Enough remained, as has been seen, to keep the nation in sad straits. There were various causes to produce the same effect. To raise the very first essential for carrying on a war, a sufficient army, had been found impossible, notwithstanding the increase of bounties and the enlistment of minors without the consent of their parents or masters; * all allurements failed. The chief reliance of the government was necessarily upon the militia, about which the same controversies continued as those already mentioned between the federal and the state authorities. Yet, to show

* Rejected, when first proposed to Congress, but afterwards carried, (December, 1814.)

the extent to which the opposition party indulged itself in embarrassing the government, an alarm was sounded against the national forces, small though they were, as threatening the liberties of the country. But the army was not the only point of difficulty. To prevent supplies to the forces of the enemy, as well as to cut him off from all advantages of commerce with the United States, a new embargo was laid, (December, 1813.) So severe were its restrictions, affecting even the coasting trade and the fishery, that Massachusetts called it another Boston port bill, and pronounced it, by her legislature, to be unconstitutional. It was repealed in a few months, and with it the non-importation act, which, in one shape or another, had hung upon the commercial interests of the nation for years, (April, 1814.) More serious by far were the financial embarrassments of the government. All efforts to relieve the treasury had been wholly inadequate. Loan after loan was contracted; tax after tax was laid, until carriages, furniture, paper, and even watches, were assessed, while other help was sought, as in a new national bank, the earlier one having expired according to the provisions of its charter. But the state to which the finances at length arrived was this, that while eleven millions of revenue were all to be counted upon, — ten from taxes, and only one from custom duties, — fifty millions were needed for the expenditures of the year, (1815.) It did not change matters when a large number of the banks of the country suspended specie payments, (August, 1814.)

Party controversies.

The opposition to the war had never ceased. It rested, indeed, on foundations too deep to be lightly moved. Below the points immediately relating to the war itself, were earlier questions. Such old topics as the relations of the national and the state government came up for fresh controversy. " The governments of the

United States," declared the federalist chief magistrate of Massachusetts, "is founded on the state governments, and must be supported by them." There might be a change of sides; federalists might stand where republicans had stood, and republicans where federalists had done; but the divisions were the same. Even those between the north and the south reappeared, and with wider lines, in the midst of the war, which, as a general rule, the south supported and the north opposed.

Hartford Convention. The idea of a convention of the party, or, as the phrase ran, of the states opposing the war, was started in Massachusetts. So little countenance did it receive, as to be dropped for several months, when increasing trials led to increasing struggles. It was then renewed, but in the more modest guise of "a conference between those states the affinity of whose interests is closest, and whose habits of intercourse from local and other causes are most frequent;" in other words, the New England States; but action upon subjects of a national nature was to be left, should the conference deem it expedient, "to a future convention from all the states in the Union." The Massachusetts legislature appointed twelve delegates to represent her in the conference, and invited her sister states of New England to do likewise, (October, 1814.) Connecticut responded by appointing seven delegates, and designating Hartford as the place for the conference to meet. Rhode Island appointed four delegates; two counties in New Hampshire and one county in Vermont, one delegate each. Twenty-six were chosen, all but two of whom were present on the opening of the conference at Hartford, (December 15.) The other two afterwards appeared, constituting, with the secretary, an assembly of twenty-seven.

Charges of disunion. So small was the body to which an immense importance was attached at and after the time, but rather by its opponents than its adherents. The latter regarded it just as it was, a meeting of men to whom the greater part of New England was glad to intrust its shattered interests, but without any deep-seated expectation of succor, so strong against them was the majority of the nation. To this majority, however, or to its mouthpieces, the assembly at Hartford wore a different aspect. It was the last desperate stake, the administration party urged, of the opposition; lost or won, it hastened the issue of disunion so long suspected as prepared. Whatever extremes the federalists may have fallen into, there is no proof of their intending to separate from their countrymen. The call of the Massachusetts authorities for this very conference at Hartford proposed such deliberations and such measures, only, as were "not repugnant to their obligations as members of the Union." That they were in earnest appears from the proceedings of the conference, or the Convention, as it is generally called.

Proceedings of the Convention.

The Convention, of which George Cabot, of Massachusetts, was the president, and Harrison Gray Otis, also of Massachusetts, the leading member, addressed itself to its work with prayer. It found two classes of "dangers and grievances," as it entitled them, to be considered: one which required present relief, the other which might be left for future redress. Of the first, the chief were the illegal course of the government in relation to the militia and the destitution of all defensive resources in which New England was left. To meet these difficulties, the Convention suggested that the New England States might be allowed to assume their own defence, and, further, that a reasonable portion of the taxes assessed upon them by the general government should be retained by them to cover the expenses of defending themselves. As to the second class of complaints, embracing most of the matters that had been urged against the republican administrations by the federalists, the Convention set forth seven amendments to the Constitution. These were all prohibitory: one against any representation of slaves; another against any embargo of longer duration than sixty days; three others against any law of non-intercourse, any war, unless it were defensive, any admission of a new state, except by a two thirds vote in Congress; a sixth against the eligibility of persons "hereafter to be naturalized" to Congress or to any civil office under the United States; and a seventh against the reëlection of a president, or the election of two successive presidents from the same state. In proposing these amendments, the Convention declared "that no hostility to the Constitution is meditated." After providing for a second Convention at Boston, in case "peace should not be concluded and the defence of these states should be rejected," the Convention adjourned, having been three weeks in session, (January 5, 1815.)

Results. The results were almost null. They might be said to have been altogether so, but for a law passed by Congress without any apparent reference to the Convention, ordering that militia should "be employed in the state raising the same or in an adjoining state, and not elsewhere, except with the assent of the executive of the state so raising the same," (January.) Otherwise, nothing followed the much dreaded Convention. The commissioners appointed to apply to the general government on the part of Massachusetts, for leave to carry out the recommendations of the Convention touching the self-defence of the states, found the war at an end when they reached Washington. The constitutional amendments were rejected by the states to which they were proposed.

Meanwhile proceedings on which far less stress has been laid than upon those of the Hartford Convention, had

Nullification in Connecticut and Massachusetts.

occurred in Connecticut and Massachusetts. The legislatures of those states passed acts in direct conflict with a recent statute of the United States regarding the enlistment of minors. So far was this contradicted by the measures in question, that the parties engaged in enlisting minors were subjected to fine and imprisonment, (January, 1815.) It was not the first time that these states had set themselves against the Union. Both had taken ground against the embargo, Connecticut by statute and Massachusetts by her judicial tribunals. Massachusetts had more lately resisted the measures of the government, as we shall see, in relation to British prisoners. Nullification was far beyond the doctrines of the Convention. That body had declared itself in this wise: "That acts of Congress in violation of the Constitution are absolutely void is an undeniable position. It does not, however, consist with the respect and forbearance due from a confederate state towards the general government, to fly to open resistance upon every infraction of the Constitution." But passions were high, and nullification came naturally to New England.

Defence of Louisiana.

Late in the summer preceding the Hartford Convention, a British party landed at Pensacola, whose Spanish possessors were supposed to be inclined to side against the United States. An attack, in the early autumn, upon Fort Bowyer, thirty miles from Mobile, was repelled by the small but heroic garrison under Major Lawrence, (September 15.) A month or two afterwards, General Jackson advanced against Pensacola with a force so formidable that the British withdrew, Jackson then resigning the town to the Spanish authorities, and repairing to New Orleans, against which the enemy was believed to be preparing an expedition, (November.) There he busied himself in raising his forces and providing his defences, until the British arrived upon the coast. After capturing a feeble flotilla of the Americans, they began their advance against the capital of Louisiana, (December.) They were ten thousand and upwards; the Americans not more than half as numerous. Jackson, on learning their approach, marched directly against them, surprising them in their camp by night, and dealing them a blow from which they hardly seem to have recovered, (December 23.) They soon, however, resumed the offensive under Sir Edward Pakenham, advancing thrice against the American lines, but thrice retreating. The last action goes by the name of the battle of New Orleans. It resulted in the defeat of the enemy, with the loss of Pakenham and two thousand besides, the Americans losing less than a hundred, (January 8, 1815.) The British retired to the sea, taking Fort Bowyer, the same that had resisted an attack the autumn before, (February 12.) Louisiana had been nobly defended, and not by the energy of Jackson alone, nor by the resolution of her own people, but by the generous spirit with which the entire south-west sent its sons to her rescue.

Martial law at New Orleans.

Jackson had hesitated at nothing in defending New Orleans. Upon the approach of the British, he proclaimed martial law; he continued it after their departure. The author of a newspaper article reflecting upon the general's conduct was sent to prison to await trial for life. The United States district judge was arrested and expelled from the city for having issued a writ of habeas corpus in the prisoner's behalf; and on the district attorney's applying to the state court in behalf of the judge, he, too, was banished. On the proclamation of peace, martial law was necessarily suspended. The judge returned, and summoning the general before him, imposed a fine of one thousand dollars. The sum was paid by Jackson, but was offered to be repaid to him by a subscription, which proved public opinion to sustain his determined course.* It was characteristic of the man and of his adherents in after years.

Reappearance of the navy.

While these events were going on by land, the sea was for a time abandoned, at least by all national vessels. Privateers continued their work of plunder and of destruction — a work which, however miserable to contemplate, doubtless had its effect in bringing the war to a close. But the navy of the nation had disappeared from the ocean. It presently reappeared in the shape of its pride and ornament, the Constitution, which, under her new commander, Stewart, got to sea from Boston, (December, 1814.) The President, Hornet, and Peacock did the same from New York, the President being immediately captured, though not without a severe combat, by the British cruisers, (January, 1815.) Her loss was avenged by the sister vessels; the Constitution taking two sloops of war at once — the Cyane and the Levant — off Madeira, (February 20;) the Hornet sloop taking the Penguin brig off the Island of Tristan d'Acunha, (March 23;) and the Peacock sloop taking the Nautilus, an East India Company's cruiser, off Sumatra, (June 30.)† All these actions were subsequent to a treaty of peace.

The war had not continued a year when the administration accepted an offer of Russian mediation, and despatched

* Refusing to receive the subscription, he was reimbursed, near thirty years afterwards, by order of Congress.

† "Thus terminated at sea," says the British historian Alison, towards the close of an account by no means partial to the American side, "this memorable contest, in which the English, for the first time for a century and a half, met with equal antagonists on their own element; and in recounting which, the British historian, at a loss whether to admire most the devoted heroism of his own countrymen or the gallant bearing of their antagonists, feels almost equally warmed in narrating either side of the strife."

Peace preliminaries.

envoys to treat of peace. The chief points to be provided for, according to the instructions, were, first, impressments, of which the settlement had been facilitated by an American law prohibiting the enlistment of British seamen in the service of the United States, and next, the matter of blockades, the only part of the anti-neutral system which had not been abandoned by the British, (March, 1813.) Great Britain declined the mediation of Russia, but offered to enter into negotiations either at London or at Gottenburg. The American government chose the latter place, and appointed five commissioners — John Quincy Adams, James A. Bayard, Henry Clay, Jonathan Russell, and Albert Gallatin — to negotiate a treaty, under much the same instructions as before, (January, February, 1814.) But on the news of the triumph of Great Britain and her allies over Napoleon, the demands of the United States were sensibly modified. The opposition alleged it to be from fear of the foe, whose power was so much increased by the issue of the European war. But the administration and its party declared that the pacification of Europe did away with the very abuses of which America had to complain; in other words, that there would be no blockades or impressments in time of peace. At all events, the envoys were directed to leave these points for future negotiation, confining themselves at present to the conclusion of a general treaty. They were also authorized to treat at London, if they thought the arrival of British commissioners at Gottenburg was likely to be delayed, (June.) The new instructions found the commissioners of both nations in session at Ghent, (August 8.)

Treaty of Ghent.

Four months and a half elapsed before coming to terms. The British demands, especially on the point of retaining the conquests made during the war, were altogether inadmissible. Fortunately, they were yielded; the disposal of the American question being desirable in the uncertain state of European affairs. "Some of our European allies," wrote Lord Liverpool, British premier, to Lord Castlereagh, British ambassador at the Congress of Vienna, then in session, "may not be indisposed to favor Americans, and if the Emperor of Russia should be desirous of taking up their cause, we are well aware that there is a most powerful party to support him." The command of the British forces in America was pressed upon the Duke of Wellington. He consented in case the war should be continued, but advised peace, being satisfied, as he said, that there was "no vulnerable point of importance belonging to the United States" which could be held by the British "except New Orleans." Nor even this, as Sir Edward Pakenham soon afterwards found. Castlereagh wrote from Vienna that the American war made little sensation there. But when it was terminated by the negotiations at Ghent, those at Vienna were carried forward with much less difficulty than Great Britain had previously experienced. The treaty of Ghent restored the conquests on either side, and provided commissioners to arrange the boundary and other minor questions between the nations, (December 24.) As for the American objects of the war, according to the declarations at its outbreak, they were not mentioned in the articles by which it was closed; yet the United States did not hesitate to ratify the treaty, (February 18.) Within a week afterwards, the president recommended "the navigation of American vessels exclusively by American seamen, either natives or such as are already naturalized;" the reason assigned being "to guard against incidents which, during the periods of war in Europe, might tend to interrupt peace."

Protection of foreigners.

Though much was waived for the sake of peace, one principle, if no more, had been maintained for our country. In the first year of the war, the British had set out to treat some Irishmen taken while fighting on the American side, not as ordinary prisoners of war, but as traitors to Great Britain. On their being sent to be tried for treason in England, Congress aroused itself in their behalf, and authorized the adoption of retaliatory measures. An equal number of British captives was presently imprisoned, and when the British retorted by ordering twice as many American officers into confinement, the Americans did the same by the British officers in their power. The British government went so far as to order its commanders, in case any retaliation was inflicted upon the prisoners in American hands, to destroy the towns and their inhabitants upon the coast. It was at this juncture that Massachusetts, as already alluded to, appeared in the lines of nullification. The federalist majority in Massachusetts, caring little for the fate of the Irish prisoners, forbade the use of the state prisons for the British officers now ordered to be confined, (February, 1814.) The matter was set at rest by the retraction of the British government, who consented to treat the Irishmen as prisoners of war. Proclamation was made pardoning all past offences of the sort, but threatening future ones with the penalties of treason; a threat never attempted to be fulfilled, (July.)

Indian treaty.

Some months after the treaty of Ghent, a treaty was made with the Indians of the north-west. Such as had been at war agreed to bury the tomahawk, and to join with such as had been at peace in new relations with the United States, (September.)

Algerine treaty.

Another treaty had been made by this time. It was with the Dey of Algiers, who had gone to war with the United States in the same year that Great Britain did. The United States, however, had paid no attention to the inferior enemy until relieved of the superior. Then war was declared, and a fleet despatched, under Commodore Decatur, by which captures were made, and terms dictated to the Algerine. The treaty not only surrendered all American prisoners, and indemnified all American losses in the war, but renounced the claim of tribute on the part of Algiers, (June.) Tunis and Tripoli being brought to terms, the United States were no longer tributary to pirates.

Exhaustion. Madison was reëlected president, with Elbridge Gerry as vice president, in the first year of the war. If he really consented to war as the price of his re-election, he had his reward. The difficulties of his second term, more serious than those of any administration before him, weighed upon him heavily. He welcomed peace, as his party welcomed it, — in fact, as the whole nation welcomed it, — with the same sensations of relief that men would feel if the earth, yawning at their feet, should suddenly close. To see from what the government and the nation were saved, it is sufficient to read that systems of conscription for the army and of impressment for the navy were amongst the projects pending at the close of the war, and that the public debt had been increased by one hundred and twenty millions — a far larger sum in those days than in these. Some parts of the country had suffered more than others; some industries, like those of commerce, had vanished. But as a whole, the people were in a state of temporary exhaustion.

Independence. It was not so much in vain as it sometimes seems. Indirectly, almost unconsciously, our fathers had perfected their independence of other nations. Never after, as before the treaty of Ghent, did the United States hang in suspense upon British orders or French decrees; never again did the people, or their parties, shape their course merely according to foreign movements. Not the war itself, so much as what went before, bore this fruit; the war was merely the forcing process by which the fruit was ripened.

CHAPTER III.

Missouri Compromise.

Recovery. The depression at the close of the war was not so great as the elation at the return of peace. Men every where resumed their old enterprises, or entered upon new ones, without fear of the past or the future. The government addressed itself at once to the restoration of national prosperity. A new tariff was adopted, partly to increase the revenue, and partly to protect domestic manufactures. Internal taxes were gradually abolished. A new Bank of the United States was chartered, (March, 1816.) All this was not done in a day; nor was the revival of the nation uninterrupted. But the general tendency was towards recovery from the disorders into which the country had been plunged by the recent war.

Administrations. Madison's troubled administration came to an end. James Monroe was the president for the next eight years, (1817–25,) with Daniel D. Tompkins as vice president. Monroe, once an extreme, but latterly a moderate republican, so far conciliated all parties as to be reëlected with but one electoral vote against him. Old parties were dying out. The great question of the period, to be set forth presently, was one with which republicans and federalists, as such, had nothing to do.

Seminole war. The new administration had but just opened, when the Seminole war, as it was styled, broke out with the Indians of Georgia and Florida. It began with massacres on both sides, and ended with a spoiling, burning, slaying expedition, half militia and half Indians, under General Jackson, the conqueror of the Creeks in the preceding war, (March, 1818.) On the pretext that the Spanish authorities countenanced the hostilities of the Indians, Jackson took St. Mark's and Pensacola, not without some ideas of seizing St. Augustine. He also put to death, within the Spanish limits, two British subjects accused of stirring up the Indians, (March, May.) So that the war, though called the Seminole, might as well be called the Florida war. The Spanish minister protested against the invasion of the Florida territory, of which the restitution was immediately ordered at Washington, though not without approbation of the course pursued by Jackson.

Acquisition of Florida.

Florida was a sore spot on more accounts than one. The old trouble of boundaries had never been settled; but that was a trifle compared with the later troubles arising from fugitive criminals, fugitive slaves, smugglers, pirates, and, as recently shown, Indians, to whom Florida furnished not only a refuge, but a starting point. The Spanish authorities, themselves by no means inclined to respect their neighbors of the United States, had no power to make others respect them. "This country," said President Monroe, referring to Florida, "had, in fact, become the theatre of every species of lawless adventure." Matters there were not improved by the uncertain relations still continuing between the United States and Spain. Former difficulties, especially those upon American indemnities, were not settled; while new ones had gathered in consequence of South American revolutions, and North American dispositions to side with the revolutionists. The proposal of an earlier time to purchase Florida was renewed by the United States. Its acceptance was impeded chiefly by differences on the boundary between Louisiana and the Spanish Mexico, but this being settled to begin at the Sabine River, a treaty was concluded. On the payment of five millions by the American government to citizens who claimed indemnity from Spain, that power agreed to relinquish the Floridas, East and West, (February 22, 1819.) It was nearly two years, however, before Spain ratified the treaty, and fully two before Florida Territory formed a part of the United States, (1821.)

New states. The State of Connecticut, hitherto content with her charter government, at length adopted a new constitution, in which there was but little improvement upon the old one, except in making suffrage general and the support of a church system voluntary, (1818.) New constitutions and new states were constantly in process of formation. Indiana, (December 11, 1816,) Mississippi, (December 10, 1817,) Illinois, (December 3, 1818,) and Alabama,* (December 14, 1819,) all became members of the Union.

Proposal of Missouri. Before the actual accession of Alabama, Missouri was proposed as a candidate for admission. It was a slaveholding territory. But when the bill authorizing it to frame a state constitution was before Congress, a New York representative, James W. Tallmadge, moved that no more slaves should be brought in, and that the children of those already there should be liberated at the age of twenty-five. This passed the House of Representatives, but failed in the Senate. Then another New York representative, John W. Taylor, moved to prohibit slavery in the entire territory to the north of latitude 36° 30′; but this, too, was lost. A bill setting off the portion of Missouri Territory to the south of the line just named,

* The eastern half of the Mississippi Territory became the Territory of Alabama in 1817.

as the Territory of Arkansas, was passed. But nothing was done towards establishing the State of Missouri, (February, March, 1819.)

Intense agitation. Had it been an outbreak of hostilities, had it been a march of one half the country against the other, there could hardly have been a more intense agitation. A large number felt that the time had come to make a stand against the extension of slavery. On the other hand, the attempted prohibition of slavery was denounced as violating the rights of the slaveholding states; nay, more, as the preliminary to a negro massacre, a civil war, a dissolution of the Union. The aged Jefferson wrote, despondingly, "The Missouri question is a breaker on which we lose the Missouri country by revolt, and what more God only knows. From the battle of Bunker's Hill to the treaty of Paris we never had so ominous a question." John Adams was more sanguine: "I hope it will follow the other waves under the ship, and do no harm." Public meetings were held; those at the south to repel the interference of the north, those at the north to rebuke the pretensions of the south. The dispute extended into the state tribunals and legislatures, the northern declaring that Missouri must be for freemen only, the southern that it must be for freemen and their slaves.

Question of slavery. It was certainly a great question. "Scarcely ever," said a Massachusetts representative, "was so great a question before a human tribunal." Not only Missouri, but the rest of that vast region originally called Louisiana, was to be opened or closed to slavery. Not only the few thousand slaves within the territory claiming to become a state, but the thousand thousands to follow them, in the state and beyond it, were to be disposed of by the decision that must soon be reached. The party of freedom insisted upon the right and the duty of

Congress to make Missouri free; the party of slavery was equally urgent that Congress had no right to interfere, that a state alone could determine whether it would be slaveholding or not in any case, and that in this particular case it had no option, being bound by the treaty under which Missouri, as a part of Louisiana, had been acquired, and by which the inhabitants, being admitted to all the rights of United States citizens, had been admitted to all the rights of United States slaveholders. There was also a numerical argument. The Union now consisted of twenty-two states, eleven free, eleven slaveholding; and as the last, Alabama, had been slaveholding, the next ought to be free. When Congress re-assembled, and Maine sought to be received as a state, Massachusetts consenting, (1820,) the argument from numbers was turned, and Missouri was to be slaveholding, because Maine was to be free.

The Compromise. The Senate united Maine and Missouri in the same bill and on the same terms; that is, without any restriction upon slavery. But a clause introduced on the motion of Jesse B. Thomas, of Illinois, prohibited the introduction of slavery into any portion of the Louisiana Territory as yet unorganized, leaving Louisiana the state and Arkansas the territory, as well as Missouri, just what they were; that is, slaveholding. The line of 36° 30′, proposed the year before, was again proposed, save only that Missouri, though north of the line, was to be a Southern State. This was the Missouri Compromise. It came from the north. On the part of the north, it yielded the claim to Missouri as a free state; on the part of the south, it yielded the claim to the immensely larger regions which stretched above and beyond Missouri to the Pacific. Thus the Senate determined, not without opposition from both sides. The House, on the contrary, adopted a bill admitting Missouri, separately from Maine, and under the northern restriction concerning slavery. Words continued to run high. Henry Clay, still in the House, wrote that the subject "engrosses the whole thoughts of the members, and constitutes almost the only topic of conversation." A committee of conference led to the agreement of both Senate and House upon a bill admitting Missouri, after her constitution should be formed, free of restrictions, but prohibiting slavery north of the line of 36° 30′, (March 3, 1820.) Maine was admitted at the same time, (March 3-15.)

Different interpretations. The Compromise prohibited slavery in the designated region forever. This was the letter; but it was under different interpretations. When President Monroe consulted his cabinet upon approving the act of Congress, all but his secretary of state, John Quincy Adams, inclined to read the prohibition of slavery as applying only to the territories, and not to the states that might arise beyond the prescribed boundary. This was not a difference between northern and southern views, but one between strict and liberal constructions of the Constitution; the strict construction going against all power in Congress to restrict a state, while the liberal took the opposite ground. So with others besides the cabinet. Among the very men who voted for the Compromise were many, doubtless, who understood it as applying to territories alone. The northern party, unquestionably, adopted it in its broader sense, preventing the state as well as the territory from establishing slavery. That there should be two senses attached to it from the beginning was a dark presage of future differences.

Admission of Missouri. Present differences were not yet overcome. Missouri, rejoicing in becoming a slaveholding state, adopted a constitution which forbade the legislature to emancipate slaves or to allow the immigration of free negroes. On this being brought before Congress, towards the close of the year, (1820,) various tactics were adopted; the extreme southern party going for the immediate admission of the state, while the extreme northern side urged the overthrow of state, constitution, and Compromise, together. Henry Clay, at the head of the moderate men, succeeded, after long exertions, in carrying a measure providing for the admission of Missouri as soon as her legislature should solemnly covenant the rights of citizenship to "the citizens of either of the states," (February, 1821.) This was done, and Missouri became a state, (August 10.)

Slave trade. While the nation thus refused to arrest slavery within its limits, it resisted the extension of the slave trade. Upwards of fourteen thousand slaves were said to have been imported in a single year, (1818.) Upon this an act of Congress attached fresh and severer penalties to the slave dealer, and provided for the return of his unhappy victims to their native country, (1819.) Another act denounced the traffic as piracy, (1820.)

CHAPTER IV.

THE MONROE DOCTRINE.

Independence of Central and South America.

THREE years after the treaty of Ghent, the foreign secretary of the British government asked the American minister, Richard Rush, at London, what the United States would do about Spanish America. He meant the colonies of Spain in Central and South America, which had some time before declared their independence, and afterwards maintained it in arms, but which the European powers desired to see restored to their former colonial condition. It was a time of reaction against freedom throughout Europe and European possessions. The Holy Alliance of Russia, Prussia, and Austria, to which France and Great Britain more or less adhered, had undertaken to remove all traces of the French revolution and its kindred movements; and of these the rising throughout Spanish America was one. The confidence of the American minister in the independent spirit of the government he represented, appeared in his reply to the question of the British secretary, that "the only basis" upon which the United States would negotiate concerning the Spanish colonies was their "independence." Four years later, this independence was formally recognized by the United States government, (1822.)

The Monroe Doctrine.

It was a brave act. The European allies were evidently preparing to interfere, first with Spain herself, where fresh revolutions had broken out, and then with her revolted colonies. Only Great Britain was drawing back, and from her alone could the United States expect any sort of acquiescence in the recognition of the American states. Her foreign secretary, then George Canning, proposed to Mr. Rush, still minister at London, a concurrent declaration of Great Britain and the United States in opposition to the course of the continental powers. In a later interview, Canning spoke of the question as "a new and complicated one in modern affairs," and, while seeking action, seemed to fail in finding any which could be adopted, or, if adopted, be effectual. A month or two later, (December 2, 1823,) President Monroe sent his seventh annual message to Congress, and here announced that, in negotiations with Russia, his administration had asserted, "as a principle in which the rights and interests of the United States are involved, that the American continents, by the free and independent position which they have assumed and maintained, are henceforth not to be considered as subjects for future colonization by any European powers." "We owe it," continued the president, "to candor, and to the amicable relations existing between the United States and those powers, to declare that we should consider any attempt on their part to extend their system to any portion of this hemisphere as dangerous to our peace and safety. With the existing colonies or dependencies of any European power we have not interfered, and shall not interfere. But with the governments who have declared their independence, and maintained it, and whose independence we have on great consideration and on just principles acknowledged, we could not view any interposition for the purpose of oppressing them, or controlling in any other manner their destiny by any European power, in any other light than as the manifestation of an unfriendly disposition towards the United States." Such was what has since been called the Monroe Doctrine.

Authorship. If it had borne the name of its immediate author, it would have been called after John Quincy Adams, then secretary of state, rather than the president. But the real authorship is to be traced, beyond any individual, to the nation, or to the thinking part of the nation. Such were the times, and such the politics of Europe, so adverse to every political principle which an American republican held dear, that he longed to have his government committed to a better course. "There will be, I trust," said Daniel Webster, "an American policy." As he was speaking a month after the message, he might have said, There is an American policy.

Purpose. Its purpose, as far as the Monroe Doctrine went, was twofold. It showed the intention of the United States to prevent the European powers from extending their system across the Atlantic either to destroy free institutions where they existed, or to set up their own institutions wherever a spot could be found. The first point was to protect the republics of Central and South America. The second was to protect the yet unoccupied regions of the entire continent. As to the first, Mr. Rush wrote home from London, that it was expected and well received; but as to the second, he declared that it was unexpected, and would not be acquiesced in by England. It was of much greater consequence that the purpose of the Doctrine should be sustained at home. Congress declined to take any formal action; but, as Webster said, some time later, the tone of the president's message "found a corresponding response in the breasts of the free people of the United States."

Aid to Greece. The same message which spoke for freedom in the new world spoke for it in the old. Two years before, the Messenian Senate had appealed to the United States for aid to the Greeks in their struggle against the Turkish yoke. Sympathy had been won, subscriptions and personal services had been given by individuals, and now the message expressed the national concern. Webster followed it up by one of his great speeches in the House, urging the appointment of a commissioner to Greece, and all the moral support that could be lent to a righteous cause.

Lafayette's visit.

A few months later Lafayette arrived, on national invitation, to behold the work which he had aided in his youth. The French government, as its ambassador at London confessed, did not like the invitation, or the American frigate that was placed at the disposal of the guest, for the government was of the then prevailing temper, while Lafayette was identified with all that was liberal, or, as his opponents would say, revolutionary in Europe. His visit, therefore, was not merely a proof of American gratitude towards himself, but of American sympathy with the principles which he represented more than any other man alive. "The other day," he says, "at Boston, God was prayed to give liberty to the two hemispheres; and a devotion like this suits me better than the anti-revolutionary anathemas of Europe." From the day of his landing (August 16, 1824) to that of his departure, (September 7, 1825,) a period of more than a year, he was, as he described himself, "in a whirlwind of popular kindnesses of which it was impossible to have formed any previous conception, and in which every thing that could touch and flatter one was mingled." "A more interesting spectacle, it is believed," said President Monroe, "was never witnessed, because none could be founded on purer principles, none proceed from higher or more disinterested motives." To make some amends for his early sacrifices, pecuniary as well as personal, in the American cause, Congress voted Lafayette a township of the public domain, and a grant of two hundred thousand dollars.

Congress of Panama. When John Quincy Adams had risen to the presidency, (1825,) an invitation was received by the government from some of the Central and South American states to unite in a congress at Panama. The objects, ranging from mere commercial negotiations up to the Monroe Doctrine, were rather indefinite; but Adams appointed two envoys, whom the Senate confirmed, and for whom the House made the necessary appropriations, though not without great opposition, (December, 1825 — March, 1826.) One of the envoys died, the other did not go upon his mission; so that the congress began and ended without any representation from the United States, (June — July.) It adjourned to meet at Tacubaya, near Mexico, in the beginning of the following year. The ministers of the United States repaired to the appointed place, and at the appointed time, but there was no congress.

CHAPTER V.

TARIFF COMPROMISE.

Nullification. THE alleged right of a state to nullify any act which it deemed unconstitutional on the part of the general government was but another form of asserting that the state, and not the nation, was the sovereign authority according to the Constitution. It had been maintained, as we have seen, by Jefferson and Madison in 1798, and by the New England federalists in 1814 and 1815. It was now renewed, and became the great question before the country during the administrations of Adams and Jackson.

In Georgia. Many years before, Georgia had ceded her western lands, covering the present Alabama and Mississippi, on condition that the United States government would buy and transfer to her the large tracts still held by the Creeks and Cherokees within her borders. This the government began to do; but some difficulty with the Creeks, who had not been fairly dealt with, delayed the execution of the contract. The governor of Georgia hinted at anti-slavery motives on the part of the administration, and called upon the adjoining states to stand by their arms. President Adams communicated the matter to Congress, asserting his intention "to enforce the laws, and fulfil the duties of the nation by all the force committed for that purpose to his charge." Whereat the governor wrote to the secretary of war, "From the first decisive act of hostility, you will be considered and treated as a public enemy," (1827.) Fortunately, the winds ceased. The state that had set itself against the nation more decidedly than had ever yet been done returned to its senses. As for the unhappy Indians, not only the Creeks, but all the other tribes that could be persuaded to move, were gradually transported to more distant territories in the west.

Tariffs. Other causes were operating to excite the states, or some of them, against the general government. The tariff of 1816, intended to assist the nation in recovering from the losses of war, had also been intended to protect domestic manufactures against importations from abroad. It was urged by the Southern States in the opinion that cotton would command higher prices if manufactured at home, and was resisted by the Northern, especially the New England States, whose interests were then commercial rather than manufacturing or agricultural. But after the adoption of the tariff, the Northern and Middle States devoted more and more of their capital to manufactures, while the cotton-growing states continued to raise the raw material without attempting to manufacture it; so that the northern and southern sections gradually changed front, until the southern became violently opposed to protective duties, by which, as one of its chief leaders declared, its interests had been shamefully sacrificed, while, on the other hand, the manufacturers, not merely of cotton, but of woollen, hemp, iron, and other materials, in the Eastern and Middle States, demanded protection; "and it matters not," they said at a convention in Harrisburg, (1827,) "if it amounts to prohibition." The controversy resulted in the triumph of the protective, or, as its supporters called it, the American, system in the tariff of 1828.

Exposition and protest of South Carolina.

Several of the Southern States declared this to be unconstitutional. South Carolina did more, and her legislature issued an Exposition and Protest, in which the resistance of the state to the general government was not only threatened, but justified, (December, 1828.) "The existence," it was argued, "of the right of judging of their powers, clearly established from the sovereignty of the states, as clearly implies a veto or control on the action of the general government on contested points of authority; and this very control is the remedy which the Constitution has provided to prevent the encroachment of the general government on the reserved rights of the states. . . . There exists a case [the tariff] which would justify the interposition of this state, and thereby compel the general government to abandon an unconstitutional power." It was at this same time, "in December, 1828," wrote Daniel Webster, "I became thoroughly convinced that the plan of a southern confederation had been received with favor by a great many of the political men of the south." Secession was the inevitable consequence of nullification.

Jackson's first acts.

Andrew Jackson succeeded to the presidency, (1829.) His first act was to remove hundreds of public officers in order to provide for his followers. In this he had no example among his predecessors, for all the six together had made just sixty-four removals from office, and no more. His next act of importance was to recommend Congress to modify the tariff of the year before, which was the same as to recommend concession to the demands of South Carolina and other discontented states. Some months later, (May, 1830,) Congress adopted a few modifications, that would have been unimportant but for the precedent of giving way on the part of the nation.

Webster's defence of the nation.

But before this action was taken, the nation and its sovereignty had been nobly defended in the Senate of the United States. Senator Foot, of Connecticut, offered a resolution at the close of the previous year, (1829,) concerning the disposition of the public lands; but these were soon lost sight of in the debates which followed concerning the relative powers of the states and the national government. Robert Y. Hayne, a senator from South Carolina, appeared in support of the theories to which his state was committed; but every one knew that he was speaking for a greater leader, John C. Calhoun, vice president of the United States under Jackson, as he had been under Adams, and yet more influential as the head and front of nullification. Hayne's first speech on this question (January 19, 1830) was answered by Webster the next day, and with such effect that Hayne's rejoinder was not completed for several days, when Webster spoke the second time, (January 26,) and with greater effect than had or has ever been witnessed in either house of Congress. His purpose was to lay the axe at the root of nullification; and this he did by a close and decisive argument that the national government is not a compact among sovereign states, but a government established by the people, and to be resisted, if at all, only by appeal from one of its branches to another, or by the right of revolution against them all. "I trust," said the great orator, to whom the proud title of Defender of the Constitution was given by his grateful countrymen, "the crisis has in some measure passed by," (1831.)

Bad temper.

But not even Webster could then see how perilous the crisis continued. A visitor at Washington, early in 1831, describes the temper in Congress; and the temper there prevailed elsewhere: "When we entered the House, there was a debate going on relative to reduction of duty on salt. Some southern members spoke with great vehemence, but nobody on the floor paid any attention to them. They spoke of their oppression, of throwing themselves on the sovereignty of their states, of being goaded to rebellion, of the time being near when Vengeance should stalk about these halls. It was melancholy to see such feelings aroused among our countrymen, and more painful to see them quite disregarded."

South Carolina nullifies.

A year and more later, the storm long brewing broke upon the country. Congress, having reduced the high duties upon some articles, but left them upon others, refused to abandon protection in the new tariff of 1832. The South Carolina members of Congress immediately united with Vice President Calhoun in an address declaring their conviction "that the protecting system must now be regarded as the settled policy of the country," and recommending "a struggle" to transmit to posterity "the rights and liberties received as a precious inheritance from an illustrious ancestry." The legislature of South Carolina summoned a convention of the state, which met at Columbia, under the presidency of Governor Hamilton, (November 19.) A few days sufficed to pass an ordinance declaring "that the several acts, and parts of acts, purporting to be laws for the imposing of duties on importation . . . are unauthorized by the Constitution of the United States, and violate the true intent and meaning thereof, and are null and void, and no law, nor binding upon the State of South Carolina, its officers and citizens; . . . and that it shall be the duty of the legislature to adopt such measures and pass such acts as may be necessary to give full effect to this ordinance, and to prevent the enforcement and arrest the operation of the said acts, and parts of acts, of the Congress of the United States within the limits of the state," (November 24.)

And threatens to secede.

In all this there was nothing new. But South Carolina went further than any of her predecessors in nullification. "We, the people of South Carolina," concluded the ordinance of the convention, "do further declare that we will not submit to the application of force, on the part of the federal government, to reduce this state to obedience, but that we will consider the passage by Congress of any act . . . to enforce the acts hereby declared to be null and void, otherwise than through the civil tribunals of the country, as inconsistent with the longer continuance of South Carolina in the Union; and that the people of this state . . . will forthwith proceed to organize a separate government."

Resolution of government.

If the state was resolute, the general government was no less so. The president was in his element. A crisis which he was eminently adapted to meet had arrived. It called forth all his independence, all his nationality. Other men — more than one of his predecessors — would have doubted the course to be pursued; they would have staid to inquire into the powers of the Constitution, or to count the resources of the government; nay, had they been consistent, they would have inclined to the support, rather than to the overthrow, of the South Carolina doctrine. Jackson did not waver an instant. He took his own connsel, as he was wont to do, and declared for the nation against the state; then ordered troops and a national vessel to the support of the government officers in South Carolina. "No act of violent opposition to the laws has yet been committed," — thus the president declared in a proclamation; "but such a state of things is hourly apprehended; and it is the intent of this instrument to proclaim not only that the duty imposed on me by the Constitution, to take care that the laws be faithfully executed, shall be performed, . . . but to warn the citizens of South Carolina . . . that the course they are urged to pursue is one of ruin and disgrace to the very state whose right they affect to support," (December.) The appeal to the South Carolinians was the more forcible in coming from one of themselves, as it were; Jackson being a native of their state. Addressing Congress in an elaborate message, (January 16, 1833,) the president argued down both nullification and secession, maintaining that "the result of each is the same; since a state in which, by a usurpation of power, the constitutional authority of the federal government is openly defied and set aside, wants only the form to be independent of the Union." He then proceeded to recount the measures which he had taken, and to propose those which he considered it necessary for Congress to take. Congress responded, after some delay, by an enforcing act, the primary object of which was to secure the collection of the customs in the South Carolina ports. To this Calhoun, who had resigned the vice presidency in order to represent South Carolina in the Senate, opposed himself in vain; while Webster argued against him as he had done against Hayne two years before, (February.)

Resolution of states.

The government did not stand alone. One after another the states, by legislative or by individual proceedings, came out in support of the national principle. The principle of state sovereignty, that might have found support but for the extremity to which it had been pushed, seemed to be abandoned. South Carolina was left to herself, even by her neighbors, usually prone to take the same side. Only Virginia came forward, appealing to the government as well as to South Carolina to be done with strife. As if to show her sympathy for the cause of the state, Virginia appointed a commissioner to convey her sentiments to the people of South Carolina. Otherwise the states ranged themselves distinctly, though not all actively, on the side of the nation.

Tariff compromise.

But on one point there was a decided reservation with many of the states. The tariff was openly condemned by North Carolina, Alabama, and Georgia; the last state proposing a southern convention, to take some measures of resistance to the continuance of a system so unconstitutional. Henry Clay took the matter up in the Senate. He had been the advocate of the Missouri Compromise, and now, in consultation with others, brought forward a tariff compromise. This proposed that the duties on all imports exceeding twenty per cent. should be reduced to that rate by successive diminutions through the next ten years, (till June 30, 1842.) Unlike the Missouri question, the tariff question was disposed of without protracted struggles. The advocates of protection opposed the compromise as a financial measure, but far graver objections were brought against it as a political measure. Webster considered it as "yielding great principles to faction," and others thought with him that it was no time to waive the national supremacy at the moment that a state was in open rebellion against it. But the compromise became a law, (March 2.) "The lightning," as one of Clay's correspondents wrote to him, was "drawn out from the clouds lowering over the country," and South Carolina returned to her former position. But that was full of insubordination, and the clouds still lowered.

The president's regret.

The president never ceased to regret that he had not done as he threatened, and arrested Calhoun for high treason. It was a regret in which many shared, believing that the time had come to test the strength of the national government, and that the trial of its second officer, on the charge of conspiring against it, would have been a better opportunity of settling the relations between the nation and the state than could be found in enforcing acts or compromises.

CHAPTER VI.

ANTI-SLAVERY.

Calhoun's basis.

CALHOUN, escaping trial, went home to tell his people that the south could not be united against the north on the tariff question. "The basis of southern union," he said, "must be shifted to the slave question."

Two periods in the anti-slavery movement.

This question had then (1833) entered upon its later phase. In the history of the movement against slavery in the United States, two periods are easily observed. The first is from the beginning of the government to the year 1831, during which anti-slavery meant opposition to an evil from which all parts of the country were suffering, and to the relief of which all must contribute. Slavery was to be removed gradually, and with compensation to the owners of slaves who might be emancipated. As a general rule, societies were the instruments to be employed in bringing about the desired results, the subject being too delicate, or too vast, or both, for individual action. All this changes in the second period, from 1831 forward. Slavery is the sin for which those only who tolerate it are to pay the penalty; it is to be wiped out at once, and without compensating those who have upheld it; and as its abolition is to be effected only at great risks and in defiance of powerful traditions, it must be the work of individuals, who, though combined in associations, are mostly engaged in individual action.

It was a natural consequence of this contrast that while the South coöperated in anti-slavery movements before 1831, it set itself against them afterwards. Of one hundred and forty-four anti-slavery societies in 1826, one hundred and six were southern. Of the comparatively few, ten years later, all were northern.

South-ampton massacre. The dividing line between the two periods is marked by the Southampton massacre. This happened in the Virginia county of that name in August, 1831. Its leader was a slave of fanatic character, named Turner; its first victims were sixty whites, its last one hundred blacks, who fell before the state militia and United States troops sent against them. In December of the same year, the legislature of Virginia, discussing the massacre, went on to discuss its cause, and the possibility of removing it by emancipation. Various plans were proposed, and though none was adopted, though all were opposed by the eastern members, the tone of the debate was generally anti-slavery. "The hour of the eradication of the evil is advancing," said T. J. Randolph, a grandson of Jefferson; "it must come." It was the last time that any southern legislature, or assembly of any kind, suffered slavery to be treated in this style.

Lundy and Garrison. Already the changed character of the anti-slavery movement had appeared. Benjamin Lundy, a mechanic of Quaker parentage, began his journal, entitled Genius of Universal Emancipation, in 1821, and three years later, removed its office from Ohio to Maryland. There, at Baltimore, in a slaveholding community, he continued to urge the immediate abolition of slavery, and, not content with his labors as a journalist, travelled north and south to meet men face to face, and increase the number of his fellow-laborers. In Boston, he found a a young printer, William L. Garrison, working in the same cause, and willing to follow him to Baltimore. Soon after Garrison's arrival, however, an article which he wrote exposed him to arrest and fine, and being unable to pay the fine, he was imprisoned until set free by a friend at a distance. He made his way back to Boston, and to its better opportunities of writing freely, and at the beginning of 1831 established the Liberator, a paper of more outspoken and unshaken hostility to slavery than any which went before or followed after. "A greater revolution in public sentiment," it declared, "is to be effected in the free states, particularly in New England, than at the south. . . . Let southern oppressors tremble; let their northern apologists tremble. . . . On this subject I do not wish," said the determined editor, "to speak or write with moderation."

American Anti-Slavery Society.

The new school of abolitionists was neither numerous nor influential at the beginning. A few local societies were formed, and their meetings and publications increased the volume rather than the power of the movement. It gathered fresh strength from the abolition of British colonial slavery by Parliament in the summer of 1833, and early in the following winter the leading abolitionists met at Philadelphia and organized the American Anti-Slavery Society. The declaration of this body, compared by its members to the Declaration of Independence adopted in the same city fifty-seven years before, was drawn by Garrison. It recognized the right of states to legislate exclusively on slavery within their own limits, but asserted the right of the general government to suppress the slave trade from state to state, and to abolish slavery in the District of Columbia and the territories. It insisted upon the duty of the government and the people, particularly in the free states, "to remove slavery by moral and political action, as prescribed in the

Constitution of the United States." In every respect the declaration was imperative; and as not only expressing, but inspiring, the strongest anti-slavery convictions of the time, it must be forever memorable in our history. The poet Whittier said, thirty years afterwards, "I set a higher value on my name as appended to the anti-slavery declaration of 1833 than on the title page of any book."

Reaction among the people.

The abolitionists were soon beset. Men pointed at them as if they were mad or wicked. Mobs broke into their meetings and laid violent hands upon their leaders, who were sometimes rescued only by being taken to prison. The legislature of Georgia offered five thousand dollars for the arrest and conviction of the editor or publisher of the Liberator. Not Georgia alone, but Alabama, North and South Carolina, and Virginia, called upon the free states to make anti-slavery publications penal offences, and to suppress anti-slavery societies. These demands were supported by those in office and those out of office throughout the north. At Charleston, S. C., the United States post-office was attacked, and papers brought by mail from the north were seized and burned, (1835.) Instead of defending his charge, the postmaster ordered similar mail matter to be stopped thereafter, and the postmaster general of the United States, though confessing that he had no authority to ratify such an act, refused to condemn it.

In the government.

The government followed the lead of the people. President Jackson's message of December, 1835, suggested the passage of a law to prohibit the circulation of "incendiary publications" through the mails. Two months later, Calhoun, chairman of a Senate committee, reported a bill providing that when a state declared publications to be incendiary, Congress must prohibit their circulation; but this fell through, (April, 1836.) Its failure was more than made up, however, by the adoption, in the House of Representatives, of a rule which was maintained for several years, that "all petitions relating in any way to slavery be laid on the table without being printed or referred," (May 11.) These first concessions to slavery were ominous not to the slave alone, but to the free.

Murder of Lovejoy.

Among the few who stood firm on the other side was Elijah P. Lovejoy, a young New England minister, who had become the editor of the Observer, at St. Louis. He was a man of broader nature and better education than any who had become conspicuous in the anti-slavery cause. He did not profess to be an abolitionist, or to devote himself exclusively to a crusade against slavery; but his sympathies were all on the side of freedom, and he never hesitated to express them. If he was a champion of any one principle, it was of free speech, which, as we have seen, had fallen into great peril since the government and the people united against it. "So long as I am an American citizen," said Lovejoy, "so long as American blood runs in these veins, I shall hold myself at liberty to speak, to write, and to publish whatever I please on any subject, being amenable to the laws of my country for the same." He removed his paper from St. Louis to Alton, Illinois, that he might be in a free state; but the state was not free to him, or to brave men like him. Repeatedly assailed by mobs, his house stoned, his printing presses destroyed, he was in arms with a few friends to defend a new press from threatened violence, when he was shot about midnight, (November 7, 1837.) Such was the spirit of the country, that a meeting to express some natural sentiment at this murder was held with great difficulty in Faneuil Hall, and, when held, was obliged to listen to a defence of the murderers from the attorney general of Massachusetts.

Violence of abolitionists.

All this drove the abolitionists to a new and extreme position. "The grand rallying point," according to Garrison and his associates, was the repeal of the Union, (1842.) Other repeals were proposed — that of the pulpit, which had not thundered as it ought against slavery, that of the churches, which had not forced their pulpits to thunder. These passionate demands threw back abolitionism, instead of advancing it. Men willing to act against slavery were not willing to act against their country or their church, and instead of becoming abolitionists they became anti-abolitionists. Another party would have to be formed to take the lead, and this could not be done in a day.

Massachusetts missions.

For twenty years and more, colored sailors arriving in a port of South Carolina, Georgia, Alabama, and Louisiana, had been subject to imprisonment during the stay of the vessel in which they came. William Wirt, Attorney General of the United States, gave the opinion that the act of South Carolina, where this practice originated, was unconstitutional, and incompatible with the rights of other nations, (1824.) But though South Carolina yielded as far as British seamen were concerned, she refused to yield with regard to Americans; and in this she, with her sister states, was upheld by Congress when that body refused, by a large majority, to interfere, (1842.) In 1844 the Massachusetts legislature authorized the governor to appoint agents to inquire into the imprisonment of Massachusetts seamen in Charleston and New Orleans, the two great ports of the Southern States. The governor sent Samuel Hoar to Charleston, and Henry Hubbard to New Orleans, but both were driven off. South Carolina asserted her right to exclude "seditious persons or others whose presence may be dangerous," and on this ground the Massachusetts agent was expelled. The state had previously contented itself with shutting out colored citizens; it now shut out white. "Has the Constitution of the United States," asked the expelled agent in his report to the State of Massachusetts, "the least practical validity or binding force in South Carolina, except where she thinks its operation favorable to her?"

Necessity of anti-slavery.

Our narrative has not been too brief to show how great a necessity the anti-slavery movement had become, and how certain, therefore, it was to grow and spread, notwithstanding all the weakness of its friends and all the strength of its foes.

CHAPTER VII.

ANNEXATION OF TEXAS.

United States Bank. TURNING back to some events which we have passed by, we enter upon a controversy no less severe than that between freedom and slavery. It is between President Jackson and the democratic party on the one side, and on the other the United States Bank and the whig party, then in opposition, and under the leadership of Clay and Webster. After putting a veto on the renewal of the bank charter, (1832,) the president, now in his second term, (1833,) directed the secretary of the treasury to remove the treasury deposits from the bank; and when the secretary then in office declined to do so, he was displaced by another, Roger B. Taney, who consented. The Senate charged the president with violating the Constitution, and Webster called upon "all who mean to die as they live, citizens of a free country," to "stand together for the supremacy of the laws." The question was political as well as financial, and thus excited universal interest.

Finances. Financially, the country was in a singular condition. The public debt was paid off, (1835,) and twenty-eight millions of surplus revenue were distributed among the states, (1837.) But the course of trade, the speculations and disorders among business men, brought about a commercial crisis, from which almost every body suffered — capitalists failing, laborers losing employment, and families sinking into want. Specie payments were suspended by the banks, first of New York, then of other cities; and a deputation waited upon the president, now Martin Van Buren, to ask the suspension of payment in specie to the treasury, and the summons of Congress in an extra session. The extra session was held in September, but the president's proposal of a system by which the public moneys should be deposited in public offices, instead of banks, was not adopted until a later time. It was not for the government, but for the people themselves, to restore their broken fortunes.

State insolvency. One great obstacle was the financial condition of the states. In the two years preceding the crisis, state debts had been contracted to the amount of nearly one hundred millions. It soon became difficult to meet even the interest on these obligations. Indiana, Arkansas, and Illinois stopped paying interest; Maryland and Pennsylvania paid only by certificates, and by those only in part. Michigan and Louisiana ceased not merely to pay, but also to acknowledge their debts, while Mississippi repudiated five millions at once, on the ground that the bank in whose favor her bonds had been issued had sold them on terms contrary to its charter. Eight states and a territory (Florida) thus became bankrupt, or worse than bankrupt, in the course of eighteen months, (1841–2.)

Civil war in Rhode Island. Rhode Island met with a peculiar trial. Its charter government, now a century and a quarter old, had long been the object of reform. Two new constitutions were proposed, (1841,) one by a convention called by a Suffrage Association, the other by a convention which the legislature had summoned. The latter was rejected; the former was accepted by popular vote; but not having been framed according to the forms of law, it was opposed by the state authorities. Its supporters chose Thomas W. Dorr governor, who, with an armed force, attacked the arsenal at Providence, and, failing there, afterwards threw up intrenchments, ten miles off, at Chepachet. Three thousand volunteers marched against this post, but found it abandoned; and so the civil war ended, (June, 1842.) A few months later, a new constitution, providing for the reforms which Dorr and his party had sought through strife, was adopted.

New states and territories. Other states were organizing themselves more peaceably. Arkansas, the first state admitted since Missouri, (June 15, 1836,) was followed by Michigan, (January 26, 1837.) Wisconsin, organized as a single territory, (1836,) was presently divided as Wisconsin and Iowa, (1838.) Then Iowa was admitted a state, (March 3, 1845,*) and at the same date Florida became a member of the Union.

Indian wars. Relations with the Indians were frequently disturbed. A war with the Sacs and Foxes, under Black Hawk, broke out on the north-west frontier, but was soon brought to an end by a vigorous campaign on the part of the United States troops and the militia, under Generals Scott and Atkinson, (1832.) Another war arose with the Seminoles, under their chief Osceola, in Florida. It was attended by serious losses from the beginning, (1835.) On the junction of the Creeks with the Seminoles, affairs grew still worse, the war extending into Georgia and Alabama, (1836.) The Creeks were subdued under the directions of General Jessup; but the Seminoles continued in arms amidst the thickets of Florida for many years.

Foreign relations: France. The standing grievance of the United States against the European powers consisted in the indemnities long due for spoliations of American commerce. These were at last settled with Denmark, Portugal, Spain, and Naples, (1830-4.) But with France

* Again in 1846, but not actually entering until 1848.

there were some high-sounding phrases before our claims were satisfied. A treaty with the government of Louis Philippe fixed the amount at about five millions; but the Chamber of Deputies refused to provide the money, and the draft of the United States government for the first instalment was protested, (1834.) The president proposed to Congress to authorize reprisals upon French property; whereupon the French minister at Washington was recalled, and the American minister at Paris was offered his passports. More phrases followed. Great Britain offered mediation, and it was accepted; but, without waiting for it, the French government paid the five millions, (1836.)

Great Britain. Not long after this, we were in trouble with Great Britain. On the outbreak of an insurrection in Canada, (1837,) some of our people undertook to join it, and encamped on Navy Island, a British possession in the Niagara River, to which they transported arms and stores in a steamer called the Caroline. This steamer, though at the time on the American bank of the river, was destroyed by a British detachment accompanied by Alexander McLeod, sheriff of Niagara; and an American citizen lost his life in the fray. Three years afterwards, McLeod, being in New York, was arrested on a charge of murder by the state authorities. The British government demanded his release, and were sustained by the United States administration, on the ground that he had acted as an agent or soldier of Great Britain. But the authorities of New York held fast to their prisoner, and brought him to trial. Had harm come to him, his government stood pledged to declare war; but he was acquitted for want of proof, (1841.) Congress subsequently passed an act requiring that similar cases should be tried only before United States courts. The release of McLeod did not settle the burning of the Caroline on the American shore; this still remained. There had been other difficulties with Great Britain upon the Maine frontier, where the boundary line was undetermined. Collisions took place, and the Maine militia and the British troops had been but just prevented from fighting, (1839.) Nor was this all. Far away, upon the African coast, British cruisers were claiming a right to visit American vessels, in carrying out the provisions for the suppression of the slave trade. The right was asserted in a quintuple treaty, to which Great Britain, France, Austria, Prussia, and Russia were parties, (October, 1841;) but the United States denied it altogether.

Treaty of Washington.

Meanwhile William Henry Harrison, the choice of the whig party, had succeeded to the presidency, (March 1841.) On his death, a month after, John Tyler, vice president, became president. His secretary of state, Daniel Webster, proposed to the British minister at Washington to take up the question of the north-eastern boundary. The offer led to the appointment by the British government of a special envoy in the person of Lord Ashburton, (1842.) Conferences between him and the American secretary were shared by commissioners from Maine and Massachusetts upon all subjects pertaining to the boundary, but other points in controversy were separately considered. The treaty of Washington, ratified by the Senate four months afterwards, (August 20,) settled the north-eastern boundary; put down the claim to a right of visit, and in such a way as to lead to the denial of the claim by European powers who had previously admitted it; provided for the mutual surrender of fugitives from justice; and as to the affair of the Caroline, the British envoy made an apology, or what amounted to one. Even the old quarrel about impressment was put to rest, not by the treaty, but by a letter from Webster to Ashburton, repeating the rule originally laid down by Jefferson, "that the vessel being American shall be evidence that the seamen on board are such," adding, as the present and future principle of the American government, that "in every regularly documented American merchant vessel, the crew who navigate it will find their protection in the flag which is over them." In short, every difficulty was settled by the treaty, or by the accompanying negotiations, except one, the boundary of Oregon, on which no serious difference had as yet appeared. "I am willing," said Webster in the Senate, nearly four years subsequently, "to appeal to the public men of the age, whether, in 1842, and in the city of Washington, something was not done for the suppression of crime, for the true exposition of the principles of public law, for the freedom and security of commerce on the ocean, and for the peace of the world."

Republic of Texas. The field was now clear for renewing the agitation of a measure that had been planned for many years. On the south-western frontier, there lay a province of Mexico, unoccupied until emigrants from the United States began to settle there under Mexican authority, (1821.) Time and prosperity increased their numbers, and they formed a constitution, with which they sought admission, as a federal state, into the republic of Mexico, (1833.) The Mexican government refused, and sent a force to arrest the officers who had been elected under the constitution, and to disarm the people. War, or revolution, or both, ensued. The Texan Lexington was Gonzales, where the first resistance was made, (September 28, 1835.) The Texan Philadelphia was a place called Washington, where a convention declared the independence of the state, (March 2, 1836,) and adopted a constitution, (March 17.) The Texan Saratoga and Yorktown, two in one, was on the shores of the San Jacinto, where General

Houston, commander-in-chief of the insurgents, gained a decisive victory over the Mexican president, Santa Anna, (April 21.) Six months afterwards, Houston was chosen president of the republic of Texas, (October.)

Project of annexation. In his inaugural speech, he expressed the desire of the people to join the United States. Nothing could be more natural. With few exceptions, they came from the land to which they wished to be reunited. It was but natural, for the same reason, that a large number of those whom they had left behind them should wish their return. There were other motives. Though the Florida treaty of 1819 acknowledged the Spanish claim to Texas, the United States government did not lose its desire to possess the region, and twice attempted to buy it from Mexico, into whose possession it had passed. It could now be had without buying. Above all, Texas had established slavery where Mexico had abolished it, and where the interest of the American slave states, as they thought, required it to exist. It was more certain, they reasoned, to exist if Texas became one of them. But though these impulses were strong, others were stronger for a time. That portion of the American people which was set against the extension of slavery was, therefore, set against annexing Texas. That larger portion which adhered to public principle, and knew that to annex Texas was to despoil Mexico, also stood out against annexation. The independence of Texas was recognized by the United States, (1837.) But the same year its application for admission to the Union was rejected and withdrawn.

Revived. It was frequently revived. As the anti-slavery movement deepened, nothing seemed more fit to stem it than the increase of slaveholding territory; and this lay close at hand in Texas. If it were not taken, it might cease to be slaveholding; for Great Britain, as the great abolitionist power, was supposed to entertain the design of getting Texas under her control, and abolishing slavery there. "Few calamities," wrote our secretary of state, Upshur, in 1843, "could befall this country more to be deplored than the abolition of domestic slavery in Texas." "To this continent," wrote Upshur's successor, Calhoun, in 1844, "the blow would be calamitous beyond description." It thus became more and more of a settled purpose with the south to force Texas upon the north, or, as one of the South Carolina districts presented the alternative, "either to admit Texas into the Union, or to proceed peaceably and calmly to arrange the terms of a dissolution of the Union." But to this there was something to be said on the northern side; and it was said earnestly, that the character of the Union as a republic, founded for freedom and for free institutions, would be lost by acquiring territory expressly for slavery. A fresh conflict for and against slavery ensued, in which the numbers against it were evidently on the increase. What the abolitionists could not do, the slaveholders and their adherents did, by opening the eyes of the people and showing them how near they were to the brink of the precipice.

Effected

The majority went forward blindly. A treaty of annexation, concluded by Calhoun as secretary of state, was rejected by the Senate in June, 1844. Its supporters instantly carried the measure into the presidential election of that year, casting aside Van Buren, who was a candidate for renomination by the democratic party, and nominating James K. Polk, chiefly because he was committed to immediate annexation. The whigs nominated Clay because he had opposed annexation, and when he wrote a letter showing himself to be halting between two opinions, the life was taken out of his party, and they lost the election. As soon as Congress met, resolutions to annex Texas were proposed. Even southern whigs objected. "A dangerous and revolutionary precedent," said Rives of Virginia. "At the sacrifice of the peace and harmony of the Union," said Berrien of Georgia. "If we admit that the general government can interpose to extend slavery as a blessing, we must also admit that it can interfere to arrest it as an evil," said Rayner of North Carolina. What the north, or the true representatives of the north, had to object, need not be repeated. The joint resolutions of the two houses of Congress were adopted, (March 1, 1845,) approved by the president, (March 2,) and accepted by Texas (July 4,) which was finally admitted to the Union, (December 29.) No other shadow crossed the triumph of slavery than a merely verbal provision that in any states formed out of Texan territory north of the Missouri Compromise line, "slavery shall be prohibited." As Texas had no territory north of the Compromise line, the prohibition had no value.

CHAPTER VIII.

WAR WITH MEXICO.

Causes. As soon as the United States government resolved to annex Texas, the Mexican minister at Washington demanded his passports. "War was the only recourse of the Mexican government." A few months later, (August, 1845,) American troops were moved to Corpus Christi, and, six months afterwards, (March, 1846,) to the Rio Grande, with orders "to repel any invasion of the Texan territory which might be attempted by the Mexican forces." On the other side, Mexico protested altogether against the line of the Rio Grande. The River Nueces, according to Mexican authority, was the boundary of Texas. Even supposing Texas surrendered by the Mexicans, which it was not, they still retained the territory between the Nueces and the Rio Grande — a territory containing but few settlements, and those not Texan, but purely Mexican. In support of this position, the Mexican General Arista was ordered to cross the Rio Grande and defend the country against the invader, (April, 1846.)

Hostilities. As the American troops, some three thousand strong, under General Taylor, approached the Rio Grande, the inhabitants retired; at one place, Point Isabel, burning their dwellings. This certainly did not look much like Taylor's being on American or on Texan ground. But he, obedient to his orders, kept on, until he took post by the Rio Grande, opposite the Mexican town of Matamoras, (March 28, 1846.) About a month later, (April 24,) a Mexican force was sent across the stream, when a squadron of United States dragoons, reconnoitring, fell in with a much superior force, and, after a skirmish, surrendered. The next day but one, Taylor, as previously authorized by his government, called upon the states of Texas and Louisiana for five thousand volunteers. As soon as the news reached Washington, the president informed Congress that "war exists, and exists by the act of Mexico herself," (May 11.) Congress took the same ground, and gave the president authority to call fifty thousand volunteers into the field, (May 13.) It was ten days later, but of course before any tidings of these proceedings could have been received, that Mexico made a formal declaration of war, (May 23.) The question as to which nation began hostilities, must depend upon the question of the Texan boundary. If this was the River Nueces, the United States began the war the summer before. If, on the contrary, it was the Rio Grande, the Mexicans, as President Polk asserted, were the aggressors.

Oregon controversy. At the very time that these hostilities opened there was serious danger of a rupture between the United States and Great Britain. It sprang from conflicting claims to the distant territory of Oregon. Those of the United States were based, first, upon American voyages to the Pacific coast, chiefly one made by Captain Gray, in the Columbia, from which the great river of the north-west took its name, (1792;) secondly, upon the acquisition of Louisiana with all the Spanish rights to the western shores, (1803;) and thirdly, upon an expedition under Captain Lewis and Lieutenant Clarke, of the United States army, by whom the Missouri was traced towards its source, and the Columbia followed to the Pacific Ocean,

(1804–6.) Against these, the British government asserted various claims of discovery and occupancy. Twice the two nations agreed to a joint possession of the country in dispute, (1818, 1827;) twice the United States proposed a dividing line, once under Monroe, and again under Tyler. The rejection of the latter proposal had led to a sort of war cry, during the presidential election then pending, (1844,) that Oregon must be held. President Polk renewed the offer, but on less favorable terms, and it was rejected, (1845.) The next year, when matters looked darkest, Great Britain made proposals, by which the line of forty-nine degrees was made the boundary, and the right of navigating the Columbia was secured to the British, (June 15, 1846.) Thus vanished the prospect of a war with Great Britain, in addition to the war with Mexico.

Conquest of north-east of Mexico. General Taylor engaged the enemy at Palo Alto, (May 8,) and Resaca de la Palma, (May 9,) with a force so inferior, that great alarm had been felt about it, and yet he came off victor in both actions. The Mexicans at once recrossed the Rio Grande, and Taylor followed as far as Matamoras, (May 18.) A long pause ensued, to wait for reënforcements, and indeed for plans; the war being wholly unprepared for on the American side. At length, with considerably augmented forces Taylor set out again, supported by Generals Worth and Wool among many other eminent officers. Monterey, a very important place in this part of Mexico, was taken after a three days' resistance under General Ampudia, (September 21–23.) An armistice of several weeks followed. Subsequently, Taylor marched southward as far as Victoria; but on the recall of a portion of his troops to take part in other operations, he fell back into a defensive position in the north, (January, 1847.) There, at Buena Vista, he was attacked by a comparatively large army under Santa Anna, then generalissimo of Mexico ; but he was again victorious, (February 22, 23,) and Santa Anna left him master of all the north-eastern country. Six months later, Taylor sent a large number of his remaining men to act elsewhere, (August ;) then, leaving General Wool in command, he returned to the United States, (November.)

Conquest of Chihuahua.

An expedition, headed by Colonel Doniphan, marched down upon Chihuahua, taking possession of El Paso, (December 27, 1846,) and then, after a battle with the Mexicans at the pass of Sacramento, (February 28, 1847,) of Chihuahua, the capital, (March 1.) Doniphan presently evacuated his conquest, (April.) Early in the following year, Chihuahua became the object of another expedition, under General Price, who again occupied the town, (March 7, 1848,) defeating the Mexicans at the neighboring Santa Cruz de las Rosales, (March 16.)

Conquest of New Mexico.

Both Doniphan and Price made their descents from New Mexico, which had been taken possession of by the Americans under General Kearney in the first months of the war, (August, 1846.) Some months after, when Kearney had gone to California, and Doniphan, after treating with the Navajo Indians, had marched against Chihuahua, an insurrection, partly of Mexicans and partly of Indians, broke out at a village fifty miles from Santa Fe. The American governor, Charles Bent, and many others, both Mexicans and Americans, were murdered ; battles, also, were fought, before the insurgents were reduced, by Price, (January, 1847.)

Conquest of California.

Ere the tidings of the war reached the Pacific coast, a band of Americans, partly trappers and partly settlers, declared their independence of Mexico at Sonoma, a town of small importance not far from San Francisco, (July 4, 1846.) The leader of the party was John C. Fremont, a captain in the United States Engineers, who had recently received instructions from his government to secure a hold upon California. A few days after their declaration, Fremont and his followers joined the American Commodore Sloat, who, aware of the war, had taken Monterey, (July 7,) and entered the Bay of San Francisco, (July 9.) Sloat was soon succeeded by Commodore Stockton; and he, in conjunction with Fremont, took possession of Ciudad de los Angeles, the capital of Upper California, (August 13.) All this was done without opposition from the scattered Mexicans of the province, or from their feeble authorities. But some weeks later, a few braver spirits collected, and, driving the Americans from the capital, succeeded likewise in recovering the greater part of California, (September, October.) On the approach of General Kearney from New Mexico, a month or two afterwards, he was met in battle at San Pasqual, (December 6,) and so hemmed in by the enemy as to be in great danger, until relieved by a force despatched to his assistance by Commodore Stockton. The commodore and the general, joining forces, retook Ciudad de los Angeles, after two actions with its defenders, (January 10, 1847.) A day or two later, Fremont succeeded in bringing the main body of Mexicans in arms to a capitulation at Cowenga, (January 13.) California was again, and more decidedly than before, an American possession. Lower California was afterwards assailed, but under different commanders. La Paz and San José, both inconsiderable places, were occupied in the course of the year. On the opposite shore, Guaymas was taken by a naval force under Captain Lavalette, (October,) and Mazatlan by the fleet under Commodore Shubrick, (November.) It was all a series of skirmishes, fought in the midst of lonely mountains and on far-stretching shores.

And now to return to the eastern side. From the first, a blockade of the ports in the Gulf of Mexico was but poorly maintained. Then the American fleet embarked upon various operations. Twice was Alvarado, a port to the south of Vera Cruz, attacked by Commodore Conner, and twice it was gallantly defended, (August 7, October 15, 1846.) Then Commodore Perry went against Tobasco, a little distance up a river on the southern coast; but, though he took some prizes and some hamlets, he did not gain the town, (October 23-26.) The only really successful operation was the occupation of Tampico, which the Mexicans abandoned on the approach of their enemies, (November 15.)

Operations in Gulf of Mexico.

Early in the following spring the fleet and the army combined in an attack upon Vera Cruz. Anticipations of success, however high amongst the troops and their officers, were not very generally entertained even by their own countrymen. Vera Cruz, or its castle of San Juan d'Ulloa, had been asserted, in Europe as well as America, to be impregnable; but a few days' bombardment obliged the garrison, under General Morales, to give up the town and the castle together, (March 23-26, 1847.) Once masters there, the Americans beheld the road to the city of Mexico lying open before them; yet here, again, their way was supposed to be beset by insurmountable difficulties. They pressed on, nine or ten thousand strong, General Scott at their head, supported by many officers of tried and untried reputation. Elsewhere, the war had been carried into remote and comparatively unpeopled portions of the country. Here the march lay through a region where men would fight for their homes, and where their homes, being close at hand, would give them aid as well as inspiration. The march upon Mexico was by all means the great performance of the war.

March upon city of Mexico.

Battles on the way. Its difficulties soon appeared. At Cerro Gordo, sixty miles from Vera Cruz, Santa Anna posted thirteen thousand of his Mexicans in a mountain pass, to whose natural strength he had added by fortification. It took two days to force a passage, the Americans losing about five hundred, but inflicting a far greater loss on their brave opponents, (April 18–19.) Here, however, they paused; a part of the force was soon to be discharged, and Scott decided he would make his dismissals and wait for the empty places to be filled. He accordingly advanced slowly to Puebla, while the Mexicans kept in the background, or appeared only as guerillas, (May 28.) The guerilla warfare had been foretold as the one insuperable obstacle to the progress of the American army; it proved harassing, but by no means fatal. During the delay ensuing on land, the fleet in the gulf, under Commodore Perry, took Tuspan and Tobasco, both being but slightly defended, (April 18—June 15.) At length reënforcements having reached the army, making it not quite eleven thousand strong, it resumed its march, and entered the valley of Mexico, (August 10.)

In valley of Mexico. There the Mexicans stood, Santa Anna still at their head, thirty-five thousand in their ranks, regular troops and volunteers, old and young, rich and poor, men of every profession and trade, — all joining in the defence of their country, now threatened at its very heart. Behind the army was the government, endeavoring to unite itself, yet still rent and enfeebled to the last degree. Even the clergy, chafed by the seizure of church property to meet the exigencies of the state, were divided, if not incensed. It was a broken nation, and yet all the more worthy of respect for its last earnest resistance to the foe. Never had armies a more magnificent country to assail or to defend than that into which the Americans had penetrated. They fought in defiles or upon plains, vistas of lakes and fields before them, mountain heights above them, the majesty of nature everywhere mingling with the contention of man. Fourteen miles from the city, battles began at Contreras, where a Mexican division under General Valencia was totally routed, (August 19–20.) The next engagement followed immediately, at Churubusco, six miles from the capital, Santa Anna himself being there completely defeated, (August 20.) An armistice suspended further movements for a fortnight, when an American division under Worth made a successful assault on a range of buildings called Molino del Rey, close to the city. This action, though the most sanguinary of the entire war, — both Mexicans and Americans surpassing their previous deeds, — was without results, (September 8.) A few days later, the fourth and final engagement in the valley took place at Chapultepec, a fortress just above Molino del Rey. Within the lines was the Mexican Military College, and bravely did the students defend it, mere boys outvying veterans in feats of valor; but the college and the fortress yielded together, (September 12–13.) The next day Scott, with six thousand five hundred men, the whole of his army remaining in the field, entered the city of Mexico, (September 14.)

Wilmot proviso. The war had not continued three months, when the United States made an overture of peace, (July, 1846.) It was referred by the Mexican administration to the National Congress, and there it rested. In announcing to the American Congress the proposal which he had made, President Polk suggested the appropriation of a certain sum, as an indemnity for any Mexican territory that might be retained at the conclusion of the war. In the debate which followed, an administration representative from Pennsylvania, David Wilmot, moved a proviso to the proposed appropriation: "that there shall be neither slavery nor involuntary servitude in any territory on the continent of America which shall hereafter be acquired by or annexed to the United States by virtue of this appropriation, or in any other manner whatsoever." The proviso was hastily adopted in the House; but it was too late to receive any action in the Senate before the closing of the session, (August.) In the following session the proviso again passed the House, but was abandoned by that body on being rejected by the Senate.

Mexican proviso. When the American commissioner, N. P. Trist, met the commissioners on the part of Mexico, he found them reluctant to yield any territory. It went especially against their will to open any to slavery; their instructions being quite positive on the point that any treaty to be signed by them must prohibit slavery in the ceded country. "No president of the United States," replied Commissioner Trist, "would dare to present any such treaty to the Senate."

Treaty. Trist was recalled, but he took it upon himself to remain where he was, and to treat with new commissioners, two months after the entrance of the American army into the city of Mexico. The result of battles rather than of negotiations was a treaty signed at Guadalupe Hidalgo, a suburb of the capital. By this instrument Mexico ceded Texas, New Mexico, and Upper California, while the United States agreed to surrender all other conquests, and to pay for those retained the sum of fifteen millions, besides assuming the claims of American merchants against Mexico to the amount of more than three millions, (February 2, 1848.) Ratifications were finally exchanged at Queretaro, (May 30,) and peace proclaimed at Washington, (July 4.) The Mexican territory — that is, the portion which remained — was rapidly evacuated.

CHAPTER IX.

Compromise of 1850.

Old domain. The former domain of the United States was gradually organized. Wisconsin came in quietly as a state, (May 29, 1848.) Oregon was established as a territory after frequent debate upon the exclusion of slavery, and an attempt to extend the line of the Missouri Compromise to the Pacific, so that the territory south of 36° 30′ might be considered slaveholding. A trouble of quite a different sort broke out in connection with Oregon; the Indians of that territory taking up arms, to the great peril of its settlers, in the year of its organization, (1848.) The next year another territory was peaceably organized in Minnesota, (1849.)

New domain. But with regard to the new domain, there were grave difficulties. Eight hundred thousand square miles of territory had been added by the treaty of Guadalupe Hidalgo to the two millions previously belonging to the United States. To any nation this would have been an embarrassing accession; to ours it was almost overwhelming, on account of its relation to slavery. The southern people claimed the war as of their making; its spoils, therefore, were for them. Northern men, who stood for freedom, declared the war a sufficient evil in itself, without entailing the greater evil of slavery extension. So one section set itself against the other on the borders of the new domain.

Free-soil party. That the feeling in the north had become much stronger, was proved by the formation of a new party on the side of freedom. The presidential canvass began, and the whig and democratic parties entered into it with no other special purpose regarding freedom or slavery than to let both alone. But the free-soil party, in convention at Buffalo, (August, 1848,) announced "the duty of the federal government to relieve itself from all responsibility for the existence or continuance of slavery," and "the only safe means of preventing the extension of slavery . . . to prohibit its extension by act of Congress." Public opinion was touched. The whig party, or some of its northern leaders, made a show of liberal principles. The democrats, in spite of being aided by all the patronage of the administration, lost ground. Though not carrying a single state, or a single electoral vote for their own candidate, the free-soilers had much to do with determining the election of the whig candidate, Zachary Taylor, as less hurtful to freedom than his competitor.

Root's resolution. When Congress met, in December, the House of Representatives, on motion of Joseph M. Root, of Ohio, instructed its committee on territories to report a bill or bills providing territorial governments for New Mexico and California, "excluding slavery." A bill for California passed the House, but was blocked in the Senate on account of the restriction against slavery.

Convention of southern members of Congress. Calhoun, still a senator, prepared an address of the southern members of Congress to their constituents, (January, 1849.) It inveighed against the aggressions of the north, particularly its evasion of the fugitive slave law, and its abolitionism. "We ask not," wrote Calhoun, "as the north alleges we do, for the extension of slavery. That would make a discrimination in our favor as unjust and unconstitutional as the discrimination they ask against us in their favor. . . . What, then, we do insist on is, not to extend slavery, but that we shall not be prohibited from immigrating with our property into the territories of the United States because we are slaveholders." John M. Berrien, a senator from Georgia, proposed an appeal to the people of the United States, instead of one to the south alone; but the original address was adopted, (January 22.)

California constitution.

Soon after President Taylor entered office, (March, 1849,) he suggested, or adopted the suggestion of others, that the true way to meet the issue was, for the Californians to frame a state constitution; and, to encourage this, a special agent was despatched from Washington, (April.) A convention was held in California, (October,) and a constitution framed, prohibiting slavery. The president communicated it to Congress, according to the usual form, (February, 1850.) Why California took precedence in these movements, and why the interest in her course was much greater than that felt for New Mexico, or any other part of the national territory, was plain enough. In the very same month that California was ceded to the United States, gold was found on a branch of the Sacramento. The whole country was excited. Emigration to the gold fields, speculation in their products, or in the supplies which their workers required, building up San Francisco and other cities, became the great business enterprises of the time. Such a region — so rich, so attractive, and bidding fair to be so powerful — was a prize beyond any for which the free and the slave states had heretofore contended.

Clay's resolutions.

Before the California constitution was sent in, Henry Clay had presented some resolutions in the Senate, (January.) They proposed the admission of California as a free state, and the prohibition of the slave trade in the District of Columbia, as concessions to freedom, while the other side was to gain the organization of the territories without restriction concerning slavery, the continuance of slavery in the District, and the enforcement of the fugitive slave law. Upon these a long debate ensued. Webster supported them, chiefly on the ground that slavery was already excluded from the territories by "the law of nature, of physical geography." William H. Seward, senator from New York, opposed the resolutions, because their principles were repudiated, as he said, by "the law of nature written on the hearts and consciences of freemen."

Compromise. The Senate appointed a committee of thirteen, Clay being chairman, by whom the substance of his resolutions was reported in three bills. The first admitted California as a state, organized New Mexico and Utah as territories without any provision for or against slavery, and arranged the disputed boundary between New Mexico and Texas by a large indemnity to the latter. The second provided for the recovery of fugitive slaves. The third abolished the slave trade in the District of Columbia, (May 8.)

Its adoption. At the height of the controversy over these bills, President Taylor sickened and died, (July 9.) He was succeeded by the vice president, Millard Fillmore, who called about him a new cabinet, Webster at the head, and threw the whole weight of the administration in favor of the compromise. It was at first rejected. But, on the substitution of separate bills for each of the measures proposed, they were successively adopted by both houses. California was admitted a state; New Mexico and Utah were constituted territories, and the payment of ten millions to Texas, in consideration of the boundary and other questions, was voted; all on the same day, (September 9.)

Nine days after, the fugitive slave bill became a law, (September 18;) and two days later still, the slave trade in the District of Columbia was suppressed, (September 20.)

Fugitive slave act. The main feature of this compromise was no compromise at all. In the fugitive slave act, freedom yielded every thing. There was no occasion for a new law about fugitives; only one thousand slaves, or one thirtieth of one per cent. of the slave population, escaped during this very year. The author of the law now passed was believed to have drawn it in terms which would render its execution impossible, partly to humiliate the north, partly to exasperate the south by fresh instances of northern unfaithfulness to southern claims. The constitution was explicit, that a person held to service in one state, escaping into another, should be delivered up on claim of the party to whom such service might be due; but it was equally explicit that no person should be deprived of liberty without due process of law. But the act of 1850 provided no process except the hearing of the claim, without admitting the testimony of the alleged fugitive, or allowing him the benefit of a jury. Its character roused the free states from end to end. Whether for slavery or for freedom elsewhere, they were, by a large majority, for freedom on their own soil; and now their soil was no longer free to those who could be claimed as fugitive slaves. Any body could be claimed, as experience soon proved; free men and free women could be, whites could be, and they could be carried off as slaves. More seizures followed throughout the free states in one year from the passage of this act than had taken place in all the sixty years before.

Last of the compromises. One of our most eminent statesmen has said that the compromise of 1850 was a proof of infatuation. It was wonderful that the north should submit to it; it was impossible that such submission should continue. The compromise was the last of its line. Calhoun died before it was carried, (March.) Clay and Webster followed the next year but one, (1852.) The leaders perished, and their work soon perished after them.

CHAPTER X.

KANSAS.

Ten years' struggle.

THE ten years following the Compromise of 1850 witnessed greater aggression on the part of slavery, and greater resistance on the part of freedom. It was a struggle of which the aspect varied from year to year, almost from day to day, favorable now to one side and now to the other, and leaving the issue uncertain except to those who believed that the right must win at last.

Temporary success of compromise.

At first the Compromise seemed to succeed. Fugitive slaves were arrested and re-enslaved. Slavery in the District of Columbia was undisturbed. The new territories were open to slaveholders and their human possessions. The south, it is true, complained that her interest had been sacrificed, particularly in regard to California, and South Carolina held a convention to consider the expediency of secession, (1851.) On the other hand, the northern lovers of liberty felt themselves and their country disgraced by the concessions that had been made, and would have unmade them, were it possible, without delay. But the people generally accepted the situation, and, in the election of 1852, gave a large majority to the democratic candidate, Franklin Pierce, as pledged to the execution of the Compromise. It was, at least, a temporary success.

Repeal of the Missouri Compromise.

Singularly enough, the first of the important measures to follow it was the repeal of the Missouri Compromise. Under the leadership of Stephen A. Douglas, democratic senator from Illinois, Congress took up a bill organizing the territories of Kansas and Nebraska on "the principle established by the Compromise of 1850," namely, "that all questions relating to slavery in the territories and in the new states to be formed therefrom, are to be left to the decision of the people residing therein," or, as it was also styled, "the principle of non-intervention by Congress with slavery in the states and territories." To give this principle free play, Douglas thought he must do away with the intervention in which Congress had formerly indulged, and three weeks after the proposal of his bill, he proposed an amendment, by which the Missouri Compromise, "being inconsistent with non-intervention," was "declared inoperative and void." The bill, as amended, passed the Senate, (March, 1854,) and the House, (May,) and thus the territory, which had been promised to freedom in return for giving up Missouri, was laid open to slavery.

Ostend manifesto.

Foreign territory was in request for the same purpose. Just as the Kansas cloud rose in the west, another cloud appeared in the east. By direction of the secretary of state, Marcy, the United States ministers at London, Paris, and Madrid, met at Ostend to consult about the acquisition of Cuba, (October, 1854.) The island was wanted for the same reason that Texas had been wanted, and that Kansas and Nebraska were then wanted, by our slaveholders. The three ministers united in a despatch to their principal, urging the purchase of Cuba from Spain, and declaring that if Spain should refuse to sell, and Cuba, being in her possession, should "seriously endanger our internal peace, . . . then, by every law, human and divine, we shall be justified in wresting it from Spain." This manifesto, as it was called, received no rebuke from our government. But the republican convention, entering upon the next election for the presidency, pronounced it a "highwayman's plea," and "in every respect unworthy of American diplomacy."

Immigration to Kansas.

Meanwhile the question between freedom and slavery in Kansas and Nebraska was passing from the hands of politicians to those of the people. Immigration set in strongly towards Kansas, the southern territory, and therefore the better suited for occupation by slaveholders. One column entered chiefly from the neighboring Missouri, calling themselves Sons of the South, but called by their opponents Border Ruffians; their object being not so much to settle in the territory as to take up all the best land and control the elections whenever held. Where they struck, there the free-state men, or abolitionists, as termed by their adversaries, determined to make a stand. This column, mostly of New Englanders, came for the purpose of settling as well as controlling Kansas, in order that it might be a home to them and to the freemen coming after them. As they had a long way to travel, and many difficulties to encounter from the Missourians, in addition to all the ordinary difficulty of making distant settlements, an association, with headquarters in Boston, was formed to aid them; and time soon showed how much the aid was needed. It was a grave crisis, not only for Kansas, but for the whole country. As that territory cast in its lot with freedom or slavery, so, it seemed, would Nebraska, so would many another territory as yet unnamed.

Elections.

The first elections went against the free-state party. Hundreds crossed the border from Missouri, voted, triumphed, and recrossed it to their homes. Lawrence, the chief settlement of the New Englanders, had three hundred and sixty-nine legal voters. But at the election for members of the territorial legislature, (March, 1855,) seven hundred and eighty-one votes were cast for the pro-slavery candidates by a party of Missourians arriving the evening before, and encamping, with arms and cannon, on the outskirts of the town. Such means secured a pro-slavery legislature, but were far from overthrowing the free party. On the contrary, the governor of the territory, Reeder, though appointed at Washington in the interest of slavery rather than freedom, sided with the settlers against the borderers, and came out strongly for making Kansas a free state. A constitution to that purpose was framed at Topeka, (October, 1855,) but without any immediate hope of its going into operation. A few months later, (March, 1856,) a special committee of the House of Representatives, sent to investigate affairs in Kansas, reported that the elections had been carried by organized invasion, the legislature was illegally constituted, and the constitution embodied the will of a majority of the people. Whereupon the House admitted Kansas as a free state; but the Senate did not agree.

Civil war.

Left to themselves, the opposing elements in Kansas broke out in civil war. From May to September, (1856,) the conflict continued, irregular and feeble, yet passionate and destructive. Lawrence was attacked by a force of Missourians, South Carolinians, and Georgians; its printing offices were sacked, and its free-state hotel was fired, (May 21.) Other towns and villages were treated in the same manner, and a few skirmishes took place. It was not the extent of the struggle, but its mere existence, that alarmed the country. Slavery was exciting civil war, and not in Kansas alone.

Assault upon Senator Sumner. Charles Sumner, of Massachusetts, was elected as a free-soiler to the United States Senate in 1851. From the day he took his seat, he contended, sometimes single-handed, sometimes with a few adherents, in behalf of the principles which now, more than ever, needed all the championship they could command. Just as the war in Kansas was breaking out, he delivered a speech which he entitled "The Crime against Kansas," and in which he arraigned, with pitiless severity, the slave-state party and its supporters, (May 19, 20.) Two days after, being the next day after the attack upon Lawrence, (May 22,) as Mr. Sumner was sitting at his desk, though the Senate had adjourned, he was assaulted from behind, beaten over the head and back, and thrown senseless upon the floor. A representative from South Carolina, abetted by two colleagues, another South Carolinian and a Virginian, was the assailant. He was fined three hundred dollars by a Washington court, censured by the House of Representatives, and having resigned in consequence of the censure, was reëlected by his constituents without opposition. On the other hand, the Massachusetts senator, whose term was soon to expire, obtained his reëlection with far less opposition than would have arisen but for the wrong he had suffered. Slavery was not wise in its modes of warfare.

Election of 1856. The deeper feeling excited throughout the free states appeared in the presidential election of 1856. All that the free-soil party did at the election of 1852 was to throw 157,000 votes, without carrying a single state, against the Compromise of 1850. Its successor, the republican party, strong in accessions from the broken whigs, stronger still in the reaction against Kansas and Ostend, numbered 1,350,000 voters, and carried eleven states. But the democrats were still in the majority, and elected

James Buchanan, the same who, as minister to London, had taken part in the Ostend circular.

Dred Scott case. Soon after his entrance upon office, (March, 1857,) an opinion, which had been reached the year before, but reserved, probably for political reasons, was pronounced by the Supreme Court of the United States; two judges, McLean and Curtis, dissenting. Dred Scott, a slave, carried by his master from Missouri to Illinois and Minnesota, married on free soil, had one child born there, and was taken back to slave soil, with wife and child. After some time he sued for his liberty and theirs. The state Circuit Court of Missouri gave sentence in his favor; but appeals were taken to the state Supreme and United States Circuit Courts, both of which decided against him; and his case was then carried before the United States Supreme Court, at Washington. There the court decided that it had no jurisdiction, because no slave, or descendant of a slave, could become a citizen of the United States, and therefore sue at its tribunals. But though without jurisdiction, the court proceeded with an opinion, that the Missouri Compromise was unconstitutional, and consequently, that a slave did not cease to be one by being carried to territory where the Compromise prohibited slavery. This opinion committed the judiciary to the same course to which the executive and legislature, with occasional exceptions in the House of Representatives, were already pledged against freedom.

Personal liberty laws. But while the general government became pro-slavery, many of the state governments were becoming anti-slavery. Public sentiment throughout the free states was deeply moved by the Kansas struggle, and it was not calmed when the president took part with the borderers against the settlers, and endeavored to enforce a slave-state constitution. But public sentiment had been still more deeply moved by events in the free states themselves, under the very eyes of their people, whenever the fugitive slave law was put into execution; and this they determined to resist. Every state in New England, and some of the Western States, from 1850 onwards, passed acts which were known as Personal Liberty laws, and by which, generally, the state officers were forbidden to aid in the arrest or imprisonment of a fugitive slave.

Commercial crisis.

Another shadow crossed the country in the commercial crisis of 1857. Like that of twenty years before, it was the result of speculation carried beyond all bounds of prudence, not to say honesty. Specie payments were again suspended, and all material interests suffered.

Mormons.

The territory of Utah, organized under the Compromise of 1850, had been occupied only by Mormon settlers. On the appointment of a governor, and other territorial officers, (1857,) the Mormons refused obedience, but yielded on the approach of a large body of troops, (1858.)

Montgomery convention.

Meanwhile the gulf between freedom and slavery was growing greater. At a commercial convention of slaveholding states, in Montgomery, Alabama, (May, 1858,) nothing excited more interest than the report of a committee in favor of re-opening the African slave trade. The south needed more slaveholders; to have them she must have more slaves. She was losing Kansas and the national territories because she could not occupy them; her slave population being needed at home, there was none to spare for emigration. It did not suit slaveholders to lower the value of their property in slaves by importation, and the majority voted to lay the report on the table.

Lincoln's and Seward's predictions.

Almost at the same time, (June,) a speech was made at Springfield, Illinois, by Abraham Lincoln, as the republican candidate for a seat in the United States Senate. His position was the more striking because his competitor, Douglas, was identified with the repeal of the Missouri Compromise and its bitter consequences. "I believe," said Lincoln, at the outset, "this government cannot permanently endure half slave and half free." His friends entreated him to suppress the prediction, but he would not, and in after years declared that it was one of his wisest actions. A few months later, (October,) Mr. Seward made another prediction, at Rochester, N. Y. "It is an irrepressible conflict between opposing and enduring forces, and it means that the United States must and will, sooner or later, become either entirely a slave-holding nation or entirely a free-labor nation."

John Brown's raids.

Early in the same year, one of the Kansas free-state leaders, John Brown, told his friends in New England that he had been intending for twenty years to make a descent among slaveholders for the purpose of liberating their slaves. At the end of the year, (December, 1858,) he made his first attempt on the borders of Missouri, and, as he said, "without the snapping of a gun on either side," took eleven slaves, whom he conducted to Canada. Although this act was disapproved even by his neighbors in Kansas, who had suffered so much from Missouri slaveholders, Brown was encouraged to repeat it in another quarter and on a larger scale. "Twenty men in the Alleghanies," he had stated, "could break slavery in pieces in two years;" and he now had twenty-one, whom he led towards the Alleghanies, seizing Harper's Ferry and its arsenal on the way, (October 16, 1859.) "I never," he said afterwards, "did intend murder, or treason, or the destruction of property, or to excite slaves to rebellion or to make insurrection." His design, he insisted, was "to free the slaves." He held the arsenal for thirty-three hours, when, almost all his followers being killed, wounded, or scattered, and the troops, United States marines, and Virginia militia, gathering in overwhelming force, he surrendered. He was imprisoned, tried, and executed, (December.) A few years before, and such an act as his would have been all but universally condemned. Now, through the free states, it was, to a great degree, excused, and to some degree admired.

New states. The nation made a fresh purchase of territory in 1853, when the Mesilla Valley, or southern Arizona, containing about thirty thousand square miles, was bought of Mexico for ten million dollars. Minnesota was admitted a state in 1858, Oregon in 1859, and Kansas, without a slave, in January, 1861. But before the admission of Kansas to the Union, the Union had been broken.

CHAPTER XI.

SECESSION.

Lincoln elected president. ABRAHAM LINCOLN was nominated by the republican party, and, after a most stirring canvass, was elected, over three competitors, to the presidency, (November 6, 1860.) His election signified the restoration of the executive branch of the government to the side of freedom.

South Carolina prepares to secede. As such, it roused the other side to desperate action. The legislature of South Carolina, meeting, the day before the election, to cast the electoral vote of that state, received a message from the governor recommending the immediate call of a convention to adopt the only alternative within reach, and take the state out of the Union. Speeches in and out of the legislature expressed the same opinion, and when the news of Lincoln's election arrived, (November 7,) it was hailed with rejoicing, as opening the way to secession, not only in South Carolina, but in all other southern states. Five days later, (November 12,) the legislature called a convention to meet in the middle of December.

Warning in Georgia. The legislature of Georgia assembled the day but one after the election, (November 8.) Many of its members were impatient to follow the lead of South Carolina; but others hesitated, some refused. The majority were able to carry a bill appropriating a million to arm the state, (November 13,) and everything appeared to be in train for secession. At this point, Alexander H. Stephens, who had long represented Georgia in Congress, came before the legislature to warn them against proceeding farther. "In my judgment," he said, "the election of no man, constitutionally chosen to the presidency, is sufficient cause for any state to separate from the Union. . . . The president can do nothing unless he is backed by power in Congress. The House of Representatives is largely in the majority against Mr. Lincoln. In the Senate he will also be powerless. . . . Why, then, I say, should we disrupt the bonds of this Union when his hands are tied? . . . Let the fanatics of the north break the Constitution if such is their fell purpose; . . . but let not the south, let not us, be the ones to commit the aggression." Yet, against his own warning, and as if to render it ineffectual, Mr. Stephens proposed a convention, and four days after (November 18) a bill calling such a body was passed.

President's message. Other states were doing, or preparing to do, likewise, and the whole country was conscious of peril close at hand, when Congress met, and received the annual message of the president, (December 3.) Few, if any, could have expected help from it; few, therefore, were disappointed. Mr. Buchanan argued that the election which had just occurred was no sufficient cause for the movements in South Carolina and elsewhere. But they might be regarded as justified by the personal liberty laws, and could certainly be accounted for by the agitation against slavery in which many of the people had long allowed themselves to share. As for the means to meet the existing danger, the president thought that Congress had no power to coerce a state, that is, to prevent its secession or compel its return to the Union. But Congress could adopt some amendments of the Constitution, and recommend their adoption by the states, securing slavery, not only in the slave states, but in the territories, and, so far as fugitives were concerned, in the free states themselves. But the message fell dead as soon as delivered.

Crittenden compromise. Congress plunged into the conflict. The southern members spoke with pride of what their constituents were doing, and the more reckless their course, the nobler it seemed. On the other hand, the northern members faltered; what their constituents were doing was uncertain, what they might do was more uncertain still, and every thing on their side continued in suspense. After a fortnight of wrangling, a joint resolution was laid before the Senate by John J. Crittenden, of Kentucky. This proposed to amend the Constitution, in order to restore the line of 36° 30′ between the free and the slave states, and to extend it to the Pacific shore, and further, to secure the execution of the fugitive slave law, and to provide, that when it could not be executed, the value of the fugitive should be paid to the claimant from the United States treasury. This was called a compromise.

Secession of South Carolina. On the same day that Crittenden brought forward his resolution, (December 17,) the convention of South Carolina assembled. Southerners from almost every state, commissioners from Alabama and Mississippi, came to urge haste; only an address from fifty-two members of the Georgia legislature urged delay, and this address was not made public. No one doubted the result. "The secession of South Carolina," as a member of the convention said, "is not an event of a day. It is not any thing produced by Mr. Lincoln's election, or by the non-execution of the fugitive slave law. It has been a matter which has been gathering head for thirty years." Four days from the opening, a committee reported, and the convention adopted, without a dissenting vote, "an ordinance to dissolve the Union between the State of South Carolina and other states united with her under the compact entitled the Constitution of the United States of America." In the evening of the same day, the governor and legislature being invited to witness the ceremony, the ordinance was signed by every delegate, and then proclaimed by the president of the convention, who declared that "the State of South Carolina is now and henceforth a free and independent commonwealth." Greater exultation never sat upon southern lips than at the moment when South Carolina threw herself into the abyss of secession, and called it independence.

Anderson at Fort Sumter.

The same spirit prevailed throughout the south. It suffered no check from Washington, where the national authorities made less ado about the secession of a state than they had been wont to make about the admission of one. In many of the public offices, and throughout the capital, more was said for South Carolina than against her attempt to destroy the Union. Only in one spot where the government was represented, and that the nearest to the scene of insurrection, was the will of the insurgents opposed. Major Robert Anderson had been for two months in command of a garrison numbering little more than eighty men, including a band, at Fort Moultrie, not quite four miles from Charleston. After the calling of the convention, he asked the war department to occupy Castle Pinckney, close by Charleston, and Fort Sumter, on an island in the harbor, three miles and a half from the city. General Scott, the head of the army, advised compliance; but the majority of the cabinet refused, and the secretary of state, Lewis Cass, resigned in indignation. After the secession ordinance, Anderson wrote, suggesting Fort Sumter as a stronger position than that he held at Fort

Moultrie, and, receiving no reply from Washington, took the responsibility, and moved his garrison, with the women and children belonging to them, to Fort Sumter, on the evening of the day after Christmas. "He has opened war," said one of the Charleston journals. "His holding Fort Sumter is an invasion of South Carolina," said another. The new commonwealth ordered the other forts to be occupied, the arsenal, post-office, custom-house, and revenue cutter, in short every remaining possession, to be seized. This relieved the president, as he said, from the necessity he at first thought himself under of ordering Anderson out of Sumter, and on his refusing to give such an order, the secretary of war, a Virginian, resigned, and a patriotic Kentuckian, Joseph Holt, was appointed, from whom Anderson received a despatch approving his act as "every way admirable, alike for its humanity and patriotism, as for its soldiership," (December 31.) A week later a resolution of similar tone was passed by the House of Representatives. Major Anderson had taken the first step towards preserving the Union.

Star of the West.

Under the inspiration of what he had done, the government determined upon sending him reënforcements; and in order to avoid publicity, they were embarked at New York, upon a passenger steamer, the Star of the West. On its arrival off Charleston harbor, it tried to pass the bar with the soldiers under hatches; but its mission had been betrayed, and though it bore the United States flag, fire was opened from Fort Moultrie and Morris Island, as well as from an armed vessel. Anderson, being under orders not to fire unless attacked, could not interfere, and the Star of the West, being unable to return fire or to pass the batteries, put back to sea, (January 9, 1861.)

Secession of other states.

On the selfsame day, Mississippi seceded, followed in the course of the same month by Florida, Alabama, Georgia, and Louisiana, and on the first of February by Texas. None of the conventions in these states were unanimous in favor of secession, and that in Alabama threw a vote of thirty-nine out of one hundred against it. The secession of Texas was followed by the most shameless treachery, even of those treacherous days. General Twiggs, next in rank to General Scott, and intrusted with nearly half the army of the United States, besides posts of great importance, and stores of great value, surrendered the whole to commissioners appointed by the Texan convention, (February 18.) Out of all the twenty-five hundred whom Twiggs betrayed, not one common soldier deserted to the seceders. Many officers were faithless, as many both of the army and navy, at home and abroad, had already proved, and continued to prove.

Peace conventions.

On the last day of January, when six states had left the Union, and a seventh was just leaving, a convention assembled at Albany. It was called as a democratic state convention, but other parties, past or present, were represented in it. "We meet here," said the president, Judge Parker, "as conservative men. . . . The people of this state," he continued, "demand the peaceful settlement of the questions that have led to disunion. They have a right to insist that there shall be conciliation, concession, compromise." "We are advised," said Governor Seymour, "that if force is to be used, it must be exerted against the united south. . . . Let us see if successful coercion by the north is less revolutionary than successful secession by the south." Such was the sentiment of conservative men throughout the country. If they condemned secession, they also condemned every measure by which it could be resisted. One more effort of pacification was made in a peace conference, representing twenty-one states, at Washington. Meeting on the 4th of February, and continuing until the 27th, the conference debated various projects, and finally determined upon recommending Congress to submit to the States an amendment of the Constitution, substantially the same as the Crittenden compromise.

Confederate government. Another body met on the 4th of February, at Montgomery, Alabama. Six states, soon seven, were represented in a congress, by which a constitution was framed, and an executive appointed, Jefferson Davis, of Mississippi, being elected president, and Alexander H. Stephens, of Georgia, vice president, of the Confederate States of America. The acceptance of the vice presidency by a man who had resisted secession less than three months before, shows how thoroughly the Union feeling in the seceded states was extinguished. The president had been a secessionist from the start. As he now travelled towards Montgomery, he spoke again and again to shouting crowds of their brilliant prospects. "If war must come," he said, "it must be upon northern, and not upon southern soil. . . . We will carry war where it is easy to advance, where food for the sword and torch awaits our armies in the densely populated cities." But he did not believe the north would fight, while he was sure that all the slaveholding states would join the Confederacy, and that their independence would be recognized by England and France. In his inaugural address, the probability of war was admitted. "We have entered upon a career of independence, and it must be inflexibly pursued through many years of controversy with our late associates of the Northern States." In the month following, when Vice President Stephens returned from Montgomery, he spoke concerning his government to a great meeting at

Savannah. "Its foundations are laid," he said; "its corner-stone rests upon the great truth that the negro is not equal to the white man; that slavery, subordination to the superior race, is his natural and normal condition. This our new government is the first in the history of the world based upon this great physical, philosophical, and moral truth. . . . May we not look with confidence to the ultimate universal acknowledgment of the truths upon which our system rests?"

Lincoln on the way to Washington.

While the president of the Confederate States journeyed to Montgomery, the president elect of the United States was on his way to Washington. He took leave of his neighbors at Springfield, Illinois, in one of the most touching speeches ever made, saying that he was assuming a burden greater than had been laid upon any before him except Washington, and that he must depend upon Divine assistance. As he travelled on, he spoke sometimes gayly, but oftener gravely, of the situation, insisting that "nobody is suffering any thing," and that "the people on both sides must keep their self-possession." As he raised the American flag over Independence Hall, in Philadelphia, on Washington's birthday, he said, "I have often inquired of myself, what great principle or idea it was that kept this confederacy so long together;" he was alluding to the revolution. "It was not the mere matter of the separation of the colonies from the mother land, but that sentiment in the Declaration of Independence which gave liberty not alone to the people of this country, but I hope to the world for all future time. . . . If this country cannot be saved without giving up that principle, I was about to say that I would rather be assassinated on this spot than surrender it." He was aware at that moment of a plot to assassinate him as he passed through Baltimore, and to avoid the danger he made the rest of the journey to Washington by night.

Inauguration. His inauguration was protected by an unusually large body of troops against the violence which was believed to be intended, (March 4.) The most striking passage in the president's address was the following: "We find the proposition that in legal contemplation the Union is perpetual, confirmed by the history of the Union itself. The Union is much older than the Constitution. It was formed, in fact, by the Articles of Association in 1774. It was matured and continued in the Declaration of Independence in 1776. It was further matured, and the faith of all the then thirteen states expressly plighted and engaged that it should be perpetual, by the Articles of Confederation in 1777; and finally in 1787, one of the declared objects for ordaining and establishing the Constitution was to form a more perfect union. But if the destruction of the Union, by one or by a part only of the states, be lawfully possible, the Union is less than before. . . . I therefore consider that in view of the Constitution and the laws, the Union is unbroken; and to the extent of my ability I shall take care, as the Constitution itself expressly enjoins upon me, that the laws of the Union shall be faithfully executed in all the states." He concluded, "In your hands, my dissatisfied fellow-countrymen, and not in mine, is the momentous issue of civil war. The government will not assail you. . . . We are not enemies, but friends. We must not be enemies."

Contrast. History has few such contrasts as this between the chief magistrate of the United States and the leaders of the seceded states. In all their positions, in their views of their own principles and of the principles which they must combat, in their purposes and their expectations, there is something of the same difference as that dividing the day and the night. That such a man as Abraham Lincoln represented the Union, and stood ready to live or die for it, was one of the greatest blessings which God has bestowed upon this nation.

Attempt at negotiation. A week after the new administration began, two men, claiming to be commissioners from the government of the Confederate States, informed the secretary of state, Mr. Seward, that they were instructed to make overtures for the opening of negotiations. To their letter the secretary replied in a memorandum, the main point being that he "cannot act upon the assumption, or in any way admit, that the so-called Confederate States constitute a foreign power with whom diplomatic relations ought to be established," (March 15.)

Relief of Fort Sumter. A more anxious question had come up the very day after the inauguration. Major Anderson was still in Fort Sumter. He had sent away the women and children towards the end of January. All around the fort, on both sides of the harbor, extended the batteries of the South Carolinians and their comrades from other states. Thousands in arms kept watch upon the eighty men within the fort, to whom no succor had been sent since the Star of the West had been driven back. At the end of February, Anderson wrote to the war department that twenty thousand men would be needed in order to reënforce him before his provisions were exhausted, and this letter was laid before the cabinet. General Scott concurred in the opinion, and stated that the government had no such force at its control, and could have none in season to relieve the garrison. The president seems to have acquiesced, but only for a time; giving up Fort Sumter, as he afterwards declared, was "our national destruction commenced." He sent an officer directly to Major Anderson, who said that he could hold out till the 15th of April; and on receiving this assurance, the president determined to relieve him. A few days later, (April 4,) a written order was given, and a message was sent to inform the governor of South Carolina that, if provisions were suffered to reach the fort, no troops would be introduced. Several vessels, with both troops and provisions, sailed from New York and Norfolk within the next few days. They arrived, (April 11, 12,) uncertain whether they were bringing peace or war, and found war before them.

CHAPTER XII.

Civil War.

First Period.—April, 1861, to January, 1863.

Fall of Fort Sumter.

All the other forts and possessions of the United States that had been seized by the seceders, were like dust in their mouths while Fort Pickens, near Pensacola, under Lieutenant Slemmer, and Fort Sumter held out against them. The news that an attempt would be made to provision Fort Sumter determined the confederate authorities to order its reduction by General Beauregard, in command of the forces at Charleston. "Unless you sprinkle blood in the face of the people of Alabama," said an Alabamian to Jefferson Davis, "they'll be back into the old Union in less than ten days." Beauregard at once called upon Anderson to surrender, and on being met by a refusal, renewed the demand, with notice that unless it were complied with, fire would be opened. At half past four on the following morning, (April 12,) the first shot was fired, and for thirty-three hours, one hundred and twenty cannon kept up the bombardment. Anderson made no reply till seven in the morning, and closed his port-holes at dark, renewing fire early the next day; but though husbanding his strength, it was worn down, not only at the guns, but amidst the flames which repeatedly broke out within the walls. On the second day, the men breathed only by covering their faces with wet cloths; and to save

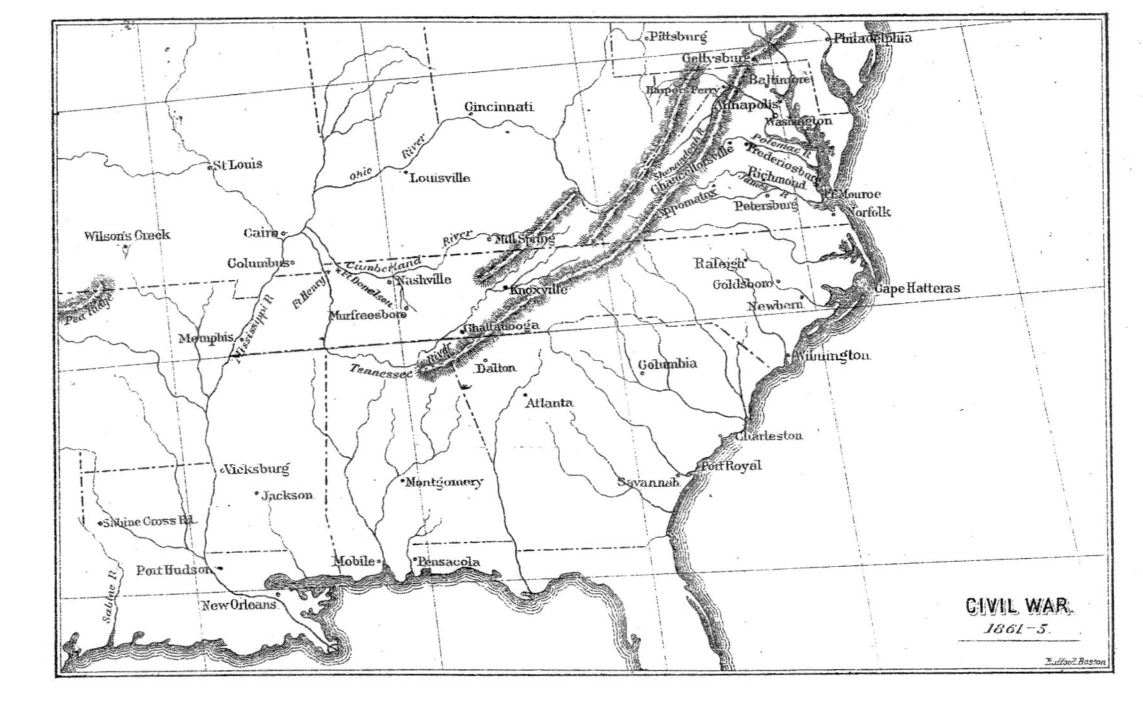
CIVIL WAR.
1861–5.
Pittsburg
Philadelphia
Gettysburg
Harpers Ferry
Baltimore
Annapolis
Washington
Potomac R.
Shenandoah R.
Chancellorsville
Fredericksburg
Richmond
James R.
Appomattox
Petersburg
Ft. Monroe
Norfolk
Cincinnati
St. Louis
Ohio River
Louisville
Wilson's Creek
Cairo
Columbus
Mill Spring
River
Cumberland
Ft. Henry
Ft. Donelson
Nashville
Knoxville
Pea Ridge
Mississippi R.
Murfreesboro
Memphis
Chattanooga
Tennessee River
Dalton
Raleigh
Goldsboro
Newbern
Cape Hatteras
Wilmington
Columbia
Atlanta
Charleston
Port Royal
Savannah
Vicksburg
Jackson
Montgomery
Sabine Cross Rd.
Sabine R.
Port Hudson
Mobile
Pensacola
New Orleans

themselves from utter destruction they were forced to throw over the powder which had been taken from the magazine, while but three cartridges were left, and no more could be made on account of the fiery shower to which every part of the fort was now exposed. The vessels sent to relieve the garrison had been seen off the harbor at noon on the first day, but they could bring no other relief than the sense of their being comparatively near, and the garrison fought on. At half past one in the afternoon of the second day, a volunteer flag of truce appeared, and various messages followed between Anderson and Beauregard. The major would not surrender, but would evacuate; that is, he would leave the fort with company and private property, and, above all, the flag, which he must have the privilege of saluting when it was lowered. To these terms Beauregard at length consented. They were carried into effect the following day, (April 14.) Anderson saluted his flag, and embarked his men on a Charleston steamer, by which they were taken to the United States steamer Baltic, off the harbor, while Te Deums were sung in the Charleston choirs, and sermons of victory were preached from the pulpits; for it was Sunday. But the rejoicings of the Carolinians had begun the night before, when their governor bade them exult that the flag which had triumphed for seventy years had been " humbled before the glorious little State of South Carolina." There was at least one reason to rejoice — that the bombardment had not cost a human life on either side.

Uprising. A proclamation, dated April 15, by the president, called forth the militia of the several states to the number of 75,000, " in order to suppress combinations" in the seceded states, and also summoned both houses of Congress to meet on the 4th of July. The militia instantly obeyed. First to reach Washington were three Pennsylvania companies, but these came unarmed, (April 18;) the first to come armed were the Massachusetts sixth, which received enthusiastic greeting along the route until reaching Baltimore, where a mob opposed their march, and lives were lost in forcing a passage through the city. Massachusetts blood, first to be shed in the war for independence, was the first to be shed in the war for union, and on the same day of the year, April 19. Other regiments followed; but the way through Washington was blocked, and until another was opened by the Chesapeake and from Annapolis, Washington was cut off from its communications. Difficulty and danger only increased the spirit of the loyal people. While the militia gathered, and went forward to the capital, other men subscribed, labored, and served as efficiently as if under arms. Women aided in making up supplies, and children brought their offerings. The national flag was raised on every public, and almost every private building; national badges were every where worn; national songs were every where sung. Meetings were held, and if speeches could have saved the country, it was safe. All spoke alike; the conservative and the radical for once used the same language, and speakers and listeners united in one universal expression of fidelity to the Union. This was the uprising of the north. That of the south was the same in fervor. Derisive laughter greeted the president's proclamation at Montgomery. Defiance was the reply to it from every point in the seceded states, and almost every point in the slaveholding states which had not seceded. One hundred guns were fired at Richmond to celebrate the fall of Fort Sumter. A few days later, and the Virginia convention, which had been in session two months, resolved that an ordinance of secession should be submitted to popular vote. But without waiting for the vote, the secessionists seized the national arsenal at Harper's Ferry and the national navy-yard at Norfolk, and placed the state in immediate hostility to the Union. It was considered a great triumph that Virginia, with all her associations and resources, should enter the Confederacy, and her capital become the capital of the new government. Nothing now remained in the south under the flag of the United States but Fortress Monroe in Virginia and three forts in Florida — Fort Pickens near Pensacola, Fort Taylor at Key West, and Fort Jefferson in the Tortugas. These, it was believed, would soon fall, and more than these. Vice President Stephens, as he hastened to Richmond, divulged the purpose of an attack on Washington, and the confederate secretary of war promised that the confederate flag should float over the dome of the Capitol before the first of May.

More secession. The secession of Virginia was followed, after some delay, by Arkansas, Tennessee, and North Carolina, (May.) All of them had been out of the Union in spirit long before they left it in the letter. Every slave-holding state was now gone but Delaware, Maryland, Kentucky, and Missouri, and the last two of these were in danger of going, while the first two showed little resolution in staying.

Rebellion or war. Before all the eleven had seceded, — in fact from the moment that fire opened upon Fort Sumter, — a question arose as to the character of the conflict. If the government could treat it purely as a rebellion, not as a war, then the seceders would be in danger of being regarded by foreign powers as rebels without the rights which international law accords to belligerents. But the president allowed them these rights without intending it, when he proclaimed the determination of the government to blockade the southern ports, (April 19,) for a government is considered to close its own ports, but to blockade only the ports of another power with whom it is at war. The proclamation of blockade was therefore held to involve the recognition of the Confederate States as belligerents on the part of the United States, and to justify other nations in making the same recognition. Great Britain was the first to make it. Without waiting the arrival of the newly-appointed American minister, Charles Francis Adams, though he was known to be on his way to London, the queen's proclamation of neutrality (May 13) gave the same belligerent rights to the disloyal as to the loyal states of the Union. France took the same course, (June 11.) Her ruler, Napoleon III., was soon known to be in favor of even stronger action, and to press upon the British government the recognition of confederate independence; but to this length Great Britain refused to go.

Two periods of the war. The war thus opening may be divided into two periods; the first from April, 1861, to January, 1863, when the cause of the struggle was reached by the emancipation of the slaves in the seceded states; and the second to April, 1865. We can here observe only the salient movements of the two.

Lyon's defence of Missouri. The first marked success on the national side was gained by Captain Nathaniel Lyon. He held the United States arsenal at St. Louis with a garrison of a few hundred regulars, and on receiving authority from the president, he enlisted several thousand volunteers, chiefly among the German population, who were readier than the native citizens to defend their state against secession. The governor of Missouri, sympathizing with the native, not the German spirit, ordered the state militia to encamp near St. Louis, with ill-concealed designs against the Union troops. On hearing that guns and ammunition had been brought to the state camp, Lyon drove thither in disguise, satisfied himself that the report was true, and returned to lead out his force at once against the militia. They yielded to his superior numbers, and surrendered themselves, their munitions and their camp, without a shot in resistance. But as Lyon was bringing back his prisoners, a mob from St. Louis fired upon his men, who fired in return, and but for his orders to cease firing, many would have lost their lives. Among those who fell was an officer, to whose widow Lyon said, "Since my boyhood it has always been my highest wish to die as your husband has;" and the words were fuel to the patriotic flame he had already kindled. The effect of Lyon's mastery over the Missouri secessionists was heightened by the associations of the day, for it was the anniversary of that on which Ethan Allen and his comrades mastered Ticonderoga, May 10, 1775, the first marked success of the revolution. Lyon was promoted to be a general, and continued to defend Missouri against secession, until his life-long wish was gratified, and he fell in battle at Wilson's Creek, (August.) He left all his property to the government which he had heroically served.

West Virginia for the Union.

Down to the secession of Virginia, the seceding states had appeared to be a unit. If opposition was tried, it soon broke down and vanished, sometimes because the Unionist believed it to be his duty to obey his state, but more frequently because he was outnumbered or overborne. But a large portion of Virginia, embracing the western counties, where soil and climate were unfavorable to slave labor, refused to be dragged out of the Union. Two conventions were held at Wheeling, the first before the ordinance of secession was ratified, the second afterwards, and in this West Virginia was declared independent of Virginia, and placed under a provisional state government, (June.) Meantime the Union arms had been successful against the confederates, who vainly endeavored to keep their hold on what they considered a rebellious population, and the campaign continued unfavorable to them, (July.) General McClellan was in command of the national forces. The civil movement, however, was far more striking than the military, and gave much greater encouragement to the government and its supporters. West Virginia was formally admitted to the Union in June, 1863.

East Tennessee. The same character of soil and climate extends south-west from West Virginia to East Tennessee. There, too, the loyalty of the people was unbroken; and though they did not declare, they really maintained their independence of the state authorities which joined the confederates. It was late in the course of the war before the Union armies occupied East Tennessee.

Extreme measures. The war had but begun when its pressure became unexpectedly severe. Volunteers were soon (May 3) called for, to serve for three years, instead of the three months required of the militia. Large numbers of vessels were taken up for transportation and blockade, while plans of a new navy were rapidly prepared. Vast quantities of arms, munitions, clothing, and stores were ordered, and demands upon the national resources increased beyond all previous experience. Yet greater sacrifices were thought necessary, and the government laid its grasp upon some of the highest rights of the citizen. In all the chief cities of the loyal states, at one and the same moment, the telegraphic messages received at the different offices during the previous year, were seized by United States marshals, (April 20,) in order to alarm, if not actually punish, such as had been accomplices in secession. A week later (April 27) the president authorized General Scott to suspend the privilege of habeas corpus, on the military line between Philadelphia and Washington. Under this warrant, the officer in command of Fort McHenry, near Baltimore, refused to obey a writ directing him to produce the person of a Maryland militia-man, (May 14.) Still more resolute was the action of General Cadwallader, commanding the Maryland department, in refusing to obey the writ of the chief justice of the United States in favor of John Merryman, a member of the Maryland legislature and when the chief justice issued a second writ, directing the United States marshal to arrest the general for contempt of court, the marshal was not allowed to enter Fort McHenry, (May 25.) These were the first measures in a course which many of the most loyal men in the country lamented. The constitution provides that habeas corpus may be suspended in case of rebellion, but not by whom it may be suspended. Whether the president possessed the power of suspension was questionable; but he continued to exercise it, and Congress ultimately sustained him. Another measure was received with more general approbation. The secretary of war directed General Butler, in command of Fortress Monroe, to refrain from surrendering to alleged masters any persons who might come within his lines, (May 30.) This was in answer to advices from the general that he had refused to surrender certain fugitives from Hampton, because employed, or about to be employed, on confederate fortifications. "They are contraband of war," he said, at another's suggestion; "set them at work within our lines." By a remarkable coincidence, this first step towards emancipation was taken where slaves had first been brought to our shores.

Congress and the president's message.

Congress met on the 4th of July. Twenty-three states were represented in the Senate, twenty-two in the House of Representatives. The president's message recommended "the legal means for making this contest a short and decisive one . . . at least four hundred thousand men and four hundred million dollars." It stated, "This is essentially a people's contest. On the side of the Union, it is a struggle for maintaining that form and substance of government whose leading object is to elevate the condition of men. . . . It is worthy of note that while large numbers of those in the army and navy favored with offices have resigned, not one common soldier or common sailor is known to have deserted his flag. . . . Our popular government has often been called an experiment. Two points in it our people have already settled — the successful establishing and the successful administering of it. One still remains — its successful maintenance against a formidable internal attempt to overthrow it. . . . And having thus chosen our course, without guile and with pure purpose, let us renew our trust in God, and go forward without fear and with manly hearts." Congress passed one bill authorizing a loan of two hundred and fifty million dollars, another calling out five hundred thousand volunteers, and a third providing that slaveholders forfeited all claim to slaves employed in aiding insurrection or resisting laws of the United States. The things to be done, said a member, are to tax, fight, and emancipate.

Bull Run. More than a month passed before the troops gathering at Washington were sent over the Potomac, (May 23.) There fortifications were thrown up, and preparations for further marches were made. Many of the loyal people became very impatient, and clamored for an advance against Richmond, now the capital of the Confederate States. But between it and the national capital lay the principal confederate army, drawn from Charleston and other quarters, and threatening Washington with the fate which confederate authorities had openly predicted. At length, the Union army being forty thousand strong at Washington, with eighteen thousand besides not far from

Harper's Ferry, General McDowell received orders to move at the head of about thirty thousand men, (July 15.) General Beauregard had twenty-six thousand confederates under his command at Manassas Junction, thirty miles southwest of Washington, and General Johnston had eight thousand more at Winchester. It was McDowell's object to engage with Beauregard before Johnston could join him, and he therefore marched directly upon Manassas. An engagement was brought on by an attempt to turn the confederate right at Union Mills on Bull Run, a small stream emptying into the Potomac, but this proved unimportant, (July 18.) Three days later, (July 21,) the battle of Bull Run was fought on either side of Young's Creek, which flows into the run. The Union army endeavored to turn the confederate left, and at first succeeded, about noon. "They're beating us back," said the confederate General Bee. "We'll give them the bayonet," replied Jackson, as he held a ridge towards which the Union troops were advancing. "Form, form," cried Bee to his disordered line; "there's Jackson, standing like a stone wall." Beauregard hurried reënforcements to the same point, and thither, at half past three, came four thousand of Johnston's men from Winchester, pouring out of the railway train which brought them, to strike the Union right, and drive it back in terrible disorder. Rout followed, and then, as the masses crossed Bull Run on the retreat towards Centreville, a panic set in, and all was lost. A small force of United States regulars prevented the confederate cavalry from pursuing, and the confederate infantry were too much disordered themselves to leave the field. Their loss was the greater; three hundred and seventy-eight killed and fourteen hundred and eighty-nine wounded, to four hundred and eighty-one killed and one thousand and eleven wounded on the Union side. But the Union army lost a large number taken prisoners, and twenty-seven out of twenty-eight cannon which had crossed Bull Run; in fact, lost everything. The confederates made little use of their victory, except to boast of it. "Our troops," said General Johnston, "believed the war ended, . . . and left the army in crowds to return to their homes." On the other hand, the Union troops rallied. Their defeat was ascribed to causes over which they had no control, to the clamor which had obliged them to move though unprepared, to the heat, dust, and exhaustion of the midsummer day on which they fought, and, above all, to the mismanagement which allowed Johnston to reënforce Beauregard. It was fortunate that such excuses could be made, or the spirit of the people might have sunk under the blow. As it was, they bore up against it, and learning the lesson taught, addressed themselves more seriously to the war which they saw before them.

Carolina and Georgia coast. The blockade of the southern coast proved far more efficient than could have been hoped or feared. Notwithstanding the immense extent over which it required to be maintained, not many vessels succeeded in running it. Among these were a few commissioned as privateers, one of which, the steamer Sumter, did great havoc among United States merchantmen. To enforce the blockade, two expeditions, military and naval, were sent southward; one in August, reducing Forts Clark and Hatteras, at Hatteras Inlet; the other in September, reducing Forts Beauregard and Walker, at the entrance of Port Royal harbor, between Charleston and Savannah. Beaufort was occupied, and Tybee Island, commanding the mouth of the Savannah River, (December.) These victories were bravely won, but feebly used.

The Trent. One of the successful blockade runners carried two commissioners from the confederate government, Mason of Virginia, and Slidell of Louisiana, the former to Great Britain, the latter to France. At Havana they took passage in the British mail steamer Trent, and made about two hundred and fifty miles, when the vessel was stopped by the United States sloop of war San Jacinto, to which the commissioners, with their secretaries, were transferred, (November 8,) and brought to the United States. The commander of the San Jacinto, Captain Wilkes, had acted on his own responsibility; but he was congratulated by the secretary of the navy, thanked by the House of Representatives on the first day of the session, (December,) and honored by almost every possible form of public and private gratitude. But the president saw what must follow. "We must stick," said he, on hearing of the capture, "to American principles concerning the rights of neutrals. . . . If Great Britain demands, we must give up the traitors." Great Britain demanded it immediately, in a despatch to Lord Lyons, minister at Washington, and without waiting a reply ordered troops and arms to Canada, ships and munitions to the North American and West India squadrons, while English journals stormed, and Englishmen seemed to lose their reason. The prince consort insisted on moderation, and the party led by Cobden and Bright took a rational position, to which more and more of their countrymen were attracted as the first flash of passion passed. Meantime, Mr. Seward had written to Mr. Adams that as Captain Wilkes had not acted under instructions, his government was free to receive any suggestion from the British government, (November 30.) Not quite four weeks later, Mr. Seward communicated to Lord Lyons a letter addressed to Mr. Adams, in which he argued that if Captain Wilkes had brought the Trent itself into port, to be adjudged a prize or liberated by a court of admiralty, he would have acted in accordance with British principles concerning neutrals; but that not having done this, and not having any warrant in American principles to interfere with a neutral as he had, his prisoners must be released by the United States. "We are asked," says the secretary of state, "to do to the British nation just what we have always insisted all nations ought to do unto us." On new year's day, the confederate commissioners and their secretaries were delivered to a British gunboat at Provincetown, Mass. The London Times, which had led the assault on Captain Wilkes and his government, now said that England would have done just as much for two negroes. Although the commissioners succeeded in reaching the capitals to which they had been accredited, they did not succeed in negotiating with either government.

Military preparations.

Immediately after Bull Run, General McClellan was called from West Virginia to take command of the broken troops at Washington. These were reorganized as the army of the Potomac, and very largely increased through the summer and autumn; but nothing followed, except a bloody repulse of a detachment at Ball's Bluff, (October 21.) General Scott resigned, and General McClellan succeeded as commander-in-chief, (November 1,) but was relieved in little more than four months. His successor, appointed the following summer, was General Halleck. But the only real commander-in-chief was Edwin M. Stanton, who took charge of the war department in January, 1862, and held it in a grasp of iron till victory was won. He was charged by many of the Union generals with prejudice and wilfulness, but few doubted his capacity, none doubted his energy or his loyalty. Under his direction the recruiting service never flagged; as fast as the armies were reduced by disease or battle, they were filled by the unwearying devotion of the people.

Campaigns in the west. From the battle of Wilson's Creek, in which Lyon fell, a succession of engagements under rapidly increasing commanders kept the balance in Missouri generally inclined towards the Union side. The confederates marched into Kentucky, and fortified various points on the Mississippi River, in the early autumn, and their repulse became a leading object with the government and its forces in the west. The victory of Mill Spring, gained by General Thomas, one of our best and most serviceable generals, on the 19th of January, 1862, was the first in the series of actions by which Kentucky, and the greater part of Tennessee were recovered. Fort Henry, on the Tennessee River, was taken by the Union gunboats, (February 6,) and Fort Donelson, with twelve thousand men, by the army under General Grant, after very hard fighting for two days, (February 16.) Nashville was immediately occupied, while the confederate posts on the Mississippi were, one after another, abandoned or surrendered, (March, April.) The battle of Pittsburg Landing, or Shiloh, near the southern border of Tennessee, was lost the first day, and won the second day, by General Grant, much aided by General Sherman of his own army, and reënforced by General Buell at the head of another army; but though very destructive, twenty thousand being killed or wounded on both sides, no results followed, (April 7, 8.) After long delays and numerous reënforcements, the army advanced under General Halleck as far as Corinth, Mississippi, which the confederates had first fortified and then evacuated, (May.) Meanwhile operations had been actively prosecuted on the Mississippi, and after several important successes, under Commodore Foote and General Pope, the Union flotilla, under Captain Davis, routed the confederates near Memphis, and took possession of that city, (June 6.) This freed the Mississippi as far south as Vicksburg.

Recovery of New Orleans.

It was also free to the same point from the mouth. A greater naval and military armament than had as yet been equipped, was directed towards New Orleans. It appeared almost impracticable to reach the city; the army, under General Butler, could not march thither without support from the fleet, and the fleet, under Commodore Farragut, found the river strongly defended by two forts, St. Philip and Jackson, with a fleet in the stream, while a chain, supported upon hulks, was stretched from one bank to the other. The chain was broken, but the forts held out unshaken by a bombardment of several days. Farragut ran by them in the night, under a cannonade which hardly any commander before him would have braved, escaped the fire-vessels sent against him, vanquished the confederate fleet, and on the day after moved his squadron abreast of New Orleans, (April 25.) The forts below surrendered, (April 28,) and the city was occupied by the Union army, (May 1.) General Butler remained in New Orleans, while Farragut ascended the Mississippi, taking Baton Rouge and Natchez, and running the Vicksburg batteries to meet the Union fleet above them, then running them again on his return to New Orleans.

Fort Pulaski.

Batteries being planted on Tybee Island by Captain Gillmore, they opened upon Fort Pulaski, and compelled its surrender on the second day, (April 11.)

Roanoke, Newbern, and Fort Macon.

Higher up the coast the forts on Roanoke Island fell before an expedition under General Burnside and Commodore Goldsborough, (February 7, 8.) The confederate fleet in Albemarle Sound was soon mastered, (February 10.) The next month, (March 14,) Newbern was captured, and the next, (April 25,) Fort Macon, so that a great part of the North Carolina coast was recovered.

Merrimac and Monitor.

When Norfolk came into the hands of the Virginia secessionists, they found, among other very valuable spoils, the steam frigate Merrimac, sunk by the officers of the navy-yard, but easily raised and converted into an iron-plated ram by her captors. Her appearance in Hampton Roads, where Union ships of war and transports were always lying, had long been feared, when she came, with five smaller vessels in her train, in the afternoon of March 8. At half past three she struck the sloop of war Cumberland, which sank discharging her guns, and carrying down her sick, wounded, and killed. At half past four she compelled the surrender of the frigate Congress, already attacked by her consorts. She then turned against the steam frigate Minnesota, that had run aground, but without immediately attacking this vessel. The Roanoke and St. Lawrence were also grounded. Enough was done for one day, and the Merrimac withdrew towards Norfolk, to return when she pleased, and to do, as it seemed, what she pleased. Hampton Roads lay at her mercy, and beyond, the sea, the Potomac, Washington, Philadelphia, New York or Boston, any harbor, any fleet, any shore upon which she might descend. But one night changed everything by bringing the Monitor to the scene of action. This was a low iron-clad, constructed under John Ericsson's direction in New York, and armed with heavy guns in a movable turret, which had been invented twenty years before by Theodore R. Timby. These are names and facts which deserve to be remembered, for the vessel thus fashioned proved the safety of the Union fleets and the Union shores. Lieutenant Worden commanded, and he laid his tub, as it appeared, full in the path of the huge Merrimac, as she came to complete her work of devastation on the morning of the 9th of March. The action was decisive, and the Monitor drove her antagonist back to Norfolk. On the abandonment of that place by the confederates, early in May, they blew up the Merrimac. The Monitor foundered at sea in September. Her brave commander, in the action with the Merrimac, received severe injuries, and as he lay helpless in Washington, the president wept over him with pathetic gratitude.

Peninsular campaign.

We have now to follow the Union forces to defeat, and that where it told the most against them and their cause. The army of the Potomac, under General McClellan, was transported to the peninsula between the York and James Rivers, at the beginning of April. It was occupied a month by the siege of Yorktown, and then led forward in such a way as to expose a part of it to great peril at Williamsburg, (May 5.) Most of its fighting was done between May 27, at Hanover Court House, and July 1, at Malvern Hill; and in the course of these five weeks, it passed from one extreme, where its advance was within four miles of Richmond, to the other, where it fought only to save itself from total destruction before reaching the James River in retreat. Fair Oaks, (May 31, June 1,) Mechanicsville, (June 26,) Gaines' Mill, (June 27,) White Oak Swamp, (June 30,) — these, with others just mentioned, are the names of its battles, all gallantly delivered, and all vainly, so far as related to the purpose of the campaign. Thousands upon thousands of brave men, as brave as any the country had, fell by disease or wounds; and when all was over, Richmond looked safer than Washington. The general threw the blame upon the government for not reënforcing him, and the government blamed the general; the army and the people were divided in opinion. But the campaign had been determined in very much the same manner, though on a much larger scale, as the battle of Bull Run. The confederate general known as Stonewall Jackson entered the Shenandoah Valley, where General Banks was in command, drove him with great loss out of the valley, (May 23–26,) then beat General Fremont at Cross Keys, (June 8,) and General Shields at Port Republic, (June 9,) — both of whom had been sent to intercept him, — and having thus alarmed Washington and the north, he prevented troops from being forwarded to General McClellan, and brought his force to swell the army defending Richmond, now under the command of General Lee; when Lee, thus strengthened, turned on the Union lines, and forced their withdrawal to the River James.

Northern Virginia.

Lee and Jackson proved a more serious combination than had as yet confronted the Union generals. The forces near Washington and in the Shenandoah Valley, augmented at first by troops from West Virginia and the Carolina coast, and afterwards by the Army of the Potomac from the James River, were organized as the army of Virginia, under General Pope, and directed towards Richmond from the north. It was a brief and pitiful movement, beginning with the defeat of General Banks at Cedar Mountain, (August 9,) and ending with the defeat of General Pope at Bull Run, (August 29,) and Chantilly, (August 31,) from which he sought safety within the fortifications of Washington. Again had Jackson's swift marches on the flank and rear of our army resulted in its overthrow. To match such a general with one like Pope was like matching the Mississippi with a creek. Yet Pope's defeat was not wholly his own work; he suffered from military jealousies among the officers who should have supported him for the sake of the country.

Defence of Maryland.

The relics of the summer campaigns, and the new regiments hurrying to the front, were gathered as the army of the Potomac, and intrusted to General McClellan. He was soon on the road in pursuit of Lee, who, flushed with repeated victories, crossed the Potomac, (September 3–6,) and called upon the people of Maryland to throw off their " foreign yoke," by which he meant the government of the United States. Ready as individuals were, the great body of Marylanders had no mind to join the confederates, and the army was disappointed in the accessions and supplies which had been confidently expected. It order to take Harper's Ferry, Lee ran the great risk of dividing his forces; but it was run safely, and Jackson, after taking the Ferry and twelve thousand men garrisoning it, (September 15,) rejoined his commander. McClellan won the battle of South Mountain on the 14th, and might have turned it into a great victory, had he followed it up before Jackson's return. But he did not, and accordingly had to fight both Lee and Jackson at Antietam, on the 17th, where they suffered sufficiently to decide their retreat to Virginia. This, in the circumstances, was equivalent to a Union victory, and the relief to the loyal country was immense, though there was great disappointment because the confederate retreat was not molested.

Defence of Cincinnati.

Just before this advance into Maryland, two confederate divisions entered Kentucky. One of them, under General E. K. Smith, defeated a body of Union troops at Richmond, (August 30), and marched towards Cincinnati. General Lewis Wallace took upon himself the almost hopeless defence of the city, and ordered all places of business to be closed, ferry-boats to stop, and citizens to work on intrenchments and enlist in an improvised army. " Any how," he proclaimed, " it must be done. The willing shall be properly credited; the unwilling promptly visited. The principle adopted is — citizens for the labor, soldiers for the battle," (September 1.) Forty thousand came forward, and in three days a line of earthworks ten miles long, armed and manned, on the southern bank of the Ohio, looked so formidable that when the confederates arrived, (September 12,) they made no attack, but retreated. The other confederate division, under General Bragg, defeated a Union force at Memfordsville, (September 17,) and being joined by Smith, retreating from Cincinnati, Bragg also retreated southward, engaging in a battle at Perryville with the Union army under General Buell, (October 8.) Of all these movements in Kentucky and Maryland, nothing stands out in such relief as the defence of Cincinnati. It was better than any battle as a proof of the resolution with which the loyal people were now armed.

Reverses. Their resolution was put to the test by repeated reverses as the year drew to a close. General McClellan gave place to General Burnside as commander of the army of the Potomac, (November 7,) and he led his brave troops to fruitless slaughter in attempting to storm Lee's works at Fredericksburg, (December 13.) General Buell gave place to General Rosecrans as commander of the Army of the Cumberland, and he, marching against the confederates, was attacked by them at Stone River, near Murfreesboro', and but for General Thomas and the centre of his army, would have been routed, (December 31.) General Grant, succeeding General Halleck in command of the army at Corinth, held that post against the confederates, and on his marching westward, General Rosecrans defended it in a well-fought battle, (October 4.) But Grant's expedition against Vicksburg was a failure. As he advanced from the east, the officer in charge of his stores surrendered, and left him no alternative but to fall back, (December 20,) while his lieutenant, General Sherman, advancing from the north, was repulsed in battle at Chickasaw Bayou, (December 29.)

Emancipation. Light was breaking from another quarter than the battle-field. The first rift in slavery was very narrow, merely emancipating slaves employed in aiding insurrection. But it was sure to widen. General Fremont, commanding the department of Missouri, issued a general order freeing the slaves of "all persons in the State of Missouri who shall take up arms against the United States," (August 30, 1861.) This, the president directed, must be "so construed as to conform with, and not to transcend, the provisions on the same subject contained in the act of Congress," a few weeks earlier, by which only such slaves were freed as were themselves employed in aiding insurrection. The next spring, (May 9,) another general order was issued by General Hunter, in command of the department of the south, or Georgia, Florida, and South Carolina: "The persons in these states, heretofore held as slaves, are declared forever free." This, too, was met by the president. "The supposed proclamation now in question," he asserted, "whether genuine or false, is altogether void. . . . I further make known that whether it be competent for me, as commander-in-chief of the army and navy, to declare the slaves of any state or states free, and whether at any time or in any case it shall have become a necessity indispensable to the maintenance of the government to exercise such supposed power, are questions which, under my responsibility, I reserve to myself, and which I cannot feel justified in leaving to the decision of commanders in the field," (May 19.) The president goes on to state that he had recommended (March) Congress to adopt a joint resolution, and that it had been adopted (April) by large majorities in both branches, declaring it the duty of the United States to coöperate, by pecuniary aid, with any state undertaking the gradual abolishment of slavery. Here, as may be remarked, he took the early anti-slavery ground in favor of a gradual and compensated emancipation. This, he continued, "now stands an authentic, definite, and solemn proposal of the nation to the states and people most interested in the subject matter. To the people of those states, now, I mostly appeal. . . . You cannot, if you would, be blind to the signs of the times." These signs were indeed plain. Congress had already abolished slavery in the District of Columbia on the principle of compensation to the slaveholder, (April 16.) It soon abolished slavery in the territories, without compensation, (June 19.) It soon after (July 17) passed an act to seize and confiscate the slaves of persons engaged in rebellion, which was what Fremont had attempted the previous year. But a greater measure than any of these was now in contemplation by the president. Early in the summer he read to his cabinet the draft of a proclamation emancipating all slaves in the seceded states. The secretary of state objected not to the act, but to the time of doing it; let it be done, he said, after victory. Time passed, bringing no victory, but deeper and deeper defeat, and at last the confederates were in Maryland. "I made a solemn vow before God," said the president afterwards, "that if General Lee was driven back from Maryland, I would crown the result by the declaration of freedom to the slaves." To a deputation from Chicago, which waited on him at this time, (September 13,) to urge emancipation, as if it were their measure, not his, he meekly replied, "The subject is on my mind by day and by night more than any other. Whatever shall appear to be God's will, that I will do." Antietam was fought, Lee was driven back, and then, on the 22d of September, came forth the president's proclamation, "That on the first day of January, in the year of our Lord one thousand eight hundred and sixty-three, all persons held as slaves within any state, or designated part of a state, the people whereof shall then be in rebellion against the United States, shall be then, thenceforward, and forever free; and the executive government of the United States, including the military and naval authority thereof, will recognize and maintain the freedom of such persons."

Effect of the proclamation.

Those few words lifted the load under which the nation had staggered from its birth. The slaves in the states which had rebelled would be free at the beginning of another year, and it could not be long after when the slaves in the slaveholding states which had not rebelled would also be free. Men could look into an early future, and see no slave in all the national domain. It did not please them all; for the moment, it did not please most of them. In the elections which soon followed throughout the loyal states, the republican majorities of the presidential vote were changed to a democratic majority against the administration; and though various causes were assigned, such as the condition of trade and the currency, the growing taxes, the arrests on political charges, and the reverses of the campaign, there can be no doubt that the most effective cause of all was the emancipation policy to which the administration stood committed. The British minister, Lord Lyons, wrote home of "a change in public feeling among the most rapid and complete that have ever been witnessed even in this country." Moreover the army and navy, or many officers and men, grumbled that the war for the Union should be turned into a war for the slave. As the president afterwards said, the good results of emancipation were not so immediate as was expected. But he stood firm, and though it was often predicted that the first of January would come and go without a second proclamation from him to give effect to the first, it brought out the following:

"I do order and declare that all persons held as slaves within said designated states and parts of states [that is, under confederate rule] are, and henceforward shall be, free. . . . And I hereby enjoin upon the people so declared to be free to abstain from all violence unless in necessary self-defence. . . . And I further declare and make known that such persons, of suitable condition, will be received into the armed service of the United States. . . . And upon this act, sincerely believed to be an act of justice, warranted by the Constitution upon military necessity, I invoke the considerate judgment of mankind and the gracious favor of Almighty God."

CHAPTER XIII.

Civil War — continued.

Second Period. — January, 1863, to April, 1865.

Finances. Long before this, the means of paying for the war became a serious question. Prosperous as was the nation, particularly the loyal part of it, when the conflict began, it could not continue so, while wealth was poured out on every side, and labor was largely turned to the battle-field. The banks sounded the first note of alarm by suspending specie payments in 1861. Congress gave the next in February, 1862, by authorizing the issue of United States treasury notes, without redemption, to the amount of $150,000,000 at first, and afterwards of $400,000,000; and these notes were declared to be legal tenders in payment of debts. The volume of irredeemable currency, thus expanding, produced its inevitable effects. In order to obviate them in very small degree, the national bank system was established early in 1863. By this the banks, hitherto state institutions, became national, and their notes were secured by deposits of government bonds at Washington. The circulation was thus materially improved, and bank notes from all parts of the country passed current every where. But the value of the currency remained that of mere paper money, irredeemed and irredeemable. It therefore soon declined. More paper dollars were needed to buy what was before bought by gold and silver, or by paper redeemable in gold and silver. Prices therefore rose, and persons of limited income found it more limited than ever, while some sank gradually into poverty. On the other hand, those who could profit by the times rose to sudden riches. Government contracts, and the speculations encouraged by the unsettled state of the money market, were turned to the creation of new fortunes. Many made money by dealing in government bonds, of which millions followed millions, as loan followed loan. By March, 1864, the national debt had reached fifteen hundred millions, and this proved just about one half of the amount expended by the nation, not counting state or local expenditures, upon the war. The secretary of the treasury, Mr. Chase, thought his operations highly successful; but the price of gold reached 195 (paper dollars for one hundred gold) in May, 1864, and 285 in July, declining afterwards.

Vicksburg.

Of all the military and naval movements of the war, none had hitherto come nearer its object than that which aimed at getting possession of the Mississippi River. One great obstacle remained, indeed more than one; but if one could be overcome, no other would cause any serious difficulty. This one was Vicksburg, once a quiet town, now a noisy stronghold, with long lines of batteries upon its cliffs, and earthworks in its rear, on the holding of which the confederates set a very high value, but not at all higher than its strategic importance merited. General Grant had failed, as we have seen, in his attempt at the close of 1862; but the new year found him intent upon the same object, and after sending a successful expedition up Arkansas River, (January, 1863,) he concentrated his efforts upon Vicksburg. All that he could do on the north and west, or river, sides of the place seemed unavailing, and when he had met with more than enough disappointment to check a commander of average firmness, he resolved upon trying an approach upon the south and east. This was so hazardous a plan that his most trusted subordinate, General Sherman, protested against it, while Grant delayed reporting it to Washington until interference from that quarter would be too late. He proposed carrying his army down the river, landing on the eastern bank, marching towards the interior, and then back towards Vicksburg, without any line of communication with the point from which he started, or any other point which he could fix upon as a base of operations. To do this merely with an army was impossible, but with the gunboats on the river, and aid from them throughout the movement, it might be executed. On two different nights, several gunboats ran the confederate batteries, eight miles long, and though suffering from the fire, were soon repaired and ready for service below the fortifications. At the same time, cavalry to the number of seventeen hundred, under Colonel Grierson, were sent to break up the railroads and telegraphs connecting with Vicksburg, and those brave riders made their way through six hundred miles of a hostile country, arriving at Baton Rouge in sixteen days from La Grange, Tennessee. "The Confederacy is a mere shell," reported Grierson. General Sherman was next directed to make a feint of attacking Vicksburg on the north, and then to join Grant on the south. All these precautions having been taken, Grant led his army down the western bank of the Mississippi, crossed at Bruinsburg, (April 30,) defeated the confederates in five battles, (May 2–17,) on the march, first to Jackson, the capital of Mississippi, then to Vicksburg, and more than all prevented General Johnston, commanding the army outside, from effecting a junction with General Pemberton, commanding inside the fortress. On gaining the position which had been intended, Sherman had the magnanimity to confess his mistake in having opposed the plan of his superior, while Grant was equally magnanimous in saying nothing of Sherman's objections, or amends. Two assaults were made, both unsuccessfully, and then reënforcements were asked for and obtained. Siege was laid, and in six weeks Vicksburg fell, with all its garrison and munitions. The surrender took place upon the 4th of July.

Port Hudson. The surrender of Port Hudson followed, (July 8.) This was a stronghold lower down the river, which an army under General Banks, now of the Louisiana department, had been assailing for some time. It could not hold out when Vicksburg yielded. The Mississippi, from source to mouth, was recovered by the Union, and the Confederacy was cut in two. In the early autumn, an expedition from Vicksburg took Little Rock, the capital of Arkansas, (September 10.)

Chancellorsville. The army of the Potomac, discouraged by reverses, changes of generals, and political controversies, was placed under the command of General Hooker, (January 26.) He undertook to reorganize it, and three months later to lead it to victory. He had hardly crossed the Rappahannock, and taken the offensive against Lee, than he suddenly changed to the defensive, waiting for the enemy, as he said, to give him battle on his own ground, at Chancellorsville. But his right was suddenly attacked on the flank by Stonewall Jackson, (May 2,) and with such effect as to determine the defeat of the whole army, though the battle was kept up for two days more, (May 3, 4.) On the next day, Hooker returned to the north side of the Rappahannock, leaving behind him thousands of killed, wounded, and prisoners. The confederates also suffered very heavily, and in Jackson, who was fired on in the dark from his own lines, they lost a general to whom they owed this and many a preceding victory. "He was as good," they said, "as ten thousand men." The army of the Potomac was soon yet more reduced by the discharge of troops whose period of enlistment expired. On the other hand, Lee's army of Northern Virginia was ready, as one of its best officers, General Longstreet, said, to undertake anything.

Gettysburg. Its temper was put to trial. Notwithstanding the yet fresh experience of the previous autumn, the confederate authorities resolved upon another expedition into the loyal states, and within a month from Chancellorsville, Lee began to move northward, (June.) As soon as this was known, Hooker followed, keeping between the enemy and Washington, and crossed the Potomac the day after Lee. Great was the alarm, not only at the capital, or in the parts of Maryland and Pennsylvania immediately threatened, but at Philadelphia, and even New York, both within striking distance, if Lee were again victorious. The disaffection of certain classes in the larger cities, and their threatened resistance to the draft which the government was about to make, added to the fears of a confederate attack; and many a flight, many a case of valuable effects, was directed to some far-off place of security. Means of defence did not abound. As soon as the president became aware of Lee's purpose, he called for one hundred thousand militia from New York, Pennsylvania, Maryland, West Virginia, and Ohio; but scarcely half that number responded, and most of those who did were ill prepared to meet the army of Northern Virginia. It did not encourage public confidence to learn that just at this crisis, when the confederates were entering Pennsylvania, the army of the Potomac was changing commanders; but General Hooker resigned, and General Meade, a tried and efficient officer, was appointed. He pressed forward without delay, and Lee, finding his communications threatened, turned from the road towards Harrisburg, and moved south-eastward to Gettysburg. Here was the watershed between the Susquehanna Valley on the north, and the Potomac on the south, and here a battle between northern and southern armies might seem intended to be decisive. General Reynolds, commanding the Union advance, was ordered to march on Gettysburg from the south, at the same moment that the foe approached from the west; and there he engaged in the forenoon of July 1, and while winning the first advantage, fell mortally wounded. At this time the main body of Meade's army was very far off, but being hurried forward, and well posted on a double ridge south of the town, it was ready for the fiercer conflict of the second day. It proved very difficult to resist the attack which the rashness of General Sickles invited on the Union left, and which, for some hours, threatened the whole army with defeat, while the Union right was also turned, and danger in that quarter became imminent. But Meade and his brave men stood fast, and when, on the third day, the confederates charged the left centre under General Hancock, and threw all their passionate vigor into one convulsive effort, they were met, broken, and compelled to give up the hard-fought field. Seventeen thousand Union soldiers, and more than twenty thousand confederates, were killed or wounded in this great battle. It was won on the same afternoon of July 3 when Pemberton was arranging the terms of his surrender to Grant at Vicksburg. On the evening of the day of that surrender, Lee began his retreat, and ten days later, amid great disorder and suffering, his army, reduced by almost one half, recrossed the Potomac. It was a great disappointment to loyal men that he should have been allowed to get back into Virginia; but the army of the Potomac was in no condition to pursue with any zeal or effect. The president called upon the people to observe a day for national thanksgiving, praise, and prayer, invoking Almighty God "to lead the whole nation, through paths of repentance and submission to the Divine will, back to the perfect enjoyment of union and fraternal peace." The day was kept on the 6th of August. Three months later, (November 19,) a part of the Gettysburg battle-field was dedicated as the burial-place of those who had there fallen in defence of the Union. The president was there, and when the ceremonies were performed, and the funeral oration was delivered by Edward Everett, he stood up and uttered a few words, consecrating the living to the great task which the dead had left, and saying, "Here let us resolve that they shall not have died in vain; that this nation shall, under God, have a new birth of freedom; and that government of the people, by the people, and for the people, shall not perish from the earth."

Attempt on Indiana and Ohio.

As in 1862, so in 1863, when Lee advanced in the east, a simultaneous attempt was made to penetrate the loyal states of the west. Thirty-five hundred cavalry, under General Morgan, who expected to be joined by a force then in East Tennessee, passed through Kentucky at the beginning of July, crossed into Indiana, and on being resisted there, turned into Ohio, but were pursued, and finally (July 26) captured, with the exception of a few hundred. It was more than twice as large a party as that under Grierson, which had made its way across two of the Southern States in April and May; but while Grierson swept all before him, Morgan himself was swept before his pursuers. The governors of Indiana and Ohio both called for volunteers, Cincinnati was placed under martial law, as in the year before, and all the country round rose to repel the foe.

Draft.

Conscription had been the chief means of filling the confederate armies from the beginning of the second year of war. It was a year later (May 8) when the president of the United States announced a draft to be made in July, according to an act of Congress in March. To this measure there was great opposition, open and secret. An association, called Knights of the Golden Circle, was believed to intend revolution in the Middle and Western States. Riots broke out in New York, and for three days and nights (July 13–15) all was anarchy. Governor Seymour stood on the steps of the City Hall, calling the rioters his friends, and telling them he had sent his adjutant general to Washington "to have the draft stopped." The riot, of course, continued, until the police and rapidly gathering militia put it down, after more than four hundred, chiefly colored persons, had been killed or wounded. Disturbances broke out elsewhere, and an epidemic of disorder seemed impending. But the army of the Potomac, in saving the nation from the evil of defeat, saved it from the greater evil of sedition. The president had received formal authority from Congress to suspend the privilege of habeas corpus, (March 3,) and he now (August 19) suspended it.

Fort Sumter. The occupation of many points along the southern coast proved highly serviceable to the blockade. It also led to various attempts upon other points not yet occupied, sometimes successful, but generally the reverse. Fort Sumter, where the war began, was like a thorn in the side of more than one commander. It was first assailed by sea alone, when (April 7, 1863) Admiral Dupont brought up his fleet of seven monitors and two iron-clads; but heavy as was their fire, it proved unavailing against that of Sumter and its encircling fortresses and batteries, so that in forty minutes the fleet withdrew, considerably injured. In the summer, Admiral Dahlgren took command, while General Gillmore was appointed to the military department in which Sumter lay. He thought it could be reached by operations on shore, the fleet assisting, and began with a few thousand men, all he had for the purpose, on Folly Island. Hence a party was sent, under General Strong, to Morris Island, at the northern end of which stood Fort Wagner, and this was assaulted, but unsuccessfully, (July 11.) Works were then thrown up on the island, and under their cover a second assault was tried, but with even more disastrous result. Strong fell mortally wounded, and other brave officers were killed, among them Colonel Shaw of the Massachusetts 54th, a colored regiment, (July 19.) More works were constructed, and after a long bombardment, a third assault was about beginning, when Fort Wagner was found to be evacuated, (September 7.) Fort Sumter, bombarded at the same time, was much injured, but not evacuated, and a boat attack by night (September 8) was repelled with great loss. The only result of these destructive operations was to close the harbor of Charleston to blockade-runners.

Colored troops. The Massachusetts regiment, which fought as bravely as the bravest at Fort Wagner, was the first recruited among the colored people of the north. Those of the south began to enlist the year before, in South Carolina and Louisiana, and Congress authorized the president to receive them into the service, (July, 1862.) But they did not generally enter it until after the emancipation of January, 1863. Willing as they were, they were hindered both by their own habitual submission and by the inveterate prejudices of their white fellow-countrymen. When the Massachusetts 54th was sent from Boston, it was by sea, in order to avoid any possible indignities in the streets of New York or other cities. Many of their white comrades shrank from them, many more treated them as inferiors, who might share in the hardships, but not in the honors, of the war. Strong as these feelings were, they yielded — they could not but yield — before the great qualities which the colored troops displayed. As the president wrote, in August, 1863, "There will be black men who will remember that with silent tongue, and clinched teeth, and steady eye, and well-poised bayonet, they have helped on." Of course, the wrath of the confederates overflowed, at times in threats, at times in cruelties, as when a garrison at Fort Pillow, near Memphis, was put to the sword, the blacks for being black, and the whites for being their comrades, (April, 1864.)

Great Britain and confederate cruisers. Relations with Great Britain, disturbed by her proclamation of neutrality, and yet more by her behavior in the Trent affair, were again stormy. Iron steamers, built at Liverpool and Glasgow, were easily turned into confederate cruisers, and employed against United States merchantmen. One called the Oreto, afterwards the Florida, was armed at Mobile; but most of them never entered a confederate port, but were equipped like the "290," afterwards the Alabama, which sailed to the Azores, and there received its armament from one British vessel, and its crew from another. These rovers generally hoisted the British flag as they approached a vessel, and then, running up the confederate, used British guns and British gunners to capture or to destroy their victims. All this had been going on for a year, and exciting the utmost indignation among American merchants and the whole American people, when it became known that two ironclad rams, the most powerful ships of war that could be built, were in construction at the same ship-yard which had sent out the Alabama; and there could be no doubt of their destination. The United States minister, Mr. Adams, had done his best to prevent the sailing of the cruisers; he now attempted to prevent the sailing of the rams. On being told by the British foreign secretary that "the government cannot interfere," Mr. Adams wrote, (September 5, 1863,) "It would be superfluous for me to point out that this is war." By taking this position, he carried the day, and the rams were detained.

Chatta-nooga. The defeat of the army of the Cumberland, under General Rosecrans, at Stone River, at the close of 1862, was redeemed at the opening of 1863, at Murfreesboro'. But though the confederate general Bragg retreated from this battle-field, he did not retreat far, nor did Rosecrans follow for six months afterwards. He then started, his principal object being to hold Chattanooga on the southern border of East Tennessee, while General Burnside, with the army of the Ohio, was to cross the northern border, and recover that loyal region. Without a battle, Rosecrans so moved as to compel the evacuation of East Tennessee by the confederates, whom Bragg soon found he needed in his own army; and further, to force Bragg and all his troops out of Chattanooga, (September 8.) Burnside entered Knoxville, (September 3,) amid a rejoicing population, men, women, and children joining in the welcome, and in offers of hospitality to the army. Nothing like it had been seen in the course of the war, for nowhere else had a people held so long, unaided, to the Union. Rosecrans, not content with what had been gained, pressed on, and without sufficient knowledge of the enemy's movements. Bragg was reënforced by Longstreet and a large body of troops from the army of Northern Virginia. With these he turned upon Rosecrans, marching by the Chickamauga, with the intention of throwing himself between the Union army and Chattanooga, which lay at no great distance. Thomas, in command of the Union left, opened the battle on the 19th, and closed it on the 20th, the centre and the right having broken and fled, Rosecrans with them. Retreat to Chattanooga was inevitable, and with the army there, and the enemy on Missionary Ridge and Lookout Mountain, — heights which commanded its communications, if not the town itself, — the campaign seemed utterly lost. So, indeed, it was; but another campaign succeeded under other direction, and the loss was repaired. A new department, the Mississippi, was created, and General Grant was appointed to its command. Under him, his army of the Tennessee, Sherman commanding, the army of the Cumberland, Thomas commanding, the army of the Ohio, Burnside commanding, and twenty odd thousand men brought from the army of the Potomac, twelve hundred miles in seven days, with Hooker at their head, all constituted an effective force, and Grant was an effective leader. Here the interest of the war was for a time concentrated; nor were circumstances wanting to give it peculiar intensity—on the one hand, the situation of the Union forces, virtually besieged in Chattanooga, and actually besieged at Knoxville, where Longstreet brought superior numbers against Burnside; on the other hand, the successive stages in their relief, Grant's arrival, (October 23,) then Sherman's, (November 15,) then the great victory of Chattanooga, part of it above the clouds on Lookout Mountain, and the whole planned and executed with extraordinary ability, (November 23–25), in consequence of which Bragg retreated from his position, and Longstreet from his at Knoxville. The combinations of the general and the achievements of the army had won a triumph as romantic as it was complete.

Grant Lieutenant General.

The victorious commander was soon appointed to a still higher charge. Congress revived the grade of lieutenant general, which had been held only by Washington, and the president immediately nominated Ulysses S. Grant. Ten days later, an executive order was issued appointing Lieutenant General Grant to the command of the armies of the United States, (March 10, 1864.) The new chief soon made it known that he had two purposes above all others of a military nature—the first, that the armies of the east and the west must act together, and the second, that they must act directly against the confederate armies.

Red River. Neither purpose was served by an expedition previously planned. Louisiana, or that part in Union possession, had been the starting-point of several military adventures, and one more was now directed against Shreveport, on Red River. It was joined by troops from the army of the Tennessee, and gunboats and iron-clads from the Mississippi. General Banks was in command, with General Franklin as his lieutenant and adviser. The whole thing failed. The army was routed at Sabine Cross Roads, (April 8,) and compelled to retreat precipitately; while the fleet, caught in low water above the falls at Alexandria, would have been lost there but for the engineering ability of Lieutenant Colonel Bailey, who, by a series of dams across the rocks, raised the water so that the vessels could pass down, (May 9-13.) The expedition ended with the removal of General Banks, General Canby succeeding.

France and Mexico. Before entering upon Grant's campaign we catch sight of a new danger. In the first year of the war, France, Great Britain, and Spain united in a convention, of which the ostensible object was to compel Mexico to resume the payment of her foreign debt. From this Great Britain and Spain withdrew in the following year; but France, or rather the Emperor Napoleon, pressed on with the intention of conquering Mexico, and creating an empire which should be more or less tributary to his own. The French arms soon prevailed, and the Austrian Archduke Maximilian became Emperor of Mexico. There could be but one opinion about this among the loyal citizens of the United States. The French emperor was their enemy, as well as the Mexicans'; he was known to favor the dissolution of the Union, and but for the prospect of that event, and the struggle against it in which the Americans were involved, he would never have exposed his troops or his government in a Mexican expedition. Resolutions were twice offered in the United States Senate declaring the expedition an act unfriendly to the United States; but the Senate would not debate them. The House of Representatives passed a resolution, (April 4, 1864,) "that it does not accord with the policy of the United States to acknowledge a monarchical government erected on the ruins of any republican government in America, under the auspices of any European power." The French minister at Washington immediately demanded an explanation of the secretary of state, while the American envoy at Paris was asked by the French foreign minister if he brought peace or war. Although the French government professed to be satisfied with the representations it received, the danger of rupture between it and the United States continued as long as occupation of Mexico by the French continued.

Virginia. Lieutenant General Grant made his headquarters with the army of the Potomac, which remained under the immediate orders of General Meade. With this army, in three corps, commanded by Generals Hancock, Warren, and Sedgwick, a fourth corps commanded by General Burnside, and the cavalry under General Sheridan, Grant began his campaign against Lee on the 4th of May. The same day, the army of the James, under General Butler, moved from Fortress Monroe towards Richmond, but was soon checked and thrown out of the combined movement. For two months Grant was in the thick of battle. The Wilderness, (May 5–12,) Spottsylvania, (12–21,) the North Anna, (21–31,) Cold Harbor, (June 1–10,) and Petersburg, (10–30,) were the centres from which circles of slaughter successively radiated. The army of Northern Virginia, reënforced from the south, never fought more stubbornly, or, considering the difference in its antagonist, more successfully. It was in its own country, strong in its defences, and moving in shorter distances than the Union army. Every attempt to pierce it, or to flank it, failed, and Grant, though proposing, on the sixth day, "to fight it out on this line if it takes all summer," changed his line on the fourteenth day, and on the thirty-second utterly abandoned it for a line on the south side of the James, which he held all summer, autumn, and winter, with headquarters at City Point. Here his first object was the capture of Petersburg; his second, to break in between Petersburg and Richmond; his third, to extend his intrenchments on the left, that is, to the south-west, in order to seize the railroad communications of the enemy. The third alone was partially gained by seizing the Weldon railroad, (August 18.) It was now nearly three months and a half since the campaign began, and this was the first positive success. Blood had flowed like water; ten thousand men had been killed, — General Wadsworth and General Sedgwick among the earliest to fall, — and fifty thousand more were wounded, many of them past recovery, on the Union side alone. The enemy, far from being absorbed in resisting Grant, was able to send a force of twenty thousand, under General Early, into Maryland and Pennsylvania, (July.) Baltimore and Washington were threatened, Chambersburg was burned, the country all around was ravaged, and Early retired to the Shenandoah Valley. There he was followed by General Sheridan, and thrice defeated, at Opequan, (September 19,) Fisher's Hill, (September 21,) and Cedar Creek, (October 19,) the last action beginning with the defeat of the Union troops, in Sheridan's absence, and ending with their victory when he placed himself at their head. Such, in its main features, was the Virginia campaign of 1864; and the closing year found Grant still before Petersburg, and still endeavoring to extend his lines to the south-west, while Lee held Petersburg, and Richmond behind it, apparently secure.

Georgia. Yet Lee had been weakened not only by the immediate pressure of Grant, but by other movements at a distance. The next day but one after the army of the Potomac began to move, General Sherman led the three armies of the Tennessee, the Cumberland, and the Ohio,—the first under McPherson, the second under Thomas, and the third under Schofield,—against the confederate army under Johnston, (May 6.) The army was Sherman's immediate object; his final object being Atlanta, in Georgia, a centre of supplies to the confederates, and about one hundred and fifty miles, by lines of march, from Chattanooga. By constantly flanking the enemy, and frequently fighting him, Sherman crossed the Alleghany range and the Chattahoochee River—a success so great, in the opinion of the confederate authorities, that Johnston was removed, and Hood put in his place, (July 17.) He was a bold, if not a skilful commander, and attacked Sherman in three successive engagements near Atlanta, (July 20, 22, 28,) McPherson falling in the second, but the Union troops victorious in all three. Then followed a month's siege of Atlanta by Sherman, then his movement towards the south, culminating in the victory of Jonesboro', (August 31,) and the evacuation of Atlanta by the confederate army, (September 2.) "Atlanta is ours, and fairly won," Sherman telegraphed to Washington. He ordered the inhabitants to leave the city, destroyed the manufactories and machine shops which had been supplying the confederate forces, and held it simply as a military position. Finding that the enemy intended to break his communications, and move towards Tennessee, Sherman sent back his best general, Thomas, to defend that state, and afterwards despatched a large part of his army for the same purpose. Meantime, he followed Hood northward and westward, until satisfied with regard to the preparations for meeting him, when he turned back to Atlanta, destroying the railroads, cutting the telegraph wire, and finally firing Atlanta, as he started on a march to the sea, (November 14.) This was his own plan, and one to which General Grant had been slow to consent. Sherman led three divisions, General Howard commanding the right, or the army of the Tennessee; General Slocum the left, or army of Georgia; and General Kilpatrick the cavalry; in all, sixty-five thousand men, moving in four columns. The distance was between two hundred and fifty and three hundred miles, and it was traversed in four weeks, without any severe fighting or serious loss. Savannah was invested December 12; Fort McAllister was taken by assault, under General Hazen, on the next day; and communications were opened with the fleet by General Sherman in person. On the 22d, Savannah surrendered, and on the 26th, the triumphant general telegraphed to the president, "I beg to present you, as a Christmas gift, the city of Savannah." His objects had been completely obtained, the Georgia railways being broken up, the manufactories, crops, and cattle of the people being swept away, "as well as," he said, "a countless number of slaves." Nor was this all. Thomas had done his part. As Hood marched northward, he was checked, in a severe battle, at Franklin, by Schofield, or rather by one of Schofield's brigadiers, Opdycke, (November 30;) and Schofield joining Thomas, the enemy pressed on to Nashville. Grant became impatient, and started from the James River, but on reaching Washington received such information from Thomas as quieted his apprehensions. That general took the offensive, and falling on Hood's left wing, defeated his whole army at Nashville, in a battle which lasted two days, (December 15, 16,) and was followed by a pursuit of the broken confederates for two hundred miles. Their Georgia army was no more.

Kearsarge and Alabama.

From the military operations of this year we turn to the naval. Foremost stands the victory of the Kearsarge over the Alabama. This steamer which sailed from Liverpool in the summer of 1862 had been for nearly two years capturing and destroying American vessels on the Atlantic, in the Gulf of Mexico, and in the Indian seas. While she was lying in the French port of Cherbourg, the United States steamer Kearsarge, Captain Winslow, arrived in pursuit, and Semmes, in command of the Alabama, accepted the opportunity of battle, (June 19, 1864,) confident that his vessel of British build, and his guns manned by gunners from a British ship of war, would win. It was, in fact, an engagement between British and American steamers, and the sympathies not only of Great Britain, but of France, were on the side of the Alabama. But in vain. An hour's conflict, off Cherbourg, and the Alabama ran up the white flag, then sank beneath the waters of the Channel, her commander escaping in a British yacht, to be honored with a public dinner and the gift of a sword by his admirers in England. The tribute to Winslow and his men was the gratitude of every heart among their loyal countrymen.

Mobile Bay.

On the 5th of August, in the early morning, Admiral Farragut brought his fleet against three forts and a confederate squadron defending the entrance to Mobile Bay. The ram Tennessee was one of the squadron, and a more powerful vessel than any of the assailants, while the channel was obstructed with piles and torpedoes. It mattered not to Farragut. Lashed to the maintop of his flagship, the Hartford, and giving his orders through a speaking tube to the deck, the admiral led the way to victory, destroying or scattering the confederate fleet in less than four hours, causing the abandonment of one of the three forts immediately, and the surrender of the other two upon the appearance of a land force. The closing of Mobile left but one port, Wilmington, where the blockade could be run.

Reëlection of Lincoln.

In the midst of war a new state, Nevada, was admitted to the Union, (October 31.) The presidential election followed, (November 8.) This was justly regarded as deciding whether the war should be continued or stopped. The democratic party, or the majority of them, wanted it stopped, and declared it a failure. They put forward, however, a candidate, General McClellan, who might think it a failure, but could not wish it stopped until it succeeded. Mr. Lincoln was the republican candidate, nominated not without open and secret opposition, and receiving a half-hearted support from many of the most earnest men in the party. But he stood for the Union, and the Union chose him its president for another term, by two hundred and twelve out of two hundred and thirty-three electoral votes, and a popular majority of more than four hundred thousand. All things considered, the long sufferings and the life-long losses of the war, and the uncertainty in which its issues were still involved, the will of the people to continue it is as really sublime as any thing in our history.

Thirteenth amendment.

It soon appeared how much more than the election itself had been at stake. Congress repealed the fugitive slave law before the election, (June, 1864;) but only the Senate would consent to the proposition of an amendment to the Constitution prohibiting slavery within the United States. After the election, the House adopted it by more than a two thirds' vote, amid rejoicings which have few parallels in congressional annals,

(January 31, 1865.) This amendment, known as the Thirteenth, was ratified in the course of the year by three fourths of the state legislatures, and became a part of the Constitution.

Slaves enlisted by the confederates.

Singular as it may seem, the confederate Congress itself was moving towards emancipation. We have passed over the straits to which the government at Richmond was gradually reduced—its want of means, its want of men. As the campaign of 1864 became more and more disastrous, the measures to which it brought the confederates became more and more remarkable. At length, Jefferson Davis proposed, and General Lee recommended, the employment of slaves as soldiers, and that those so employed should be freed, either on entering or quitting service. A bill was brought before Congress, adopted by the House, rejected by the Senate, but on the Virginia senators voting for it, in obedience to the legislature of that state, the bill was carried, (February, 1865.) "It is an abandonment," said one of the senators from Virginia, "of the ground on which we seceded from the old Union. . . . If we are right in passing this measure, we were wrong in denying to the old government the right to interfere with the institution of slavery and to emancipate slaves." There could be no clearer proof that the confederates were vanquished.

Fort Fisher.

But battles remained to be fought. One had already occurred at the mouth of the Cape Fear River, where Fort Fisher and other strong fortifications protected the approach to Wilmington. This it became important to reduce, not merely to complete the blockade at the only point where it was incomplete, but to prepare for General Sherman's advance from Georgia through the Carolinas. The first attempt failed. The fleet under Admiral Porter bombarded the fort vigorously; but General

Butler, taking command of the troops, though it was intended that they should be led by one of his subordinate generals, allowed only one part of them to be disembarked, and returned with the whole to James River, (December 24–25, 1864.) General Grant then ordered General Terry to take them back, and he landed them above the fort, intrenched their position, and then led them to a severe and successful assault, the fleet aiding by a continuous bombardment, (January 13–15, 1865.) Fort Fisher was surrendered, and all the other works at the mouth of the Cape Fear were abandoned.

Sherman in the Carolinas.

Sherman was all the while preparing to march northward. His instructions were to embark his army at Savannah for the James River, in order to combine with the forces there; but he was anxious to march by land, which would bring up the troops in better condition, and at the same time inflict a mortal blow upon the Carolinas, particularly the one which began the war. "At one stride," he promised, he would "make Goldsboro', and open communications with the sea by Newbern." Grant consented, and by the 1st of February, Sherman's army was in motion towards Columbia. It was a far more difficult march than that to Savannah. The weather was wet and cold, the roads were under water, the rivers were swollen; "we must all turn amphibious," said Sherman. But he reached his first point, the capital of South Carolina, and it was surrendered, (February 17.) On the same night Charleston was evacuated, the confederates no longer regarding it as tenable, and on the next morning the Union troops in that neigborhood entered the city and took possession of Fort Sumter, (February 18.) Both cities were fired by the confederates, and both would have been utterly destroyed but for the exertions of the Union soldiers. Sherman kept on, and crossed the line between the Carolinas, (March 8,) then entered Fayetteville, (March 11,) and communicated with the Union army on the coast. This was now under General Schofield, who, with a considerable force, had come from Tennessee, by way of Washington, to Fort Fisher, taken Wilmington, (February 22,) and moved to the interior in order to join Sherman. The junction was soon effected at Goldsboro', (March 21,) but not before Sherman had some severe encounters with the enemy, now concentrated from various quarters under General Johnston. Railroad communication was immediately established between Goldsboro' and Newbern, and Sherman left his army for a few days in order to meet the president and General Grant at City Point, and concert the final operations which were evidently at hand.

Grant's victory over Lee.

The armies on the north and south side of the James held their positions through the winter unchanged, until the left was extended as far as Hatcher's Run, (February 6.) A few weeks later General Sheridan was directed to bring a strong body of mounted men from Winchester, in the Shenandoah Valley, across the northern and western communications of Richmond, either to Sherman's or to Grant's headquarters. He came to Grant's, (March 27,) having excited great alarm at the confederate capital. Then Grant began decisive movements. The army of the Potomac had just repelled the last effort of Lee to break its line, (March 27,) and now turned upon his lines. He could not hold them, but he must be attacked before retreating, and prevented from joining Johnston, as he was believed to intend. To turn his right was Grant's first object, and Sheridan gained it in the battle of Five Forks, (April 1.) To break Lee's lines was Grant's next object, and the whole army gained it by a common and irresistible assault, in consequence of which Lee sent word to Jefferson Davis that

Richmond must be evacuated, (April 2.) It was so, amid confusion and horror, all order lost, while flames, kindled by direction of the war department, were threatening the whole city with ruin, as the Union troops came in, and instantly set about extinguishing the fire, (April 3.) That day, one long, broad thrill of exultation ran through the loyal states. The end, they knew, was near; the sacrifices, in order to attain it, were not in vain. Grant was in pursuit of the retreating army. Broken as it might be, it was still an army, still his great object; and while others made their entry into Richmond, he, and Meade, and Sheridan, and the rest, pressed on for six days more, when, at Appomattox Court House, Lee surrendered the army of Northern Virginia, (April 9.) Again the loyal states exulted, and as day succeeded day, with fresh evidences of the great victory that had been won, the country seemed secure.

Assassination of the president.

Every thing was again plunged into insecurity by the assassination of the president. He had visited Richmond, and returned to Washington full of kindly purposes towards the conquered, when an actor, named Booth, entered the box where he sat in a theatre, and shot him through the head. He lingered, unconscious, for several hours, and died early on the following morning, (April 15.) The life of the secretary of state was attempted by another hand the same night, and other high officers of government, it was believed, had been in peril. Andrew Johnson, vice president, succeeded to the presidency; but his character was not such as to reassure those who mourned for Lincoln. They were millions. If ever the heart of the nation was moved as one man, it was then; and the grief was all the deeper in contrast with the joy that had just gone before.

Close of the war.

The day before the president's assassination, the secretary of war announced his intention "to stop all drafting and recruiting in the loyal states," (April 13.) This was the same as to declare the war ended; and so it proved. Mobile, after a severe siege, surrendered to General Canby on the 12th of April, and the same day General Wilson entered Montgomery, once the confederate capital. Johnston's army surrendered to Sherman on the 26th, and would have done so much sooner but for an effort to cover other than military objects. In the following month, (May,) Taylor and E. K. Smith surrendered their armies in the south-west to General Canby. The last hostility by land was an engagement near Palo Alto, in Texas, (May 13.) The last by sea was the burning of a whaling fleet, in the Northern Pacific, by the cruiser Shenandoah, (June 28.)

Prisoners.

We have reserved to the close some of the lights and shadows in the story of the war. Among the shadows, none fell farther than the treatment of the Union prisoners by their captors. There were difficulties in the way of exchanging prisoners, at first because the government shrank from so far acknowledging the insurgents as belligerents, and afterwards because the confederates would exchange white prisoners alone, claiming a right to deal with the blacks and their white officers as criminals. These delays would have been hard enough for the prisoners and their friends in any circumstances, but in those of the southern prisons they were heart-rending. At Richmond and elsewhere, in jails, warehouses, and covered railway bridges,—at Andersonville and other places, in pens,—thousands upon thousands of Union prisoners were exposed to barbarities almost exceeding belief. "Terrible beyond description," are the words applied to the Richmond prisons in a report of a confederate congressional committee to the secretary of war, in September, 1862. "A reproach to us as a nation," reports a confederate adjutant and inspector-general to the same official, in

August, 1864, respecting Andersonville. A committee of the United States Sanitary Commission, after thorough inquiry, reported in September, 1864, that "tens of thousands of helpless men have been, and are now being, disabled and destroyed by a process as certain as poison. . . . This spectacle is daily beheld and allowed by the rebel government. . . . The conclusion is unavoidable that these privations and sufferings have been designedly inflicted." According to the statistics of the war department, one hundred and twenty-six thousand nine hundred and fifty soldiers were taken prisoners, and twenty-two thousand five hundred and seventy of these died in prison. It was often proposed to retaliate upon confederate prisoners, but better counsels prevailed.

Sanitary and Christian Commissions.

Nothing was brighter through these sad years than the persevering devotion of the people to those who fought their battles. Men had no sooner sprung to arms than other men, and women in great number, began to minister to their wants and those of their families. Several Soldiers' Aid Societies were formed, and out of these grew the United States Sanitary Commission, or, as it was styled in the order from the secretary of war, "a commission of inquiry and advice in respect of the sanitary interests of the United States forces," (June 1861.) It was not to do what the government was doing, but rather to do what the government was leaving undone, and as there was a great deal of this, the Commission was kept busy. Its headquarters were in New York, its posts all over the loyal states, its members and work-people, men and women, in every camp and every hospital, watching the well, nursing the sick, transporting the wounded, protecting the discharged, supplying medicine, food, clothing, books, and even games along the Union lines. Another organization, the Christian Commission, was formed (November, 1861) with immediate reference to the spiritual wants of the soldiers; but its agents became as active as those of the Sanitary Commission in the relief of physical necessities. Side by side, the commissions distributed what the nation gave, all kinds of supplies and subscriptions in one steady stream, sometimes from a poor woman, sometimes from a man worth millions, in individual offerings, or in various combinations. Fairs in New York, Philadelphia, and Boston were successful in raising the largest sums. At least thirty millions, in money and stores, passed through the agencies of the two Commissions.

Cost of the war.

The pecuniary cost of the war to the government and the loyal states, without counting a dollar expended by the confederates, could not have been less than five thousand millions. Indirectly it involved heavy losses in production and productive force, as every war has done; but these cannot be accurately estimated. The great cost of the war was personal — the death of thousands in battle, and hospital, and, after their discharge, of wounds or diseases contracted in service, and the pain and privation occasioned by their loss to thousands upon thousands more. Here was the real sacrifice, and in this the dying and the living shared. Yet few would have drawn back from it, had they the power; for, much as the war cost them, it repaid them with the sense of suffering in a great cause, and of contributing to great ends — the emancipation of four million slaves, the union of forty million freemen.

CHAPTER XIV.

REUNION.

Difficulties. PEACE had its difficulties no less than war. The conquered were ready to confess their defeat, the conquerors to use their victory without abusing it. But here was a nation, split in two, to be reunited; here was a society, quivering with agitation, to be calmed. One great class — the slaveholding — was broken up. Another — the slave — was suddenly thrown from slavery into freedom. The whole people were accustomed to war, and to all its consequences, public and private. Civil authority had outgrown its old traditions. The president and his cabinet, Congress, the state and municipal governments, were in the habitual exercise of more or less arbitrary powers. Large appropriations and expenditures of money were too common to excite a healthful concern. Habits and ideas were every where changing, and not at once for the better. On the contrary, the high qualities which the danger of the country called out seemed sinking beneath the corruption and indifference which set in like a flood when the danger passed. In these circumstances, reunion was not only difficult; it might be impracticable, and many predicted that it would be.

Disarming. The first obstacle in its way was removed by the disarming of the nation. In May, 1865, the army was more than a million strong. On the 22d and 23d of that month more than two hundred thousand soldiers passed in review before the president, at Washington. Fresh from their great victories, they looked as if they could do what they pleased with their unarmed countrymen. Nor were they all. The thousands who manned the national fleets were equally strong in the position they had won. Yet all these numbers dwindled, all these armies and crews were disbanded with as much ease as if they had been vanquished instead of victorious. The secretary of war reported eight hundred thousand troops mustered out in six months, while material of every kind, stores, transports, railroads and their trains, telegraphs, were disposed of, and the army placed upon a peace footing. The same reduction was effected in the navy. Soldier or sailor, the volunteer disappeared in the citizen.

Freedmen. The next obstacle to reunion could not be so rapidly removed. Three or four million freedmen were to be snatched from their former masters, or those who now threatened to master them, and trained to self-control, before the nation to which they belonged could be properly considered as united. Just as the war was closing, Congress established in the war department a bureau of freedmen, refugees, and abandoned lands, to continue during the war, and one year thereafter, (March, 1865.) A commissioner, with an assistant for each state in insurrection and a number of clerks, was charged with all subjects relating to freedmen. Until the army was reduced so that it could no longer spare its officers, it supplied commissioners to the bureau. Their functions, originally, were to provide for the sick and needy, and to distribute abandoned lands among the freedmen; but few lands proved to be abandoned, and this part of the work fell through. Relief was administered in every possible form — food, clothing, shelter, and protection. When differences arose between freedmen and their employers, the commissioners served as arbitrators, and this service was as useful as any which they rendered. In July, 1866, the bureau was continued for two years longer, and its duties were enlarged so as to include education of the freedmen and their children. In this good work individuals and associations had been engaged here and there for several years, but it was now extended all over the Southern States. In 1868 the bureau was again continued, and in 1869 it reported twenty-five hundred and seventy-one schools, thirty-two hundred and sixty-two teachers, and one hundred and sixteen thousand one hundred and ten scholars. In 1870 it came to an end, having stood between the freedmen and their trials, and enabled them to cross the gulf between their old condition and their new.

Reconstruction of states. A third obstacle to reunion was the position of the states that had seceded. Whether they were states or not, in the Union or out of it, excited a great deal of discussion to little purpose. Practically, they were separated from the states which had not seceded, and it was necessary to bring the separation to an end. As this involved all the authorities, confederate and state, all the army and navy, all the classes which had been in insurrection, it was far the most severe task before the nation. Unhappily, its severity was increased by divisions between the two branches of the government employed in it; the president insisting upon one course, and Congress upon another, until both were on the brink of failure. President Johnson entered upon office with loud threats of avenging the assassination of his predecessor, and punishing the treason that had excited civil war. Vengeance, however, was not in the minds of the people, and Mr. Johnson's tone soon softened. He issued a proclamation of amnesty to "all persons who have directly or indirectly participated in the rebellion," excepting the higher civil, military, and naval officers of the confederate service, together with various other classes, provided that all availing themselves of the amnesty should take and keep an oath of fidelity to the Constitution, the Union, and the laws and proclamations of emancipation. Next, the president appointed provisional governors of the seceded states, with instructions to call conventions, in order to amend the state constitutions, and enable the loyal people to recover their constitutional relations to the Union. This was done in each state, the conventions declaring the secession of the state null and void, and prohibiting slavery within its borders. Then the state legislatures assembled and ratified the thirteenth amendment of the Constitution of the United States. This was the president's plan of reconstruction. It left the states very much in the hands of those who had taken them out of the Union, without any other proviso in behalf of their colored people than the acceptance of emancipation. Congress met in December, 1865, and instantly began upon another plan. A joint committee, commonly called the Reconstruction Committee, was appointed, and entered upon long investigations. At the end of six months, (June, 1866,) it reported as a basis of reconstruction a fourteenth constitutional amendment. This provides that all persons born or naturalized in the United States are citizens; that the privileges of citizenship shall not be abridged by any state; that if a male citizen, being twenty-one years old, is denied the right to vote, he cannot be counted in the number to be represented in Congress; that no person who has broken his oath to support the Constitution, and engaged in insurrection, can hold office; that the validity of the public debt of the United States shall not be questioned, but that any debt in aid of insurrection, or any claim for the loss of a slave, shall be illegal. On this plan, it is evident that the hitherto ruling class at the south would retain a very limited share of authority, while the freedmen would be put in a position of political security. Freedmen were, in the first place, full citizens of the United States. If they were not full citizens of the state in which they lived, the state would suffer in its congressional representation, and would therefore be under pressure to give them full citizenship — in other words, the right to vote. Here was the essential difference between the presidential and the congressional plans; the latter sought suffrage for the freedman, the former avoided it. The legislature of Tennessee immediately accepted the fourteenth amendment, and the state was thereupon re-admitted to the Union, July 23, 1866. With regard to the other states, a long delay ensued. The quarrel between the president and Congress became bitterer, and as he encouraged the states seeking re-admission to hold to his policy instead of yielding to that of Congress, they remained where they were. Congress gave suffrage to the freedmen in the District of Columbia, (January, 1867,) and admitted the state of Nebraska only on condition that it should not deny suffrage to the freedmen within its limits, (March 1.) These, and many other acts, were passed over the president's veto. More decisive than any other measure, the reconstruction act of March 2, 1867, divided the ten states waiting admission into military districts, each with its commanding officer, and so to remain until a convention of delegates "elected by male citizens twenty-one years old and upward, of whatever race, color, or previous condition," excepting those disqualified by the fourteenth amendment, should frame a state constitution, which, being ratified by the people and approved by Congress, should go into operation, and the legislature thereupon elected should adopt the fourteenth amendment, and it should become a part of the United States Constitution. All this came to pass with seven of the states in the following year, when North Carolina, South Carolina, Georgia, Alabama, Florida, Louisiana, (June 25, 1868,) and Arkansas, (June 22,) were re-admitted. For many, if not all these states, it was a cruel experience. They were released from military rule to pass under a civil rule exercised largely not by their own people, but by mere adventurers who had come among them with sordid purposes, and whose success came very near being the ruin of the states where they succeeded. Nearly two years more passed before the other three states were re-admitted, Virginia in January, Mississippi in February, and Texas in March, 1870.

Impeachment of President Johnson.

A year before this last date President Johnson's troubled term had closed. He had taken a position so antagonistic to Congress, that Congress may be excused for all its antagonism to him. But the extreme to which it went in impeaching him can be justified on no other than party grounds. An act of 1867, regulating the tenure of certain civil offices, was intended to prevent the president from removing their incumbents, as had been the rule, without the consent of the Senate. On the president's disregarding this act, and removing the secretary of war without consulting the Senate, his opponents thought they had their opportunity of impeaching him, and he was accordingly impeached by the House of Representatives, to be tried by the Senate for high crimes and misdemeanors, (February, 1868.) After a trial lasting nearly two months, a few senators were independent enough to vote against their party, and he was acquitted, (May 26.)

Fourteenth and fifteenth amendments.

The fourteenth amendment was officially proclaimed a part of the Constitution in July, 1868. In the following February, a fifteenth amendment was adopted by Congress, to the intent that the right to vote should not be denied by the United States or by any state on account of race, color, or previous condition of servitude. In March, the adminstration of President Grant began, and at the end of a year, in March, 1870, he announced the final adoption of the amendment in a special message to Congress as completing "the greatest civil change that has occurred since the nation came into life." The freedman was now fully a citizen.

Enforcing the fourteenth amendment.

Such changes as benefited him were not accepted by many of his neighbors as benefiting them. In numerous parts of the Southern States the colored people were much harried by the whites, who often turned upon their own people likewise. An association called the Ku-Klux spread in various quarters, and violence was on the increase, when Congress passed an act to enforce the provisions of the fourteenth amendment, authorizing the president to suspend the privilege of habeas corpus, that is, to use military power wherever the constituted authorities did not suppress unlawful combinations, (April, 1871.) It may be questioned whether the remedy was not worse than the disease; but Congress had become wonted to high-handed rule. The president made proclamation exhorting "the people of those portions of the country to suppress all such combinations by their own voluntary efforts through the agency of local laws." Reluctant as President Grant was to exercise the powers which the act conferred, he suspended habeas corpus in certain parts of South Carolina, (October.) But this was not helping a real reunion.

Amnesty.

A better step was taken in May, 1872, when Congress removed all legal and political disabilities, except from senators and representatives of the thirty-sixth and thirty-seventh Congresses, (1859-63,) officers in the judicial, military, and naval service, heads of departments, and foreign ministers, who had violated their oath to support the Constitution. This left a very small number, comparatively, to pay the penalty of rebellion, and completed, as far as legislation could complete, the work of reconstruction.

Financial administration. The public debt did not reach its full proportions until some time after the close of the war. Many doubted the power, many more doubted the will, of the nation to bear so heavy a burden, without attempting to lighten it at the expense of those to whom it was due. It was, therefore, a great relief when the House of Representatives, on the day after it assembled in December, 1865, voted, one hundred and sixty-two to one, that the public debt is sacred and inviolable, and that any attempt to impair it shall be promptly rejected. But the difficulty of wisely administering the national finances was very great. The best measures involved immediate sacrifices, which financiers, public and private, were unwilling to make. Taxation was a trouble that could be remedied by means of reductions and improvements, until an easier system was established. The debt could be diminished by paying off instalments from the surplus revenue. But the paper money, which constituted the only currency, and which affected all prices and all habits of living throughout the country, could not be redeemed, or even brought near to redemption, without some temporary losses ; and these were too great for the moral force of the government, as for that of the nation. The financial administration of seven years of peace left the people almost as far from a sound financial condition as it found them.

Civil service. One administrative reform was begun upon. Congress authorized the president to prescribe such rules and regulations for the admission of persons into the civil service as would promote its efficiency, (March, 1871.)

The president appointed a commission, and received from them a scheme of rules which he communicated to Congress, (December.) That body was disposed to be inactive. The civil service, as it stood, was at congresssional disposal; its offices were filled or vacated, generally speaking, according to the demands of members of Congress, each managing his own locality, or claiming his share in general appointments. This patronage would cease with the reform of the civil service; delay in reforming it was therefore inevitable. The commission recommended the competitive examination of candidates for office, and the probationary appointment of those who succeeded at examination, together with securities for the tenure and promotion of deserving officers. It was a system vitally needed.

Indians. Another great reform was carried farther. It was the president's planning and the president's doing. He brought it forward in his inaugural address, (March, 1869,) and followed it up by active measures. A board of commissioners was created to take supervision of the Indians. In place of the agents hitherto appointed, officers of the army and persons nominated by different religious societies were intrusted with a charge which had been long abused. Some reservations were placed entirely under the immediate control of the Society of Friends and other bodies which had sent missionaries among the Indians. "I have attempted," said President Grant, "a new policy towards these wards of the nation with fair results so far as tried." Indian hostilities did not cease. They had broken out during the civil war, and after its close. They broke out again after the new policy was tried. But with this policy there came a hope, that had not come before, of winning over the Indians to civilization and peace.

Mexico and France. In turning to foreign relations, we go back to the Johnson administration. Early in 1866, Mr. Seward wrote to the French minister at Washington, reminding him that the United States desired the withdrawal of the French troops from Mexico. As the Emperor Napoleon was weary of keeping them there, he not unwillingly promised to withdraw them, and, after making some changes in his plan, finally executed it in the first months of 1867. It was the strongest assertion of the Monroe Doctrine that had been made by our government; hardly a stronger one could be made.

Alaska and Russia. On the 30th of March, 1867, a treaty with Russia transferred Alaska from that power to the United States, on the payment of a little more than seven millions. This great territory, though nominally colonized for nearly a century, contained less than five hundred Russians and Siberians in a total population of twenty-nine thousand. It can hardly be said to have a history. The first Russians to reach it came in 1731; the first to explore it came in 1741, under Behring, who soon died on the island named after him. Voyages led to trading-posts and the establishment of Russian companies for the prosecution of the fur trade, in which American merchants and seamen also engaged. There was little besides the fur trade to characterize the territory, or to render it a desirable acquisition, when it was transferred to General Rousseau, representing the United States, (October, 1867.)

Alabama claims. The claims of the United States against Great Britain, for the depredations of the Alabama and other vessels in the confederate service, formed the subject of long-continued negotiations. A treaty was concluded with the British government by the American minister, Reverdy Johnson, at the beginning of 1869, but rejected by the United States Senate. Two years later, the British minister at Washington proposed a joint high commission of the two governments to settle some questions concerning the North American fisheries, and other matters relating to the British Possessions. Mr. Fish, secretary of state, suggested the consideration of the Alabama claims by the same commission, and this was accepted. Accordingly five commissioners of each government, ten in all, met at Washington on the 27th of February, 1871, and on the 8th of May signed the treaty of Washington, which was ratified by the United States Senate on the 24th of May, and by both governments on the 17th of June. By this all the Alabama claims were referred to a tribunal of arbitration, consisting of five members, one named by the president, one by the queen, one by the king of Italy, one by the president of the Swiss Confederation, and one by the emperor of Brazil. For a basis of arbitration, three rules were laid down as binding a neutral to prevent, 1st, the equipment or departure of any vessel to carry on war against a friendly power; 2d, the use of its ports or waters as a base of naval operations, or for the renewal of supplies against a friendly power; and 3d, the violation of the foregoing obligations. Furthermore, the British commissioners were authorized to express regret for the escape of the Alabama and other vessels from British ports, and for the depredations committed by those vessels. As to other claims between the two governments, or their subjects or citizens, the treaty referred them to a commission of three members, one appointed by Great Britain, one by the United States, and one by both powers, to sit at Washington. This was a great advance upon all previous negotiations, and as the negotiators announced, "the method of adjustment is such as will set a noble example to other governments in the interest of the peace of the world." In December, 1871, the board of arbitration met at Geneva, in Switzerland, the United States being represented by Charles Francis Adams, who had served as minister to Great Britain for seven years from the beginning of the civil war. At this meeting the American and British cases were presented, and the arbitrators then adjourned, to re-assemble in June, 1872. Before that date, the treaty and the tribunal both came very near dissolution. A paragraph was found in the American case urging what was known as the indirect claims, or, as they were vaguely understood, the liability of Great Britain for all the expenses of the civil war after the battle of Gettysburg; because, after that, as was alleged, the offensive operations of the insurgents were conducted only at sea through the cruisers, and the war was prolonged for that purpose. Happily, the indignation excited by these suggestions in England was not sustained by any support to them from the American people, who had little mind to follow up such claims. The board of arbitration met on the 15th of June, 1872, and on the 28th set the indirect claims aside. On the 14th of September they gave their decision, — the British arbitrator dissenting, — that Great Britain should pay fifteen and a half million dollars as indemnity to the United States. In this decision the two governments and the two nations acquiesced.

Settlement.

Abroad and at home, the immediate consequences of the war were now settled. Legislation and negotiation had rendered the reunion of the American people possible. Only the virtue of the people themselves could render it real.

CHAPTER XV.

National Development.

Three quarters of a century.

The period from 1797 to 1872 forms a large part of our history. Three quarters of a century is a long time in any national life, and particularly in such a one as ours. In 1797, the United States, sixteen in number, were just beginning to reach over the Alleghanies towards the basins and prairies of the west; they had not even begun to approach the Gulf of Mexico. The people numbered five millions. Independent, they were yet dependent; they accepted the half subordinate position accorded to them by the European powers, and pursued a policy towards some of these powers which may almost be described as colonial, rather than national. Within their own borders, they were not altogether masters; the soil had not yet yielded half its treasures; the rivers, even of the east, were but partly navigated; the great lakes undotted by a sail; the highways rough and infrequent; the mails slow, though light; the resources of the nation hardly touched, in fact, hardly known. In 1872, the states numbered thirty-seven. The territory embraced three million square miles, stretching from ocean to ocean, besides more than five hundred thousand in the north-west of the continent. The population reached all but forty millions. Immigration brought in eight millions during the period, and their children and descendants swelled the increasing numbers. The nation stood face to face with the greatest states of Europe on equal terms. It handled its own possessions with vigor, cultivating its lands, working its mines, multiplying its fabrics, covering its waters with vessels, traversing its plains with railways, multiplying its facilities, and using its opportunities. There had been interruptions. Wars broke out, and commercial crises occurred at intervals, but the injuries they caused seemed to be repaired by the prosperity which soon followed them. The three quarters of a century, taken as a whole, was one long growth in size, and strength, and riches.

Causes at work. Nothing like it was to be seen elsewhere. Europe grew, and European colonies grew, but not as the United States, not as rapidly, not as widely. Indeed, the difference is so great, the growth of the United States is so wonderful, that there has been some difficulty in accounting for it. The Americans are not so evidently braver, or wiser, or more industrious, or more ambitious, than their contemporaries, as to be fitted to outstrip them. Nor is the country so much more productive, or any of its natural advantages so superior, as to explain its exceptional development. The causes at work have been partly physical, but chiefly political. The climate, soil, extent of territory waiting occupation, easy communication from one part to another, have all contributed to the great result. But it would never have been so great had it not been yet more furthered by the national institutions, and particularly by the principle of self-government on which they rest. Of all people, ancient or modern, none have been left to govern themselves so much as the American. None have been trained to such independence, to such mobility, to such power of improving the circumstances in which they may be placed. It is this which has remedied, as well as produced, the defects in the national character, and the errors in the national life; it is this, more than any other single cause, which has brought the national development to its present point.

Public schools. The self-relying spirit of the nation is fed by the public schools, as a stream by its fountain. 1. As a system of administration, the schools, being left to local management, favor the exercise of local authority. The only schools under control of the general government are those in the District of Columbia, the Military Academy at West Point, (1802,) and the Naval Academy at Annapolis, (1845.) A Bureau of Education, recently connected with the department of the interior, has no other function than to collect and distribute educational information. All that the government has to do with the schools throughout the country is to make over that share of the public land in each township which Congress has reserved for the support of public education. The state governments, as a rule, control only the normal and charitable schools of their foundation, and by no means all of these. The great mass of schools is under municipal administration. 2. As a system of instruction, the public schools tend to develop the national traits in their scholars. They give the same privileges to every child, training the native and the foreigner, the Teuton, the Celt, and the African, on equal terms. After the emancipation of 1863, and more particularly after the extension of the Freedmen's Bureau in 1866, provision for that great class before unprovided for was made first by the national, afterwards by local authority, and children of color were taken into the schools. The instruction of all classes at the south was much encouraged by the munificence of George Peabody, who placed three and a half millions in the hands of trustees in order to promote southern education, (1866–9.) There still remain great gaps, not in any one section, but almost every where ; yet the general working of the school system is beneficial to a degree that can hardly be overestimated. It gives a stamp to the mind and life of its children which it is difficult to see how they would otherwise receive. It fits them if native born, and doubly fits them if foreign born, for the citizenship that awaits them, for the self-government to which, one by one, and all together, they are called.

Higher education. Institutes, colleges, and universities — the latter including professional and scientific schools — are chiefly of private foundation. Here, too, in more or less connection with the common schools, the self-governing principle is maintained. The higher institutions of learning were very few and very feeble at the beginning of the period. They have become more numerous and more vigorous; but they are still in a state of transition to better things.

Public libraries. Till within the last quarter of a century, libraries were private, or belonged to private corporations, except those of Congress and the state governments. The Astor Library, founded by its first librarian, Joseph G. Cogswell, rather than by the merchant who endowed it, led the long line of public libraries which have arisen in many of our smallest towns as well as our largest cities. Though not always wisely collected or wisely used, they have supplied what was always needed to accompany or to follow the studies of the schools.

Art museums. Just as the period closes, a new movement begins with the foundation of art museums in New York and Boston. These, also, will supply a great want in education.

Letters. The literature that produced but little in the seventeenth and eighteenth centuries continued to produce but little in the early part of the nineteenth; then it became more fruitful. Washington Irving was the first of our men of letters, properly so called. He wrote history, biography, travels, and legendary and sentimental tales, all in a sunshiny style, which gave our literature a new charm. Cooper wrote his stories of Indians and backwoodsmen, seamen and soldiers, with a fervor which made one forget the unnaturalness of his characters. Maria Brooks wrote the impassioned verse of Zophiel; Lydia Sigourney was less poetic, but perhaps more winning in her simpler strains. Percival and Halleck were happy in their lyric efforts. William Croswell wrote poems as flowers dropped along the path of priestly offices; yet, had they been his work, instead of his pastime, he would not have lived in vain. Almost the same thing may be said of Andrews Norton, whose little cluster of hymns will move many a heart beyond the reach of the theological and critical labors in which he spent his days. Webster's speeches were the great landmark in our political literature. None of our public men compared with him in breadth of thought or force of language. Everett's orations were the graceful work of a rhetorician rather than a statesman. Kent and Story were the great expounders of our laws. Jared Sparks gave his honest toil to the history and biography of the nation. His editions of Washington's and Franklin's Writings revived the interest in them and their times. Prescott turned to the brilliant episodes of Spain, and the Spanish possessions in America, and gave them so picturesque a treatment, as to win readers every where, at home and abroad. Ticknor was the historian of Spanish literature, and on so comprehensive a plan, as to set a new example to American scholars. Nathaniel Hawthorne sought out a mythical background for his creations, and then filled in their wavering outline with deep color and solemn shade. Fiction became more and more attractive to our writers, and they wrote with increasing mastery. Poetry put on a new aspect as it was interpreted by Bryant and Longfellow, Whittier, Emerson, and Lowell, to whom the nation owes a very large proportion of what is best in its intellectual life. History continued to find followers, and Bancroft, Motley, Palfrey, and Parkman were among the most successful.

Science. Scientific culture was very greatly on the increase. Its two foremost names are of foreign origin. John James Audubon, born in Louisiana long before its acquisition by the United States, was the author of a work on the Birds of America, far surpassing any similar publication before attempted in this country. Audubon belongs to the former half of the period under review, Agassiz to the latter. This eminent naturalist, not so much a Swiss as an American, has published important volumes on the natural history of the United States; but his most important work is the foundation of the Museum of Comparative Zoölogy at Cambridge. Nathaniel Bowditch deserves to be remembered as the translator and commentator of the Mécanique Céleste of La Place. The United States Coast Survey and Observatory have been of great benefit to science. Universities and scientific schools, or those upon their staffs who have been active in research, have stimulated scientific studies in almost every direction.

Art. Gilbert Stuart was the great portrait painter, not only of his own day, but of the whole period. His faces live and speak like those of the greatest masters. Washington Allston was at once the portrait and the historical painter, the landscape and the ideal artist, in whom all that is most sublime and all that is most delicate found full expression. He stands in our artistic, like Irving in our literary history, the first to give American art its charm. Crawford came later, the most imaginative of our sculptors, but with less power to execute his conceptions than they deserved. Greenough and Powers, Story and Ball, have all won high places in sculpture. Cole, Kensett, Hunt, and many more, form a group of painters to whom the country is more indebted than it knows. Music has taken strong hold upon some of our communities. It has come with the musically educated immigrants, and grown among the American born, particularly since it was introduced into the public schools. But it has as yet inspired no great composers of our own.

Inventions. The best American ideas are often said to be those of our inventors. Eli Whitney's cotton gin, Hoe's printing press, McCormick's and other reapers, Howe's and other sewing machines, the numerous improvements in all sorts of machinery and manufactures, — these are levers by which the national development has been very greatly promoted. Fulton's steamboat, the Clermont, appeared on the Hudson in 1807. First of our railways was the Quincy, in Massachusetts, a single track between three and four miles long, for transporting granite from a quarry to the water's edge, (1827.) First of our locomotives was one upon the Hudson and Mohawk Railroad in New York, (1832.) First of our and all other electric telegraphs was that constructed by Morse between Washington and Baltimore, and its first message was, "What hath God wrought!" (1844.) The first Atlantic cable was laid in 1858, but failed after a momentary success; the second parted in mid-ocean, (1865,) and the third succeeded, (1866.) No one man deserves the credit of this great enterprise so much as Cyrus W. Field.

Expeditions. The expeditions of survey and discovery, mostly undertaken by the government, form a striking feature of the period. That of Lewis and Clarke, to which we referred in connection with Oregon, was a very remarkable achievement for the time. It occupied more than two years (1804–6) and crossed the continent from the Mississippi to the mouth of the Columbia. Thirty years later (1838–42) an exploring expedition, consisting of several vessels under the command of Lieutenant Charles Wilkes, and carrying a corps of scientific men, sailed on a long cruise through the Antarctic and Pacific Oceans. Lieutenant William F. Lynch, of the navy, made exploration of the Jordan and the Dead Sea, (1847.) Two Grinnell expeditions, so called from Henry Grinnell, through whose liberality they were mainly fitted out, sought for the English voyagers under Sir John Franklin, then missing in the Arctic Seas. The first was commanded by Lieutenant De Haven, of the navy, (1850–51 ;) the second by Dr. Kane, also of the navy, who had served on the first as surgeon, (1853–5.) A squadron, under Commodore Perry, brother of the Perry of Lake Erie, was sent to Japan to negotiate a treaty, by which the ports of that country were opened to American commerce, (1852–4.) Later expeditions explored our western and south-western territories, or traversed Central America and the Isthmus of Darien, with the view of cutting a canal to connect the Atlantic with the Pacific. Of all the expeditions, none have honored the nation or humanity more than those which carried succor to foreign lands. When Ireland was starving, in 1847, Madeira, in 1852, and the cotton manufacturing shires of England, in 1862, supplies were sent from our people as to fellow-countrymen. In some of these succors the government shared by providing vessels from the navy to carry the food furnished by private benevolence.

Charities. Our national charities began at home. Societies to relieve the poor, the sick, and the prisoner, existed in the foregoing century ; they were largely extended in this. Schools and asylums were opened for all suffering classes, beginning with the American Asylum for the

Deaf and Dumb in Hartford, (1817,) the Perkins Institution and Massachusetts Asylum for the Blind in Boston, (1832,) and the Massachusetts School for Idiotic and Feeble-minded Youth, also in Boston, (1848.) Associations for the care of destitute or vicious children, erring women, and the aged of both sexes, have done their various work in all quarters. Missions to the ignorant and outcast have been unwearied in reclaiming them. Bible and tract societies have distributed their publications wherever an opening could be found. Besides these organizations, individuals have labored, openly or secretly, in relieving the spiritual and physical necessities of their neighbors. Could it be fairly described, the ministry to every form of want and crime would make the best pages in our history.

Drawbacks. To all this national development there have been, and there still are, very serious drawbacks. They spring, to a great degree, from the development itself. Corruption follows hard upon growth in society, as in nature, and its effects are as fatal in one as in the other. Wealth grows, and the passion for it grows faster. Labor struggles not only with capital, but with labor; trade is tainted with dishonest practices; life itself is lowered by the readiness with which men forsake its higher callings because they are less lucrative than the lower. Power increases, and the lust for it increases likewise. Candidates for office stoop to mean conditions. Office-holders stoop yet lower, and whether in town or city, state or national government, degrade themselves and their authority. For some of our forms of disgrace, new words, or words with new meaning, are required, and strangers and children ask what is a *ring*, or a *lobby*, and sometimes fail to understand it when explained. If the results of political corruption were confined to those who indulge in it, the injury would be far less formidable. But they spread on every side, they infect our institutions, they poison the spirit of our people. These evils are not new. They were lamented when the nation was born, in the very throes of the revolution, while such as loved the country were pledging to it their lives, their fortunes, and their sacred honors, and others were making money out of its trials, or turning its agonies to their own preferment. It is only that the evils are more apparent than they used to be. They have a larger area, a more numerous following; and so the shadows which they cast seem to shut out more of the light that should be shining. There is but one way to dispel them — by consecrating the nation to a higher service, and giving ourselves to it, one and all.

INDEX.

A.

D.

E.

F.

G.

H.

I.

J.

N.

O.

P.

Q.

R.

S.

T.

U.

V.

W.

Y.

Z.

www.ingramcontent.com/pod-product-compliance
Lightning Source LLC
LaVergne TN
LVHW021304110826
845150LV00003B/478

* 9 7 8 1 4 2 5 5 5 9 6 5 6 *